MOON

GREAT SMOKY MOUNTAINS NATIONAL PARK

HIKING · CAMPING
SCENIC DRIVES

JASON FRYE

Contents

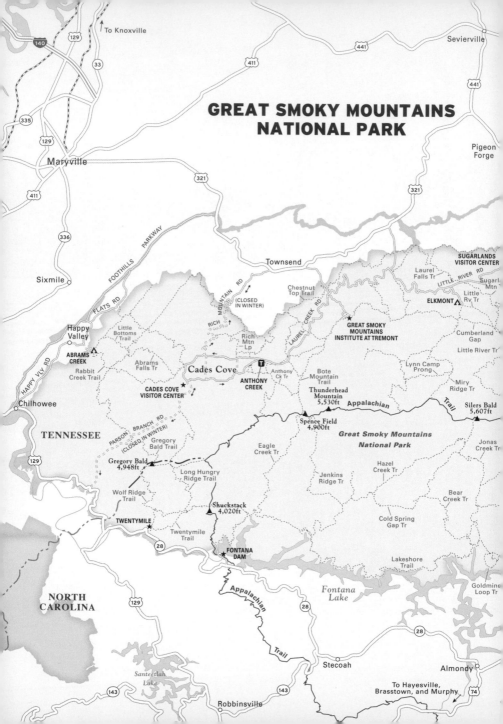

GREAT SMOKY MOUNTAINS NATIONAL PARK

To Knoxville

Sevierville

Maryville

Pigeon Forge

Sixmile

Townsend

SUGARLANDS VISITOR CENTER

Laurel Falls Tr

LITTLE RIVER RD

Sugarl Mtn

Chestnut Top Trail

ELKMONT

Little Rv Tr

Happy Valley

Little Bottoms Trail

RICH MOUNTAIN RD (CLOSED IN WINTER)

Rich Mtn Lp

GREAT SMOKY MOUNTAINS INSTITUTE AT TREMONT

Cumberland Gap

Little River Tr

FOOTHILLS PARKWAY

FLATS RD

ABRAMS CREEK

Lynn Camp Prong

Rabbit Creek Trail

Abrams Falls Tr

Cades Cove

ANTHONY CREEK

Anthony Ck Tr

LAUREL CREEK RD

Bote Mountain Trail

Miry Ridge Tr

Chilhowee

CADES COVE VISITOR CENTER

Thunderhead Mountain 5,530ft

Appalachian

Trail

Silers Bald 5,607ft

HAPPY VLY RD

Spence Field 4,900ft

TENNESSEE

PARSON BRANCH RD (CLOSED IN WINTER)

Gregory Bald Trail

Great Smoky Mountains National Park

Jonas Creek Tr

Gregory Bald 4,948ft

Long Hungry Ridge Trail

Eagle Creek Tr

Hazel Creek Tr

Jenkins Ridge Tr

Bear Creek Tr

Wolf Ridge Trail

Shuckstack 4,020ft

Cold Spring Gap Tr

TWENTYMILE

Twentymile Trail

FONTANA DAM

Lakeshore Trail

Goldmine Loop Tr

NORTH CAROLINA

Appalachian

Fontana Lake

Stecoah

Almondy

Santeetlah Lake

Trail

To Hayesville, Brasstown, and Murphy

Robbinsville

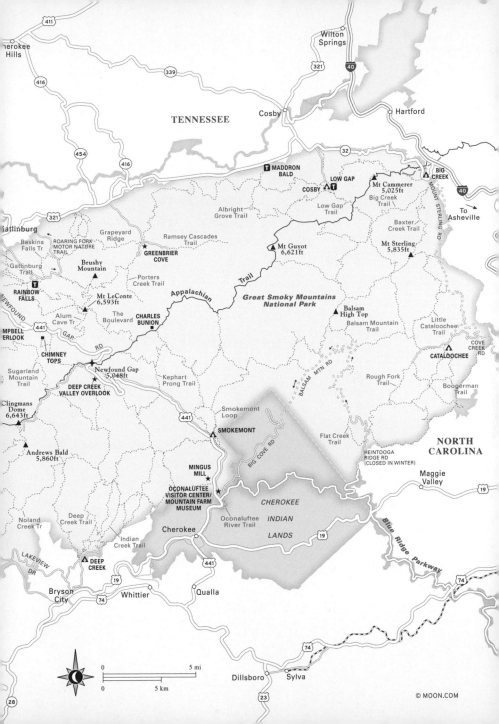

DISCOVER

Great Smoky Mountains National Park

The national parks are called America's Best Idea, and I think Great Smoky Mountains National Park is the best of the bunch. But I may be biased.

My earliest vacation memories are of these green mountains in summer and their blazing color in fall, of rushing streams and black bears lazing in the afternoon sun and the fields of Cades Cove filled with deer. On one morning ride across Newfound Gap Road, I learned why these mountains are called the Smokies. The mist rising from the coves and hollows and hidden places in the hills looked like smoke: tendrils of it rose like the sure sign of a chimney or a campfire; drifts of it formed miniature cloudbanks.

The Smokies are a colorful place. In the summer, the mountains are emerald green. In the fall, the leaves are a riot of color. Spring is a time when wildflowers blanket high mountain meadows and secret glades. Thickets of rhododendron, galax, mountain laurel, and flame azalea bring flowery breath to the trails and paths throughout the park. In the winter, there's the beauty of a red fox running across a field white with snow, the crystalline shine of ice at the waterfalls, the

Clockwise from top left: hiking in the Smokies; maple tree in front of Cable Mill; black bear cub; Cades Cove Loop; mountain laurel blooming in early summer; Newfound Gap after sunset in the summer

jewel-like glint of snow in the morning sun, and the surprising yellow blooms of witch hazel.

There's a smell to this place too—rich, wet, and fertile, the smell of dirt and decades of leaves. Moss tinges the air near the springs, seeps, and waterfalls. In the autumn, the faint cinnamon smell of leaves perfumes the breeze, and the sound as they crunch underfoot announces your passage.

Birds, cicadas, the rush of water, and the sigh of wind create a layered sonic landscape. When the elk bugle and call to one another, when a turkey gobbles, or when a hawk keens, it punctuates the soundtrack of the Smokies.

There's other music—banjos and dulcimers and guitars and voices raised in song. That music sounds so at home it feels like it's been here as long as the streams or birds or wind, but it's just evidence of us. We drive the roads and hike the trails, fish in the streams, take photos of the sunsets and vistas, adding our voices to the music of the place.

When we leave, this song stays with us. We hum it to ourselves, recalling the place, the breeze, the sun on our faces, and the smell of fall on the air. We sing because this place is song-worthy, a place like no other.

This is why we go back: to learn a new verse, to find a place or experience missed on a previous trip. I go not to lose myself in the wilds of the Smokies, but to find myself there.

Clockwise from top left: fresh cut flowers at the Market Square Farmer's Market; Indian Flats Falls; Mountain Farm Museum near the Oconaluftee Visitor Center; Hi-Wire Brewing in Asheville

8 TOP EXPERIENCES

1 **Watch the Sky Change from Clingmans Dome:** From the highest point in the park, sunrises and sunsets tint the mountains, the mist, and the sky in quiet, breathtaking moments you shouldn't miss (page 45).

2 **See Why They're Called the Smoky Mountains:** Mist fills the valleys and tendrils of fog rise from secret coves and hollows in the mountains. Driving **Newfound Gap Road** just after dawn or as the sun sets will show you exactly what makes these mountains "smoky" (page 44).

3 **See the Firefly Light Show:** Elkmont's colony of synchronous fireflies is world-renowned. With a little luck you can catch them blinking in unison every night for a couple of weeks in early summer (page 78).

>>>

^
^
^

4 **Find Fall Color:** To see the mountains awash in color, bike or drive **Cades Cove Loop** (page 81), hear the leaves crunch underfoot on **Deep Creek Loop Trail** (page 90), or hike to **Andrews Bald** (page 49).

5 **Go Wildlife-Watching:** Want to see owls, elk, deer, and even bears? You'll find them in **Cades Cove,** in **Cataloochee,** and at the **Oconaluftee Visitor Center.** Just remember to bring your binoculars or zoom lens if you want to get up close with the park's full-time residents (page 30).

<<<

6 **Hike to a Waterfall:** There are tons of hikes in the Smoky Mountains, so why not hit the trail and head to Hen Wallow Falls, Abrams Falls, Deep Creek, or Grotto Falls (page 27)?

7 **Go for a (Thrill) Ride in Dollywood:** Dolly Parton's mountain theme park is full of roller coasters and waterslides, ready to deliver the thrills you want (page 123).

8 **Say "Cheers!" in Asheville:** Asheville's vibrant brewery and restaurant scene makes for the perfect reward after a few days on the trail. Head to civilization for a celebratory pint (page 193).

<<<

Planning Your Trip

Where to Go

Great Smoky Mountains National Park

Great Smoky Mountains National Park, the **most-visited national park** in the country, straddles the North Carolina-Tennessee border and encompasses an incredible and varied landscape. Here you'll see rounded peaks and jagged mountaintops that are among the tallest in the eastern United States; white-water rivers and crystal-clear streams loaded with trout; **wildlife** like elk and bears, turkeys and deer in meadows and balds throughout the park; morning mist and **evening firefly shows** that delight millions of visitors every year. It's a hiker's paradise crisscrossed by more than 800 miles of **trails** and studded with **waterfalls** that make for the perfect place to rest and refresh.

NEWFOUND GAP

Newfound Gap bisects the park and connects Cherokee, North Carolina, with Gatlinburg, Tennessee. This beautiful drive draws just about every visitor to the park, and for good reason. With the **overlooks** that give big views of the eastern and western Smokies, sunrise at **Clingmans Dome,** quiet wooded strolls and **short day hikes,** spring wildflowers, and stellar fall color, it's where you can say, "I went to Great Smoky Mountains National Park and it was great" and mean every word.

WESTERN SMOKIES

In the western Smokies you find some busy spots like **Cades Cove, Fontana Lake,** and **Deep Creek** (a little less visited, but still busy), and a

Gatlinburg

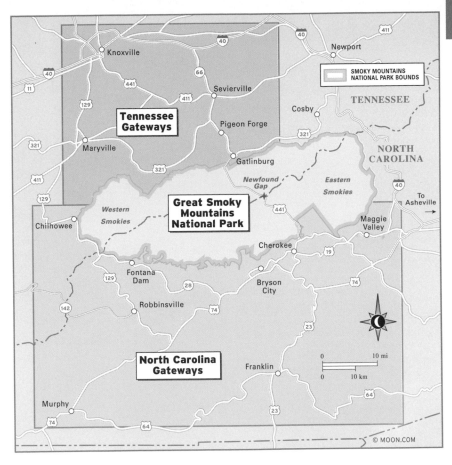

few places, like **Abrams Creek,** where visitors are infrequent. **Fly-fishing** is outstanding here, as the creeks flow into various rivers and into Fontana Lake. Long-distance hikers come here for the **Appalachian Trail, Lakeshore Trail,** and other big backpacking adventures.

EASTERN SMOKIES

The eastern Smokies are less visited, but spots like **Cosby, Cataloochee, Balsam Mountain,** and **Greenbrier** offer the remoteness and rugged beauty that characterize this park. **Camping, day hikes,** and **backpacking** adventures are the norm here. While many casual visitors don't frequent this region, serious outdoorspeople do. The **wildlife-viewing** alone makes this part of the park worth every minute you spend here.

Tennessee Gateways

Gatlinburg, the western gateway to the Smokies, has delighted families for generations, and nearby **Pigeon Forge** is home to **Dollywood,** the mountain-themed amusement park from the country music legend. **Knoxville,** a big-time college town and one of Tennessee's music cities, offers a taste of city living at the edge of the Smokies. All three towns are tourist draws in their own right, and their blend of Southern

- **Backpacking:** Make overnight reservations in advance to backpack to Mount LeConte, or hike a section of the Appalachian Trail and stay in one of the backcountry campsites.

- **Bicycling:** Get up early to rent a bike from the Cades Cove Store and ride the loop car-free on Wednesdays during summer.

- **Camping:** The Cataloochee Valley offers solitude; or time it right to see fireflies at Elkmont Campground.

- **Hiking:** Follow the easy Hen Wallow Falls Trail to a lovely waterfall, take in the views from the top of Andrews Bald, or make the trek to Rocky Top, a mountain immortalized in song. Adventurous souls can step foot on the Appalachian Trail.

- **Historic Sites:** Watch living history demonstrations at the Mountain Farm Museum or explore the chapel and cemetery of Cataloochee's former communities.

- **Scenic Drives:** Cruise along Newfound Gap Road for epic views and scenic overlooks. Drive through Roaring Fork Motor Nature Trail for close-up views of the hills and hollows.

hiking along Abrams Creek

- **Solitude:** Camp at Abrams Creek or Cosby Campgrounds, drive along Balsam Mountain Road, or take a midday hike in the Cataloochee Valley.

- **Waterfalls:** Hike to Grotto Falls, gear up and head to Abrams Falls, or get ready to take a dip in Midnight Hole while you hike along Big Creek Trail.

hospitality, humor, and mountain culture makes quite the impression.

North Carolina Gateways

Newfound Gap Road begins in **Cherokee,** North Carolina. This place is the ancestral home of the Eastern Band of Cherokee Indians, and they celebrate their history and culture, past and present, on the **Qualla Boundary.** Between Cherokee and Asheville, appealing small towns like **Dillsboro** and **Sylva** are rich with history and culture, while a town like **Bryson City** has embraced its place as an outdoor center and doorway to the park.

Located between the Blue Ridge and Smokies, with easy access to the mountains, **Asheville** is home to the lauded **Biltmore Estate,** some of the best **restaurants and breweries** in the South, and a number of cool **inns** and **B&Bs.** Only 90 minutes away, staying in Asheville makes getting to Great Smoky Mountains National Park easy.

When to Go

High Season

SUMMER (JUNE-AUG.)

Summer draws a **big number of visitors** escaping the summer heat at cooler high elevations and spending their vacation days in a beautiful part of the world. Beat the heat by tubing in **Deep Creek** or going **white-water rafting** on the Nantahala or Pigeon Rivers, or head to spots like Cades Cove for **early morning bike rides** or even **mountaintop hikes** throughout summer. Plan for **warm weather** and pack shorts, light tops, and plenty of water as well as sunscreen and bug spray.

AUTUMN (SEPT.-MID-NOV.)

Autumn is the obvious season to visit the mountains. With leaves showing their last—and brightest—bit of **fall color** from the end of **September** through **October,** you can have as long a season of leaf-peeping as you want. This is prime time to hit some of the park's **back roads**—Balsam, Heintooga Ridge, Little Greenbrier, Rich Mountain, and Heintooga Round Bottom Roads—for great views before the **routes close (early to mid-Nov.).** Every hike becomes a color study, and around every bend you'll find towering trees and sky-scraping mountainsides alive with gold, red, even purple leaves.

Most days are warm and sunny in the daytime, chilly in the evening, and even cold at night in the highest elevations. You'll be fine in long sleeves and a vest or light jacket most of the time, but you'll want something a little heavier if you're visiting late in the season.

Low Season

WINTER (MID-NOV.-FEB.)

Winter in this region varies by elevation. At the highest points, the temperatures drop—plummet, even—and the chance of snow or ice is real. It's a little warmer at the lowest elevations, but make no mistake, it's still winter. **Clingmans Dome Road** and **Roaring Fork Motor Nature Trail close** in late November when inclement winter weather has the potential to arrive, but the other main roads stay open as weather allows.

Expect snow several times throughout the season, with a few significant snowfalls; come with some warm layers, a hat, and gloves.

SPRING (MAR.-MAY)

Spring rains bring **wildflowers** and **waterfalls** back to life. Though trails can be muddy, it's a fabulous time to visit, especially for **wildlife-watching.** In **Cades Cove** and **Cataloochee,** you'll see bear cubs, deer fawns, and elk calves trailing their mothers at the woods' edge. The park's back roads—Balsam, Heintooga Ridge, Little Greenbrier, Parson Branch, Rich Mountain, and Heintooga Round Bottom Roads—and **Roaring Fork Motor Nature Trail** and **Clingmans Dome Road reopen.**

Spring temperatures are similar to fall, with warm days and cooler or even cold evenings, so pack accordingly—just remember to throw in a rain jacket.

Before You Go

Park Fees and Passes

Great Smoky Mountains National Park (www.nps.gov/grsm) is free to visit. Backcountry campgrounds require permits and reservations through the **Backcountry Information Office** (Sugarlands Visitor Center, 865/436-1297, https://smokiespermits.nps.gov, 8am-5pm daily, permits $4 pp per night, $20 maximum) up to 30 days in advance.

Entrance Stations

There are three main entrances to Great Smoky Mountains National Park. Each entrance is easily accessed from a nearby gateway town:

- From **Gatlinburg, Tennessee,** follow U.S. 441 south 2 miles to the north entrance to the park.

- From **Cherokee, North Carolina,** drive 2 miles north along U.S. 441 to the south entrance to the park.

- From **Townsend, Tennessee,** take Highway 73 east for 3 miles to enter the park near Cades Cove.

Reservations

Reservations are recommended at most **campgrounds** and required at others in the national park and along the Blue Ridge Parkway, especially during the peak seasons of summer and fall. Reservations for **hotels and B&Bs** in the gateway towns of Cherokee, Bryson City, and Asheville, North Carolina, or Gatlinburg, Pigeon Forge, and Knoxville, Tennessee, are recommended during summer and fall.

In the Park

Visitors Centers

The busiest information center in the park is **Sugarlands Visitor Center and Park Headquarters** (1420 Fighting Creek Gap Rd., Gatlinburg, TN, 865/436-1291, www.nps.gov/grsm, 9am-5pm daily Jan.-Nov., 9am-4:30pm daily Dec.), located in Gatlinburg, Tennessee, at the north entrance to Newfound Gap Road.

If you're entering from the North Carolina side, **Oconaluftee Visitor Center** (1194 Newfound Gap Rd., Cherokee, NC, 828/497-1904, www.nps.gov/grsm, 9am-5pm daily Jan.-Nov., 9am-4:30pm daily Dec.) is just 2 miles north of Cherokee at the south entrance to Newfound Gap Road.

Where to Stay

LeConte Lodge (865/429-5704, www.lecontelodge.com, late-Mar.-mid-Nov.) is the only true lodging in the park, accessible via a 5-6.8-mile hike. Even though there is no running water or electricity, the lodge books quickly. Reservations are via lottery up to **one year in advance.** For more amenities, plan to stay in the gateway towns of **Cherokee, North Carolina,** or **Gatlinburg, Tennessee.**

There are 10 developed campgrounds in the park. **Campground reservations** (877/444-6777, www.recreation.gov, $17.50-27) are accepted up to **six months in advance** for the following sites:

- **Elkmont Campground** (220 sites, Gatlinburg, TN, Mar.-Nov.), located west of Sugarlands Visitor Center, is the largest campground and one of the most visited.

- **Smokemont Campground** (142 sites, Cherokee, NC, year-round) is just off Newfound Gap Road, 3.2 miles north of the Oconaluftee Visitor Center.

Cataloochee Creek

- **Cades Cove Campground** (159 sites, Townsend, TN, year-round) is a popular spot located near the entrance of Cades Cove Loop.

- **Cosby Campground** (157 sites, Cosby, TN, Apr.-Oct.) is the park's third-largest campground, located in the quiet northwest corner of the park.

- **Cataloochee Campground** (Cataloochee, NC, Mar.-Oct.) has only 27 tent and RV sites in a valley on the west side. Reservations are required.

All other developed park campgrounds are a mix of **first-come, first-served** and **reservation only,** and are typically open April-October.

Getting Around

There are no park shuttles or public transportation available within the park—you will need **your own vehicle** (though there are a few for-hire hiking shuttles). There are also **no gas stations** in the park; fill up first in Cherokee, North Carolina; Gatlinburg, Tennessee; or Townsend, Tennessee.

Best of the Smokies

What do you do in Great Smoky Mountains National Park? Seeing how the park is mountainous and wild, with trails rather than roads leading into every corner, cove, and holler, it can be puzzling. But don't worry; we have plenty of ideas on how to spend a week you'll never forget in Great Smoky Mountains National Park.

Day 1
NEWFOUND GAP ROAD

Base yourself in **Gatlinburg,** Tennessee, where you'll have all manner of accommodations options and tempting entertainments easily at hand. Begin your exploration of the Smokies at the **Sugarlands Visitor Center,** a mere 2 miles from Gatlinburg at the northern end of Newfound Gap Road, where you can pick up maps, trail advice, and tips on where to spot the best wildflowers and wildlife.

As you drive **Newfound Gap Road** through the park, think about what kind of hike you want to stop and take. Is it something easy like a stroll along the **Kephart Prong Trail?** Or something challenging like the 10-mile (round-trip) hike to **Alum Cave Bluffs** or the 10-mile (round-trip) trek to the top of **Mount LeConte?** Along the way you'll pass trailheads and marked paths aplenty, and there's something to suit your hiking style.

Stop at any overlooks that catch your interest as you climb to the crest of the mountains on Newfound Gap Road. When you reach the gap, take the time to visit **Clingmans Dome,** the highest peak in the park. From the viewing platform at the top (an easy walk), you'll have a jaw-dropping view of the surrounding country. If you haven't taken a hike yet, **Andrews Bald** is nearby, and a moderate 3.5-mile round-trip trek will lead you to a high mountain meadow often ablaze with wildflowers.

Take Newfound Gap Road to the **Oconaluftee Visitor Center** in Cherokee, North Carolina.

the summit of Mount LeConte

Best of the Park in One Day

Mountain Farm Museum

If all you have is one day to spend in Great Smoky Mountains National Park, don't sweat it. You can still see a lot (and plan a return trip as soon as you can).

- Start the day in Gatlinburg with a stop at Sugarlands Visitor Center to pick up maps and find out about special events. Follow Little River Road west toward Cades Cove. You never move too fast on this curvy road, so slow down and take your time to soak up the views.

- At Cades Cove, grab a map and a driving guide for the scenic 11-mile Cades Cove Loop, one of the most popular drives in the park. Though there may be company—crowds, even—this wide, verdant valley ringed by tall peaks is the very picture of calm rural beauty. Stop for a walk to John Oliver Cabin, the Methodist Church, or one of the many cabins that showcase the history of settlement here. Once you've seen Cades Cove, return to grab lunch in Gatlinburg.

- Newfound Gap Road connects Gatlinburg, Tennessee, to Cherokee, North Carolina. Follow Newfound Gap Road up and over the Smokies. Along the way, stop at the Kephart Prong Trail or one of the other quiet walkways,

and head into the woods for a short, easy walk that'll have you immersed in nature in no time. In 23 miles, you'll reach the turnoff to Clingmans Dome, the highest peak in the park. If the weather is good, you'll be able to see the observation tower at the summit as you drive up Newfound Gap. After the 8-mile drive to the parking area, make the short, steep hike to the top. If the summit is shrouded in clouds (and it may well be), continue south along the crest of the Smokies.

- Stop at Newfound Gap to check out the Rockefeller Memorial, the place where President Franklin Delano Roosevelt dedicated the park in 1940. As you continue east toward Cherokee, stop at any of the scenic overlooks along the way—you can't go wrong.

- You'll draw close to the Oconaluftee Visitor Center in North Carolina by the end of the day. Perfect timing, as elk make an appearance every evening in a field adjacent to the visitors center and the Mountain Farm Museum. While checking out the collection of historic structures at Mountain Farm, keep an eye out for elk; they will often cross right through the middle of this recreated farmstead on their way to dinner.

Stop here to check out the historic cabins and structures at the **Mountain Farm Museum** and scan the field for the herd of elk that call these hills home before returning to Gatlinburg. Once you're back in Tennessee, it's time for dinner at **Local Goat** or **Smith & Son Corner Kitchen** before you hit **Sugarlands Distilling** or **Ole Smoky** for a little moonshine to calm your nerves.

Day 2
ROARING FORK

In the morning, have breakfast at the **Pancake Pantry,** and then head for the **Roaring Fork Motor Nature Trail** for today's hike. Depending on how adventurous you feel, this can be a half-day exploration of a waterfall or two, or a strenuous 14-mile trek to **Mount LeConte** and back. Either way, start off by hiking to **Rainbow Falls,** an 80-foot waterfall on LeConte Creek. For a short hike, turn around and hoof it back to the trailhead once you've seen the falls; to reach the summit of Mount LeConte, continue on the trail but be ready for a long, hard day of it. **Baskins Creek Falls** is a smaller waterfall—only 30 feet—but few people make the tough hike in to see it, so it's a bit of a hidden gem.

Since you've earned your supper, go for a Southern classic—the meat and three—at **Puckett's Grocery & Restaurant** before making your way to **The Island in Pigeon Forge,** where you can ride the **Great Smoky Mountain Wheel,** try an escape room, sample some moonshine, and get a late-night snack.

Day 3
COSBY

Head northeast to **Cosby** for a night of camping at **Cosby Campground,** where you'll have your choice of beautiful day hikes. **Hen Wallow Falls** and **Albright Grove** offer easy, wildflower-filled hikes. The trip to the stone fire tower at the top of **Mount Cammerer** is a long, tough day on the trail, but well worth it. If you've brought your fishing gear (and license), catch dinner in **Cosby Creek.**

late afternoon on a quiet country road in Cades Cove

Family Fun

cycling Cades Cove Loop

Great Smoky Mountains National Park is an ideal place to show kids the wonders of the great outdoors and the importance of our national parks. In addition to the Junior Ranger Program and ranger-led activities, there are several places that are perfect for kids.

- **Mountain Farm Museum:** This life-size model of a working mountain farm gives kids a feel for life here years ago.

- **Synchronous Fireflies:** These rare fireflies blink in unison as they fly above a field near the Elkmont Campground for a couple of weeks each summer. And if you miss the synchronous fireflies, keep your eyes peeled for their more typical cousins in any field around dusk.

- **Elk Watching:** Visit Cataloochee to see the elk herd there or stick around the Oconaluftee Visitor Center, where they make their appearance at dusk if not before.

- **Wednesday Bike Ride:** Head to Cades Cove on Wednesdays (May-Sept.) when the road is closed to cars but open to bicycles and foot traffic. Rent a bike and spend the day admiring Cades Cove at a slower pace than usual.

- **Big Creek Trail:** This gentle hike includes wildflowers galore, a stream for wading, a swimming hole, and a 35-foot waterfall cascade.

- **Go Fish:** Try your hand at fly-fishing. Cherokee, North Carolina, has weekly fishing contests for kids and adults. Fontana Lake is full of fish in the deep water and feeder streams. All along Little River you'll find plenty of places to wet a line, and in Bryson City, North Carolina, you can fly-fish downtown in the Tuckasegee River.

Day 4
CATALOOCHEE

In the morning, break camp and head north on Highway 32 for breakfast in Cosby at **Janice's Diner.** From Cosby, follow Foothills Parkway east to I-40 and take the scenic route south to **Mount Sterling Road,** a drive of about an hour. Along Mount Sterling Road, roll down the windows, relax, and breathe deeply—you're almost at one of the most secluded areas of the park.

In **Cataloochee,** register at the campground (reserve a site in advance), set up your tent, and enjoy a picnic lunch before lacing up your boots and heading into the valley. Look for **elk** in the field across from **Caldwell House,** or hike to **Palmer Chapel, Little Cataloochee,** or the

Steve Woody House. Anglers can wet a line in one of the nearby creeks and try to catch dinner. Sunset signals time for chow and **stargazing**—there's so little light pollution that the celestial show is breathtaking. Sit back and enjoy.

Day 5
CADES COVE

Today, we head west to **Cades Cove,** a mountain community that was one of the first places settled by Europeans on the western side of the Smokies. The 11-mile **Cades Cove Loop** leads through the former settlement and a collection of homes and structures. Take a moderate hike to **Abrams Falls,** a 20-foot waterfall, or follow the **Rich Mountain Loop,** a big day hike; either way, you'll find plenty of scenery. Take your time exploring because you're pitching a tent in **Cades Cove Campground** (reserve well in advance) tonight. Once it's dark, be sure to take a walk and admire the stars.

Day 6
FONTANA LAKE AND DEEP CREEK

The next day, follow **Rich Mountain Road** out of Cades Cove to its junction with U.S. 321 near Townsend. Soon you'll get on the **Foothills Parkway** and skirt the southern edge of the park before crossing the border into **North Carolina** at **Deals Gap.**

After Deals Gap, follow Highway 28 east along Cheoah Lake and past **Twentymile** to Fontana Village. To stretch your legs, turn north toward **Fontana Dam,** at the western end of Fontana Lake, and the trailhead for **Shuckstack Mountain,** a strenuous hike along the **Appalachian Trail.**

Or stay eastbound on Highway 28 and U.S. 74 all the way to **Bryson City, North Carolina.** Stop for lunch at the **River's End Restaurant** at the **Nantahala Outdoor Center** before turning north for your overnight at the **Deep Creek**

Tube Center and Campground. For a short hike, follow the trail to **Juney Whank Falls,** or head to the **Road to Nowhere,** an abandoned highway project that terminates with a tunnel through the mountain, and hike alongside Fontana Lake.

After a long day, relax at the campground in Deep Creek, which offers a relaxing treat: **tubing.** Wash away the sweat and trail dust with a float trip and some splashing in the creek. If you need more refreshment, head back to Bryson City to call on **Nantahala Brewing Brewpub, Mountain Layers Brewing Company,** or the **BCOutdoors Taproom** at **Bryson City Outdoors** for a pint or two.

Day 7
CHEROKEE, NORTH CAROLINA

For your final day, head to Cherokee, the ancestral heart of the Cherokee Nation and home of the Eastern Band of Cherokee Indians. The drive from Deep Creek is a short one, so you'll have a full day to explore. Start by visiting the **Museum of the Cherokee Indian,** where you'll learn the Cherokee creation story, hear songs and legends, and discover the heartache of the Trail of Tears. Across the street at the **Qualla Arts and Crafts Mutual,** browse the traditional arts and crafts made by Cherokee artisans and craftspeople, then head up the hill to the **Oconaluftee Indian Village** to see how the Cherokee people lived in the 18th and 19th centuries.

For lunch, grab a burger from **BJ's Diner** or get a pizza from **Wize Guyz Grille.** In the evening, head to **Harrah's Cherokee Casino,** where you can entertain yourself at table games or slots before dining at one of the on-site restaurants. The casino has overnight accommodations, or you can spend a quiet night at **Panther Creek Cabins.**

In the morning, it's a 1.5-hour drive to the airport in Asheville and the flight home.

Best Hikes

There are so many wonderful hikes that it can be hard to choose. Here are some bonus details to keep in mind when searching for your perfect trail.

If You're Looking For . . .

Waterfalls:

- The popular **Grotto Falls Trail** (2.6 miles round-trip) leads to a picture-perfect waterfall off the **Roaring Fork Motor Nature Trail.**

- In **Cosby** (a few miles northeast of Gatlinburg), you'll find **Hen Wallow Falls Trail** (4.4 miles round-trip), which leads to a delicate waterfall some 90 feet high.

- **Deep Creek Loop Trail and Juney Whank Falls** (5.5 miles round-trip) is a double loop hike that will take you past a trio of waterfalls and alongside a stream perfect for wading. It's

easy enough to give everyone in your party a good time on the trail.

- A hike suited to just about anyone? That leads to a great waterfall? The hike to the 20-foot **Abrams Falls** (5 miles round-trip) is the one—and it's in **Cades Cove,** so you know you'll drive right by the trailhead.

Wildflowers:

- **Andrews Bald** (3.5 miles round-trip) is a trail that starts at **Clingmans Dome,** a few miles off Newfound Gap Road, and leads to a high mountain meadow filled with wildflowers and shrubs that bloom throughout summer, making it one of the most rewarding hikes you'll find.

- Over in **Cades Cove,** head to **Rich Mountain Loop** (8.5 miles round-trip) and take on all or some of the hike; it's loaded with wildflowers from mid-April through summer. Spring's a

hikers rest at Abrams Falls

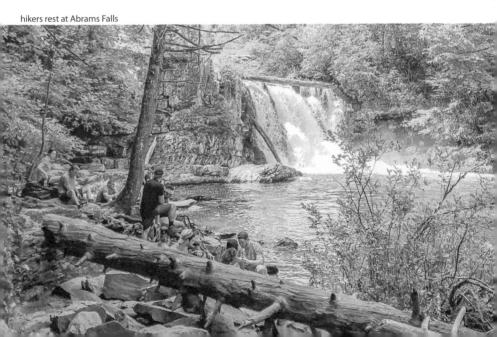

Escape the Crowds

The park sees record numbers of visitors year after year, especially during fall when the changing leaves bring visitors by the million. There are times that the most popular areas, and especially the most popular trails, can feel crowded. So what can you do?

Grab your warmest gear and plan to visit in **winter,** when it'll seem you have the park to yourself. The waterfalls will be magnificent, and if you're lucky, you'll be hitting the trails when the forest is hushed with falling snow. You can also plan to be at trailheads **early in the morning,** or you can pick **long trails,** like Lynn Camp Prong, where most visitors will turn back less than a mile in, making it easy to hike your way out of the crowds. Pockets of the park—like Cades Cove—are popular in spring when bears and deer are out with their young, but if you **camp** there, you'll have the loop road to yourself all day on Wednesday and early morning before they open the gates at dawn.

Here are some other less-crowded areas to consider:

• **Balsam Mountain Road:** The road's location off the Blue Ridge Parkway means people tend to forget this beautiful corner of the park. Head here in the fall to immerse yourself in foliage and escape the typical leaf-peeping traffic.

• **Mount Cammerer:** This strenuous hike is avoided by many, but it rewards with an unparalleled view. The few folks on this trail are here to be surrounded by the Smokies—and to dodge the crowds.

• **Lynn Camp Prong:** Start this trail near the Great Smoky Mountains Institute at Tremont, where a short hike will lead you to some photogenic cascades and dreamy wildflowers. Continue on to Indian Flats Falls at mile 4, then turn back.

• **Big Creek:** An almost-forgotten campground and some awesome hikes in a corner of the park most visitors overlook? That's Big Creek. Camp here, backpack to Mount Sterling, or check out the suited-for-everyone Big Creek Trail.

• **Abrams Creek:** This seasonal campground is rarely full; even if it is, several great hikes originate here. Hit the Rabbit and Abrams Creeks Loop or hike the easy, wildflower-rich Little Bottoms Trail.

hot time here, with wildflowers peaking in early May, but you'll see plenty anytime you hike here.

• Along the first mile of the **Chestnut Top Trail** (8.6 miles round-trip), the number and variety of wildflowers is surprising, making it a favorite of Spring Wildflower Pilgrimage visitors.

• When you hike from **Brushy Mountain to Mount LeConte** (11.8 miles round-trip), your time on the **Porters Creek Trail** takes you past a riot of wildflowers. Along the first mile of this trail, you'll find yellow trilliums, wild geraniums, and more.

Wildlife:

• **Rich Mountain Loop** (8.5 miles round-trip) in **Cades Cove** is a long one, but it gives you views of Cades Cove and plenty of wildlife-watching opportunities, making it one of the top hikes in the park.

• Keep **Little River Trail** (12.3 miles round-trip) short and sweet as you follow an old logging road alongside Little River and through the home of the **synchronous fireflies,** or follow the whole trail for an out-and-back day hike.

• The family-friendly **Oconaluftee River Trail** (3 miles round-trip) follows the Oconaluftee River near the Mountain Farm Museum and a field frequented by elk, which you can spot on the trail, crossing the trail, and even basking in the river. Remember to be careful and not get too close when you see an elk nearby.

Swimming Holes:

• **Big Creek Trail** (10.6 miles round-trip) follows a onetime logging road through the woods on a steady, easy incline that soon reaches **Midnight Hole,** a popular, and deep, swimming hole fed by a small waterfall; continue on the trail to see the 35-foot Mouse Creek Falls.

- **Chimney Tops Trail** (4 miles round-trip) leads to a fantastic view, but when you're hot from spending time on the trail, nothing is more refreshing than jumping into one of the deep holes in the creek for a shock of cold mountain water.

- Don't think **Little River Trail** (12.3 miles round-trip) is just for the synchronous fireflies; there's an excellent swimming hole with rocks for sunbathing near the trailhead, and several swimming holes up the trail.

- **Alum Cave Bluffs Trail** (4.6 miles round-trip) follows LeConte Creek for a little way, and along the first 1.5 miles of this trail, you'll find a few swimming holes that are four or five feet deep, which is plenty to cool you off.

Views:

- **Mount Cammerer Trail** (11.2 miles round-trip) is a tough hike to the summit, but you're rewarded with some of the best views in the park, courtesy of a **stone fire tower** built in the 1930s.

- More of a really steep path than a proper trail, the trek to the observation platform on the summit of **Clingmans Dome** (1 mile round-trip) is a must-do for anyone who wants big mountain views. Be sure to check the weather before you get started: Your view could vary between 7 yards and 70 miles (when you can see seven states), depending on cloud cover.

- The trail to **Baskins Creek Falls** (3.2 miles round-trip) leads you to a lovely view—the 30-foot namesake waterfall—but along the way you'll be rewarded with wildflowers filling meadows, the remnants of old homesites standing in the forest, and the chance to spot a white-tailed deer or two.

Alum Cave Bluffs Trail

fall colors along the Chimney Tops Trail

Wildlife-Watching

Seeing a bear and her cubs, an antlered elk grazing in a field, or a herd of white-tailed deer delivers quite the thrill. Fortunately, there are lots of places to see wildlife in the park and take a photo or two that'll help you remember the moment.

- One of the best places to see wildlife is **Cades Cove.** Bears, deer, turkeys, foxes, and even the elusive bobcat make an appearance, and birders will spot dozens of species here.

- On **Rich Mountain Road,** leading out of Cades Cove toward Townsend, you'll find bears and deer throughout the year, but especially in midsummer as wild berries and other food ripen.

- Bears can often be seen on **Newfound Gap Road,** crossing from one side to the other or hanging back in the woods near the road. Occasionally you can see one at a trailhead or in a parking lot, but not often.

- In **Cataloochee Valley,** at the north end of the park, you'll find a herd of elk. The area is an isolated and wildlife-rich spot, so you run a good chance of seeing bears, foxes, and other creatures while you're there.

elk on the riverbank in Cherokee

- Another herd of elk tends to hang out in the big field near the **Oconaluftee Visitor Center and Mountain Farm Museum** in Cherokee. Rangers and park volunteers are often on hand to help keep the proper distance between you and the elk.

It's important to remember that these are wild animals, and they should stay that way. Wherever you see wildlife, here are a few easy rules to follow to help keep you and the animals safe.

- **Keep your distance.** Try to keep at least 50 yards between you and the wildlife. Elk, deer, and bears are fast, so if you get too close and they don't like it, they may charge. Use a zoom lens, a spotting scope, or binoculars to get a close-up view.

- **Never feed the wildlife.** Once animals learn to associate humans with food, they look to every human for a bite to eat, which can lead to aggressive, food-seeking behavior. When that happens, the park is forced to take action, which often means euthanizing the animal. Don't lure animals to your car by offering a piece of food

through the window, and don't lay out treats as bait.

- **Don't disturb the animals.** As the rules say, "Feeding, touching, teasing, frightening, or intentionally disturbing wildlife is prohibited." That means it's a big no-no. If you approach an animal and it changes its behavior, you're too close.

- **Dispose of your trash responsibly.** Use the bear-proof trash receptacles and never litter.

- **Store food properly.** Don't know how? Ask a ranger; they're happy to help.

- **Report nuisance wildlife behavior to park officials.** See some aggressive bears or elk, a deer going from car to car for a snack, or a raccoon or bobcat behaving weirdly? Tell a ranger when and where as soon as you can.

Be responsible, and let's ensure there's wildlife for the next visitor—or generations of visitors—to enjoy.

Great Smoky Mountains National Park

Great Smoky Mountains National Park wears a
well-earned title: Great.

In its lifetime, the park has seen more than 570 million visitors, with more than 12.5 million people calling on the park in 2019 and 12.1 million in 2020. Why do they come? The mountains, the sky, the wildlife, the waters, the peaks, the stories—all of it. The Smokies are laced with trails; rivers, streams, and waterfalls trace their courses through the wrinkled mountains; and wildlife, from rare salamanders to huge elk to black bears, call this place home.

Straddling the North Carolina-Tennessee state line, Great Smoky Mountains National Park's 522,427 acres are nearly equally split between the two states. On the slightly larger North Carolina side, the

Highlights

Look for ★ to find recommended sights, activities, dining, and lodging.

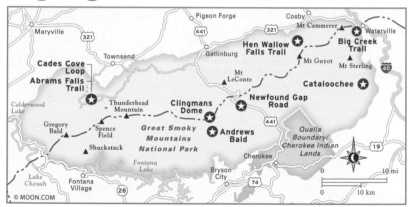

© MOON.COM

★ **Drive Newfound Gap Road:** Bisecting the park, this 33-mile route offers plenty of long views, short hikes, and streamside driving (page 43).

★ **Catch the View from Clingmans Dome:** From this third-highest peak in the eastern United States, you can see up to 100 miles on a clear day (page 45).

★ **Hike Andrews Bald:** Hike to one of the prettiest high-altitude meadows in the Smokies (page 49).

★ **Hike Hen Wallow Falls Trail:** An easy out-and-back day hike leads to one of the loveliest waterfalls in the park (page 62).

★ **Hike Big Creek Trail:** This creek-side trek is perfect for young and beginner hikers. Make it a 2- or 10-mile hike that includes waterfalls and wildflowers (page 66).

★ **Camp in Cataloochee:** Spending the night in this secluded valley—with its Milky Way views, solitude, and frequent elk sightings—is bliss (pages 71 and 74).

★ **Drive Cades Cove Loop:** The most-visited spot in the park provides plenty of wildlife viewing and its largest collection of intact historic structures (page 81).

★ **Hike Abrams Falls Trail:** This Cades Cove hike brings you through the forest to the 20-foot Abrams Falls, where a picnic lunch is in order (page 84).

mountains pile up against one another, making for tall peaks, steep slopes, and deep coves. It's wild here and more sparsely populated than on the Tennessee side, but throughout the park you'll find places so remote and so isolated they've remained undisturbed by humans for impossible stretches of time, or at least they feel that way. As wild and secret as these mountains are, you'll also find places like Cades Cove, a wide, fertile valley where people have lived for a long time. Today the remote places are still remote, requiring sometimes considerable effort to reach, but Cades Cove is a sightseer's delight with its preserved historic churches, schools, and homesteads, and in the fall, droves of visitors come for one of the most impressive color shows in the eastern United States.

The park comprises more than 800 square miles of cloud-ringed peaks and rainforest. It was designated an International Biosphere Reserve in 1976 and a World Heritage Site in 1983, and researchers, like the nonprofit organization Discover Life in America (www.dlia.org), come here to study the flora and fauna. Tens of thousands of species of plants and animals reside here, with 80 species of reptiles and amphibians alone, which is why the park is sometimes called the Salamander Capital of the World. More than 200 species of birds nest here, and 60-plus mammals—from mice to mountain lions (though the mountain lions are unofficial denizens, you can hear tales of a sighting now and again)—roam these hills. Discover Life in America's All-Taxa Biodiversity Inventory (a census of all nonmicrobial life forms) of Great Smoky Mountains National Park has turned up 970 species of plants and animals previously unknown to science.

The deep wilderness here makes an awesome refuge for outdoor enthusiasts, and the accessibility of the park's absolutely ravishing scenery makes it ideal for visitors of all ability levels and nearly all interests.

PLANNING YOUR TIME

Many visitors devote a single day to the park, driving Newfound Gap Road, taking a short hike along the way, and circling Cades Cove before moving on. To give the park a fair shake, devote at least **three days** to exploring. Spend a day in the north end of the park in Cataloochee Valley, then devote another day to savoring the sights of Newfound Gap Road, including a stop by Clingmans Dome and time to drive Cades Cove. On the third day, pick a waterfall to visit or trail to hike; on the Roaring Fork Motor Nature Trail, you'll find both.

Within the park, **lodging** is limited to camping—unless you want to pack your sleeping bag and hike to the rustic LeConte Lodge just below the summit of Mount LeConte—so your best bets for hotels, motels, inns, cabins, and B&Bs are the **Tennessee towns** of Gatlinburg, Pigeon Forge, Townsend, and Knoxville; or the **North Carolina towns** of Cherokee, Bryson City, Maggie Valley, Sylva, Dillsboro, and Asheville.

When to Go

Seasonal considerations have a big influence on park visitation. Crowds arrive for the blooming of **spring** wildflowers, and each **autumn** the park is crawling with people who want a good long look at the mountains blazing with red, yellow, and burgundy leaves. **Summer** brings visitors for hiking and that cool mountain air, while **winter** finds the park more empty than full, but no less beautiful.

Weather can vary wildly across the park in any season, due in part to the elevation, which ranges from 900 feet at the lowest point to more than 6,600 feet at the highest. Clingmans Dome, the highest point in the park, has an average high temperature of only 65°F in July; the only months you're guaranteed *not* to see snow flurries are June-August. In contrast, on the same day temperatures can

---

Previous: approaching Clingmans Dome from Andrews Bald; Hen Wallow Falls Trail; Cades Cove in autumn

Great Smoky Mountains National Park

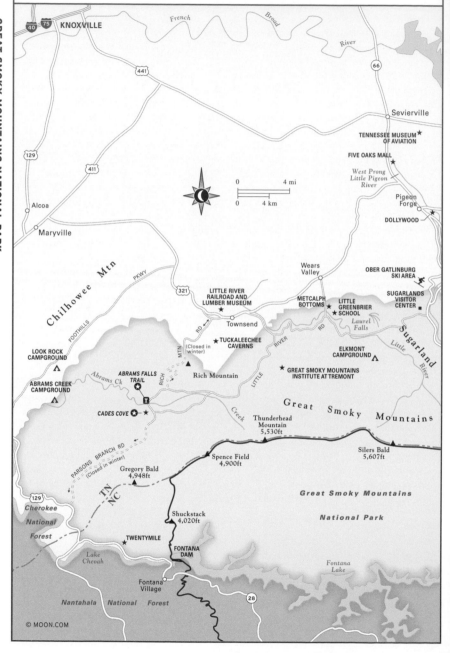

KNOXVILLE

French

Broad

River

Sevierville

TENNESSEE MUSEUM OF AVIATION

FIVE OAKS MALL

West Prong Little Pigeon River

Pigeon Forge

DOLLYWOOD

Alcoa

Maryville

0   4 mi
0   4 km

Wears Valley

OBER GATLINBURG SKI AREA

SUGARLANDS VISITOR CENTER

Chilhowee Mtn

FOOTHILLS PKWY

LITTLE RIVER RAILROAD AND LUMBER MUSEUM

METCALPH BOTTOMS

LITTLE GREENBRIER SCHOOL

Laurel Falls

Sugarland

Townsend

TUCKALEECHEE CAVERNS

(Closed in winter)

ELKMONT CAMPGROUND

Little River

LOOK ROCK CAMPGROUND

Abrams Ck

RICH MTN

Rich Mountain

GREAT SMOKY MOUNTAINS INSTITUTE AT TREMONT

ABRAMS FALLS TRAIL

ABRAMS CREEK CAMPGROUND

CADES COVE

LITTLE RIVER

Creek

Great   Smoky   Mountains

Thunderhead Mountain 5,530ft

Silers Bald 5,607ft

PARSONS BRANCH RD
(Closed in winter)

Spence Field 4,900ft

Gregory Bald 4,948ft

Great Smoky Mountains

National Park

TN
NC

Shuckstack 4,020ft

Cherokee

National

Forest

TWENTYMILE

FONTANA DAM

Lake Cheoah

Fontana Lake

Fontana Village

28

Nantahala   National   Forest

© MOON.COM

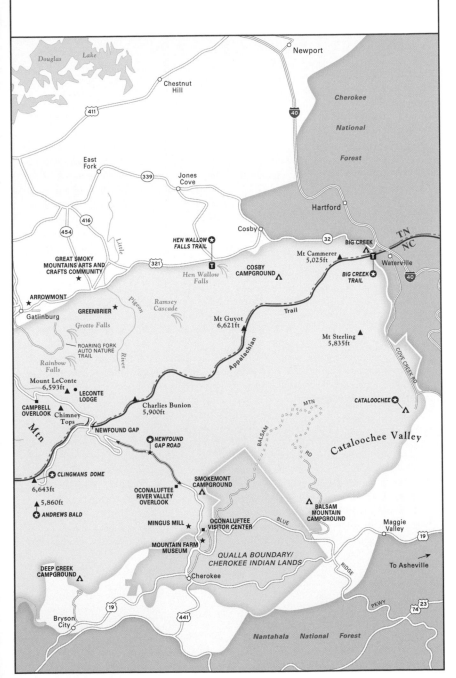

Newport

Douglas Lake

Chestnut Hill

411

Cherokee

National

Forest

I-40

East Fork

339

Jones Cove

416

Hartford

454

Cosby

32   BIG CREEK

TN
NC

HEN WALLOW FALLS TRAIL

Mt Cammerer 5,025ft

Waterville

GREAT SMOKY MOUNTAINS ARTS AND CRAFTS COMMUNITY

321

Hen Wallow Falls

COSBY CAMPGROUND

BIG CREEK TRAIL

I-40

ARROWMONT

Pigeon

Ramsey Cascade

Trail

Mt Sterling 5,835ft

COVE CREEK RD

GREENBRIER

Gatlinburg

Grotto Falls

Mt Guyot 6,621ft

ROARING FORK AUTO NATURE TRAIL

River

Appalachian

Rainbow Falls

CATALOOCHEE

Mount LeConte 6,593ft

LECONTE LODGE

MTN

CAMPBELL OVERLOOK

Charlies Bunion 5,900ft

Chimney Tops

BALSAM

Cataloochee Valley

Mtn

NEWFOUND GAP

NEWFOUND GAP ROAD

RD

CLINGMANS DOME

6,643ft

SMOKEMONT CAMPGROUND

5,860ft

OCONALUFTEE RIVER VALLEY OVERLOOK

ANDREWS BALD

BALSAM MOUNTAIN CAMPGROUND

Maggie Valley

MINGUS MILL

OCONALUFTEE VISITOR CENTER

BLUE

19

MOUNTAIN FARM MUSEUM

QUALLA BOUNDARY/ CHEROKEE INDIAN LANDS

To Asheville

DEEP CREEK CAMPGROUND

RIDGE

Cherokee

19

441

PKWY

74   23

Bryson City

Nantahala   National   Forest

be in the upper 60s on Clingmans Dome but in the low 90s with some intense humidity in Cades Cove.

If ever there was a place for wearing layers, this is it. Be sure to pack long sleeves or a light jacket and your rain gear, regardless of the season. Keep these extremes in mind in terms of safety as well: A snowstorm can bring two feet of snow to the highest elevations and leave ice on the curvy mountain roads while temperatures at the foot of the mountains are considerably warmer and snow-free. Thick fog and isolated storms are also a possibility year-round.

SPRING

Spring wildflowers begin to appear in late **March** and peak in mid- to late-**April.** This time of year, rain is common and there's a chance of a spring snowstorm (especially at higher elevations, but even at the base of the mountains) or a strong spring thunderstorm. It's a muddy time to hit the trail, and you'll want to pack layers and foul-weather gear if you plan on heading into the woods. Temperatures begin to climb in spring, working toward summer's warmth, but it happens in fits and starts, another reason to keep a sweater or jacket handy when visiting in the spring.

The wildflower display bleeds over into early summer as azaleas, mountain laurels, and rhododendrons put on their best show just after the season transitions to summer, but due to the park's extensive microclimates, it's possible to see flame azaleas blooming early, peaking **April-July.** Mountain laurels come next, blooming **May-June,** and rhododendrons come last with a burst of color in **June-July.** The wildflowers bloom from the bottom of the mountains to the top, with patches of color and reports of blooms occurring first at lower elevations and ending at the high balds and ridgelines.

SUMMER AND FALL

Summer and fall constitute the park's high season; the busiest times to visit are **mid-June to mid-August** and throughout **October.** In summer, the most popular hiking trails don't quite resemble a queue, but you're guaranteed to encounter many groups of hikers of all ages and ability levels coming and going. In fall, these same trails are busy with picture-takers; if fall color is on your agenda, consider spending more time on the gravel roads and long hikes and in seldom-seen corners of the park's extreme north and south ends.

Fall color is on everyone's mind when they visit in October. The mountaintops are the first to reveal signs of the season's best and brightest show as they begin to turn in early October. Colors bleed down the mountains, descending until early November, when the trees from the foot to the crest of the mountains are aflame with color. Note that the arrival and departure of this seasonal display isn't set; summer heat can alter the schedule for wildflower blooms and fall color, and rainfall can do the same. It's best to call the park or check regional websites to see how fall color is progressing. It's a safe bet to visit in **mid-October** for a solid color show.

Temperatures throughout summer and fall can get as high as the low 90s (F) at the lowest elevations, though high temperatures and humidity are relatively rare. There is an extreme of temperature to consider, though. Spots like Clingmans Dome can be chilly even in the summer, with as much as a 30°F difference from peak to valley floor. Those temperature extremes also give rise to the park's namesake "smoky" effect as layers of fog can fill valleys or wrap the peaks. If you visit Clingmans Dome and find it enshrouded in fog, try again in an hour or two, or even the next day, and the weather will likely reward you.

WINTER

Winter can be a fantastic time to visit the park, especially if you're there for a bit of snow. The crowds are nearly nonexistent, and maintained roads like Cades Cove Loop and Newfound Gap are starkly beautiful. Along the mountain ridges, trails, and streams, as well as among the historic structures, you'll find lovely, lonely sights.

Temperatures can hit highs of 50°F, but more often than not it's cold, with nighttime temperatures at or below freezing (32°F, and colder at high elevations) and daytime temperatures in the 40s. Snow is possible, with most significant snow occurring in **January-February.**

Several roads in the park are closed in the winter, though closing dates vary. Among these are Balsam Mountain, Clingmans Dome, Little Greenbrier, Rich Mountain, and Heintooga Round Bottom Roads, and the Roaring Fork Motor Nature Trail. The **Blue Ridge Parkway,** which starts (or ends) in Cherokee, North Carolina, also closes in the winter. **Newfound Gap Road** remains open in all but the most serious of weather; however, road crews work to maintain it in the winter. Before you set out, check current road conditions (865/436-1200, ext. 631, or on Twitter by following @SmokiesRoadNPS) and the weather (865/436-1200, ext. 630).

Exploring the Park

Great Smoky Mountains National Park (GSMNP, 865/436-1200, www.nps.gov/grsm) was the first—and the largest—of three National Park Service units established in the southern Appalachians. The park was founded in 1934, followed in 1935 by the Blue Ridge Parkway and in 1936 by Shenandoah National Park. These sister facilities include some 600 miles of contiguous roads and close to 800,000 acres of land, all of it acquired from private landholders, and all of it standing testament to the wild, rugged beauty of the Appalachian Mountains and the people who helped tame these places.

Great Smoky Mountains National Park is the most-visited national park, with visitor numbers of more than 12 million each year. In the 522,427-acre park, there are 850 miles of hiking trails, including 71 miles of the Appalachian Trail; 16 mountains over 6,000 feet; 2,100 miles of mountain streams and rivers; and an astoundingly diverse set of flora and fauna.

More than 17,000 species have been documented here, including more than 100 species of native trees, 1,500 flowering plant species, 200 species of birds, 66 types of mammals, 67 native species of fish, 39 varieties of reptiles, and 43 species of amphibians. And that's not even counting the mushrooms, mollusks, and millipedes. Researchers believe an additional 30,000-80,000 species may exist. No other area of a similar size in a similar climate can boast a higher number of species. A multitude of factors are believed to have contributed to this astounding diversity, including the wide elevation range (875-6,643 feet), which provides a large variance in temperature, as well as the fantastic growing conditions created by summer's high humidity and abundant rainfall (apart from the Pacific Northwest, these are the rainiest mountains in the country). Plus, as some of the oldest mountains in the world—it is believed they were formed some 200-300 million years ago—the Smokies have seen a number of dramatic climatic changes. During the last ice age (10,000 years ago), the glacial intrusion into the United States didn't reach the Smokies, making them a refuge for species of plants and animals displaced from homes farther north.

VISITORS CENTERS

Begin your exploration of Great Smoky Mountains National Park with a stop at one of the park's four visitors centers. You'll find rangers who know the trail and road conditions as well as what's blooming where. You can also grab detailed maps and trail guides.

Sugarlands Visitor Center

The busiest information center in the park is

Blooms and Foliage

trillium

Spring wildflowers begin to appear in late March, peaking in mid- to late-April, blooming first in lower elevations, then creeping up the mountains. **Fall colors** appear in the opposite order, with the mountaintops the first to show autumn's arrival in early October. The colors bleed down until mid- to late-October and early November, when trees from the foot to the crest of the mountains are alight with color. Summer heat can throw the schedule for springtime blooms and fall colors off a bit, as can rainfall levels.

Keep in mind that the dates for wildflower blooms and fall color displays are only guidelines. Call the Great Smoky Mountains National Park or check with regional websites to find out how the seasons are progressing.

· **Catawba rhododendron:** Grows at elevations above 3,500 feet; blooms in June.

· **Flame azalea:** This wild shrub blooms at lower elevations in April-May, at higher elevations through June-early July.

· **Mountain laurel:** Blooms early May-June.

· **Rosebay rhododendron:** Blooms in lower elevations in June-July.

· **Trillium:** This wildflower comes in several colors and blooms in late spring and summer at low and mid-elevations.

· **Witch hazel:** Blooms in late fall and into winter at low and mid-elevations.

· **Yellow fringed orchid:** Blooms throughout summer at lower elevations.

also the first stop for visitors entering the park from Tennessee. **Sugarlands Visitor Center and Park Headquarters** (1420 Fighting Creek Gap Rd., Gatlinburg, TN, 865/436-1291, www.nps.gov/grsm, 9am-5pm daily Jan.-Nov., 9am-4:30pm daily Dec.) is located just inside the park, only 2 miles from Gatlinburg. Here you'll find the usual visitors center information as well as a 20-minute film introducing you to the park.

The **Backcountry Information Office** (865/436-1297, https://smokiespermits.nps. gov, 8am-5pm daily, permits $4 pp per night, $20 maximum) is located at the Sugarlands

Visitor Center. This is the place to get back-country permits, as well as thru-hiker permits for the Appalachian Trail. Facilities include restrooms, snack machines, and a **Great Smoky Mountains Association** (www.smokiesinformation.org) bookstore and shop.

Oconaluftee Visitor Center

If you're entering Great Smoky Mountains National Park from the North Carolina side, **Oconaluftee Visitor Center and Mountain Farm Museum** (1194 Newfound Gap Rd., Cherokee, NC, 828/497-1904, www.nps.gov/grsm, visitor center 9am-5pm daily Jan.-Nov., 9am-4:30pm daily Dec.; Mountain Farm dawn-dusk daily), just 2 miles north of Cherokee on U.S. 441 (Newfound Gap Rd.), is the best place to begin your tour.

You'll find public restrooms, snack machines, and a bookstore and shop operated by the **Great Smoky Mountains Association** (www.smokiesinformation.org). Adjacent is the **Mountain Farm Museum,** a collection of log structures that include a farmhouse, a barn, a smokehouse, and other homestead structures; demonstrations of early farm life are held here regularly.

Clingmans Dome Visitor Contact Station

Along Newfound Gap Road is the turnoff to Clingmans Dome and the **Clingmans Dome Visitor Contact Station** (Clingmans Dome Rd., off Newfound Gap Rd., 25 miles from Cherokee, NC, and 23 miles from Gatlinburg, TN, 865/436-1200, www.nps.gov/grsm, 10am-6pm daily Apr.-June and Sept.-Oct., 10am-6:30pm daily July-Aug., 9:30am-5pm daily Nov., closed Dec.-Mar.). Clingmans Dome is the highest peak in Great Smoky Mountains National Park and features a fantastic viewing platform. At the visitor contact station, you'll find information on the park, a bookstore operated by the Great Smoky Mountains Association (www.smokiesinformation.org), and restrooms.

Cades Cove Visitor Center

In Cades Cove, about halfway around the ever-popular Loop Road, is the **Cades Cove Visitor Center** (686 Cades Cove Loop Rd., Townsend, TN, 865/436-7318, 9am-4:30pm daily Dec.-Jan., 9am-5pm daily Feb., 9am-6:30pm daily Mar. and Sept.-Oct., 9am-7pm daily Apr.-Aug., 9am-5:30pm daily Nov.). Indoor and outdoor exhibits illustrate Southern mountain life and culture, and there are a number of historic structures to photograph and explore. You'll also find a gift shop and restrooms at the Cades Cove Visitor Center.

Backcountry Information Office

The knowledgeable folks at the **Backcountry Information Office** (1420 Fighting Creek Gap Rd., Gatlinburg, TN, 865/436-1297, https://smokiespermits.nps.gov, 8am-5pm daily) are a good first resource when planning a hiking or backcountry camping trip. There are more than a dozen shelters and approximately 100 backcountry campsites sprinkled throughout the park at convenient intervals. Those on multiday hikes or interested in backcountry camping can **reserve tent sites** and shelter space (https://smokiespermits.nps.gov, permits $4 pp per night, $20 maximum) up to 30 days in advance of their trip. Hikers, campers, anglers, and equestrians are asked to follow Leave No Trace practices.

Field Schools

Two Tennessee-based organizations affiliated with Great Smoky Mountains National Park offer ways to get to know the park even better. The **Smoky Mountain Field School** (865/974-0150, www.outreach.utk.edu/smoky, from $70) teaches workshops and leads excursions to educate participants in a wide array of fields related to the Smokies. One-day classes focus on the history and cultural heritage of the park, the lives of some of the park's most interesting animals, folk medicine and cooking of the southern Appalachians, and much more. Instructors also lead one-day and

By the Numbers

Great Smoky Mountains National Park puts up some impressive numbers, from the staggering number of visitors—12.1 million in 2020—to the incredible biodiversity—970 plant and animal species new to science have been discovered within the park. Its other numbers are just as impressive.

- Size: 522,427 acres

- Elevation: From 875 feet at the mouth of Abrams Creek to the towering summit of Clingmans Dome at 6,643 feet

- 16 peaks standing at more than 6,000 feet elevation

- 850 miles of hiking trails, including 70 miles of the Appalachian Trail

- More than 400,000 hikers annually

- Only 384 miles of roadway in the park; 146 miles are unpaved

- 1,000 front-country campsites

- 730 miles of fish-bearing streams

- And all this with only 240 permanent employees

overnight hikes into the heart of the park. This is a great way to discover the park far beyond what you would be able to do on your own, so check their schedule and sign up for a class that interests you. Unfortunately, current regulations from the University of Tennessee mean Field School programs are closed to minors, a situation we hope will change soon.

The **Great Smoky Mountains Institute at Tremont** (9275 Tremont Rd., Townsend, TN, 865/448-6709, www.gsmit.org) teaches students of all ages about the ecology of the region, wilderness rescue and survival skills, and even nature photography. Many of the classes and guided trips are part of Road Scholar travel programs, kids' camps, or teacher-training institutes; however, there are also rich opportunities for unaffiliated learners.

PARK ENTRANCES

In the National Park System, Great Smoky Mountains National Park is unusual in that it has **no entrance fee,** so if you see a Friends of the Smokies donation box and you're so

inclined (or so moved by what you see around you), toss a few bucks their way.

Main Entrances

There are three main entrances to Great Smoky Mountains National Park that access the busiest parts of the park. Each entrance is easily approached from a nearby gateway town:

- From **Cherokee, North Carolina,** drive 2 miles north along U.S. 441 into the park.

- From **Gatlinburg, Tennessee,** follow U.S. 441 south 2 miles into the park.

- From **Townsend, Tennessee,** take Highway 73 3 miles east into the park.

Remote Entrances

There are 17 additional points at which you can enter the park via automobile. The majority of these are gravel roads in varying states of maintenance that require different degrees of driving confidence and skill. If you're up for an adventure, these roads can lead you into some beautiful corners of the park that few others experience.

Note that though these secondary entrances enter the national park, they don't have access to the extensive trail systems and historic and recreational opportunities provided by the main entrances.

ROARING FORK MOTOR NATURE TRAIL

From **Gatlinburg, Tennessee,** turn off the main parkway in Gatlinburg at traffic light number 8 and follow Historic Nature Trail Road to Cherokee Orchard and the entrance to the national park, about 1 mile from Gatlinburg. Soon after you pass the Rainbow Falls Trailhead, you can enter **Roaring Fork Motor Nature Trail** (open Apr.-Nov.) or turn back to Gatlinburg. All told, it's a drive of 6.5 miles.

Roaring Fork Motor Nature Trail is in the western-central part of the park, to the east of Newfound Gap Road. From here, you can access several trails to waterfalls as well as trails leading to **Mount LeConte;** you'll also find several historic structures and homesteads along this one-way road that give visitors a taste of the wild, rugged nature of these mountains.

RICH MOUNTAIN ROAD

Rich Mountain Road (open Apr.-Nov.) roughly follows the course of an old trading and horse trail over the mountains from Cades Cove to Townsend, Tennessee. It's a one-way gravel road, and the forest is thick here. As you climb out of Cades Cove, there are one or two spots where the views open up and you look out across the valley, but the rest is heavily wooded. Toward the end you'll reach a point where the road widens to two lanes, providing access to a pair of trails at the parking area here.

From **Townsend, Tennessee,** follow Highway 73 (West Lamar Alexander Pkwy.) to Old Tuckaleechee Road, then turn left on Dry Valley Road (Old Cades Cove Rd.) and follow it to where the pavement gives way to a gravel road. Soon after, it changes to a gravel road; you'll find a small parking area

and signs indicating a one-way road. This is Rich Mountain Road coming in from **Cades Cove.**

This entrance is only 7 miles from Townsend, 0.5 miles from the nearest house, and just inside the national park boundary, but it will feel much more isolated because the forest is thick and wild here. From the parking area, you can access both **Ace Gap Trail** and **Rich Mountain Trail.**

HAPPY VALLEY ROAD

From **Walland, Tennessee,** follow Highway 73 (East Lamar Alexander Pkwy.) to Foothills Parkway; take the Foothills Parkway south, then turn left onto Butterfly Gap Road, right on Flats Road, then follow Happy Valley Road to the unpaved **Abrams Creek Road,** a trip of 17.1 miles.

This entrance takes you into the southwestern portion of the park, just over the mountain from Cades Cove into the headwaters of Abrams Creek. The **Abrams Creek Campground** (late May-Oct., $17.50) has 16 first-come, first-served campsites and can accommodate RVs up to 12 feet.

DEEP CREEK ROAD

From **Cherokee, North Carolina,** follow U.S. 19 south to Bryson City, then turn right on West Deep Creek Road until you enter the park and reach the Deep Creek Campground. At **Deep Creek Campground** (877/444-6777, www.recreation.gov, mid-May-Oct., $25) the 92 campsites fill up fast, so make reservations early if you want to explore the trails and waterfalls of the southeastern edge of the park. It's only 2.2 miles from downtown Bryson City.

LAKEVIEW DRIVE

From **Cherokee, North Carolina,** follow U.S. 19 south to Bryson City; the road name changes to Old River Road, then Deep Creek Road. Turn left on Ramseur Street and then right on Depot Street. Finally, turn onto Everett Street (which changes to Fontana Road). Follow **Fontana Road** to the end, where there is a parking area a short walk from a tunnel through the mountain.

This 18.5-mile drive is known to locals as the **Road to Nowhere** (or, more properly, Fontana Road) for its strange intrusion into the national park. The road earned this name when the national park scrapped plans to build Lakeview Drive, a 26-mile parkway along the shores of Fontana Lake. The project built this first part of the road and completed a tunnel through the mountain before stopping. Today hikers, mountain bikers, and anglers use this point to access the streams and trails along the shores of **Fontana Lake.**

HEINTOOGA RIDGE ROAD

From the **Blue Ridge Parkway,** turn onto paved Heintooga Ridge Road (open mid-May-Nov.) at milepost 458.2. You'll be on the Blue Ridge Parkway for the first 4 miles but will abruptly enter Great Smoky Mountains National Park at **Black Camp Gap.** The road continues 5 miles, passing **Balsam Mountain Campground.** It terminates at the **Heintooga Overlook.**

Look for the one-lane gravel road at Heintooga Overlook and you've found **Heintooga Round Bottom Road** (May-Nov.). This gravel track takes you on an hour-long, 14-mile trip along **Balsam Mountain** and down into Straight Fork Valley on the lands of the Eastern Band of Cherokee Indians (the Qualla Boundary). Keep an eye out for wildlife along this seldom-traveled road, or stop for a short hike along the trails that branch off the road. This road is closed to vehicles longer than 25 feet or passenger vehicles towing trailers.

COVE CREEK ROAD

From **Asheville, North Carolina,** follow I-40 west to exit 20, then follow Highway 276 to Cove Creek Road into the Cataloochee Valley, a trip of 42 miles.

From **Knoxville, Tennessee,** follow I-40 east to exit 20, then take Highway 284 to Cove Creek Road into the Cataloochee Valley, a trip of 80 miles.

Cove Creek Road skirts the edge of the **Cherokee National Forest** before plunging into the park. The road is narrow but paved for half the drive; it changes to a well-maintained gravel track that, while still narrow, is open to two-way traffic. The road enters **Cataloochee Valley** in the extreme northern end of the national park, where there is camping, plenty of hiking, wildlife viewing (including herds of elk), and historic buildings.

MOUNT STERLING ROAD

From **Cataloochee Valley, North Carolina,** take the gravel Mount Sterling Road north and west out of the valley to I-40, a drive of 16.4 miles. The road is narrow but well maintained, and it winds its way out of the **Cataloochee Valley** up toward **Mount Sterling,** then back down to cross the Tennessee state line where you access I-40.

COSBY PARK ROAD

From **Gatlinburg, Tennessee,** take U.S. 321/Highway 73/East Parkway northeast to Cosby, then turn right on Highway 32 and right again onto Cosby Park Road to the **Cosby Campground** (127 Cosby Park Rd., Cosby, TN, info 423/487-2683, reservations 877/444-6777, www.recreation.gov, mid-May-Oct., $17.50), a trip of 21 miles. Cosby Park Road provides access to the campground in the northwestern quadrant of the park and also to the hiking trails and waterfalls nearby, namely Hen Wallow Falls, the hike to the top of Mount Cammerer, and as a way to connect to the Appalachian Trail.

GREENBRIER ROAD

From **Gatlinburg, Tennessee,** take U.S. 321/Highway 73/East Parkway northeast 5.4 miles, then turn right into the park. This narrow but paved two-lane road leads to the **Ramsey Cascades** trailhead, some excellent wildflower viewing, and trout fishing. The paved road eventually gives way to a maintained gravel road that leads to additional trailheads.

DRIVING TOURS
★ Newfound Gap Road
33 MILES

While many visitors use this 33-mile road that bisects Great Smoky Mountains National Park as a mere thruway, it's actually one of the prettiest drives anywhere. The curvy road alternates between exposed and tree-enclosed, and a number of **scenic overlooks** provide spectacular views of the Smokies. Stop at one that has a **trail** (more than half of them do) and take a short walk into the woods or eat a picnic lunch at one of the mountainside overlooks. Whatever you do on this road between **Cherokee** and **Gatlinburg,** take your time and enjoy the ride.

Cades Cove Loop
11 MILES

This 11-mile loop around a broad and picturesque valley ringed by high peaks is about as pretty as it gets. The fields, forests, those high peaks, wildlife, and historic structures are just some of the highlights of the **Cades Cove Loop** (closed to vehicles Wed. May-Sept.). Expect crowds at one of the park's most popular spots in any season, especially in the fall. To avoid the crowds, show up early. Hikes include gentle strolls to homesteads, cabins, and churches, or longer hikes to **Abrams Falls.** The road is paved and very well maintained, and although it's **one-way,** there are two points where you can cut across the valley to shorten the drive or circle back for one more look, whichever strikes your fancy.

Rich Mountain Road
8 MILES

Rich Mountain Road (open Apr.-Nov.) is a photographer's dream. Running north from Cades Cove over Rich Mountain to **Tuckaleechee Cove** and **Townsend,** this **one-way gravel road** provides a few stunning views of Cades Cove and Tuckaleechee Cove. You're likely to see bears, deer, turkeys, and other wildlife along the way. The road is typically in good condition and isn't too challenging as far as back roads go, but I'd avoid tackling this drive in a low-clearance vehicle or your economy rental car; instead, go with a truck or SUV (no 4WD necessary). Know that the road gets a little steep once it passes outside park boundaries, but it's nothing too hair-raising.

If you're stuck with a rental or you aren't confident in your off-road driving abilities, you can always enjoy similar views on the 8.5-mile Rich Mountain Loop hike, a great way to see Cades Cove without the high-season gridlock.

Heintooga Round Bottom Road/Balsam Mountain Road
14 MILES

This 14-mile one-way gravel road goes by two names—**Heintooga Round Bottom Road** and **Balsam Mountain Road** (open mid-May-Nov.)—but they're one and the same. Accessed from Blue Ridge Parkway milepost 458.2 (just a few miles from the Cherokee, NC, entrance), this is an often-overlooked road through a high and wild part of Great Smoky Mountains National Park. In the spring and summer wildflowers bloom, and in the fall the road is awash in color. The drive takes a little more than an hour from the **Blue Ridge Parkway** back down into **Cherokee;** as off-roading experiences go, it's an easy one. The road is well maintained and generally in good condition, but don't try it in your low-clearance rental or the family minivan. You'll be fine in a truck or even a small SUV.

Roaring Fork Motor Nature Trail
5.5 MILES

The 5.5-mile **Roaring Fork Motor Nature Trail** (open Apr.-Nov.), just a few miles from the heart of Gatlinburg, has everything Smoky Mountain visitors are looking for: rushing creeks, waterfalls, hikes, historic structures, and plenty of photo opportunities. This **one-way road** stays busy, but is seldom bumper-to-bumper, though some of the parking areas may make you feel differently. If you're looking for an **easy drive** with some **short walks** to homesteads and waterfalls (which make them perfect for those with mobility concerns), this is the one you need. Head there just after a rainfall to see a roadside waterfall called **Place of a Thousand Drips.**

Foothills Parkway
31.6 MILES

The scenic **Foothills Parkway** skirts the Tennessee side of the park, giving you views of the Smokies once reserved for locals. Originally intended to be a 72-mile byway running along the park's western flank, it's incomplete thanks to a 34-mile gap in the middle. That said, there's plenty to see along the **Foothills Parkway West**—a 31.6-mile stretch from Tallassee to Wears Valley—and even on the 5.6-mile **Foothills Parkway East** connecting Cosby with I-40. Four overlooks on the East section have views of Inadu Knob, Mount Cammerer, Stone Mountain, and English Mountain before you reach the interstate. The longer West section has 19 overlooks, the best of which is at **Look Rock,** where a 0.5-mile stroll to an observation tower gives your legs a stretch and affords some awesome views. Other stops of note include the **Caylor Gap and Great Smoky Mountains Overlooks,** though it's hard to find a bad view along the Foothills Parkway.

Newfound Gap Road

Easily the most heavily traveled route in the Smokies, Newfound Gap Road (U.S. 441) connects Cherokee with Gatlinburg and sees thousands of visitors a day. Newfound Gap Road is the perfect introduction to Great Smoky Mountains National Park: Contour-hugging curves, overlooks with million-dollar views, easy hikes right off the roadway, and a 3,000-foot elevation change give you a great overview of these mountains and this spectacular park. During peak times in the summer and fall, it's not uncommon to encounter a traffic jam or two along this 33-mile scenic route, especially when bears are taking their time to cross the road.

Newfound Gap Road earned its name in 1872 when Swiss geographer Arnold Henry Guyot determined that a newly found gap was the lowest pass through the Great Smoky Mountains. Lower in elevation and easier to access than the former passage at Indian Gap, 1.5 miles away, the name Newfound Gap was soon used to refer to the entire route.

SIGHTS
Oconaluftee Visitor Center

As you begin your trip along Newfound Gap Road through the park from the North Carolina side, your first stop will probably be the "Welcome to Great Smoky Mountains National Park" sign, but the **Oconaluftee Visitor Center and Mountain Farm Museum** (1194 Newfound Gap Rd., Cherokee, NC, 828/497-1904, www.nps.gov/grsm, visitor center 9am-5pm daily Jan.-Nov., 9am-4:30pm daily Dec.; Mountain Farm dawn-dusk daily), just 2 miles north of Cherokee on U.S. 441 (Newfound Gap Rd.), will likely be the second stop you make. You can pick up a park map, grab the schedule of ranger-led programs, and see exhibits on the people who called these hills home long before the park was in existence. The visitors center and adjacent comfort station are LEED Gold certified.

Oconaluftee Visitor Center is also a hot spot for **elk sightings.** In the field next to the visitors center, the elk come to graze, rest, and put on a show for park visitors. You might see a pair of young bull elk bugling back and forth before crashing their antlers together. Or elk calves running and playing. There may even be a few deer or turkeys in the elk entourage. Regardless of who shows up, the field is a great spot for photography and as close to a guarantee for elk sightings as you'll get. Just show up early in the morning or from late afternoon into evening and you'll find the herd there.

Mountain Farm Museum

Next to the visitors center is **Mountain Farm Museum** (dawn-dusk daily year-round, free), which showcases some of the finest farm buildings in the park. Most date to the early 1900s, and among them are a barn, an apple house, and the Davis House, a log home built from chestnut wood and constructed before the American chestnut blight decimated the species. This collection of structures is original to the area and dates back to the turn of the 20th century. Though the barn is the only structure original to this site, the other buildings were moved here from inside and adjacent to the park and arranged much like those on a typical farm of the era. If you visit during peak times, you'll see living-history interpreters in costume, demonstrating the day-to-day chores that would have occurred on this farm: preparing meals, sewing, maintaining and harvesting the garden, taking care of the hogs, and the like.

Mingus Mill

A half-mile north of the Oconaluftee Visitor Center and Mountain Farm Museum, you'll find **Mingus Mill** (9am-5pm daily Apr.-Nov.). This historic grist mill was built in 1886; rather than use a water wheel to power the machinery and mill in the building, it uses a water-powered turbine to generate power. This cast-iron turbine still works! A miller is on hand to demonstrate how the machinery turns corn into cornmeal (for sale on-site). Walk along the millrace (the wooden trough that carries water to power the turbine), check out the abundant seasonal wildflowers, and take a good look at how well the National Park Service restored the structure—it looks like it was built just a few years ago.

Deep Creek Valley Overlook

The **Deep Creek Valley Overlook,** 14 miles from the Oconaluftee Visitor Center (and 16 miles from Sugarlands Visitor Center if coming from the other direction), is one of the most popular overlooks in the park for good reason. From here you'll have a long view of the mountains, which roll away from you for as far as you can see.

Oconaluftee River Valley Overlook

Halfway through Newfound Gap Road is the **Oconaluftee River Valley Overlook,** a spot where you can spy the deep cut of the valley formed by the Oconaluftee River. This place is ideal for a picnic, so if you're hungry and you've brought your blanket and something to eat, spread out and relax for a few minutes.

Newfound Gap

One of the most-visited overlooks is at **Newfound Gap.** This is the highest elevation on Newfound Gap Road, at 5,048 feet, and though the views here are fantastic, the first thing you'll probably notice is the **Rockefeller Memorial,** a simple stone terrace that straddles the Tennessee-North Carolina state line and commemorates a $5 million gift made by the Rockefeller Foundation to acquire land for the park. In 1940, President Franklin D. Roosevelt dedicated the park from this site. Plan to spend a little time here, especially early in the morning or near sunset. At sunset, you can see the Smokies' namesake haze settling into the folds and wrinkles of the mountains, and in the early morning, the mountains emerge from a blue haze in a subtle display of color that's been the subject of many a postcard and computer desktop background.

TOP EXPERIENCE

★ Clingmans Dome

At 6,643 feet, Clingmans Dome is the third-highest mountain in the eastern United States and the highest in the Great Smoky Mountains. A flying saucer-like observation

tower at the end of a long, steep walkway gives 360-degree views of the surrounding mountains, and on a clear day, that view can be as far as a hundred miles. More often, though, it's misty up here in the clouds, and Clingmans Dome receives so much precipitation that its woods are actually a coniferous rainforest. The road to the summit is closed December 1-March 31, but the observation tower remains open for those willing to make the hike. To get to Clingmans Dome, turn off Newfound Gap Road 0.1 miles south of Newfound Gap and then take **Clingmans Dome Road** (closed in winter), which leads 7 miles to the parking lot. The peak is near the center of the park, due north from Bryson City.

Campbell Overlook

The **Campbell Overlook** is only 3 miles from the Sugarlands Visitor Center, and it is home to one of the best views of Mount LeConte along the road. LeConte is an interesting mountain. At 6,593 feet, it's the third-highest peak in the Smokies, but it's the tallest mountain east of the Mississippi in that it rises more than a mile from the foot of the mountain to the summit.

Sugarlands Visitor Center

The **Sugarlands Visitor Center and Park Headquarters** (1420 Fighting Creek Gap Rd., Gatlinburg, TN, 865/436-1291, www.nps.gov/grsm, 9am-5pm daily Jan.-Nov., 9am-4:30pm daily Dec.) is the most popular visitors center in the park due to its proximity to Gatlinburg. There's the usual visitors center stuff—restrooms, maps, guidebooks, a few gift items, some snacks—and it's also the origin point for the 1.9-mile Gatlinburg Trail.

RECREATION
Hiking

Great Smoky Mountains National Park contains hundreds of miles of hiking trails, ranging from family-friendly loop trails to strenuous wilderness treks. Before embarking on any of these trails, obtain a park map and talk to a park ranger to ascertain trail conditions and gauge whether it's suited to your hiking skills.

No dogs or other pets (other than service animals) are permitted on park trails except the Gatlinburg Trail and Oconaluftee River Trail, though they are allowed in front-country campsites and picnic areas so long as they remain on-leash.

OCONALUFTEE RIVER TRAIL

Distance: 3 miles round-trip
Duration: 45 minutes
Elevation gain: 70 feet
Difficulty: easy
Trailhead: Oconaluftee Visitor Center

This trail by the Oconaluftee River runs 1.5 miles from the **visitors center** to the outskirts of Cherokee. Flat except for a bridge or two and a few gentle rises, the Oconaluftee River Trail is a lovely walk. In the spring the banks of the Oconaluftee are blanketed with wildflowers, and throughout the year you may see a herd of elk crossing the river at any number of places. Bring bug spray because it can get a bit buggy right by the river on a still day. This is a great option for walking or jogging and is one of only two paths in Great Smoky Mountains National Park where you can walk your **dog** or ride your **bike.**

KEPHART PRONG TRAIL

Distance: 4 miles round-trip
Duration: 2 hours
Elevation gain: 840 feet
Difficulty: easy/moderate
Trailhead: 6.9 miles north of Oconaluftee Visitor Center along Newfound Gap Road or 8.7 miles south from Newfound Gap. Trail begins on the east side of the road.

Kephart Prong offers an easy trail experience for those looking to stretch their legs a little or get more familiar with hiking in the Smokies. The trail crosses the Oconaluftee River, then

---

1: view from Newfound Gap Road 2: the ramp to the viewing platform on Clingmans Dome 3: well-preserved structure on Roaring Fork Motor Nature Trail 4: Mingus Mill

follows the Kephart Prong (stream) for most of the hike, crossing it four times on log bridges. This hike ends at the Kephart Shelter, where the trail meets the Sweat Heifer Creek Trail and Grassy Branch Trail.

Begin by crossing Oconaluftee River via a **footbridge** and follow the wide, nearly flat trail. (Once this was a Jeep road, so you may spot bits of old asphalt along the way.) At 0.25 miles into the hike, you'll pass through a **Civilian Conservation Corps Camp** with ruins such as foundations, chimneys, and other evidence of the camp's use in the 1930s. Continue along the path and cross **Kephart Prong,** then begin to climb, passing the remains of a fish hatchery in 0.6 miles. Three more crossings of the Kephart Prong await, and you can ford the stream (use caution) or use the **log bridges** (they're narrow; use caution) at each crossing. As you continue the hike to **Kephart Shelter,** you'll pass evidence of a long-gone logging operation in the form of narrow-gauge railroad tracks. When you reach the shelter, catch your breath and get ready for the easy hike back.

APPALACHIAN TRAIL TO MOUNT LECONTE

Distance: 16.2 miles round-trip
Duration: 8-10 hours
Elevation gain: 1,600 feet
Difficulty: strenuous
Trailhead: Appalachian Trail trailhead at the Newfound Gap Road Overlook

This is a tough hike. The trail largely follows the crest of the mountains, and thus rises and falls several times with some significant elevation gains and losses.

From the start, the trail climbs for 2 miles. You'll be on a steady incline, but there are views aplenty to give you a little boost. At 1.7 miles, just before the junction with **Sweat Heifer Creek Trail,** you'll have a good look at Mount LeConte to the north. At 2.8 miles, **The Boulevard** forks off to the left.

Continue along The Boulevard, ignoring the sign for the Jump-Off Trail (you can hike that 1-mile trail on the return trip if you

want). Soon you'll drop down to an elevation around 5,500 feet, after which the trail bounces back and forth between 5,500 and 6,000 feet until you begin to properly climb **Mount LeConte** and make your way to the lodge there and the 6,593-foot summit. If you're staying overnight, you'll need reservations (which are notoriously hard to get); otherwise, it's a long hike back to the trailhead.

You can turn this into a daylong, 13.2-mile point-to-point hike if you leave a car at the Alum Cave Bluffs Trail on Newfound Gap Road and hike down from Mount LeConte to the Alum Cave Trailhead. To do this, descend from Mount LeConte via Alum Cave Bluffs Trail. In 2.5 miles you'll reach the bluffs, and in another 1.5 miles you'll reach Arch Rock and the natural tunnel there; from here it's only 1.4 miles to the trailhead and parking area where your ride awaits.

CHARLIES BUNION

Distance: 8.1 miles round-trip
Duration: 7-8.5 hours
Elevation gain: 1,700 feet
Difficulty: moderate
Trailhead: Appalachian Trail trailhead at the Newfound Gap Road Overlook

Originally named Fodderstack, the rock formation of Charlies Bunion earned its new name when two men, Charlie Conner and Horace Kephart, were hiking here. According to legend, they stopped to rest at Fodderstack and Conner removed his boots and socks, revealing a bunion that Kephart felt resembled the rocks around them. Impressed, Kephart promised Charlie that he'd get the name of this place changed on official maps in honor of the bunion.

The first leg of this trail follows the **Appalachian Trail** and **The Boulevard** to **Mount LeConte.** The trail climbs for 2 miles. At 1.7 miles, you'll come to the junction with Sweat Heifer Creek Trail. At 2.8 miles, The Boulevard forks off to the left; continue straight to reach Charlies Bunion.

The **Icewater Spring Shelter,** aptly named for the cold spring that flows out of the mountain here (treat the water before you drink it), is just 0.25 miles from the junction and is a good spot to rest. From the spring, continue a little less than a mile to a short **spur trail** on your left that leads out to the rock outcrop known as **Charlies Bunion.**

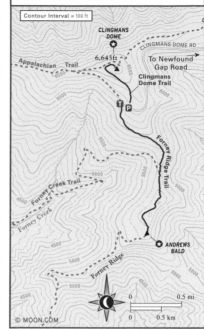

Trails to Clingmans Dome and Andrews Bald

Contour Interval = 100 ft

© MOON.COM

TOP EXPERIENCE

★ ANDREWS BALD

Distance: 3.5 miles round-trip
Duration: 3 hours
Elevation gain: 1,200 feet
Difficulty: moderate
Trailhead: Clingmans Dome parking area at the end of Clingmans Dome Road

The highest grassy bald in Great Smoky Mountains National Park, Andrews Bald is a beautiful sight at the end of a nearly 2-mile hike from Clingmans Dome. Balds are meadows found higher up on mountains, and this one is absolutely lousy with flame azalea and rhododendron blooms in the summer. Note that Clingmans Dome Road is closed in the winter.

Before trail renovations, the Andrews Bald hike had some of the most rugged sections of rocky trails in the park. Thanks to the Trails Forever program, work crews fixed drainage issues, rebuilt parts of the trail, and even built a few stairways from native rocks and trees. Now the hike is easier and safer and leads to a spectacular view of the Smoky Mountains. A bonus: The hike is just long enough to discourage some potential hikers, but it's still short enough to be doable by everyone in your party.

The **Forney Ridge Trail** starts in a spruce-fir forest that was once beautiful but unfortunately now is dead or dying. That's because the forest has been ravaged by a tiny bug—the balsam woolly adelgid—that devours Fraser firs. However, there is a certain beauty in the white bones of the tree trunks jutting up from the land. Don't worry, though; the views get considerably better in a short time. Around 1.6 miles into the hike you'll reach the edge of **Andrews Bald,** where the forest opens

up into a fantastic panorama. In spring and summer, there is a proliferation of wildflowers, flame azaleas, and rhododendrons.

SILERS BALD

Distance: 9.8 miles round-trip
Duration: 6-7 hours
Elevation gain: 2,100 feet
Difficulty: moderate/strenuous
Trailhead: Clingmans Dome parking area at the end of Clingmans Dome Road

This hike is a highlight for many (even though Andrews Bald is the showier of the high-altitude meadows) because it offers a nice day hike along the **Appalachian Trail.** The hike begins at the parking area for Clingmans Dome, the highest peak in Great Smoky Mountains National Park; on the way back, you can divert your path just a little and pay a visit to the summit here. While the Clingmans Dome parking area is a big lot, it can get crowded. Get here early, especially in peak seasons. Note that Clingmans Dome Road closes in winter.

Begin at the far end of the Clingmans Dome parking area and descend along **Forney Ridge Trail.** Follow this rocky path 0.1 miles to a junction: Forney Ridge leads to the left; Clingmans Dome leads to the right. Take Forney Ridge left for 0.6 miles to **Mount Buckley** and the **Appalachian Trail.** Here you can turn right to reach the summit of Clingmans Dome (which you can do on the return trip), or continue left (west) to Silers Bald.

As you continue west along the Appalachian Trail, you'll pass through wildflowers and flowering shrubs mixed with a fir and spruce forest until you reach a **clearing** 0.9 miles into the hike. The clearing has good views, so catch your breath and keep following the ridgeline. Descending, the trail passes through clearings and back into the woods. At 2.6 miles, you'll reach the junction with **Goshen Prong Trail** (which descends toward Elkmont); continue straight along the Appalachian Trail.

At **Double Spring Gap,** in 3.4 miles, there is an **Appalachian Trail shelter** and two springs (hence the name). The gap is the low point on the trail, so begin climbing into a forest where the fir trees give way to beeches. Top out at **Jenkins Knob,** then descend through another gap. At 3.9 miles, the trail crosses an open ridge and grassy area that again provides some great views of the Smokies.

Continue along the trail to a section known as **The Narrows** (4.2 miles), and push on to your final ascent toward Silers Bald. Pass the **Welch Ridge Trail** at 4.5 miles, then climb steeply to **Silers Bald,** 4.9 miles into the hike. Enjoy the view and catch your breath—or continue along the trail another 0.3 miles to the **Silers Bald Shelter** and a spring alongside the Appalachian Trail.

Despite the blooming wildflowers and shrubs along the path, Silers Bald receives some deserved criticism. The once wide-open bald is shrinking as the forest seeks to reclaim it. There's a small debate on what to do—let the forest take it back or maintain it as

a bald—but it's a beautiful spot and a worthwhile hike no matter what.

When ready, reverse course and head back to Clingmans Dome. To divert to the summit and add 0.7 miles or so to your trip, continue along the **Appalachian Trail** when you reach **Mount Buckley.** The trail gets steep here, but it leads to a spot 50 yards or so from the ramp to the lookout tower at the summit of **Clingmans Dome.**

ALUM CAVE BLUFFS TRAIL TO MOUNT LECONTE

Distance: 10 miles round-trip
Duration: 6-7 hours
Elevation gain: 2,560 feet
Difficulty: moderate/strenuous
Trailhead: Alum Cave Trailhead

As one of the most popular hikes in the park, this trail receives a lot of wear and tear, which can leave the trail in bad shape. Fortunately, repairs have left the trail in better condition, and hikers will find sturdy handholds along the stone stairs and narrow exposed sections at the upper end of the trail.

The trail starts off fairly gently as it climbs up to Arch Rock. **Alum Cave Creek** runs alongside the trail for a while, and here you'll have the chance to snap pictures of several cascades and beautiful rhododendron thickets (which bloom in late June-July). You'll reach **Arch Rock,** which is less arch and more natural tunnel, around 1.5 miles in.

Here the trail begins to climb more steeply. A set of stone steps leads out of Arch Rock, and the forest changes from hemlock and hardwood to spruce and fir trees. In another 0.5 mile you'll reach **Inspiration Point,** where the view opens onto one of the mid-elevation balds.

When you reach **Alum Cave Bluffs,** you're halfway to Mount LeConte. The rock formations aren't caves but rather deep overhangs that create an impressive shelter from the rain. The Smokies receive more than 85 inches of rain a year, yet the majority of the soil under the bluffs remains dry and dusty, an arid spot in one of the nation's wettest forests.

Smokies Hikes for Healing

As the Black Lives Matter movement sparked anew in 2020, Great Smoky Mountains National Park's superintendent, Cassius Cash—the first Black person to hold this position at the park—had an idea: to hold difficult conversations around race and diversity in one of the most biodiverse places on the planet, harnessing the healing powers of nature. Smokies Hikes for Healing (www.smokieshikesforhealing.org) was born, and a new avenue for exploration now awaits in the Smokies.

On Smokies Hikes for Healing expeditions, small groups join Cash and a facilitator on the trail to discuss the complexities of race relations, unintended biases, social justice, and growth in difficult times. Hikes are short—never more than 4 miles round-trip—but the impacts of the experience are long-lasting.

To participate in a healing hike, you'll need to apply online, selecting your preferred dates and answering a few questions (for example, "Why do you want to attend this hike?"). You'll be notified if you're selected. Lace up your boots, follow the leader into the wilderness, and let nature clear your mind and calm your spirit. Then the conversation begins.

Most hikers turn around at Alum Cave Bluffs, but if you're pushing on to Mount LeConte, the path steepens and grows more challenging as you gain elevation. The trail narrows to a set of rock ledges where **steel cables** have been bolted into the mountain for use as a handhold. The drop may be precipitous, but the views are fantastic. Soon the trail intersects with **Rainbow Falls Trail,** leading you to the summit of **Mount LeConte** in short order.

If you plan on hiking to Mount LeConte and back in a day, or spending the night at the lodge, it's in your best interest to arrive early so you can get a parking space.

CHIMNEY TOPS

Distance: 4 miles round-trip
Duration: 3.5 hours
Elevation gain: 1,400 feet
Difficulty: moderate/strenuous
Trailhead: Chimney Tops trailhead on Newfound Gap Road

Chimney Tops takes its name from the twin knobs that rise from ridge-like chimneys. These rocky summits are rare in the Smokies, but that's not the draw—what brings people up this steep, challenging trail is the 360-degree

view. And it's incredibly steep, gaining nearly 1,000 feet in the last mile. To reach the pinnacles, the actual Chimney Tops, requires a very steep scramble over bare rock, which can be dangerous, and it's easier to climb up than to come back down.

Many people explore the first few hundred yards of this trail because it's right off Newfound Gap Road. The cascades, pools, and boulders found along **Walker Camp Prong** are picturesque and good for wading and sunbathing. As you climb, you'll cross **Road Prong,** another stream, twice. Just after the second crossing, the trail splits, with one part following Road Prong and the other heading to Chimney Tops. Stay right to head to the chimneys.

After a brief ascent, the trail steepens significantly. Take a breather here before tackling this long, straight climb. The trail continues and narrows as you walk the ridgeline. Soon, you'll be at the foot of the **Chimney Tops,** and you'll see a sign from the National Park Service warning you to proceed at your own risk. Heed this sign, as the last bit of "trail" to the summit is a **scramble** that doesn't require any specialized equipment but is quite risky if you're inexperienced in such terrain.

GATLINBURG TRAIL

Distance: 3.8 miles round-trip
Duration: 2 hours
Elevation gain: 20 feet
Difficulty: easy
Trailhead: Sugarlands Visitor Center

This is one of only two trails in the park to allow **pets** and **bicycles** (the other is the Oconaluftee River Trail in Cherokee). More of a walk than a hike, the Gatlinburg Trail follows the **West Prong Little Pigeon River** and Newfound Gap Road for most of the trip. It's pretty and not especially challenging, but the optional walk to **Cataract Falls**—a few hundred yards up **Cove Mountain Trail,** which splits off the Gatlinburg Trail near the trailhead—can provide some photo opportunities and a pretty, easy-to-reach waterfall.

SMOKEMONT LOOP

Distance: 6.1 miles round-trip
Duration: 3-3.5 hours
Elevation gain: 1,400 feet
Difficulty: moderate
Trailhead: Smokemont Campground D section

This horse-friendly trail is an enjoyable hike along forest roads and trails, but the elevation gain pushes it to moderate difficulty.

Starting at the far end of the D section of **Smokemont Campground,** you'll see a sign marking the **Bradley Fork Trailhead;** follow this trail along Bradley Fork. In the spring, this creek-side section is packed with wildflowers, and many folks will just hike the first 0.5 miles of the trail. At 1.2 miles, the trail forks, with Chasteen Creek Trail going right and the **Bradley Fork-Smokemont Loop Trail** continuing left.

At 1.6 miles you meet up with **Smokemont Loop Trail** proper. Follow this trail left and cross **Bradley Fork** via a foot log. (Be careful; this one can be a little bouncy.) As soon as you cross, the trail forks again; the left fork follows the creek. Turn right and begin an uphill climb to **Richland Mountain.** This climb will keep going for another 2 miles at a steady incline, so pace yourself.

Once you pass through a small saddle,

you'll hear the **Oconaluftee River** and, likely, cars traveling Newfound Gap Road. At the 3.4-mile mark, the trail takes a sharp left turn, marking the place you've been waiting for—the end of the climb and start of the descent. From here you have a 2-mile-long downhill trail. As you get closer to the end, you'll see the **Bradley Cemetery,** with a spur trail leading to it at 5.3 miles. At the Cemetery Trail, **Smokemont Loop** meets a gravel road leading back to the campground in another 0.2 miles.

Fishing

Smallmouth bass and rock bass are fairly abundant in Smokies' waters. Look for smallmouth bass along the **West Prong of the Little Pigeon River,** near Gatlinburg and the park's western entrance, and in the **Little Pigeon River** near Greenbrier. Smallmouth and rock bass are found in the **Little River** on the way to Cades Cove, **Abrams Creek,** and **Fontana Lake,** specifically the feeder creeks like Noland, Hazel, and Eagle Creek.

Horseback Riding

Three commercial stables in the park offer "rental" horses (around $40 per hour). **Smokemont** (135 Smokemont Riding Stable Rd., Cherokee, 828/497-2373, www.smokemontridingstable.com) is in North Carolina near Cherokee. Two are in Tennessee: **Sugarlands Riding Stables** (1409 E. Parkway, Gatlinburg, 865/436-3535, www.smokymountainridingstables.com) and **Cades Cove** (10018 Campground Dr., Townsend, 865/448-9009, http://cadescovestables.com).

ACCOMMODATIONS AND CAMPING

As big as Great Smoky Mountains National Park may be, there are few places to stay within its boundaries—and nearly all are either campsites or backcountry shelters. The

---

1: the Appalachian Trail near Clingmans Dome
2: Alum Cave Bluffs Trail sign

1

2

ALUM CAVE TRAIL
Arch Rock   1.4
Alum Cave Bluffs 2.3
Mt. LeConte   5.0

lone exception is LeConte Lodge, a collection of cabins and small lodges with a central dining room and lodge. It's only accessible by hiking in, so you have to be dedicated to stay there.

LeConte Lodge

Just below the 6,593-foot peak of Mount LeConte is the only true lodging in Great Smoky Mountains National Park, the ★ **LeConte Lodge** (865/429-5704, www.lecontelodge.com, late Mar.-mid-Nov., $159 adults, $88 ages 4-12, includes breakfast and dinner). Like the mountain's summit, the lodge is accessible only via the network of hiking trails that crisscross the park. And if the accessibility limitation isn't rustic enough for you, this collection of cabins has no running water or electricity. What it does have are views for days and the seclusion of the Great Smoky Mountains backcountry.

For the most part the environs hark back to the lodge's 1934 opening. LeConte Lodge has no hot showers. In every cabin there is a bucket for a sponge bath—which can be surprisingly refreshing after a hot day on the trail—that you can fill with warm water from the kitchen, though you need to supply your own washcloth and towel. There are a few flush toilets in a separate building, and the only lights, aside from headlamps and flashlights, are kerosene lanterns. Your room does come with two meals: dinner and breakfast. Both are served at the same time every day (6pm for dinner and 8am for breakfast) and feature food hearty enough to fuel another day on the trail.

The lodge doesn't lack for charm, but it is short on comfort, so if you're the five-star-hotel, breakfast-in-bed type, this may not be the place for you. Catering to hikers who are happy to have a dry place to sleep and a bed that's comfier than their sleeping bag, it's short on luxury amenities. Rooms are, in truth, bunk beds in small, drafty cabins. But if you're a hiker or if you just love to have a completely different experience when you travel, this is a one-of-a-kind accommodation.

RESERVATIONS

Accommodations for LeConte Lodge are made via **lottery** (www.lecontelodge.com). The lottery is competitive, but it's easy to enter; simply go to the website and fill out the online form, including your desired dates and the number in your party. If your application is chosen in the lottery, you will receive an invoice with your accommodation information.

horses at a stable in Cades Cove

Booking information for the following season becomes available online in midsummer, so keep an eye out and get your application in early.

If you want to stay at LeConte Lodge but you're late to the lottery party, try to get on the wait list. The process is the same, but the dates are limited—typically weeknights and the larger cabins are all that's available.

You can try one other method: calling 865/429-5704. Cancellations made with less than 30 days' notice skip the wait list and are instead offered to the first inquiry that matches availability. Frequent calls are a good way to snag these last-minute reservations.

GETTING THERE

The **Roaring Fork Motor Nature Trail** (open Apr.-Nov.) at the foot of Mount LeConte is the starting point for a trio of hiking trails that lead to LeConte Lodge. **Bull Head Trail** is a 6.8-mile trip from the trailhead to the lodge, as is **Rainbow Falls Trail.** Bull Head and Rainbow Falls Trails share a trailhead at the designated parking area on the Motor Nature Trail. **Trillium Gap Trail,** the trail used by the lodge's pack llamas, passes by beautiful Grotto Falls on its 6.7-mile route; the trailhead is at the Grotto Falls parking area on the Roaring Fork Motor Nature Trail. Each of these three trails requires a four-hour hike to reach the lodge from the trailhead.

Three other trails lead to Mount LeConte from various points in the park. **Alum Cave Bluffs Trail** (5 miles one-way) enters from Newfound Gap Road; it's the shortest and easiest to access, but it's also the steepest.

Alternatively, **The Boulevard** connects the Appalachian Trail to LeConte Lodge (8.1 miles one-way from Newfound Gap Overlook). The Boulevard is relatively easy with little elevation change, but there's the issue of exposure on this trail—the rock path has more than a few dizzying drops right beside the trail. These drops, combined with The Boulevard coming in from the Appalachian Trail, deter most day or overnight hikers from its use. **Brushy Mountain Trail** (11.8 miles round-trip) leads to the summit from the Porters Creek Trailhead off Greenbrier Road (closed in winter). Despite the significant elevation change, this is a relatively easy trail.

Camping

Smokemont Campground (877/444-6777, www.recreation.gov, year-round, $25) is just off Newfound Gap Road, 3.2 miles from the Oconaluftee Visitor Center. The 142 sites include tent campsites and RV sites. It's on the banks of the Oconaluftee River and thus can get quite buggy, so be prepared.

Eastern Smokies

The eastern side of Great Smoky Mountains National Park was settled by Europeans before the western side, so there are plenty of coves and hollows with historic structures or the ruins of cabins, barns, and other buildings in the fields and woods and along creek banks and floodplains. There are also many herds of elk, introduced beginning in 2001 in an attempt to revive the species that once roamed these hills.

ROARING FORK
Roaring Fork Motor Nature Trail

One of the most beautiful drives in Great Smoky Mountains National Park is the **Roaring Fork Motor Nature Trail** (open Apr.-Nov.). This one-way loop (5.5 miles) passes through rhododendron thickets and dense hardwood forests as it follows the old roadbed of the Roaring Fork community. To get here, turn onto Historic Nature Trail (Old Airport Rd.) at traffic light number 8 in

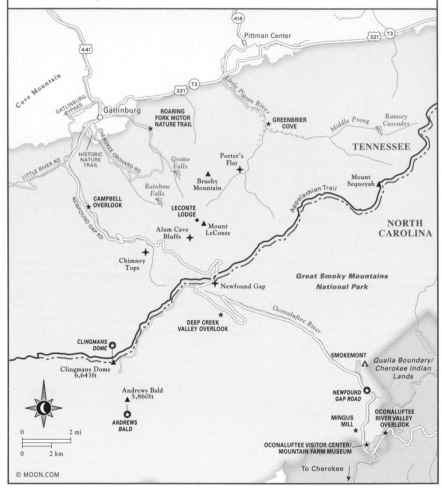

Roaring Fork and Greenbrier Cove

416

Pittman Center

321 73

441

73

321 73

Little Pigeon River

Cove Mountain

GATLINBURG
BYPASS

Gatlinburg

ROARING
FORK MOTOR
NATURE TRAIL

GREENBRIER
COVE

Middle Prong

Ramsey
Cascades

TENNESSEE

CHEROKEE ORCHARD RD

LITTLE RIVER RD

HISTORIC
NATURE
TRAIL

Grotto
Falls

Porter's
Flat

Mount
Sequoyah

Appalachian Trail

Rainbow
Falls

Brushy
Mountain

CAMPBELL
OVERLOOK

NEWFOUND GAP RD

LECONTE
LODGE

Alum Cave
Bluffs

Mount
LeConte

**NORTH
CAROLINA**

Chimney
Tops

Newfound Gap

**Great Smoky Mountains
National Park**

Oconaluftee River

DEEP CREEK
VALLEY OVERLOOK

CLINGMANS
DOME

SMOKEMONT

Qualla Boundary/
Cherokee Indian
Lands

Clingmans Dome
6,643ft

Andrews Bald
5,860ft

NEWFOUND
GAP ROAD

ANDREWS
BALD

OCONALUFTEE
RIVER VALLEY
OVERLOOK

MINGUS
MILL

0   2 mi

0   2 km

OCONALUFTEE VISITOR CENTER/
MOUNTAIN FARM MUSEUM

© MOON.COM

To Cherokee

Gatlinburg and follow the signs. Before you reach the trail, you'll drive a short distance on Cherokee Orchard Road, which runs through what was an 800-acre commercial orchard in the 1920s and 1930s. Shortly after the orchard, you'll be at the head of the trail and have the chance to purchase an inexpensive tour booklet from a roadside exhibit.

The roadbed here was built by hand in the 1850s, which explains both its narrowness and serpentine route. Around 25 families

lived here, and though it may look quaint and primitive to our eyes, a few of the homes had running water thanks to the system of troughs—some of which are still standing—that carried water right to the houses.

As the road climbs through the forest, roll down your windows and take in a few deep breaths of that fresh, cool mountain air. There is a pair of **overlooks,** though they're overgrown and in poor repair. When you stop, take in the silence. You'll soon find yourself surrounded by the sounds of nature: wind, birds calling, and streams rumbling and echoing through the forest.

Be sure to stop at the cabins still standing here. **Ogle Place,** a two-room cabin surrounded by rhododendrons; **Ephraim Bales Cabin,** which is smack in the middle of a boulder field; and **Alfred Regan Cabin,** which has an amazing trough system still in place, are all worth spending a few minutes exploring and photographing.

Hiking

Three waterfalls are within hiking distance of the Motor Nature Trail: **Rainbow Falls** (the most popular of the hikes), **Grotto Falls,** and **Baskins Creek Falls.** If you're not up for a hike, **Thousand Drips Falls** (sometimes called the Place of a Thousand Drips) is just off the road. In wet times, it's a great cascade plummeting down the mountain; during drier times, it's much more tame.

RAINBOW FALLS TRAIL
Distance: 5.4 miles round-trip
Duration: 3.5-4 hours
Elevation gain: 1,700 feet
Difficulty: strenuous
Trailhead: Roaring Fork Motor Nature Trail, 3.3 miles from Gatlinburg traffic light number 8, at the Rainbow Falls and Bull Head Trail parking area

This trail is strenuous due to how steep and rocky it is and how slick it can become in places where the trail nears the water and as you get closer to the falls. Note that Roaring Fork Motor Trail is closed in winter.

As you leave the parking area, you'll cross **Trillium Gap Trail** and begin to climb alongside LeConte Creek. Follow the trail as it goes through a couple of switchbacks and then crosses the creek on a **log bridge.** Here you'll enter a stretch with some impressive trees. Soon you'll cross LeConte Creek again. At this crossing you can see **Rainbow Falls** above you. Continue up the trail to a spot just below the falls.

Here LeConte Creek plunges 80 feet to the rocks below. During that plunge, the water becomes more of a heavy mist, giving us the name Rainbow Falls. Though you can get some good photography from the trail, there are other interesting shots from different angles around the falls. If you scramble around the falls, keep in mind that the rocks are slick and you could slip and hurt yourself. With a 2.7-mile hike back to the car, who wants to do that? If you decide to explore the area around the falls, use caution and stay safe.

You may notice that the **Rainbow Falls Trail** continues on past the waterfall itself. It is possible to take this trail to the summit of Mount LeConte, but that is a strenuous, steep, full-day hike of close to 14 miles.

GROTTO FALLS TRAIL
Distance: 2.6 miles round-trip
Duration: 2-2.5 hours
Elevation gain: 585 feet
Difficulty: easy/moderate
Trailhead: Roaring Fork Motor Nature Trail, about 2 miles into the trail, Grotto Falls parking area on the left

From the parking area, you'll follow a short unnamed spur before joining **Trillium Gap Trail,** which leads to **Grotto Falls** before continuing to the top of **Mount LeConte.** As you hike, you'll notice the path is hard-packed. That's because this trail is the resupply route for **LeConte Lodge,** so it sees traffic from the llama trains carrying supplies up to the lodge. If you're lucky, you'll see one of these trains.

The forest was once composed mostly of hemlock trees, but thanks to a nasty little bug—the hemlock woolly adelgid—many of these trees are dead or dying. Even though some of the trees are being ravaged, the forest is still thick, and it opens dramatically where the stream plunges 25 feet to form Grotto Falls.

The most intriguing part of Grotto Falls is the grotto. Trillium Gap Trail passes behind the falls thanks to a hefty rock overhang. It provides some interesting photographic opportunities that make it one of the most popular waterfall hikes on this side of the park.

BASKINS FALLS TRAIL

Distance: 3.2 miles round-trip
Duration: 3 hours
Elevation gain: 950 feet
Difficulty: moderate
Trailhead: Roaring Fork Motor Nature Trail, on the left near the Jim Bales Place

This 30-foot waterfall is like a little secret hidden along the popular **Roaring Fork Motor Nature Trail** (closed in winter). Seldom visited, it's almost a forgotten hike, meaning you can have the falls to yourself.

As soon as you start the hike, you'll pass a cemetery before making a climb up to a ridgeline. A steep descent from the ridge will take you to **Baskins Creek.** Cross the creek (be careful, especially in high water) and make the steep climb over another ridge. From here you can see what's left of an old chimney standing in the woods. Just beyond a tiny, wildflower-filled meadow is the side path leading to the base of the falls. On the right side of this trail is an old **homesite,** followed by a steep descent to the **falls.**

Many hikers turn around here and return to their car, but it is possible to continue along this trail another 1.5 miles and arrive near the entrance to the Roaring Fork Motor Nature Trail. If you do this, know that you will have a 3-mile walk along the road back to your car.

Backpacking

This backpacking trip will take you from Roaring Fork to the summit of Mount LeConte, the third-highest peak in the park (and sixth-highest in the Appalachians). Spend the night at either the LeConte Lodge or LeConte Shelter; reservations are required for each.

RESERVATIONS

A backpacking trip to Mount LeConte from Roaring Fork requires some preparation. First, you'll need to register with the **Backcountry Information Office** (865/436-1297, https://smokiespermits.nps.gov, 8am-5pm daily, permits $4 pp per night, $20 maximum) for a permit, then make a site reservation over the phone.

On Mount LeConte, you'll have only two options: LeConte Lodge, which is a hot ticket and books up early, and the LeConte Shelter, which is much easier to secure. ★ **LeConte Lodge** (865/429-5704, www.lecontelodge.com, late-Mar.-mid-Nov., $159 adults, $88 ages 4-12) includes breakfast and dinner. The LeConte Shelter is reserved through the Backcountry Information Office; reservations may be made up to 30 days before your stay. Contact the office as soon as possible to make a reservation; it's one of the park's most popular shelters.

MOUNT LECONTE VIA GROTTO FALLS

Distance: 13.5 miles round-trip
Duration: overnight
Elevation gain: 4,000 feet
Difficulty: strenuous
Trailhead: Roaring Fork Motor Nature Trail at the Grotto Falls Trail parking area

From the parking area, the path begins across **Roaring Fork Motor Nature Trail** for 0.1 miles before it meets with **Trillium Gap Trail.** Climb Trillium Gap Trail for 6.6 miles (and some 4,000 vertical feet) to the summit of **Mount LeConte.** Now you're an easy 1.3 miles to **Grotto Falls,** one of the prettiest waterfalls in the park, which is named for the grotto behind the veil of water making up the falls. The hike leads through the remains of a hemlock forest (the trees have been killed by the hemlock woolly adelgid) before it reaches the falls. At the falls you may encounter a strange sight: llamas. LeConte Lodge uses a pack train of llamas for resupply; if you're on the trail early enough, you'll see them at the waterfall.

Passing Grotto Falls, the trail will grow steeper. You'll cross a couple of small streams, but the trail is a typical woodland path with the usual rocks and roots underfoot and a decent incline. As you approach Trillium Gap, you'll begin to see patches of grass along the trail. At 3.1 miles, you'll reach **Trillium Gap**

Mount LeConte Trails

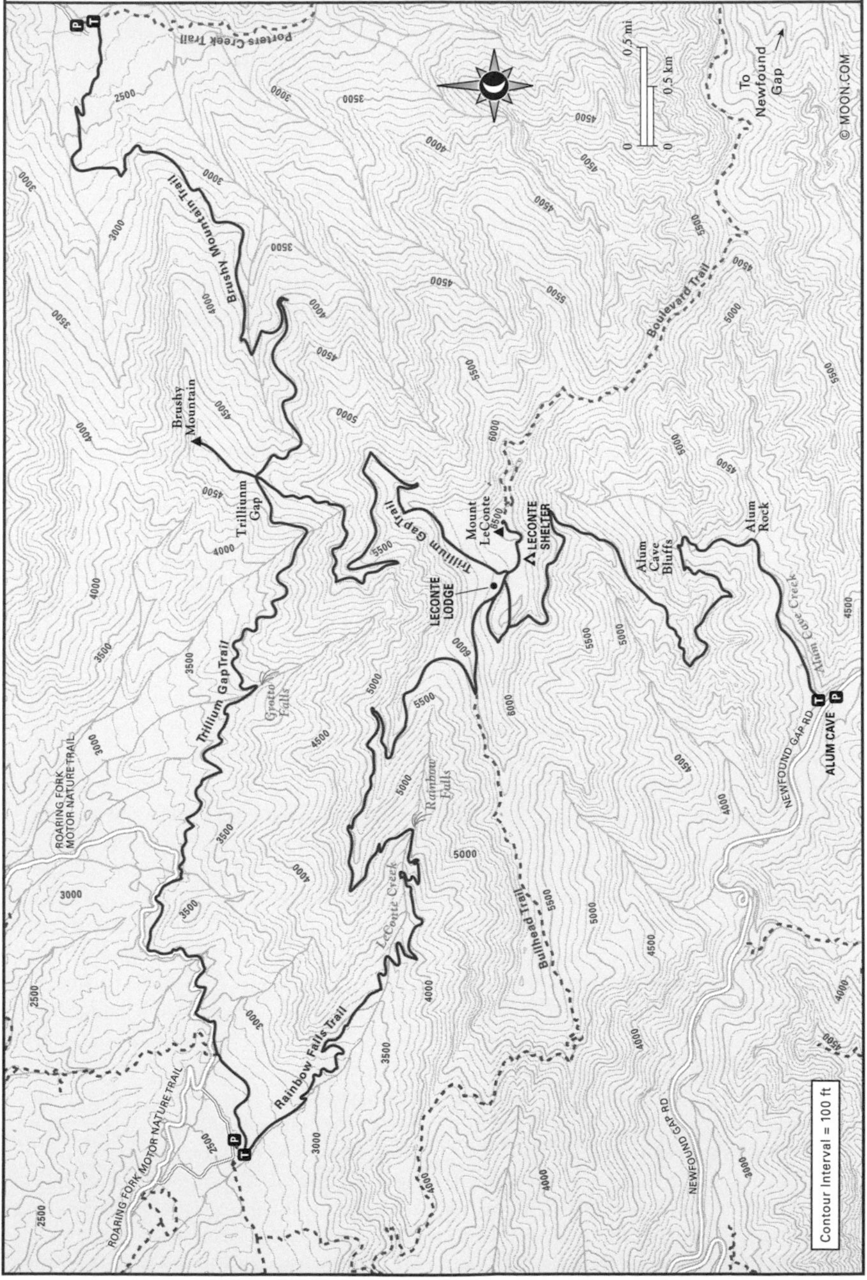

© MOON.COM

0.5 mi

0.5 km

To Newfound Gap

Porters Creek Trail

Brushy Mountain Trail

Brushy Mountain

Trillium Gap

Trillium Gap Trail

Trillium Gap Trail

Boulevard Trail

Mount LeConte

LECONTE SHELTER

LECONTE LODGE

Alum Cave Bluffs

Alum Rock

Alum Cave Creek

Grotto Falls

Rainbow Falls

LeConte Creek

Rainbow Falls Trail

Bullhead Trail

NEWFOUND GAP RD

ALUM CAVE

NEWFOUND GAP RD

ROARING FORK MOTOR NATURE TRAIL

ROARING FORK MOTOR NATURE TRAIL

Contour Interval = 100 ft

Ramsey Cascades Trail

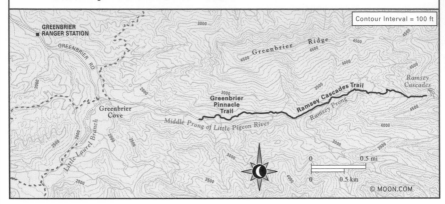

proper and the intersection with **Brushy Mountain Trail.** Peak baggers can add another 0.8 miles for the round-trip hike to the summit of Brushy Mountain. Otherwise, continue along Trillium Gap Trail.

From Trillium Gap, the trail grows steeper and rockier, but the forest is quite lush. When the moss, ferns, and smaller vegetation give way to fir trees, you know you're close to LeConte Lodge. After passing a spring, you'll hit **LeConte Lodge.** Just ahead, the trail will intersect with **Bullhead Trail** and **Boulevard Trail;** turn right to approach LeConte Lodge and the spur trail leading to the summit. It's another 0.4 miles to the summit and back.

If you're staying at LeConte Lodge, check in and rest. If you've made a reservation at the **LeConte Shelter,** backtrack to the junction of Bullhead, Trillium Gap, and Boulevard Trails and continue down Boulevard Trail for another 0.2 miles.

GREENBRIER COVE

Greenbrier Cove, like many other coves in the park, was once home to a mountain community. This area was settled by Europeans in the early 1800s, and families farmed, trapped, and hunted the land until the establishment of the national park. This cove has an interesting footnote: Dolly Parton's ancestors, Benjamin

C. and Margaret Parton, moved here in the 1850s, and their descendants left when the park was formed.

Greenbrier is stunning, especially in the spring. The cove is known as a wildflower hot spot, but don't underestimate the beauty of this place in any season.

Hiking
RAMSEY CASCADES TRAIL
Distance: 8 miles round-trip
Duration: 5.5 hours
Elevation gain: 2,375 feet
Difficulty: moderate/strenuous
Trailhead: Ramsey Cascades Trailhead at the Greenbrier park entrance, 6 miles east of Gatlinburg off U.S. 321

Ramsey Cascades is the tallest waterfall in Great Smoky Mountains National Park, spilling 100 feet in a series of steps before collecting in a pool at the base. As if that wasn't reason enough to undertake this hike, this section of the park is known as a wildflower paradise, so a springtime visit is highly recommended.

The first portion of this trail is a continuation of the gravel road you took to the parking area. You'll soon cross **Little Laurel Branch** and, almost immediately after, the Middle Prong of Little Pigeon River via a long **footbridge.** If you've timed your hike with the wildflower bloom, the next half mile will be a riot of color.

The hiking here is easy until you reach the 1.5-mile mark, where the Jeep trail you're on ends. To the left (north) is the **Greenbrier Pinnacle Trail,** a trail that's not maintained by the park; **Ramsey Cascades Trail** continues on through a rhododendron thicket.

Past this point you find yourself on a trail where roots and rocks are more the norm, so watch your footing. Continue along this trail; it will turn steep, you'll cross the **Ramsey Prong** and a side stream, and you'll know you've arrived when you hear the waterfall. The final approach is rocky and slick, with a lot of scrambling, so use caution. When you've taken in all of the **Ramsey Cascades** you can handle, simply reverse your course to the trailhead.

BRUSHY MOUNTAIN TO MOUNT LECONTE

Distance: 11.8 miles round-trip
Duration: 6-7 hours
Elevation gain: 3,000 feet
Difficulty: moderate/strenuous
Trailhead: Porters Creek Trailhead on Greenbrier Road, 6 miles east of Gatlinburg off U.S. 321
Directions: From traffic light number 3 in Gatlinburg (junction of U.S. 441 and U.S. 321), travel east on U.S. 321. Drive 6 miles and then turn right on Greenbrier Road, which becomes a gravel road. At the fork in the road 3.1 miles in, continue straight 1 mile to the Porters Creek Trailhead.

The first mile or so of this trail follows an old gravel road, the **Porters Creek Trail.** In the spring, trilliums are profuse here. You'll pass a **cemetery** and several stone walls and then cross a **footbridge** at a fork in the road. Turn left at the fork. You'll meet another fork 100 yards or so down the trail, at which you turn right onto **Brushy Mountain Trail.**

The trail continues for 4.5 miles, climbing some 2,500 feet as it does. At 5.5 miles, you'll meet **Trillium Gap Trail**. Go left on the Trillium Gap Trail and you'll reach **Mount LeConte.** Turn right and you can reach the summit of **Brushy Mountain** in 0.6 miles.

GRAPEYARD RIDGE

Distance: 15.6 miles round-trip
Duration: 8-10 hours
Elevation gain: 3,250 feet
Difficulty: strenuous
Trailhead: Grapeyard Ridge Trailhead in Greenbrier, 6 miles east of Gatlinburg off U.S. 321

This beautiful hike reveals some intriguing sights, such as the remains of a Civilian Conservation Corps (CCC) camp, stone walls, a cemetery, and an old steam engine. The route connects the Greenbrier area of the park with Roaring Fork Motor Nature Trail (closed in winter); it's best to do this as an end-to-end shuttle hike (park a car at one end, drive to the other, and hike back to the car you left). Otherwise, you'll have to arrange transport back to your trailhead or hike back.

Begin the hike along **Greenbrier Road** (closed in winter) and plunge right into a forest thick with galax and mountain laurel. You'll climb quickly, gaining nearly 300 feet in little more than 0.5 miles. At 0.1 miles, pass a spur trail to a **cemetery.** At 0.4 miles, the trail begins to descend, and you'll make the first of many crossings of **Rhododendron Creek** at 0.5 miles. This crossing has no bridge; you'll have to ford the stream without aid, so watch the water levels and only cross if you're confident in your ability and footing. Over the next 1.2 miles, you'll **cross the stream** four more times.

The trail splits from the creek and begins climbing toward James Gap at the 2.1-mile mark, going through a few rhododendron tunnels that give it an eerie feel. You'll reach **James Gap** at 2.9 miles, then quickly descend to **Injun Creek** and the wreck of an old steam engine. The name of the creek comes from the steam engine, not the native people. The engine was part of a logging operation in the 1920s; the steam-powered tractor slipped into the creek on the way out and stayed there, too heavy to move.

Turning back here makes this a nice little day hike. If you press on, you'll pass **Backcountry Campsite 32** in 0.3 miles. Here begins another steady uphill climb to

Grapeyard Ridge at the 4-mile mark. Rather than follow the true ridge, the trail traces a path just below it. This path offers better views and a profusion of wildflowers in each little cove you dip into.

The trail descends toward Grapeyard Branch, meeting with **Dudley Creek** at 4.8 miles. Prior to reaching the creek, you'll see fence posts and other signs of habitation; at Dudley Creek there is a low rock wall and evidence of a homestead. The junction with **Big Dudley Trail** at 4.9 miles marks the next point where the trail climbs as it continues on toward Roaring Fork.

A sign for **Roaring Fork** appears at 6.1 miles; the highest point of the trail is at 6.6 miles. Begin your descent into Roaring Fork. At 7.3 miles, a trail leads to Trillium Gap Trail, but continue straight and you'll soon reach the Bales Place and **Roaring Fork.** If you've stashed a car nearby or have arranged for a shuttle, you're at the end of the hike. Otherwise, take a breather, get some water, and head back.

PORTERS CREEK TRAIL

Distance: 7.2 miles round-trip
Duration: 3.5-4 hours
Elevation gain: 1,500 feet
Difficulty: moderate
Trailhead: Greenbrier Road 0.9 miles beyond the Ramsey Cascades Trailhead

From the traffic loop 0.9 miles up the road from the **Ramsey Cascades Trailhead,** begin hiking along a gravel road. Rock walls and evidence of homesites are all around; soon you'll cross a small creek and find an old **cemetery.** Cross a larger stream by wading (if the water's not too high) or using the foot log.

In 1 mile an **old traffic turnaround** indicates the start of the trail. **Porters Creek Trail** is the trail to the far left. (Brushy Mountain Trail is the middle trail, and the trail on the far right leads to a historic farm site that you can explore on the way back.)

Once you begin Porters Creek Trail, you'll cross Porters Creek in 0.5 miles. If you're hiking in the spring, you'll be treated to a carpet of wildflowers. **Fern Branch Falls** awaits 0.4 miles farther, adding to the beauty of this hike. The waterfall is surprisingly high at 35 feet, and the surrounding area is thick with moss and wildflowers in the spring.

Continue past the waterfall to the end of the hike and **Backcountry Campsite 31** at 3.6 miles. Explore the creek for a little while, and when you're ready, head back downhill to the trailhead.

COSBY

For the first half of the 20th century, Cosby was known as the moonshine capital of the world. The national prohibition on liquor turned many locals to making their own. When scientists and workers began to come to Oak Ridge to work on secret military ventures like the Manhattan Project, they weren't accustomed to Tennessee's dry-county laws, and the demand for moonshine skyrocketed. Today there isn't much by way of moonshine production in town, and most of the visitors come here for the national park.

Cosby's present reputation is as a friendly town with one of the less-used park entrances. That's good for you, because when autumn leaves begin to change and the crowds pack Gatlinburg and clog the easy-to-access trails along Newfound Gap Road, you can head to Cosby. In town you'll find a few restaurants and a handful of cabin rentals, but the park is the real treasure.

Hiking
★ HEN WALLOW FALLS TRAIL

Distance: 4.4 miles round-trip
Duration: 3.5 hours
Elevation gain: 900 feet
Difficulty: easy/moderate
Trailhead: Gabes Mountain Trailhead, across the road from the Cosby Campground picnic area

From the outset, **Gabes Mountain Trail** is a steady climb on a path that's at times rugged. Follow this trail until you see a sign for the **side trail** leading to the waterfall (2.1 miles into the hike). The 0.1-mile side trail is a little steep, but not problematically so.

Hen Wallow Falls Trail

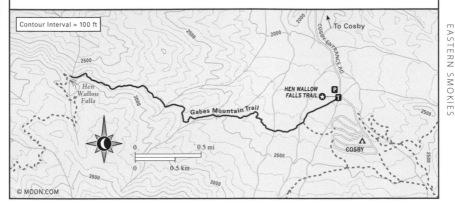

Hen Wallow Falls tumbles 90 feet into a small pool below, where there are plenty of salamanders to see. The falls themselves are only 2 feet wide at the top but fan out to 20 feet at the bottom; during dry months, the falls are still pretty, though less wow-inducing.

To get back to the trailhead, just retrace your steps.

MOUNT CAMMERER TRAIL

Distance: 11.2 miles round-trip
Duration: 7-7.5 hours
Elevation gain: 2,740 feet
Difficulty: moderate/strenuous
Trailhead: Low Gap Trailhead, just beyond the Cosby Campground amphitheater area

To start, park in the group parking area and walk along the road to where it curves into the B section of the campground. Just before **campsite 92** you'll see a trailhead; follow it for a short distance until it crosses Cosby Creek, then turn right on **Low Gap Trail.** From here, the trail climbs a little less than 3 miles up the mountain via a series of winding switchbacks until you reach the Appalachian Trail.

Turn left to join the **Appalachian Trail** for 2.1 miles. The first mile of this trail is more level, so it gives you a chance to catch your breath or make up some time. You'll know when you reach the junction with the **Mount Cammerer Trail** because the Appalachian

Trail descends to the right; you want to stay straight. The **summit** is 0.6 miles from where you leave the Appalachian Trail.

At the summit is a **stone fire tower** built in the 1930s and restored by volunteers throughout the years. The view from the deck here is awe-inspiring—it's one of the best in the park.

ALBRIGHT GROVE TRAIL

Distance: 6.8 miles round-trip
Duration: 3.5-4 hours
Elevation gain: 1,400 feet
Difficulty: moderate
Trailhead: Maddron Bald Trail
Directions: From Gatlinburg, drive 15.5 miles east on U.S. 321. Turn right onto Baxter Road; at 0.3 miles, turn right onto a gravel road. Park near (but don't block) the gate at the dirt road.

Begin hiking on **Maddron Bald Trail,** an old wagon road, which climbs immediately uphill. At 0.7 miles, you'll get your first chance for a breather when you reach a one-room **cabin** on the right. Keep climbing and, at 1.2 miles, you'll meet up with **Old Settlers Trail** (continues right) and **Gabes Mountain Trail** (continues left). Stay straight on Maddron Bald Trail, following the old roadbed for another mile before the wagon road ends at a traffic circle. Here the path begins in earnest.

Cross **Indian Camp Creek** 0.5 miles past

the old traffic circle, keeping an eye out for **Albright Grove Loop Trail,** which appears in another 0.1 miles. Since Albright Grove is a loop, you can take this entrance, make the loop, and then descend along Maddron Bald Trail. Or you can climb up another 0.3 miles to the upper junction with Albright and take Maddron Bald Trail back.

Many consider Albright Grove to be a great example of old-growth forest in the national park. Though many of the huge hemlock trees have died from a pest infestation, they've left gaps in the canopy, allowing in sunlight. You'll still see many fine and big trees here, evidence of the forest as it once stood.

After you've explored Albright Grove, head back down Maddron Bald Trail to the trailhead.

Fishing

Anglers can bring their gear to **Cosby Creek,** which has several spots where wild trout are abundant. If you find other anglers along the creek and want some isolation, hike upstream into the headwaters, where small brook trout await.

In the spring you'll catch fish along Cosby Creek, but in the summer you'll want to venture into the headwaters. Fall fishing is spectacular, thanks to that distracting and beautiful leaf show, and in the winter you'll catch fish along the stream on all but the coldest days (because you'll be snug and warm somewhere else).

Camping

Cosby Campground (127 Cosby Park Rd., Cosby, TN, info 423/487-2683, reservations 877/444-6777, www.recreation.gov, mid-May-Oct., $17.50) has 157 sites for tents and RVs. Despite being home to the park's third-largest campground, Cosby is known as the quietest of the park's gateways. A number of trails originate from the campground.

At the northern end of Great Smoky Mountains National Park, you're close enough to the **Cherokee National Forest**

(www.fs.usda.gov/cherokee, free) to camp in the Pigeon River Recreation Zone. Dispersed camping is allowed provided that campers are 100 feet away from water, trails, parking areas, and developed recreation areas.

Accommodations

Cosby has a few accommodations, but selections are limited. Fortunately, a couple of spots stand out.

Creekwalk Inn and Cabins at Whisperwood Farm (166 Middle Creek Rd., 423/487-4000, www.whisperwoodretreat.com, $289-389) is a seven-room bed-and-breakfast with inn rooms and several cabins all set on a 50-acre mountain farm. There are hiking trails and creeks to explore, and a killer breakfast is served every morning. Best of all, the individual cabins are separated, providing privacy for guests, and the B&B rooms are so cozy you'll forget anyone else is there. Until breakfast, that is, when everyone shows up for cast-iron skillet cornbread with peach jam, fried potatoes, sausage, and eggs cooked on a wood stove.

For a sample of mountain life but with electricity, **Garden of Eden Cabins** (467 Laurel Springs Rd., 423/487-2617, www.gardenofedencabins.com, $95-105) has three cabins in the woods near the national park. They are comfortable and homey, though the decor could use a bit of an update (common in B&Bs and cabins in these parts). Two of the cabins have two bedrooms, making them natural choices for couples traveling together, families, or small groups. Each cabin is pet-friendly and has a fire ring and a picnic area with outdoor seating; two cabins overlook the creek, which makes quite the lovely lullaby.

At **Cosby Creek Cabins** (4376 Cosby Hwy., 800/508-8844, www.cosbycreekcabins. com, $145-343 plus cleaning fee), you'll find larger and slightly more luxurious cabins scattered around Cosby, with several closer to Pigeon Forge and Gatlinburg. The three dozen cabins range from one to four bedrooms and

---

1: Hen Wallow Falls 2: Cosby Campground

include options like game rooms, fireplaces, and hot tubs; some are pet-friendly.

Food

Dining options are few, and all are of the country cookin' variety. But the food is both filling and tasty, though vegetarians may have a hard time finding a meatless meal.

For an early breakfast at **Janice's Diner** (2765 Cosby Hwy., 423/613-5515, 7am-8pm daily, $7-20, cash only), skip the front room (it's a little dull) and head straight for the homey, welcoming dining area in back. The food is somewhere between diner fare and homestyle cooking, which means a hearty breakfast and everything from cheeseburgers to cheesesteaks to fried chicken—plus a few salads for good measure—on the menu. The portions are big and everything's affordable, making it ideal to fill up your tank pre- or post-hike.

Magnolia Tree Restaurant & Country Market (4925 Hooper Hwy., 423/487-2519, 11am-8pm Thurs.-Tues., $7-20) is one of those dual-purpose places that feels like the inspiration for Cracker Barrel. You know the type: Eat a home-cooked meal in the dining room, then buy some fudge or whimsical country gift in the shop. While that may sound a little corny, you can pick up some road or trail snacks here and get a decent meal. Specials like brisket and smoked chicken hit the spot, but on the regular menu, try the cheesesteak, the BLT, and the chicken potpie, though not all at once—that's a lot of food and you'll have no room for dessert.

Over at **Dock's 321 Café & Marketplace** (4752 Hooper Hwy., 865/617-4656, noon-7pm, Thurs.-Sat., $6-15), they made a menu with character, which is what you expect from a place with this much personality. The restaurant—an old school bus turned eatery—sits surrounded by signs, random bits of yard art, and holiday lawn ornaments, letting you know from the start that it doesn't take itself too seriously. A couple of vegetarian menu options appear in the middle of barbecue; a Cubanesque panini; some sandwiches named for rock stars like Janis Joplin and Jerry Garcia; and slices of smoked pies (you read it right; they're smoked and they're tasty). The sandwiches are sizable and the pie excellent, and you can eat your meal here or grab it to go and enjoy in the park.

BIG CREEK

Big Creek is the site of a beautiful and seldom-visited front-country campground and has one of the best hikes for beginning day hikers and backpackers. The Big Creek Trail is more of an easy creek-side walk than a hike, but it's long enough to make you feel accomplished when you're done.

For more of a challenge, turn Big Creek into a big overnighter by including a summit of Mount Sterling, or you can take on Mount Sterling from a couple of different routes, all accessible from this region.

Hiking
★ BIG CREEK TRAIL
Distance: 10.6 miles round-trip
Duration: 5-6 hours
Elevation gain: 600 feet
Difficulty: easy
Trailhead: Big Creek Campground and Picnic Area off I-40 at Waterville (exit 457)

Big Creek Trail follows an old motor road built by the Civilian Conservation Corps (CCC) in the 1930s, so it's smooth and wide with a very gentle grade for its entire length. The difficult part of this trail is the distance, so be sure to bring plenty of water and something to eat.

Roughly 1 mile in from the trailhead, you'll see **Rock House,** an impressive rock cliff that has sheltered more than a few loggers, Civilian Conservation Corps workers, hunters, and hikers from a rainstorm. Just beyond Rock House is **Midnight Hole,** where Big Creek flows through a narrow chute in the rock, then drops 6-7 feet into a deep, dark pool perfect for swimming before flowing on.

Two miles in, you'll see **Mouse Creek Falls,** a 35-foot cascade that drops right into Big Creek. It's a fantastic spot to sit, relax, take some pictures, and enjoy the woods. It's also a great spot to turn around if you may not be up for the whole 10-mile trip.

Push on past Mouse Creek Falls and you'll come upon **Brakeshoe Spring.** In another 2.5 miles you'll reach **Walnut Bottoms** and **Campsite 37.** This is one of the best campsites in the park if you're going to make this hike an overnighter. From here, it's time to retrace your steps back to the trailhead.

MOUNT STERLING VIA BAXTER CREEK TRAIL

Distance: 12.2 miles round-trip
Duration: 5-6 hours
Elevation gain: 4,200 feet
Difficulty: strenuous
Trailhead: Big Creek Campground and Picnic Area off I-40 at Waterville (exit 457)

You can reach the summit of Mount Sterling from a number of trails—but this one is perhaps the most direct. This hike is strenuous not because of any technical or steep sections of the trail (it's actually well maintained), but because it's a steady uphill climb with a 4,200-foot elevation gain until you turn around for the return trip. At the summit, you're rewarded with a fire tower to climb, giving you massive views of this section of the park.

At the trailhead, cross a **footbridge** over Big Creek, which you'll follow for 0.5 miles until the trail begins to climb the lower slopes of Mount Sterling. Before the uphill section, you'll pass an unmarked **spur trail** at 0.3 miles; it leads to a rock wall and huge stone chimney, the remains of a lodge once owned by a lumber company.

After crossing Baxter Creek (around the 0.7-mile mark), you'll pass through some spectacular old-growth forest and one of the largest (if not the largest) tulip trees in the park at more than 175 feet tall. There are several massive trees here, including more champion tulip trees, the largest northern red oak, and the Carolina silver bell.

The hike is straightforward for the length of the trail: Keep climbing, keep passing amazing trees and lovely spring wildflowers until you reach the summit. At the 5,842-foot summit, you'll notice three things: wind, the temperature, and a **fire tower.** It's cooler, and the summit can be quite windy, which makes the thought of climbing the 60-foot fire tower seem daunting. If you climb, do so carefully and remember the view you'll get at the end. On clear days you can see Balsam Mountain to the west, Mount Guyot to the northwest, Max Patch (along the Appalachian Trail on the Tennessee-North Carolina border) to the east, and Cataloochee Valley just below to the south. When you've had your fill of the views, follow the path back to the trailhead.

BIG CREEK TRAIL AND MOUNT STERLING LOOP

Distance: 17.4 miles round-trip
Duration: 10 hours
Elevation gain: 4,200 feet
Difficulty: strenuous
Trailhead: Big Creek Campground and Picnic Area off I-40 at Waterville (exit 457)

You can make this a rewarding day hike or break it up into a one- or two-night backpacking experience. All three options follow the same route, with access to backcountry campsites.

Begin by following **Big Creek Trail,** which uses a Civilian Conservation Corps motor road to guide hikers to Rock House (an impressive rock cliff), Mouse Creek Falls, and Brakeshoe Springs. From **Brakeshoe Springs,** hike 2.3 miles to the junction with **Swallow Fork Trail.** If you plan to stay overnight, continue 0.2 miles to **Campsite 37** and Walnut Bottoms. Campsite 37 is one of the park's best backcountry sites, so consider a night here if you're backpacking.

If pressing on, take Swallow Fork Trail and begin a gradual climb, crossing a couple of small streams along the way. You will reach **Swallow Fork** 1 mile in; cross it on a foot log and you'll reach **McGinty Creek** and the remains of what was once a sawmill. This section is lousy with wildflowers in the spring, so take your time and enjoy it when the blooms are out.

From McGinty Creek, hike approximately 1 mile before making one more stream crossing,

Big Creek Trail and Mount Sterling Loop

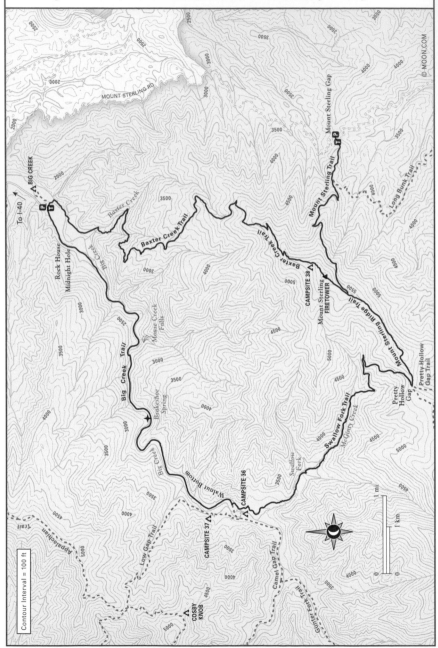

© MOON.COM

MOUNT STERLING RD.

BIG CREEK

To I-40

Mount Sterling Gap

Mount Sterling Trail

Long Bunk Trail

Rock House

Midnight Hole

Baxter Creek

Baxter Creek Trail

Big Creek

Baxter Creek Trail

CAMPSITE 38

Mount Sterling
FIRETOWER

Mouse Creek Falls

Mount Sterling Ridge Trail

Pretty Hollow Gap Trail

Brakeshoe Spring

Big Creek Trail

Pretty Hollow Gap

Swallow Fork Trail

McGinty Creek

Swallow Fork

Big Creek

Walnut Bottom

CAMPSITE 36

Appalachian Trail

Low Gap Trail

CAMPSITE 37

Camel Gap Trail

Gunter Fork Trail

COSBY KNOB

Contour Interval = 100 ft

1 mi

1 km

then start a steep climb to **Pretty Hollow Gap.** At the gap, the **Mount Sterling Ridge Trail** intersects with Pretty Hollow Gap Trail (which reaches Cataloochee in a few miles); turn left (east) for Mount Sterling.

After turning onto Mount Sterling Ridge Trail, you'll find another steep climb, but it's only 0.5 miles and it eases up once you reach the top of the knob. From the top, it's 0.4 miles to the summit and the **fire tower.** Adjacent to the summit is **Campsite 38,** for a first or second night in the backcountry. If you're camping, note that it's often windy here and cooler due to the elevation, so pack appropriate sleeping gear.

At the summit, the trail becomes **Baxter Creek Trail,** which you'll follow back to the Big Creek Trailhead. It's a steady downhill with a couple of notable landmarks. The first is a spring 0.2 miles from the summit, which you'll reach in 150 yards or so off the trail. The second landmark is 2 miles from the summit, where the trail makes a hairpin turn and plunges into another section of old-growth forest. Continue through some impressive and thick woods until arriving back at the trailhead.

MOUNT STERLING

Distance: 5.4 miles round-trip
Duration: 5-6 hours
Elevation gain: 1,900 feet
Difficulty: moderate/strenuous
Trailhead: Mount Sterling Trailhead at Mount Sterling Gap
Directions: From I-40, take the Waterville exit (exit 457) and cross the Pigeon River. Stay left and follow the road 2 miles to Mount Sterling. Turn left and drive the curvy 6.7 miles to Mount Sterling Gap. The trailhead is on the west side of the road.

This hike starts off steep and it doesn't relent for a long time. Begin hiking up the trail to a junction with **Long Bunk Trail** in 0.5 miles. Continue climbing until you reach **Mount Sterling Ridge** at 2.3 miles. You have a little climbing left—0.4 miles—before you reach the **summit.** There's an additional 60-foot climb if you visit the fire tower, which

has quite a view. On clear days you can see Balsam Mountain to the west, Mount Guyot to the northwest, Max Patch to the east, and Cataloochee Valley just below to the south. When ready, retrace your steps back to the trailhead.

Camping

The **Big Creek Campground** (off Hwy. 284/Mt. Sterling Rd., 12 sites, Apr.-Oct., $17.50) is located off Highway 284. Amenities include a ranger station, pay phone, drinking water, restrooms with flush toilets, a picnic area, and a group camp, as well as equestrian sites (reservations at 877/444-6777 or www.recreation. gov, campground inquiries 865/436-1261, $29). Trailheads to Baxter Creek Trail, Big Creek Trail, and the Chestnut Branch of the Appalachian Trail lead from the campground.

Big Creek is close enough to the **Cherokee National Forest** (www.fs.usda. gov/cherokee, free) to camp in the Pigeon River Recreation Zone. Dispersed camping is allowed provided that campers are 100 feet away from water, trails, parking areas, and developed recreation areas. To get there, take I-40 west into Tennessee and the national forest.

It is also possible to drive farther north to the French Broad River Recreation Zone for more camping, hiking, and fishing opportunities. To get there within Tennessee, take Highway 701 north to Highway 107, which leads to several trailheads and recreation opportunities.

CATALOOCHEE VALLEY

Nestled in the folds of the mountains and encircled by 6,000-foot peaks, the Cataloochee Valley was settled by Europeans in the early 1830s. This isolated valley on the northeastern edge of Great Smoky Mountains National Park was home to two communities—Big and Little Cataloochee—and more than 1,200 people in 1910. By the 1940s all but a few were gone, having left the valley for hills and hollows nearby. Today this is one of the more beautiful spots in the national park, and a

Cataloochee Valley

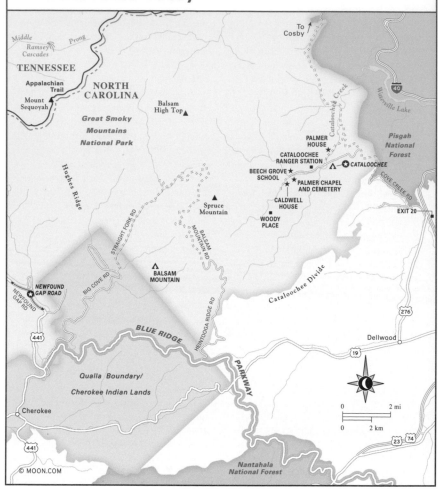

few historic structures are all that remain of the communities that thrived here, save a few memories and stories that were written down.

Cataloochee Valley is not far from I-40, but it can be a little difficult to find because the signage directing you here is poor at best. From I-40, take exit 20 onto U.S. 276. Take an immediate right onto Cove Creek Road. The condition of the road—it's alternately gravel and paved—and the narrow, winding route will make you doubt you made the right turn,

but you did. Zigzag up this road for about 12 miles, and suddenly it will open up into the wide, grassy expanse that is Cataloochee Valley. Before you begin your descent into the valley, stop at the overlook just past the intersection with Big Creek Road. From here you can marvel at the valley sweeping away before you, and the mountains rising up all around.

The valley is open to vehicle traffic 8am-sunset daily, so keep that in mind if you're visiting without plans to camp. Though less visited than other areas, such as Cades Cove on the western side of the park, Cataloochee sees its fair share of visitors. Most arrive in the evenings shortly before sunset to see the elk grazing in the fields. If you don't plan on camping and you'd rather avoid the crowds, as small as they may be, visit in midday and take a hike to see if you can find the elk in the woods; it's where they go to escape the heat.

★ Cataloochee

Four prominent structures still stand in Cataloochee Valley: two homes, a school, and a church. A few other structures and ruins, cemeteries, fences, and walls remain throughout the valley as well. The most prominent building is the **Palmer Chapel and Cemetery.** The chapel was built in 1898, and a regular service hasn't been held here for some time. Today the chapel sees sporadic use, the most regular being the annual reunion of the descendants of some of the oldest Cataloochee families. Descendants of the Barnes, Bennett, Caldwell, Noland, and Palmer families gather here to eat, hold a short church service, and maintain the cemetery. Throughout the year there are some great opportunities to photograph the chapel in all sorts of lighting, weather, and seasonal conditions.

Across the road is the **Beech Grove School,** the last of three schools to serve the children of the valley. It's empty save for a few artifacts. Beech Grove School operated on a very different school schedule than what we're familiar with: The only regular school sessions were held November-January, sometimes February, and rarely into March. This odd schedule was built around the seasons and freed children for planting and harvesting, as well as hunting and preserving food—staple activities for many living in the mountains.

Just up the road is the **Caldwell House.** We know from records that the owner, Hiram Caldwell, was prosperous, but you could tell that just by comparing this 1906 home with the other historic homes in the park, which are, by and large, log cabins. The Caldwell House is frame-built (similar to houses now), with paneling on the interior walls.

The final structure is the **Palmer House,** located off Big Creek Road, not far from the Cataloochee Ranger Station. This was once a log home—two, actually, connected by a covered walkway called a dogtrot—but as the owners came into money in the early 1900s, they began making improvements and remodeling the home. They covered the exterior and interior with weatherboarding and began using fancy wallpaper in some rooms; scraps of the wallpaper are there today. When the son inherited the property, he remodeled it, adding rooms to the home and operating it as a boardinghouse. Renters were primarily anglers who came to fish in the 3 miles of stocked trout stream the family owned.

Hiking
BOOGERMAN TRAIL
Distance: 7.4-mile round-trip
Duration: 3.5-4 hours
Elevation gain: 1,050 feet
Difficulty: moderate
Trailhead: just past Cataloochee Campground

This loop isn't named for some fearsome and mythical creature from the woods; it's named for Robert "Boogerman" Palmer, the former owner of much of the land along this hike. Palmer is rumored to have earned his nickname in school, where he told his teacher that he wanted to be "the Boogerman" when he grew up. This trail is anything but fearsome, and in the summer you'll likely see a few other hikers; if it's solitude you're seeking, hit the trail during the shoulder seasons.

Start the hike by crossing **Palmer Creek.** Follow Caldwell Fork upstream for nearly a mile and you'll come to **Boogerman Trail.** Turn left onto the trail and begin a gentle climb. When you reach a lower ridgeline, the path levels out, then descends through a grove of pine trees before ascending again. Soon the trail makes a steep ascent to another

Boogerman Trail

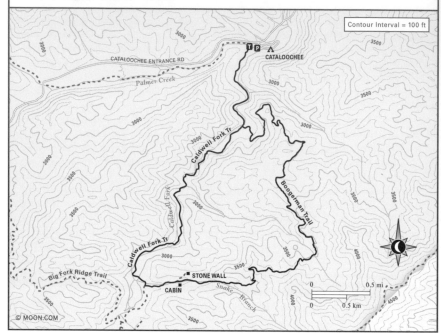

Contour Interval = 100 ft

CATALOOCHEE ENTRANCE RD

CATALOOCHEE

Palmer Creek

Caldwell Fork Tr

Boogerman Trail

Caldwell Fork

Caldwell Fork Tr

Big Fork Ridge Trail

STONE WALL

CABIN

Snake Branch

© MOON.COM

0   0.5 mi
0   0.5 km

level ridge. This section features some of the largest trees, mostly poplars, that you'll see on this hike.

As you continue on this short ridgeline section, you'll encounter some signs of human settlement, the first of which is a **stone wall.** Continue your descent and cross the stream you're following a few times, passing more rock walls along the way. If the wildflowers aren't too high, you may spot a large, strange piece of metal just off the trail. It's the remnant of some sort of homesteading equipment, perhaps a sluice gate for a water flume or maybe a piece from a sawmill. Whatever it is, it's alien here.

When you pass the decayed remains of a **cabin,** you're close to the junction with Caldwell Fork Trail. At **Caldwell Fork Trail,** turn right and cross Snake Branch (the stream you've been following), and soon thereafter, Caldwell Fork. You'll cross Caldwell Fork several more times before reaching the junction

with **Boogerman Trail** and the path back to the trailhead.

ROUGH FORK TRAIL

Distance: 2 miles round-trip
Duration: 1 hour
Elevation gain: 50 feet
Difficulty: easy
Trailhead: Rough Fork Trailhead at the end of Cataloochee Road

One of the easiest hikes in the whole park, the Rough Fork Trail follows a gravel road for nearly the entire length of the trail. Three stream crossings on foot logs are highlights of the hike, which ends at the Steve Woody House.

The trailhead begins on the other side of a gate that marks the end of the paved road and the start of the gravel road. Follow the wide, flat road as it goes through the woods. The path parallels Rough Fork until it crosses on a **foot log.** (Foot logs are long logs that have

The Return of Native Elk

tourists viewing elk herd at the Oconaluftee Visitor Center

Elk are native to the mountains of North Carolina and Tennessee, but overhunting decimated their population across the region. In North Carolina, the last elk was believed to have been killed in the late 1700s; in Tennessee, in the mid-1800s. In 2001, the National Park Service reintroduced elk to the park by bringing 25 elk to Great Smoky Mountains National Park from Land Between the Lakes National Recreation Area in Kentucky. The next year, they brought in another 27 animals. Today they believe somewhere between 150 and 200 elk live in the park.

The majority of the elk can be seen in the **Cataloochee Valley,** though a small herd lives near the **Oconaluftee Visitor Center** and **Smokemont Campground** and can be seen wading across the river and grazing in the fields and forest there.

Adult males, called bulls, weigh 600-700 pounds, while females, referred to as cows, weigh around 500 pounds. Some bulls have antlers that are five feet across. They're territorial, and bulls sometimes see humans as a threat and may charge. It's best to watch the elk from a safe distance. In Great Smoky Mountains National Park it is illegal to approach elk within 50 yards (150 feet) or any distance that disturbs or displaces the animals.

At certain times of the year, you may see calves walking close by their mothers. Never approach or touch a calf. If an elk calf feels threatened and its mother is not nearby, its natural defense is to lie down and be still. It may look orphaned, but mom is within earshot, so back away slowly.

Elk are most active in the early morning and evening, much like deer. Also like deer, their diet is primarily grass, bark, leaves, and acorns. There are no natural predators of elk in the Smokies today, though sick, injured, and young elk are sometimes targets of opportunity for black bears, coyotes, or even the boldest of bobcats.

been flattened on the top to create a walkway; they often have handrails on one side and can be a little bouncy.) The foot logs across Rough Fork are a bit bouncy but are fun and safe to cross.

Cross Rough Fork twice more via **footbridges,** then continue following the stream on the right as you make your way to the former home and springhouse (a small wooden shed built over a spring) of **Steve Woody.** Be careful around the springhouse because snakes are frequent visitors.

LITTLE CATALOOCHEE TRAIL

Distance: 12 miles round-trip
Duration: 6-8 hours
Elevation gain: 2,400 feet
Difficulty: moderate/strenuous
Trailhead: Pretty Hollow Gap/Cataloochee Horse Trail Trailhead, adjacent to Beech Grove School

Little Cataloochee Trail is 6 miles one-way, so you'll need to arrange a car shuttle back to the trailhead if you don't want to hike the full 12 miles. Alternatively, take a shorter hike from the other end of the trail.

Begin at the **Cataloochee Horse Camp** (you may have to park 0.2 miles back down by Cataloochee Entrance Rd.) and follow an old road that parallels Palmer Creek. At 0.8 miles, you'll reach the junction with **Little Cataloochee Trail.** Turn right (northeast) and follow Little Cataloochee to the end at Highway 284.

As you hike, you can look for signs of former homesteads in the form of cultivated flowers like daffodils, yucca plants, and fruit trees. There are many **homestead sites** along the trail, but most are grown over, though you can spot them.

For a while the trail will be steep; at approximately 3 miles, you'll meet up with an old roadbed that makes the hike easier. At 3.3 miles, you'll reach **Dan Cook Place,** a cabin that was reconstructed after the original was destroyed by vandals in the mid-1970s. Continue along the trail to the **Little Cataloochee Baptist Church** and **cemetery.** The original church has been maintained and is the site of occasional services.

From the church, the road descends rather steeply, passing the former community of **Ola.** Follow the road to a short side trail leading to **John Hackson Hannah Cabin,** then a junction with **Long Bunk Trail.** It's another 1.1 miles to the end of the trail at Highway 284. Use a car shuttle to return to the trailhead, or hike back along the road (which adds another 3 miles or so), or backtrack to make this a big 12-mile day.

For a shorter hike that sees a few historic structures, drive to the end of the trail on Highway 284 (the trailhead is marked) and hike to the Little Cataloochee Baptist Church and Dan Cook Place (6 miles round-trip).

Fishing

Fishing is plentiful off **Cataloochee Creek** and its tributaries, with the main quarry being wild trout.

Camping

The ★ **Cataloochee Campground** (campground 828/497-9270, reservations 877/444-6777, www.recreation.gov, mid-Apr.-Oct., reservations required, $25) has 27 tent and RV sites. There is a horse camp with seven sites not far up the valley; down the valley there's a group campground with three sites and room for much larger parties. This highly recommended campsite is one of the most secluded you'll find in the front country.

BALSAM MOUNTAIN ROAD

Since most of the crowds who visit Great Smoky Mountains National Park use Newfound Gap Road exclusively, it's nice to find a route that's less traveled and possibly more beautiful. One such route is **Balsam Mountain Road** (open mid-May-Nov.), also called Heintooga Round Bottom Trail, a lovely drive where you may be lucky to see 10 other cars.

Accessible only from the Blue Ridge Parkway near Soco Gap, the road traverses 14 miles of ridgeline. To reach Balsam Mountain Road, turn off the Parkway at milepost 458 and follow Heintooga Ridge Road to the Heintooga Overlook and Picnic Area; here the road changes names to Balsam Mountain Road and turns to gravel.

As soon as it turns into Balsam Mountain Road, it becomes one-way, so you're committed to follow it to its end. This will take about 1.5 hours (if you don't stop to hike or take in the scenery), primarily because the gravel

1: elk grazing in a field in Cataloochee Valley
2: Palmer Chapel in Cataloochee **3:** Caldwell House in Cataloochee **4:** trail in Cataloochee

road forces you to slow down. It's narrow but well maintained, so you can drive most cars along the route. If you're in doubt of the road's condition or are concerned about your vehicle's clearance, check online (www.nps.gov/grsm) for road closures and advisories.

Balsam Mountain Road is an excellent place to see spring wildflowers, summer rhododendrons, and fall leaves. At these times, traffic may pick up, but the idea of a gravel road discourages enough visitors to keep this road the one less traveled.

When you've driven about 13 miles along Balsam Mountain Road, it becomes two-way again. Here, it begins to follow Straight Fork, which will lead you right onto Straight Fork Road (closed in winter), which cuts through the Qualla Boundary to U.S. 441.

Hiking
FLAT CREEK TRAIL
Distance: 5.2 miles round-trip
Duration: 3.5-4 hours
Elevation gain: 900 feet
Difficulty: moderate
Trailhead: Heintooga Overlook and Picnic Area

You can hike Flat Creek Trail as a 5.2-mile out-and-back trail or do it as a 6.2-mile loop. If following the loop, note that the last 3.6 miles are along Heintooga Ridge Road (closed to vehicles Nov.-May).

From the picnic area, walk out to **Heintooga Overlook** for a great view. Just past the overlook, the trail forks; go right and follow **Flat Creek Trail** as it descends, crossing the creek and entering a rhododendron thicket. Soon the forest opens up and becomes grassy, a sign of previous logging activity.

At 1.9 miles, you'll reach a path (right) that leads to Flat Creek Falls, but don't bother—the views aren't good and it's difficult (and dangerous) to try. Stay on Flat Creek Trail as the trail enters a thick forest, descends, and then crosses a fork of **Bunches Creek.** Shortly after Bunches Creek, you'll climb up to **Heintooga Ridge Road.** Turn around and head back, or continue hiking up the road for a 6-mile hike.

BALSAM MOUNTAIN TRAIL
Distance: 8.2 miles round-trip
Duration: 6 hours
Elevation gain: 3,000 feet
Difficulty: moderate/strenuous
Trailhead: Balsam Mountain Road, 8.2 miles from the end of Heintooga Ridge Road at Pin Oak Gap

You have two choices for this hike: a long day hike or an overnighter with a stay at Laurel Gap Shelter. The route is the same no matter which you hike. Laurel Gap Shelter is only 4.1 miles from the trailhead, so if you chose to stay, you'll either have two easy days or one long day if you decide to hike to the summit of Balsam High Top and then go on to the shelter for water and rest.

The straightforward trail climbs aggressively uphill for 1.9 miles, where you'll reach the now-overgrown **Ledge Bald** and begin to ascend. In 0.4 miles is the junction with **Beech Gap Trail,** which comes in from the left (west) and leads back to Balsam Mountain Road after a 2.5-mile hike. Ignore the trail and press on, ascending again until you reach the ridge. Follow the ridge through a hardwood forest to a grove of fir trees, the mountain's namesake balsam trees. These trees mark **Balsam High Top,** the 3.5-mile mark on the trail. To visit the summit (no views, just do it if you're a peak bagger), you'll have to go off-trail. Otherwise, keep hiking another 0.6 miles to **Laurel Gap Shelter** and the spring there. Make camp or get a little water, have a snack, and rest up. When you're ready, hike out by backtracking the trail.

Camping
The front-country campground at **Balsam Mountain** (46 sites, first-come first-served, May-Oct., $17.50) is located off Balsam Mountain Road at Heintooga Ridge Road. Amenities include an amphitheater, a small section for tents only, restrooms, and a ranger station with nearby access to Round Bottom Picnic Area and the Flat Creek Trailhead.

An equestrian-friendly campground at **Round Bottom Horse Camp** (Round Bottom-Straight Fork Rd., 865/436-1261 or

877/444-6677, www.recreation.gov, Apr.-Oct., $23) has five campsites, pit toilets, stalls, and bedding for horses. Its location north of Cherokee, just inside the park and far up narrow Big Cove Road, makes it perfect for long rides with larger groups.

Western Smokies

The western Smokies are a bit wilder than the eastern Smokies. As European settlers moved in from the east, they first settled the coves and hollows there, then found passes through the Smokies and settled there. The mountains are tall and steep, and the valleys deep, and where there are coves and meadows, they're broad, rich-soiled places that, before the national park, were home to several small communities.

LITTLE RIVER ROAD
Elkmont

At the **Elkmont Campground,** only 8 miles from Gatlinburg, drifts of male fireflies rise up from the grass to flash their mating signal, but they don't do so as individuals—they blink in coordinated ways that still baffle researchers. For a two-week window every summer (often **late May-early June,** but it depends on a variety of factors), their nightly light show delights crowds. It starts slowly, with only a few of these insects showing off. Then more join in, and more, until they reach a crescendo. Slowly, they begin to synchronize until, at the peak, whole fields may flash all at once, giving you a sudden and startling blink of light and just as sudden darkness. Or they may flash in waves moving around the fields and hillsides. Or large groups may appear to flash their lights at one another and wait in the darkness for a response. Whatever the reason for their display, the synchronous fireflies are amazing little creatures. Nineteen species of fireflies live in Great Smoky Mountains National Park, but these are the only fireflies in the park to synchronize their flashing.

The synchronous fireflies may be one reason Elkmont developed a nascent tourism industry in the early 1900s. A hotel—The Wonderland Park Hotel—and a number of cabins and cottages were built for vacationers and honeymooners, who frequented the area for decades. Over the years, disrepair and deferred or disregarded maintenance took a toll on the structures, leading the Park Service to slate them all for demolition, but a successful bid to create the **Elkmont Historic District** held the bulldozers at bay. In the early 2000s, The Wonderland Hotel collapsed, and the Park Service drew up restoration plans; before work could begin in earnest, the hotel burned and a few of the cabins were lost. Today 18 of the cabins stand, though only 4 cabins have been rehabilitated and are open for the public to check out.

One building, the **Appalachian Clubhouse** (500 Elkmont Rd., 877/444-6677, www.recreation.gov, Apr.-Oct., venue rental $250 daily), has been restored to its 1930s glory. The clubhouse hosts a number of special events every year. The enormous meeting space is anchored by a stone fireplace at one end; doors along the east side open to a large covered porch. A sizable caterer's kitchen (it's bare-bones: outlets and counters only, no appliances or refrigerators) means the building can easily house a large meeting, wedding reception, or get-together of any kind.

The **Spence Cabin** (500 Elkmont Rd., 877/444-6677, www.recreation.gov, Apr.-Oct., venue rental $150 daily), also called River Lodge, is another restored historic Elkmont building that serves as a base for special events and gatherings. Smaller than the Appalachian Clubhouse, this restored cabin shows off what it was like to vacation here in the 1920s and 1930s. Meeting rooms are smaller, with no large central gathering place.

Neither the Appalachian Clubhouse nor Spence Cabin lacks for charm, but these are not overnight accommodations; rather, they

The Firefly Lottery

Viewing the synchronous fireflies at Elkmont is deservedly popular—so much so that in 2016 the park instituted a lottery system to control access and limit traffic congestion. The new lottery, which opens in late April, assigns parking passes for specific times during the synchronous fireflies' mating season (late May-early June). Hopeful visitors can apply online for the **lottery** (877/444-6777, www.recreation.gov, one pass per household, application fee $1). If your number is picked, you'll be charged an additional $24 for the parking pass. Once the lottery closes, results become available about a week later. Up to 800 parking passes will be made available for about 100 cars per day. The lucky winners will receive a parking pass for one vehicle with up to seven passengers, good for their specific date at the Elkmont Viewing Area, adjacent to the campground. You check in at the Elkmont Campground kiosk, and attendants will direct you to a parking area. Be sure to stay on-trail, use a low-powered red flashlight or headlamp, and keep the car lights (interior and exterior) to a minimum until it's time to leave. Follow the advice and directions of park volunteers and staff on hand, and you'll be in for a beautiful show.

are event spaces ideal for day-long events like family reunions, Scout troop meetings, and corporate retreats.

Hiking

LAUREL FALLS TRAIL

Distance: 2.5 miles round-trip
Duration: 1.5-2 hours
Elevation gain: 400 feet
Difficulty: easy
Trailhead: parking area 3.9 miles west of Sugarlands Visitor Center on Little River Road

As the shortest and possibly easiest waterfall hike in Great Smoky Mountains National Park, Laurel Falls is the most popular of such hikes. The trail is paved, the grade is gentle (after you get past a short, steep section at the start of the trail), and the falls are a little over 1.3 miles from the trailhead.

Prepare to be dazzled when you reach the falls. Laurel Falls drops 75 feet in a wide, picture-perfect cascade. It's a gorgeous spot to photograph, but you have to be there early in the day to get a shot of the falls without people in it.

SUGARLAND MOUNTAIN

Distance: 12.3 miles end-to-end
Duration: 6 hours
Elevation gain: 5,308 feet
Difficulty: strenuous
Trailhead: Fork Ridge Trailhead 3.5 miles west on Clingmans Dome Road

At 12.3 miles, this is a long hike, and you'll need to arrange for a car shuttle at one end of the trail (unless you want to hike all the way back). Fortunately, the hiking is all downhill, but that can be pretty taxing, so watch your footing and hike at a sustainable pace. There have been numerous bear sightings around this trail, so keep your eyes and ears open.

Drive 3.5 miles along Clingmans Dome Road (closed in winter) and park at the Fork Ridge Trailhead on the south side of the road. Cross to the other side of Clingmans Dome Road, where the trail begins with a short access trail to the Appalachian Trail. Turn left on the **Appalachian Trail** and hike 0.3 miles to a junction with Sugarland Mountain Trail. Turn right and take **Sugarland Mountain Trail,** your path for the next 12 miles.

The first mile is a rocky trail through a spruce-fir forest that is somewhat reminiscent of the Forest Moon of Endor from *Return of the Jedi*. About 0.3 miles after the start is the **Mount Collins backcountry shelter**—other than that, it's just wildflowers and songbirds. After 1 mile, you'll begin to climb. Views open up here and there, giving you a glimpse of Mount LeConte and the

Chimneys, and, in the distance, Pigeon Forge and Gatlinburg.

The trail passes below the summit of **Sugarland Mountain** (5,494 feet) at 2.3 miles. It's an off-trail scramble to reach the true top, so it's best to stick to the trail.

From here the trail descends and then, at the 3.5-mile point, begins to climb slightly, making a sharp western turn. At this point, you should have a good view of Gatlinburg and the Chimneys (if the weather's clear). Continue downhill; the trail becomes easier as the woods change from fir-dominant to a hardwood forest. At 8.3 miles is what was once **Campground 21.** You'll reach **Huskey Gap Trail** in 9.3 miles and a view of Mount LeConte that may be overgrown.

At 11 miles is **Mids Gap** and an 0.5-mile-long uphill stretch. After a downhill day, it will feel big. Once you top out, begin a steep descent down to the trailhead and your shuttle car.

LITTLE RIVER TRAIL

Distance: 12.3 miles round-trip
Duration: 5-6 hours
Elevation gain: 1,100 feet
Difficulty: moderate/strenuous
Trailhead: Elkmont Campground

This hike looks long, and it can be if you hike the whole length. Or you can follow as much of it as you want for a hike of 1, 2, or 10 miles. In the spring, the trail is filled with wildflowers; in October, it's a fall-color extravaganza; and year-round you'll see anglers fly-fishing in the water by the path. But in **late spring,** this is the place to be to see the **synchronous fireflies.** The path here was once used for logging, and you'll see evidence of this all along the route—look around and you'll notice there's no old growth as in some sections of the park.

The first mile passes through the homeland of the synchronous fireflies, those curious fireflies that blink in unison during their spring mating season; the rest of the hike is a trek alongside the **Little River.** At times the path is a bit more like a trail than a road, but it always follows the logging roadbed.

Most hikers turn around at the 3.7-mile mark, the point where Little River Trail meets **Goshen Prong Trail.** I recommend pressing on a little farther, only 0.2 miles or so to a **bridge** over the river, which is quite scenic.

CUCUMBER GAP AND LITTLE RIVER LOOP

Distance: 5.5 miles round-trip
Duration: 2.5-3 hours
Elevation gain: 800 feet
Difficulty: easy/moderate
Trailhead: Elkmont Campground

This hike makes a loop using Cucumber Gap Trail and a portion of Little River Trail. It's a lovely hike for wildflowers in spring and fall color in October. The trails are easy; the railroad bed of Little River Trail and the typical forest trail of Cucumber Gap make a good combination, and the length is just about perfect for a day hike.

Just past the **Little River Trailhead** is a second parking area to the right of the gate; park here to start the trail on the gravel road past the gate on **Jakes Creek Trail.** There's a steep but short climb to the junction with Cucumber Gap. **Cucumber Gap** will give you a break from climbing—it's a long, gentle ascent through the tulip tree-dominated forest. Cross **Huskey Branch** just a little way above the waterfall, which you'll see in a few moments. After reaching the junction with Little River Trail, turn left and cross Huskey Branch again, this time right at **Huskey Branch Falls.** From here it is 2 easy miles back to the Little River trailhead and parking area.

Backpacking

The **Great Smoky Mountains Institute at Tremont** (9275 Tremont Rd., Townsend, TN, 865/448-6709, www.gsmit.org) offers a range of outdoor and Smoky-centric educational opportunities. Classrooms and offices are located just off Highway 73/Little River Road (0.2 miles beyond the intersection to Townsend). At the end of this road is a long but excellent hike that will get you on the

Appalachian Trail and provide some of the best photo opportunities the park has to offer.

LYNN CAMP PRONG

Distance: 21 miles round-trip
Duration: 12 hours or 1-2 days
Elevation gain: 3,650 feet
Difficulty: strenuous
Trailhead: Road near the Great Smoky Mountains Institute at Tremont

This hike is picture-postcard perfect (seriously, you'll see shots from this trail on park postcards and calendars)—and brutal. If you want to get deep in the Smokies and experience the rugged, wild nature of this place, this hike is for you. If you'd rather get some trail miles in and see some beautiful scenery, you can do that too, but the hike will be considerably shorter and take much less time.

At first, this trail seems easy as it follows a gravel road and old railroad grade for the first 0.5 miles. At 0.5 miles, you'll see a photographer's dream: **Lynn Camp Prong,** a large set of cascades on the stream. For the next 0.2 miles or so, you'll have plenty of chances for some great photos—don't be surprised if you see a number of other photo hounds out here.

After passing the cascades, the trail continues to follow the creek for 3 more miles, where a bridge crosses **Indian Flats Prong.** Now the trail begins to grow steep. If you're thinking of cutting the hike short, push on through this steep section to **Indian Flats Falls** (4 miles), then turn around.

Continue on and turn left (north) on **Lynn Camp Prong Trail.** Campsite 28 is another 1.5 miles up the trail. To stay the night, reserve a campsite in advance through the **Backcountry Information Office** (Sugarlands Visitor Center, 865/436-1297, https://smokiespermits.nps.gov, 8am-5pm daily, $4 pp per night, $20 maximum). You can also push on to Derrick Knob Shelter along the Appalachian Trail, another 6 miles or so up the trail.

From Campsite 28, it's a nonstop 2.2-mile climb to the ridgeline and the junction with **Miry Ridge Trail.** Turn right at the junction

and continue 2.5 miles to a junction with the **Appalachian Trail.** Turn right and face the steepest climb of the hike as you ascend **Cold Spring Knob.** Finally, descend to a junction with **Greenbrier Ridge Trail.** (If you're staying at Derrick Knob Shelter, it's another 0.3 miles down the trail.) To continue, turn right and hike northeast down Greenbrier Ridge Trail.

As you descend, you'll encounter a pair of lovely stream crossings that may distract you with their beauty, but pay attention, especially in high water. The footing can be tricky and the water strong. After passing the second creek crossing, you're now within 0.5 miles of **Indian Flats Falls** and the easy hike alongside Lynn Camp Prong back to the trailhead.

Fishing

Anglers take note: This area of the park offers some fantastic fishing. Along the east prong of **Little River** and all along Little River proper, you can reel in trout, smallmouth bass, and rock bass. The formation of the bottom along the East Prong and along Little River is right for smallmouth and rock bass: rocky, heavy with roots and some debris, filled with plenty of nooks and crannies to hide, but with plenty of deep pools and slow currents where the feeding is good. In the headwaters you can find places that trout love.

Camping

The **Elkmont Campground** (434 Elkmont Rd., Gatlinburg, TN, 877/444-6777, www.recreation.gov, Apr.-late Nov., $25-27) has 220 campsites, 55 of them along the Little River, with front-row seats to the firefly light show for those here at the right time. This is the largest campground in Great Smoky Mountains National Park, and one of the most visited. In addition to the firefly show and the attraction of Little River, this site also serves as a good base for exploring the area.

CADES COVE

Easily the most popular auto tour loop in Great Smoky Mountains National Park, Cades Cove receives around two million visitors a

Cades Cove and Fontana Lake Area

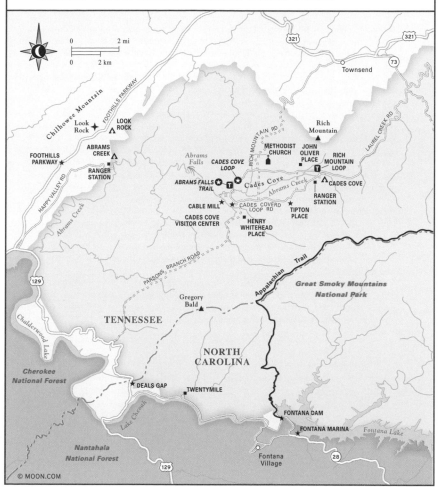

year. They come for the scenery—a long, wide, grassy-bottomed valley surrounded by undulating mountains—and the handful of preserved homesteads and historic structures, and because it's one of the park's best, and most reliable, spots to see wildlife.

TOP EXPERIENCE

★ Cades Cove Loop

The **Cades Cove Loop** is approximately 11 miles long, but in the summer and especially in the fall when the leaves are at their best, expect to spend three hours or more on this one-way road through the valley floor—and that's if you don't stop to photograph the wildlife or explore the historic structures. If you're the curious type or find the light is perfect for taking pictures, you can easily double the amount of time you spend here. When you do stop, be sure to pull off the road and leave enough room for traffic to pass. One source

Black Bears

Biologists estimate there are more than 1,500 black bears living in Great Smoky Mountains National Park, and if you know where and when to look, your chances of seeing one in the wild are quite good. Even if you don't know where to look, if you're in the park in spring or early summer, odds are you're going to spot one as you drive through the park.

Though I've seen bears in a number of spots, one of the most reliable places to see them is **Cades Cove.** Here, in the early morning and as dusk settles, the bears are more active, prowling the forest's edge and even eating apples that have fallen from the trees.

As awesome as it is to see a bear, they can present a problem to park visitors, just as we can present a problem to them. With the great number of visitors to Great Smoky Mountains National Park, many bears have grown accustomed to seeing people and have lost their natural fear of humans, automobiles, and horses. As they grow more used to people, we decide to give them "treats" to lure them closer to our cars and our campsites with food. Bears that are too accustomed to people, especially bears that have been fed a few times, can grow bold, even aggressive, searching campsites and open cars for food or even approaching open car windows or picnic tables. Now, with the rise of Instagram and the ease of sharing photos and video, a few visitors put themselves into dangerous spots just to get something to post online. That puts park visitors in danger from the bear, and it places the bear in danger of being put down for aggressive behavior.

Fortunately, serious incidents with black bears are rare, but they do occur. In 2000, a mother bear and her cub attacked and killed a camper near the Elkmont Campground. Every year, campsites and trails are closed due to bear activity and the potential for interaction between bears and visitors.

Park staff and volunteers do their best to educate visitors on proper human-bear interaction. Throughout the park you'll see signs and placards advising you on how to properly store and dispose of food and reminding you not to approach bears. Remember that bears are wild animals and unpredictable, and keep these tips in mind:

of traffic jams in Cades Cove is visitors who stop in the middle of the road to ooh and aah at the wildlife and scenery.

The popularity of this drive is well deserved. In the hours around dawn and dusk, wildlife is especially active. Vast herds of white-tailed deer are the most common sight (I once tallied 50 in a field before I quit counting), but black bears are also frequently spotted. The bears like to cozy up to the apple trees that dot the cove, and you'll occasionally spot them and their cubs napping or eating in the branches.

You may notice that the fields look especially manicured. They are, to an extent. Far from being mown and maintained like a golf course, the fields in Cades Cove are allowed to run wild, but only so wild. The National Park Service maintains the fields and fences, mowing, repairing, and reseeding as necessary to keep the valley looking much as it did when settlers lived here.

To take this lovely-in-any-season drive, follow Little River Road west from the Sugarlands Visitor Center for 17.2 miles; there it will turn into Laurel Creek Road and lead you into Cades Cove in another 7.4 miles. You can also access Cades Cove by entering the park at Townsend on Highway 73, then turning right on Laurel Creek Road, following it for 16 miles to the entrance to the cove. Cades Cove is closed to vehicle traffic Wednesdays from May-September. On those days, the loop is open exclusively to bicycle and foot traffic. The rest of the year the road is open to motor vehicles from sunrise to sunset daily, weather permitting.

Sights

According to some historians, the Cherokee people had hunting camps and possibly even a small settlement in Cades Cove, long before European settlers arrived. In fact, the name

- **Do not approach** within 50 yards or any distance that disturbs a bear, and do not allow a bear to approach you. For a good view, invest in a pair of binoculars.

- **Never feed bears.** It only gets them used to humans and causes them to think of us as a source of food.

- **Store food** in appropriate containers and in the proper places when camping. If you're not sure of the proper procedure, ask a ranger.

- **Dispose of garbage** in bear-proof receptacles.

- **Report** nuisance bear behavior or visitors breaking these rules to park officials.

In the unlikely event that **a bear approaches you,** stand tall, wave your arms, and make as much noise as possible. If you need to, throw sticks or rocks at the bear. In most cases, this will intimidate the bear and deter it from coming any closer. If the bear charges, don't run—

black bear

they can sprint 30 miles per hour, so you don't stand a chance. Instead, keep making noise and back away slowly, never turning your back to the bear. Often, bears will make bluff charges, so this is likely what you're seeing. If a black bear actually makes contact, fight back with anything and everything available to you; with a loud-enough and fierce-enough fight, the bear may see you as too much to deal with and leave you alone.

Cades Cove is believed to have come from Chief Kade, a little-known Cherokee leader. By the early 1820s, the first Europeans were here, building cabins and barns and carving homesteads out of the forest. More settlers arrived, having heard of the rich, fertile bottomland in Cades Cove, and by 1850 nearly 700 people called the valley home. As the collection of cabins and homesteads grew into a community, buildings like churches and schools were constructed. Families lived here even after the National Park Service began purchasing land. The last remaining school in Cades Cove closed in 1944, and the post office closed in 1947.

Today several historic structures remain standing along the valley floor. Among them is the most-photographed structure in the park, the **Methodist Church.** From time to time a wedding is held here, though it's more

common for visitors to leave handwritten prayers on scraps of paper at the altar.

The **Cable Mill Area** is the busiest section of the loop. Here you can see an actual mill in operation, and can even buy cornmeal or flour ground on-site. In addition to the mill and Methodist Church, the area contains two other churches, a few barns and log houses, and a number of smaller structures.

Halfway around the loop, you'll find the **Cades Cove Visitor Center** (Cades Cove Loop Rd., Townsend, TN, 865/436-7318, daily 9am-5pm Jan.-June, 9am-7pm July-Aug., 9am-6:30pm Sept.-Oct., 9am-5:30pm Nov., 9am-4:30pm Dec.), which has a good bookstore and gift shop. Most important, it also has one of two public restrooms you'll find on the tour (the other is at the Cades Cove Campground Store at the entrance).

GREAT SMOKY MOUNTAINS NATIONAL PARK
WESTERN SMOKIES

Hiking

★ ABRAMS FALLS TRAIL

Distance: 5 miles round-trip
Duration: 3 hours
Elevation gain: 350 feet
Difficulty: easy/moderate
Trailhead: Turn right onto a gravel road 4.9 miles from the start of the Cades Cove Loop; a parking area and the trailhead are at 0.4 miles in.

Several trails lead off into the woods from this parking area, but it's obvious which route to take—the most well-worn trail you see. If you're in doubt, follow the group in front of you, as Abrams Falls is the destination for most hikers who set off from this lot. Only a few steps from the trailhead is a **kiosk** that will set you on the right path.

The trail is pretty straightforward—it follows **Abrams Creek** all the way to the waterfall. The only real elevation gains come when you thrice leave the creek to climb up and around a ridge, crossing a feeder stream in the process. The first stream is Arbutus Branch, then Stony Branch, then Wilson Branch, which is very close to the falls.

After you cross Wilson Branch on a **log bridge,** you'll follow the trail downstream, cross Wilson Branch once again, and arrive at the falls.

Abrams Falls is pretty, and in wet weather it can be downright thunderous. Slick, mossy rocks make up the wall where the 20-foot waterfall, which has the largest volume of water of any waterfall in the park, tumbles into the pool below. Tempted as you may be to take a dip after a sweaty hike, don't do it; the currents are strong, and a few folks have drowned here.

ROCKY TOP AND THUNDERHEAD MOUNTAINS TRAIL

Distance: 13.9 miles round-trip
Duration: 7-8 hours
Elevation gain: 3,665 feet
Difficulty: strenuous
Trailhead: Anthony Creek Trailhead at the Cades Cove picnic area

Hiking to the famed Rocky Top is borderline brutal—you gain more than 3,500 feet in elevation, and on the trail's first few miles you share the path with horses, so it can get quite muddy and slippery. However, this exceptional hike is worth it. Time your hike for mid-June to see the rhododendrons and mountain laurels in full bloom.

Shortly after starting the **Anthony Creek Trail,** you'll reach Crib Trail Junction, then **Anthony Creek Horse Camp** (reservations required, 877/444-6777, www.recreation.gov, mid-May-early Nov., $23). Follow Anthony Creek Trail 3.5 miles to the **Bote Mountain Trail,** where hikers will turn right.

Climbing Bote Mountain Trail, you'll enter a long series of rhododendron "tunnels," and at 5.1 miles in, you'll reach **Spence Field** and the **Appalachian Trail.** Turn left and you'll get some stunning views of North Carolina and equally stunning views of hillsides and meadows covered in mountain laurels. Continue east along the Appalachian Trail to reach Rocky Top and Thunderhead Mountain.

Thunderhead Mountain is made up of three distinct summits. The first summit is **Rocky Top,** 1.2 miles from the Bote Mountain-Appalachian Trail junction and arguably the best view in the park. Next is the middle peak, sometimes called **Rocky Top Two,** just 0.3 miles beyond Rocky Top. Finally, another 0.3 miles brings you to the unremarkable summit of **Thunderhead.** Many hikers turn around at Rocky Top, never summiting Thunderhead.

RICH MOUNTAIN LOOP

Distance: 8.5-mile round-trip
Duration: 4.5-5 hours
Elevation gain: 1,740 feet
Difficulty: moderate
Trailhead: Park at the entrance gate to Cades Cove; the trail begins in the opposite parking lot.

The first part of this hike passes one of the meadows that make Cades Cove such a fabulous place. For 1.4 miles you'll walk through the woods and along the edge of the meadow until you reach the **John Oliver Cabin.**

The trail continues behind the cabin and

Rich Mountain Loop

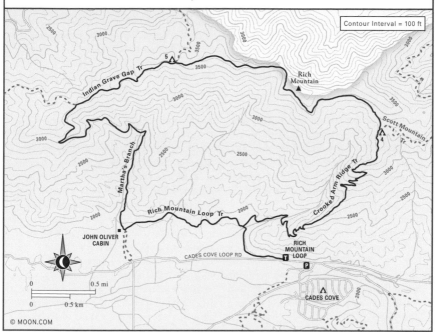

soon meets up with **Martha's Branch** and begins to climb. As you climb, you'll cross the branch a number of times. At mile 3, you'll find a place where you have a tight view of Cades Cove; don't sweat it, as better views are coming.

Continue 0.3 miles to **Indian Grave Gap Trail** and turn right. In 0.8 miles is **Campsite 5** (for backpackers) and the junction with Rich Mountain Trail. The saddle here has nice views.

Avoid the junction and follow Indian Grave Gap Trail 0.3 miles to a side trail. This path is only about 100 yards long and takes you to the highest point on Rich Mountain, **Cerulean Knob,** and the foundation of the former fire tower. Views are okay but not fantastic. Get back to the main trail and continue east, where you'll find a much better view than on the top.

When you reach a power-line clearance, you're almost at **Scott Mountain Trail** and **Campsite 4.** From the junction of these trails, continue straight ahead on **Crooked Arm Ridge Trail** (it's what Indian Grave Gap Trail turns into). This trail is steep and rutted and littered with the evidence of horses, so watch your step—that horse evidence can be slippery.

This trail leads back to **Rich Mountain Loop Trail,** 0.5 miles from the parking area.

CHESTNUT TOP TRAIL

Distance: 8.6 miles round-trip

Duration: 8 hours

Elevation gain: 1,950 feet

Difficulty: moderate

Trailhead: Chestnut Top trailhead, 100 yards north of the Townsend fork in the road where Little River Road meets Highway 73

Chestnut Top Trail can be tackled two ways: as an end-to-end hike with a shuttle vehicle at either end (5.4 miles), or as an out-and-back (8.6 miles), which makes for a longer hike. Either way, this hike is filled with wildflowers in the spring and is quite lovely.

After parking across Highway 73 from the **trailhead,** lace up and get ready to go. The first 0.6 miles is a steady climb. In the spring, the forest is carpeted with wildflowers; the first flowers appear in early March, and flowers will continue to bloom for the next two months.

As soon as you wrap up this strenuous climb, the trail levels out a little. That soon ends as you begin climbing again toward **Schoolhouse Gap** along **Chestnut Top Lead. Tuckaleechee Cove** is to the right of the trail; you'll catch glimpses of it through summer foliage and have good views of it the rest of the year.

At 4.3 miles you'll reach a junction with **Schoolhouse Gap Trail.** Turn around here for an out-and-back hike of 8.6 miles (which is almost all downhill), or turn left on Schoolhouse Gap Trail and continue hiking 1.1 miles to the **Schoolhouse Gap Trailhead** on Little River Road (requires a shuttle car).

Biking

The **Cades Cove Campground Store** (near Cades Cove Campground, 865/448-9034, www.cadescovetrading.com, 9am-6pm daily) rents bicycles in summer and fall (adult bikes $10 per hour, kids' bikes $6 per hour). Plan to get there early—well before the campground store opens. (I showed up 30 minutes before the store opened and took my place 40 deep in line. I did not rent a bike that day.) To accommodate a growing number of cyclists, the Cades Cove Store has begun to take reservations for bikes on Wednesdays only. Call them (865/488-9034), reserve your bikes, pay by phone, and be there by 7am to pick up your ride.

In 2020, **Cades Cove Loop** started a new program: On Wednesdays from May to September, the loop is **closed to automobile traffic**. This meant cyclists, joggers, and hikers could explore without the risk of cars and drivers distracted by the scenery and wildlife. In previous years, Cades Cove would close to cars on Wednesday and Sunday mornings (sunrise-10am) from May to the second-to-last Saturday in September, but this change has proven successful for cyclists and visitors on an auto tour, and I hope they make it a long-term change.

Camping

The **Cades Cove Campground** (10042 Campground Dr., Townsend, TN, information 865/448-4103, reservations 877/444-6777, www.recreation.gov, year-round, $25) is a popular spot where you'll definitely want to reserve a campsite. Although the occupancy is a little lower in the dead of winter, you'll still find a few intrepid visitors taking refuge from the cold in one of the 159 campsites here. Hikers take note: There are several backcountry campsites off the trails in Cades Cove, making it a good base for overnight trips.

At the **Cades Cove Campground Store** (865/448-9034, www.cadescovetrading.com, 9am-6pm daily), you can grab a light bite for breakfast, a sandwich or wrap, pizza, and other snack-bar items as well as a very limited selection of groceries and camping supplies.

Parsons Branch Road

Parsons Branch Road (spring-fall) is a great drive when it's open; in addition to being closed in winter, deferred maintenance and occasional fallen trees can close the road. Call ahead for closures and conditions (865/436-1200, ext. 631). Take a right turn just beyond the Cades Cove Visitor Center parking area and you'll find yourself on a 10-mile-long one-way gravel road leading to U.S. 129 and Deals Gap on the extreme southwestern edge of the park. Pothole-riddled and with 18 or so small stream crossings along the way, the road is a slow one, taking around an hour to drive. If you're careful, the drive is doable in a sedan, but you may feel more comfortable in a vehicle with a little more clearance.

The road passes **Henry Whitehead Place,** an odd-looking pair of conjoined cabins with an interesting backstory. Henry Whitehead, a widower with three daughters, married Matilda Shields Gregory after she and her small child had been abandoned by her husband. During the crisis, the community rallied and built her the small cabin, which is in back of the main structure that Whitehead built after they married.

You'll cross the same stream several times before climbing to the crest of the drive. Here you'll find the trailhead for **Gregory Bald Trail.** This is the halfway mark of the road, and it is, as they say, all downhill from here.

GREGORY BALD TRAIL

Distance: 11.4 miles round-trip
Duration: 6-7 hours
Elevation gain: 3,370 feet
Difficulty: strenuous
Trailhead: Cades Cove, 2 miles down Parsons Branch Road

The hike to Gregory Bald is a tough one. The trail is steep, you gain more than 3,000 feet, and to finish in a reasonable amount of time your pace has to be quick and constant. Tackle this trail if you're confident in your endurance or if you have a little extra time to spare in case it takes longer to complete. Note that Parsons Branch Road may close seasonally.

Start off with an easy uphill—think of it as a warm-up—to the top of a short knob before the trail levels off. Cross **Forge Creek,** then enter an old-growth forest thick with rhododendrons. How thick? So thick that even though you'll be close to the creek for a little way, you won't often see or hear it. Follow this trail and cross the creek twice more.

Soon you'll pass **Campsite 12** and begin to climb a steep ridge via a set of switchbacks. The rhododendrons give way to galax and mountain laurels, even blueberry bushes, as you climb. Moderate your pace because it's all uphill until you're within 0.2 miles of **Rich Gap.**

At Rich Gap you'll find a four-way intersection. Straight ahead leads to Moore Spring; left leads to the Appalachian Trail at Doe Knob (2.1 miles). Turn west (right) on **Gregory Bald Trail** and follow the ridgeline to Gregory Bald.

From Gregory Bald, you'll have some great views—provided it's not too foggy in the valley. To the northeast you can see Cades Cove; to the southwest are the Unicoi Mountains and Joyce Kilmer-Slickrock Wilderness; to the south are Fontana Lake and Shuckstack Tower. Unfortunately you can't see anything to the west because of the trees. Turn back and retrace your steps to return to the trailhead.

ABRAMS CREEK

Abrams Creek is in the southwestern corner of the park, 20 miles west of Townsend via the Foothills Parkway and 33 miles north of Fontana Dam (via Hwy. 28 and Happy Valley Rd.). Getting here is easy considering the remoteness of the area and the relatively few visitors.

Look Rock is a concrete observation tower that offers a good look at the Smokies. A short hike (just under 1 mile) leads to the tower, and if you're in this part of the park, it's worth the trip.

Hiking
RABBIT AND ABRAMS CREEKS LOOP TRAIL

Distance: 15.2 miles round-trip
Duration: 7-8 hours
Elevation gain: 4,000 feet
Difficulty: strenuous
Trailhead: Abrams Creek Campground near the ranger station
Directions: From the Abrams Creek Campground, turn right on Happy Valley Road and drive 2.3 miles; turn right onto Flats Road and continue for 0.6 miles. Turn left at the Foothills Parkway sign and follow the signs to the parking area.

Though the mountains are rugged and this hike gains 4,000 feet in elevation, it's a gentle if long hike that has earned a reputation for being strenuous due to its length. Begin the hike by following Rabbit Creek, where wildflowers are plentiful in spring. After 2.5 miles you meet Hannah Mountain Trail; ignore it and keep straight on **Rabbit Creek Trail,** which leads to Cades Cove and the Abrams Falls Trailhead.

At the **Abrams Falls Trailhead,** follow this path to the popular waterfall. You'll reach **Abrams Falls** in 2.5 miles and will have some great photo opportunities. After you've had your fill of waterfalls, continue along the trail as it ascends to **Hannah Mountain Trail.** Turn left to cross the creek and follow Hannah Mountain Trail 1.8 miles to an intersection with Rabbit Creek Trail. Turn right onto **Rabbit Creek Trail** to return to where you started.

LITTLE BOTTOMS TRAIL

Distance: 6.2 miles round-trip
Duration: 3 hours
Elevation gain: 930 feet
Difficulty: easy/moderate
Trailhead: Cooper Road Trail Trailhead at Abrams Creek Campground

Little Bottoms Trail follows Abrams Creek, then descends into Cades Cove near Abrams Falls. As with many trails in the Abrams Creek Campground area, you can use this hike to access Cades Cove, or you can hike it as an out-and-back hike of easy length. This creek-side hike is amazing during the spring wildflower bloom and offers several great opportunities for leaf-peeping and fall photography.

Start off on **Cooper Road Trail,** another trail that leads into Cades Cove. Follow the trail 0.9 miles to where **Little Bottoms Trail** branches off to the right. Turn right and follow Little Bottoms up a moderate ascent as you crest a ridge, then begin a steep descent down into the valley to follow the course of Abrams Creek. There are **five crossings** of feeder streams along this hike; shortly after the fifth crossing, you'll reach a junction with **Hatcher Mountain Trail.** Turn around and return to the campground.

Camping

Abrams Creek Campground (Abrams Creek Campground Rd., Tallassee, TN, 865/436-1200, late Apr.-late Oct., $17.50) sits in the southwestern corner of the park just off the Foothills Parkway. Though this campground is at a pretty low elevation of only 1,125 feet, the mountains here are quite rugged and the woods thick. Not many people visit this section of the park, so if you want a little solitude and a sound night's sleep, put this campground on your to-do list.

The 16 primitive sites are first-come, first-served, and the only real amenity is a restroom. Backpackers and backcountry campers take note: The trail system branching out from Abrams Creek Campground offers access to several **backcountry campsites,** including Campsites 1, 17, 15, and 16.

DEEP CREEK

Just south of Cherokee and just north of Bryson City, Deep Creek is a spot that may be more popular with locals and Bryson City day-trippers than most park visitors, but that shouldn't be the case. Deep Creek is relatively placid, aside from a couple of waterfalls a ways upstream. If you're not into wading or tubing, don't worry—this is a lovely place to picnic and hike or even camp away from the crowds found in some of the more popular spots in the park. Two of the trails here, Indian Creek Falls Trail and Deep Creek Loop, are among the only trails in the park to allow bicycles, so if you're up for a leisurely ride (don't expect as rugged a ride as some of the hikes in the park), you're in for a treat.

Hiking

There are two nice waterfalls here. Juney Whank Falls (what a name, right?) is less than 0.5 miles from the Deep Creek Campground and cuts an impressive figure as it drops a total of 90 feet in two stages. Indian Creek Falls is a stunning 60-foot-high set of falls and cascades located 1 mile from the campground.

JUNEY WHANK FALLS TRAIL

Distance: 0.6-mile round-trip
Duration: 30 minutes
Elevation gain: 120 feet
Difficulty: easy
Trailhead: parking area at the end of Deep Creek Road across from the campground

---

1: taking a break at Cable Mill in Cades Cove
2: Abrams Falls 3: Indian Flats Falls

Juney Whank Falls supposedly got its name from Junaluska "Juney" Whank, a Cherokee leader said to have been buried near the falls. The path here is pretty straightforward: it's a short, and at times steep, loop, and at the end, it's a little slick. You'll walk across a log bridge to get a look at the tall, skinny falls, which actually descend in two stages. The first stage drops 40 feet to a stone outcropping, then flows beneath the log bridge to fall and cascade another 50 feet.

INDIAN CREEK FALLS TRAIL
Distance: 2 miles round-trip
Duration: 1 hour
Elevation gain: 160 feet
Difficulty: easy
Trailhead: parking area at the end of Deep Creek Road across from the campground

This easier but longer hike takes you past a smaller waterfall, Tom Branch Falls, on your way to Indian Creek Falls. For about a mile, you'll follow a gently graded roadbed, and soon you'll arrive at the falls. Really, Indian Creek Falls is more of a steep, long, slick cascade of water than an actual waterfall, but it's quite serene.

TOP EXPERIENCE

DEEP CREEK LOOP TRAIL
Distance: 4.9 miles round-trip
Duration: 2.5-3 hours
Elevation gain: 900 feet
Difficulty: easy
Trailhead: Deep Creek Campground

This short hike is excellent for new hikers; the trail is easy and in good shape, plus you'll hike past Tom Branch Falls and Indian Creek Falls. The trail starts on a gravel road. Almost immediately, you'll pass **Tom Branch Falls,** which you can see well in autumn and winter. After crossing a **bridge** at the junction with **Indian Creek Trail** (to the right), pass **Indian Creek Falls,** which is more of a long cascade but no less attractive. Continue hiking along Indian Creek Trail, then pass **Stone Pile Gap Trail.** Staying on Indian Creek Trail, you'll

pass a junction with **Sunkota Ridge Trail** and begin to descend to **Deep Creek Trail.** Turn left on Deep Creek Trail and follow it back to the start of the trail.

Fishing
Along **Deep Creek** you'll find some primo trout fishing. Bring a fly rod and get ready to reel in a few brown, rainbow, and brook trout. Anywhere along the creek is fine to cast a line, but some of the best spots are in the places where people aren't. This means hiking up **Deep Creek Trail,** a 14.2-mile trail that follows the creek back to Newfound Gap Road. The trail is straightforward as it follows an old roadbed that turns into a true trail, but it is beside the creek for nearly the entire length.

Camping
At the end of Deep Creek Road are the trailheads leading to the waterfalls. You'll also find the **Deep Creek Campground** (877/444-6777, www.recreation.gov, Apr.-Oct., $25). There are nearly 100 campsites here, many of which fill up with locals. If you want to camp here, arrive early or reserve well in advance.

Deep Creek Tube Center and Campground (1040 W. Deep Creek Rd., Bryson City, NC, 828/488-6055, www. deepcreekcamping.com, camping $31-58, cabins $89-325) is a charming collection of tent and RV campsites and cabins for rent; the two largest cabins sleep 10, and one is pet-friendly. As the name implies, they rent tubes (all-day $7) for use on Deep Creek. Rentals are cheap, so you can play in the water as long as you like.

Road to Nowhere
An odd place to visit is the so-called **Road to Nowhere.** Just south of the Deep Creek entrance outside Bryson City, a short stretch of highway leads north into Great Smoky Mountains National Park. Lonely, even spooky, the road is all that remains of a parkway planned to trace a path through the

1: floating down Deep Creek **2:** Juney Whank Falls **3:** horseback riding on a trail **4:** Tom Branch Falls on Deep Creek

Smokies along Fontana Lake. Construction was started on the parkway before being abandoned. Today the road stops quite abruptly about 6 miles inside the park, at a stone tunnel. Though hard feelings over the failed parkway have softened, many families still hold a grudge against government officials who vowed to build a road along the lake to provide access to old family cemeteries there.

Cars are prohibited from using the tunnel at the end of the Road to Nowhere, but visitors on foot are welcome to stroll right through. After passing through the tunnel, there's a hike waiting for you that clocks in at 36.5 miles. Fortunately, it follows the northern bank of Fontana Lake, giving you a little reward for the effort.

The Road to Nowhere is accessible from Bryson City. To get here, drive north on Everett Street, which becomes Fontana Road, then Lakeview Drive, before arriving at a parking area in about 9 miles. A tunnel marks the end of the road. Be sure you have a flashlight, headlamp, or your phone with you because you'll need a light as you walk through the tunnel.

GOLDMINE LOOP TRAIL

Distance: 3.1 miles round-trip
Duration: 2.5-3 hours
Elevation gain: 400 feet
Difficulty: easy
Trailhead: Lakeview Drive Tunnel at the end of the Road to Nowhere

Though this hike actually begins on the far side of the tunnel, it really begins when you walk through the tunnel and emerge on the other side to find the two-lane road just ends. As you step off the road, walk a short way on a roadbed to follow the proper trail. In a little less than 0.2 miles you'll meet **Tunnel Bypass Trail,** and soon after that you'll reach **Goldmine Loop Trail.** To follow the trail, turn left and begin a steep descent as it traces a path along a ridge, then heads down to a minuscule stream.

Cross the stream and take a look around— you'll see a chimney in a field, evidence of the homes that once stood here. There are many such signs along the trail, so keep a keen eye on the woods for other signs of the former homes.

Drawing closer to the lakeshore, you'll see a short trail to **Campsite 67** (on the left); pass this and continue along Goldmine Loop. After a short hike you'll reach the shores of **Fontana Lake,** deep in a little cove, which makes for some excellent fall photos. The trail climbs back up alongside **Tunnel Branch,** a small creek that feeds the lake. The ascent grows steep until you meet the other end of **Tunnel Bypass Trail.** Continue along the trail, and in 0.4 miles you'll be back at the tunnel.

LAKESHORE TRAIL, FULL HIKE

Distance: 35.6 miles end-to-end
Duration: multiple days
Elevation change: 1,230 feet
Difficulty: strenuous
Trailhead: Lakeview Drive Tunnel at the end of the Road to Nowhere

The Lakeshore Trail runs along the northern shoreline of Fontana Lake. The 36.5-mile route is doable as a day hike in sections, but it is best done as a multiple-night backpacking trip. Arrange for transportation before you set out; this means a car shuttle at the end of the trail, or parking your own shuttle cars at opposite ends.

The total elevation gain for this hike is nearly 11,000 feet as you climb up and down, up and down as you crest 10 ridges and knobs in excess of 2,250 feet, with lots of elevation variance along the way.

The trail begins at the tunnel at the end of the Road to Nowhere. After passing through the tunnel, follow a short bit of road to the point where it turns into a trail. You'll reach your first potential campsite, **Campsite 74,** in just over 2 miles at **Forney Creek Trail.** (Skip it unless you plan on making this a weeklong backpacking trip.)

In 6.6 miles, you'll reach Anthony Branch and Chambers Creek; just after crossing Chambers Creek, approach the lakeshore to find a 0.1-mile trail to **Campsite 98.** This can be a good stopping point if this is a two-night trip. **Campsite 77** is just over 15 miles in, making it a good stopping point if you're aiming for a one-night trip. Or you can press on to **Campsite 76** at the 11-mile mark.

From Campsite 77, it is 4.2 miles to **Campsite 81** on the south side of the trail. (The trail is lakeside, but the campsite is still 0.2 miles from the water; don't expect a lake view.) Continue on 3.6 more miles to the junction with Hazel Creek Trail and **Campsite 86. Campsite 85** is 2 miles up Hazel Creek Trail, and **Campsites 84 and 83** are 4.5 and 5.3 miles up the trail, respectively. This is a good place to stop for a two-night trip, but Campsite 86 can see a good bit of traffic. You may want to press on another 1.4 miles to **Campsite 88.**

All along the trail, spur trails lead to the coves and shoreline. These vary in length, but feel free to follow them at your leisure. **Hazel Creek Trail** is one of the larger trails in this region of the park; it forms part of a bigger network of trails on which you could have a 100-mile, 10-night campout if you wanted. There's plenty to see and do if you're a hardcore hiker, and one trip here will certainly lead to another—this is a beautiful part of the park.

From Campsite 88, it is 3 miles to Flint Gap and Eagle Creek Trail (**Campsites 89 and 96** are a couple of miles up the trail). Another 0.5 miles leads to **Campsite 90** on the banks of Eagle Creek. A small spur trail leads down to the cove, if you want to see the water. In another 0.4 miles, you'll reach the intersection with Lost Cove Trail (**Campsite 91** is 1 mile down the trail). Lost Cove leads 2.7 miles to the Appalachian Trail at Sassafras Gap, just north of Shuckstack; from there it's 3.7 miles south to the trailhead at Lakeview Drive West.

Continue along **Lakeshore Trail** and you'll be on the final leg of the hike, a winding 5.2-mile trek that crosses more than a dozen creeks and streams before it reaches Lakeview Drive West and the parking area. On the off chance that Fontana Dam is closed

for repairs or security reasons, you may have to hike down Lakeview Drive and cross the dam to get to your car on the other side, adding almost 2 miles to the hike.

LAKESHORE TRAIL, DAY HIKE
Distance: 6.6 miles round-trip
Duration: 1.5 hours
Elevation change: 661 feet
Difficulty: easy
Trailhead: Lakeview Drive Tunnel at the end of the Road to Nowhere

Lakeshore Trail is a monster of a hike if done in its entirety. Most people opt to do a portion of it to get a taste. I recommend hiking from the tunnel on the Road to Nowhere out to backcountry Campsite 74 at Forney Creek. It's a straightforward out-and-back hike with an optional detour (0.4 miles round-trip) to one of the old family cemeteries here and two options for hiking down to the shores of Fontana Lake.

From the **tunnel,** continue following the pavement until it turns into a trail. You'll share this trail with hikers and horses, so stay alert for riders ahead and the little gifts horses like to leave on the trail. At 0.5 miles in, you'll see the Tunnel Bypass Trail on your left, and at 0.6 miles, you'll pass the start of Goldmine Loop Trail. Ignore these and continue on Lakeshore Trail, following it uphill and crossing five streams that make up **Goldmine Branch** as you go. Keep climbing, then descend after you reach a little **ridge** 1.3 miles in (it's only 2,300 feet in elevation and marks a good spot for a water break and a breather).

As you descend, you'll cross a branch of **Gray Wolf Creek** at 1.5 miles, then cross it again at 1.7 miles; almost immediately after the second crossing, you'll see White Oak Branch Trail climbing up to your right. Cross Gray Wolf Creek again, and at 1.9 miles you'll be at the start of a 1.2-mile round-trip **spur trail** that parallels Gray Wolf Creek and leads to the lake. Cross Gray Wolf Creek once more and you'll find the **short spur** (0.4-mile round-trip) leading to the Woody Cemetery. From here, you're 0.7 miles from **Campsite 74.**

When you reach the campsite, make the 0.4-mile round-trip stroll along the creek down to the lake; it's a gorgeous spot for photos and to rest and refuel. To head back, simply reverse course, keeping Lake Fontana on your right as you return.

BACKCOUNTRY PERMITS

Because so many trails branch off Lakeshore Trail, this region is a hotbed of backcountry campsites. There are eight backcountry campsites—72, 73, 76, 77, 78, 81, 87, and 98—on or near Lakeshore Trail; four of those (72, 73, 78, and 87) are boat-access only. Another eight campsites are within a day hike of Lakeshore Trail.

Recently, bear activity has increased in this section of the park. One camper was injured when a bear pulled him from his hammock in 2015, leading to the temporary closure of several backcountry campsites and a shelter along the Appalachian Trail. At that time, bears were spotted in a number of locations including campsites, picnic areas, and crossing the road. Bears usually aren't aggressive, just curious, but be wary in bear country, and be sure to check with rangers for bear activity and trail closures. Review proper etiquette regarding bears and proper handling of food in and around your campsite.

To camp backcountry, you'll need a permit from the **Backcountry Information Office** (Sugarlands Visitor Center, 865/436-1297, https://smokiespermits.nps.gov, 8am-5pm daily, $4 pp per night, $20 maximum). They can also answer any questions you have about the campsites, and they're quite helpful—don't be shy.

FONTANA LAKE AREA

At the southern edge of Great Smoky Mountains National Park lies Fontana Lake, a 10,230-acre reservoir created in the 1940s by the Tennessee Valley Authority (TVA) as part of its efforts to supply electricity to the various communities and government and industrial facilities in the region.

Fontana Dam

Fontana Lake is on the southern border of the national park. The 480-foot-tall, 2,365-foot-wide Fontana Dam, complete with three hydroelectric generators, was completed in 1944, providing much-needed electricity to the factories churning out materials for World War II, including in Oak Ridge, Tennessee, where research leading to the atomic bomb was conducted.

To build Fontana Dam, the TVA purchased more than 1,000 tracts of land and relocated around 600 families in five communities. Those folks left behind homes, schools, churches, and barns, all of which were covered by the lake. This displacement of so many families and elimination of these small communities was part of the trade-off that resulted in the modernization of the region. Electric power became cheap and readily available, and many jobs were created to complete the project. The dam also provides much-needed flood control to a region that receives between 55 and 82 inches of rainfall each year. Today the TVA can regulate the depth of the lake by releasing water as they anticipate flood events, and the water level of Fontana Lake can vary by as much as 50 feet.

Fontana Dam is the highest concrete dam east of the Mississippi, and it offers great recreational opportunities. The Appalachian Trail crosses the dam itself, and thousands of boaters and anglers take to the lake each year. There are more than 238 miles of shoreline along Fontana Lake and over 10,000 acres of water surface. If you have your own boat, you can launch it from the **Fontana Marina** (40 Fontana Dam Rd., Fontana Dam, NC, 828/498-2017, www.fontanavillage.com), or you can rent a kayak, canoe, or paddleboard ($15-20 per hour, $60 per day) as well as a pontoon boat ($65-85 per hour, $300-400 per day) or fishing boat ($70 per hour, $300 per day). If you need a slip, you can rent one ($5-40 per day). Shuttles to backcountry sites ($30-95 one-way, $50-190 round-trip) and seasonal tours of the lake ($30 adults, $15 ages 3-12) are also available.

The exhibits at the **Fontana Dam Visitor Center** (Fontana Dam Rd., off Hwy. 28 near the state line, www.tva.com, 9am-7pm daily Apr.-Aug., 9am-6pm daily Sept.-Oct., free), about 45 minutes from Bryson City, tell the story of the region and the construction of the dam. The center also has a small gift shop and a viewing platform overlooking the dam. Hikers take note: They sell backcountry camping permits and have showers in the back.

FISHING AND BOATING

Fishing is big on Fontana Lake. Trout love the feeder streams and headwaters that flow into the lake, and largemouth, smallmouth, and rock bass are all throughout. You'll even find walleye and muskies in the deep water (and it gets deeper than 400 feet in some points). On any given day, you'll spot anglers on boats and in kayaks, and more than a few fly rods strapped to the backpacks of hikers headed out to try the streams along the north banks of the lake.

At the **Fontana Marina** (40 Fontana Dam Rd., Fontana Dam, NC, 828/498-2017, www.fontanavillage.com), you can rent a kayak, canoe, or paddleboard ($15-20 per hour, $60 per day) as well as a pontoon boat ($65-85 per hour, $300-400 per day) or fishing boat ($70 per hour, $300 per day). If you brought your own boat, slip rentals are available ($5-40 per day). Shuttles to backcountry sites ($30-95 one-way, $50-190 round-trip) and seasonal tours of the lake ($30 adults, $15 ages 3-12) are also available.

Fontana Lake is partially in the national park and partially outside it, which makes fishing here a little more complicated. If you plan on fishing in the lake, you have two options: Get a **North Carolina fishing license** (www.ncwildlife.org) and review the guidelines (to be on the safe side), or rely on a fishing guide to supply a license and understand the rules (most do).

GUIDES

Fontana Guide Service (3336 Balltown Rd., Bryson City, 828/736-2318, www.fontanaguides.com, full-day trips $300-600, depending on group size) has a number of choices that vary by season, interest, and skill level, including options to fish in the national park. In addition to fly-fishing excursions, they offer kayak fishing, bass and lake fishing, night fishing in select spots, family-friendly trips, and general sightseeing cruises (which are especially lovely in fall).

Fontana Lake

At **Up-Close Outfitters** (828/273-0286, www.upcloseoutfitters.com, $275-600), they'll make sure your day on the water or in the woods is one for the books. Lake fishing trips visit Lake Fontana as well as nearby Lakes Hartwell and Jocassee. They also offer fly-fishing in waters south of Asheville, as well as hunting trips for turkey and white-tailed deer in nearby national forests (half- and full-day trips available). Up-Close doesn't have a storefront; your guide will meet you at the appointed place with equipment in tow.

Fly Fishing the Smokies (157 Everett St., Bryson City, 828/488-7665, www. flyfishingthesmokies.net, $200-850) has a number of guides and options for a day or more of fly-fishing the streams on the north shore of the lake and other trout waters. Go bass fishing on Fontana, wade the streams with them, or try a float trip. Half- and full-day options are available for most trips. Other options are to go fly-fishing in Great Smoky Mountains National Park, or up the ante with some backcountry camping and fly-fishing in the park (both guided and unguided trips available).

Root Hog Fishing Guide Service (828/862-7958, www.fontanafishingguide. com), $160-275) runs 4-, 6- and 8-hour fishing charters on Lake Fontana and as well as 4- and 6-hour fly-fishing trips. Owner and guide Dwight Pigman has been fishing here for decades, so he knows where to find the fish.

Accommodations and Food

Just outside the park, **Fontana Village Resort** (300 Woods Rd., Fontana Dam, 828/498-2211 or 800/849-2258, www. fontanavillage.com, lodge $119-179, cabins $159-339, camping $15-40) offers a place to lay your head in your choice of accommodations: lodge rooms, one- to three-bedroom cabins, and tent or RV camping. There are 100 lodge rooms, 110 cabins, and 20 campsites.

Mountainview Bistro (828/498-2211, 7am-10am daily, 5pm-9pm Thurs.-Sat., breakfast $4-9, dinner $14-28) at the resort serves steaks, chicken, and a nice selection of seafood that includes several preparations of trout. Reservations are recommended during weekends and in peak season. Also at the resort, **Wildwood Grill** (828/498-2211, noon-9pm daily Apr.-Oct., $8-20) serves pizza, burgers, and an array of fried appetizers. In the summer, concerts on the deck give visitors a little listening enjoyment to go with dinner.

TWENTYMILE

One of the remotest sections of the park, Twentymile is on the southern end, just past Fontana Lake and Dam and alongside the smaller Cheoah Lake. Despite the name, Twentymile Trail only goes 5 miles into Great Smoky Mountains National Park, but you can make it into a 20-mile journey by combining it with other trails, or you can keep it to a manageable day hike of around 8 miles by doing a smaller loop. Though this part of the park is out of the way, Twentymile is a popular hike, so expect to see some fellow hikers, especially on weekends and through the week on beautiful days in summer and autumn. There is a trio of **backcountry campsites** (reserve at www.smokiespermits.nps.gov) at Twentymile Trail: campsites 13, 92, and 93.

Hiking
TWENTYMILE LOOP TRAIL
Distance: 7.6-mile round-trip
Duration: 3.5-4 hours
Elevation gain: 1,200 feet
Difficulty: easy
Trailhead: Twentymile Ranger Station
Directions: Twentymile Ranger Station is 6 miles west from Fontana Dam on Highway 28. Turn at the sign for Twentymile.

This hike is very easy, following a roadbed and a well-maintained trail along Twentymile Trail, Twentymile Loop Trail, and Wolf Ridge Trail. There are a number of stream crossings along this route, and though log bridges span Moore Springs Branch and Twentymile Creek, floods may wash them away. If you're there before repair crews can fix the bridges, you may have to wade across.

From the trailhead, go 0.5 miles to where

Wolf Ridge Trail branches off to the left. Follow Wolf Ridge Trail for 1.1 miles to **Twentymile Loop Trail.** Along Wolf Ridge, you'll cross Moore Springs Branch five times as you climb. Along the way, there are abundant wildflowers, including bloodroot, fire pink, and trilliums, and the opportunity to see bears, deer, and other wildlife.

After following Wolf Ridge just over 1 mile, you'll see Twentymile Loop Trail branching off to the right. Cross Moore Springs Branch and follow the trail 2.9 miles along an easy grade before descending to a crossing of Twentymile Creek and the junction with **Twentymile Trail.**

Turn right on Twentymile Trail to descend back along the creek and to the trailhead. From here, it's just over 3 miles back to your car.

GREGORY BALD VIA TWENTYMILE TRAIL

Distance: 15.7-mile round-trip
Duration: 9 hours
Elevation gain: 3,650 feet
Difficulty: strenuous
Trailhead: Twentymile Ranger Station
Directions: Twentymile Ranger Station is 6 miles west from Fontana Dam on Highway 28. Turn at the sign for Twentymile.

This hike makes Twentymile live up to its name, even though it's a mere 15.7 miles. It's doable in a day, but it's a long, hard day, so camping for a night in the backcountry is recommended.

From the trailhead, follow **Twentymile Trail** for 0.5 miles until it intersects with **Wolf Ridge Trail.** Turn here and follow Wolf Ridge Trail 6.3 miles to **Gregory Bald Trail.** The grade of Wolf Ridge Trail is somewhat steep, but more than that, it's a relentless uphill climb all the way to where you crest the ridge before reaching **Parson Bald.** As you approach the ridge and Parson Bald, you'll find copious amounts of blueberry bushes, and, if they're in season, a fair number of bears enjoying blueberries. The same holds true at Parson Bald, just over the ridge. If you're on the trail in August, when the blueberries tend to ripen, be cautious.

When you reach Parson Bald, it's a short, easy walk to Sheep Pen Gap, where you'll find **Campsite 13** and the end of Wolf Ridge Trail. Turn right on Gregory Bald Trail and climb just under 0.5 miles to **Gregory Bald.** There are azaleas in great abundance, and during midsummer the bald is a riot of blooms. But even if you come when there's not a bloom to be found, the views make the hike worth it.

From here, keep heading east to **Rich Gap,** where you'll come upon a four-way trail junction. Follow **Long Hungry Ridge Trail** to the right, heading south. This trail is pretty flat for the first mile; then it begins to descend, and the descent becomes increasingly noticeable as you move down the trail. You'll find **Campsite 92** at 3.4 miles from Rich Gap. Once you've reached the campsite, you've left the steepest part of the hike behind you.

Continue down Long Hungry Ridge Trail to the place where it meets Twentymile Trail, following Twentymile Creek 2.6 miles back to the junction with Wolf Ridge Trail. At this point, you're only 0.5 miles from the trailhead.

Transportation and Services

CAR

The 33-mile-long Newfound Gap Road (U.S. 441) bisects the park from north to south. It's the most heavily traveled route in the park and provides a good introduction for first-time visitors. Newfound Gap Road starts at the southern terminus of the Blue Ridge Parkway, just outside Cherokee, North Carolina, and ends in Knoxville, Tennessee, 70 miles to the northwest through Great Smoky Mountains National Park.

From Cherokee, you can head straight to the eastern entrance of Great Smoky Mountains National Park via Newfound Gap Road. Take U.S. 441/Highway 71 north through Great Smoky Mountains National Park to Gatlinburg, Tennessee. It's easy to make the trip from one end to the other in an afternoon, though it may take a little longer in peak seasons. Knoxville, Tennessee, is 36 miles northwest of Great Smoky Mountains National Park along U.S. 441 and Highway 71.

There are **no gas stations** along Newfound Gap Road. You'll need to fuel up and buy snacks in Cherokee or Gatlinburg.

AIR

Asheville Regional Airport (AVL, 61 Terminal Dr., Asheville, NC, 828/684-2226, www.flyavl.com) is about one hour east of Cherokee. **McGhee Tyson Airport** (TYS, 2055 Alcoa Hwy., Alcoa, TN, 865/342-3000, www.flyknoxville.com) is about one hour west of Gatlinburg.

SERVICES

Groceries and camping supplies are limited in Great Smoky Mountains National Park. Food is virtually nonexistent, so bring snacks. The Sugarlands and Oconaluftee Visitor Centers have a small selection of vending-machine beverages and a few convenience items (batteries, memory cards), but little else.

Medical

If you find yourself in an emergency situation in the park, dial 911 if you have cell access. When speaking with the 911 operator, inform the operator that you are in Great Smoky Mountains National Park, and give your location as best you can (if you're in the backcountry, that means the trail name and the campsite or shelter nearest to you). The operator will send rangers and emergency responders. If you don't have cell service, send another hiker or driver for help.

The nearest hospitals are **LeConte Medical Center** (742 Middle Creek Rd., Sevierville, TN, 865/446-7000, www. lecontemedicalcenter.com), about 25 minutes from the western park entrance; **Blount Memorial Hospital** (907 E. Lamar Alexander Pkwy., Maryville, TN, 865/983-7211, www.blountmemorial.org), an hour away from the western park entrance; the Cherokee Indian Hospital (1 Hospital Rd., Cherokee, NC, www.cherokeehospital. org, 828/497-9163), minutes away from the Oconaluftee Visitor Center in Cherokee; and **Swain Community Hospital** (45 Plateau St., Bryson City, NC, 828/488-2155, www. myswaincommunity.org), a little less than 30 minutes from the eastern park entrance in Cherokee.

RANGER PROGRAMS

Few of us will ever have the opportunity to get to know a park as well as a park ranger. Every day they're immersed in the landscape, the culture, the history, and the beauty of their respective park, and they work with a legion of volunteers to create enrichment programs that will expand the use and appreciation of parks (and the outdoors as a whole) by the public. Great Smoky Mountains National Park has some mighty fine park rangers, and they work hard to introduce every visitor to the beauty, the stories, and the flora and fauna of the park. Through the **Junior Ranger Program,** they get kids ages 5-15 excited about the Smokies; through their Not-So-Junior Ranger Program, they get everyone ages 13-130 involved too.

Rangers lead daily hikes along nature trails and creek-side paths, take visitors on nighttime hikes of Cades Cove, host campfires and storytelling sessions, lead hayrides and history lessons, introduce us to the animals—from furry to slimy—of the park, and celebrate the history and culture here. A full schedule of seasonal programs is available online (www.nps.gov/grsm).

Guided Hikes

Hiking in the Smokies is as simple as picking up a map, choosing a trail, and heading into the woods; however, some people prefer to

Calendar of Events

- **Wildflower Pilgrimage** (Apr.): Hikes, talks, and photography sessions explore the park's abundant and diverse wildflowers (www.springwildflowerpilgrimage.org).

- **Junior Ranger Day** (late Apr.): Get the kids started on their Junior Ranger Badge with this park-wide celebration of youthful discovery—then keep it going with the weekly Junior Ranger programs throughout the year.

- **Women's Work Festival** (mid-June): At Mountain Farm Museum, learn about the role women played in the making and maintaining of a mountain home and farm.

- **Mountain Life Festival** (mid-Sept.): Mountain Farm Museum comes alive with demonstrations of domestic and cultural life—from music to demonstrations of domestic chores such as soapmaking and cooking.

- **Music of the Mountains** (mid-Sept.): This three-day festival celebrates the musical traditions of the Appalachians with demonstrations and concerts at the Sugarlands Visitor Center, as well as locations in Cosby and Townsend.

- **Festival of Christmas Past** (mid-Dec.): Get a taste of the holidays in the Smokies with demonstrations of arts and crafts (spinning, weaving, and quilting); music, singing, and storytelling; and children's activities like games and toy making.

- **Holiday Homecoming** (mid-Dec.): Music and old-fashioned Christmas traditions bring holiday cheer to the Oconaluftee Visitor Center.

hike with a group and a guide. Fortunately, the park trail system accommodates both styles. Several organizations lead outings and excursions—from day hikes to trip-planning assistance to overnight backpacking trips.

FRIENDS OF THE SMOKIES

Friends of the Smokies (North Carolina office 828/452-0720, Tennessee office 865/932-4794, www.friendsofthesmokies.com) is one of my favorite groups; they provide support to the Trails Forever program and help with trail repairs and maintenance. The group leads hikes (Mar.-Dec., members $20, nonmembers $35) along some of the classic trails in the park. Hikes include spots like Little Cataloochee Trail and Grotto Falls, overnighters to places like Mount LeConte, and trips to Mount Sterling. Each hike highlights one of the programs supported by Friends of the Smokies. Look at their schedule for upcoming trips and registration information.

SMOKY MOUNTAINS HIKING CLUB

Smoky Mountains Hiking Club (www.smhclub.org) runs weekly outings in the Smokies and in East Tennessee, though their primary mission is to assist with the maintenance of the Appalachian Trail within the park. They've been around since 1924 and currently have more than 600 members, so these hikes are always with a group of experienced and knowledgeable outdoors enthusiasts. The weekly outings are free and open to anyone who wants to participate; trips include on- and off-trail hikes as well as workdays. Check the website for the schedule and to register.

A WALK IN THE WOODS

Several commercial outfitters lead walks, hikes, and overnight trips in the park in addition to providing trip-planning assistance and hiker shuttles. **A Walk In The Woods** (865/436-8283, www.awalkinthewoods.com, $25-500) is a guide company offering nature walks, half-day hikes, full-day hikes, backpacking trips (discounts if supplying your own equipment), and hiker shuttles (cost varies depending on trailhead and time of day), which make those extra-long hikes a bit easier, especially when you only have one car.

MINDFUL MEANDERS

With **Mindful Meanders** (www.mindful-meanders.com, free), your time on the trail takes on a different angle. Rather than a straightforward hike, guides take you on slow, observation-focused walks that deepen your connection with nature. This is a bit of forest therapy or *shinrin-yoku,* a Japanese practice that translates to "forest bathing," and it has proven benefits like lowering blood pressure and stress levels, improving creativity and sleep, and giving the immune system a boost. And the Smokies is an ideal place to give it a try.

Appalachian Trail

From Georgia to Maine, the Appalachian Trail's nearly 2,200 miles traverse some rugged, lonesome, and picturesque landscapes, cresting ridges and summiting peaks, crossing streams and rivers, passing through bogs and marshes, climbing near-vertical peaks, and even following city streets.

Cutting through the heart of Great Smoky Mountains National Park, the Appalachian Trail runs along the high ridgeline that forms the border between North Carolina and Tennessee. There are 71.6 miles of the Appalachian Trail in Great Smoky Mountains National Park, and it's a highlight for thru-hikers (those taking the Appalachian Trail north to Maine or south to Georgia, all in one enormous hike), segment hikers (those hiking the whole thing one piece at a time), and day hikers (the rest of us).

This guide to the Appalachian Trail within Great Smoky Mountains National Park doesn't cover the trail mile by mile but includes enough to get you out for a multiday backpacking trip. For the lowdown on the Appalachian Trail, contact the **Appalachian Trail Conservancy** (www.appalachiantrail. org) or visit the **National Park Service** (www.nps.gov/appa), where you'll find trip-planning information, maps, trail reports, and more.

Most people hike the Great Smoky Mountains National Park section as a 7-day trek, though you can tailor this trek to suit your hiking style and the time you have—stretching it out to 10 or 12 days with a little planning, or pushing the pace to complete it in 3 brutal days.

Permits

Though no fees are required to hike the Appalachian Trail, there are requirements when hiking the Appalachian Trail in Great Smoky Mountains National Park. Thru-hikers are eligible for a **thru-hiker permit** (www. smokiespermits.nps.gov, $20); thru-hikers must begin and end their hike at least 50 miles from the border of the park and travel only on the Appalachian Trail while in the park.

Segment hikers and backpackers need a permit from the **Backcountry Information Office** (Sugarlands Visitor Center, 865/436-1297, https://smokiespermits.nps.gov, 8am-5pm daily, $4 pp per night, $20 maximum). A permit is not required for day hikers.

Trail Shelters

For Appalachian Trail thru-hikers, there's only one choice for where to stay in Great Smoky Mountains National Park: **Appalachian Trail shelters.** Of the 12 sites at each shelter, four spots are reserved for thru-hikers only, and they're first-come, first-served. If you're thru-hiking and find a shelter full, you are permitted to pitch your tent next to the shelters.

Segment hikers and backpackers can

reserve spots in these Appalachian Trail shelters or at any of the numerous backcountry campsites along and near the Appalachian Trail.

There are too many backcountry campsites near the Appalachian Trail, as well as other backcountry shelters, to list here. For a complete list, consult a **park trail map** (www.nps.gov/grsm).

A dozen shelters are located along the Appalachian Trail in the park. South to north:

- Mollies Ridge at 4,570 feet, 10.3 miles
- Russell Field at 4,360 feet, 13.1 miles
- Spence Field at 4,900 feet, 15.9 miles, has a privy nearby
- Derrick Knob at 4,890 feet, 22 miles
- Silers Bald at 5,460 feet, 28 miles
- Double Spring Gap at 5,507 feet, 29.5 miles, has a privy nearby
- Mount Collins at 5,870 feet, 35.8 miles, has a privy nearby
- Icewater Spring at 5,920 feet, 43.3 miles, has a privy nearby
- Pecks Corner at 5,280 feet, 53.7 miles
- TriCorner at 5,920 feet, 55.9 miles, has a privy nearby

- Cosby Knob at 4,700 feet, 63.6 miles, has a privy nearby
- Davenport Gap at 2,600 feet, 70.7 miles

DAY HIKING

Day hikers are drawn to the Appalachian Trail for its fantastic balds (high natural and agricultural meadows), like Andrews Bald and Silers Bald; peaks like Mount Cammerer and Rocky Top (yes, the one from the Osborne Brothers' song); and just to say they've hiked part of the Appalachian Trail. The route through the park is always high and at times rocky, at other times steep, at times both, but the views are worth it.

Day hikers who want to log a few miles of the Appalachian Trail will find a few opportunities to get their boots muddy. Notable day hikes include:

- **Charlies Bunion** (8.1 miles round-trip): Access the Appalachian Trail north from the trailhead at the Newfound Gap Road Overlook.
- **Mount Cammerer** (11.2 miles round-trip): Take the Low Gap Trail at the Cosby Campground to the Appalachian Trail, then proceed to the summit and a stone

the Appalachian Trail

fire tower. Note: Only 4.2 miles are on the Appalachian Trail.

- **Rocky Top** (13.9 miles round-trip): Follow the Anthony Creek Trailhead from the Cades Cove picnic area to Bote Mountain Trail. At Spence Field, you'll meet up with the Appalachian Trail; follow it to Rocky Top and spectacular views. Note: Only the last portion is on the Appalachian Trail.

THRU-HIKING

From Fontana Dam to Davenport Gap, the Appalachian Trail brushes past peaks surpassing 5,000 feet in elevation, including the highest point along the entire trail, the 6,643-foot Clingmans Dome. Gaps (low points in the mountains) along this stretch top out at nearly 4,000 feet.

Most thru-hikers begin in Georgia in the spring and hike north to Maine. These hike descriptions follow that northbound flow of foot traffic. The Appalachian Trail is broken down into two hikes: one from Fontana Dam to Newfound Gap, the other from Newfound Gap to Davenport Gap. Notations and mileage markers are given for the Appalachian Trail shelters, as well as points where other trails connect with or cross the Appalachian Trail.

Western Smokies
FONTANA DAM TO NEWFOUND GAP

Distance: 40.3 miles one-way
Duration: multiple days
Elevation gain: 4,900 feet
Difficulty: strenuous
Trailhead: Fontana Dam

This section of the Appalachian Trail hits the highest peak in the Smokies, Clingmans Dome, which is also the highest point along the entire length of the trail. There are seven **shelters** along this route: Mollies Ridge (mile 10.3), Russell Field (mile 13.1), Spence Field (mile 16), Derrick Knob (mile 22.3), Silers Bald (mile 27.8), Double Spring Gap (mile 29.5), and Mount Collins (mile 35.8).

Begin the hike at **Fontana Dam** and get ready for a big uphill push; you'll gain 3,035 feet in the first 11 miles. After crossing

Fontana Dam, you'll leave the paved road at 0.6 miles and begin to climb **Shuckstack Mountain.** At 3.2 miles, you'll reach the gap between Shuckstack and Little Shuckstack; at 3.8 miles, you'll hit a viewpoint that offers a great look at Fontana Lake.

When you reach 4 miles, a road on the east side of the trail leads to a fire tower at the top of Shuckstack Mountain. Make the side trip if you want; otherwise, keep hiking and descend to Sassafras Gap and the intersection with Lost Cove Trail to the east and Twentymile Trail to the west.

You'll continue up and down as you follow the terrain. At 7.5 miles you'll reach the summit of Doe Knob (4,520 feet), then descend some steep 300 feet to Mud Gap at 7.9 miles, only to climb again to Ekaneetlee Gap (3,842 feet) at 8.9 miles. Keep climbing and you'll reach **Mollies Ridge Shelter** at 10.3 miles. Depending on your pace, the time allotted for your hike, and your reservations (if necessary), make camp here.

At 10.9 miles you'll reach Devil's Tater Patch (4,775 feet) and begin a long section of what's often referred to as a "roller-coaster" section, meaning it's up and down as the trail follows the undulating ridgeline. You'll have frequent and steep ascents and descents, but little overall change in elevation between here and the 25-mile mark at Buckeye Gap.

From Devil's Tater Patch, descend to Little Abrams Gap (4,120 feet), then to Big Abrams Gap (4,080 feet) at 12.7 miles. At 13.1 miles you'll reach **Russell Field Shelter** and a spring. At 13.8 miles you'll reach McCampbell Gap (4,328 feet).

When you hit the 15.9 mile mark, you've reached the south end of **Spence Field;** the shelter is 0.1 miles on, then 250 yards down Eagle Creek Trail on the east side of the Appalachian Trail. Bote Mountain Trail intersects with the Appalachian Trail at 16.4 miles, where you meet Jenkins Ridge Trail, marking the north end of Spence Field.

As the trail begins to climb from Spence Field, you might as well start humming "Rocky Top" as you're approaching the

Fontana Dam to Newfound Gap

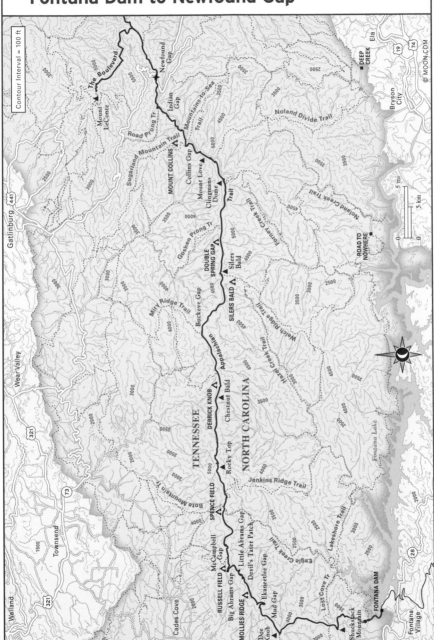

Contour Interval = 100 ft

© MOON.COM

5 mi

5 km

summit of the mountain made famous in the Osborne Brothers' song. Rocky Top's 5,441-foot peak awaits at 17.2 miles, then the summit of Thunderhead (5,527 feet) 0.6 miles farther. The views from Rocky Top are great but absolutely nonexistent from Thunderhead.

From here to Derrick Knob you'll pass through five additional gaps, then, at 22 miles, reach Chestnut Bald; **Derrick Knob Shelter** is 0.3 miles ahead on the west side of the trail.

At 25.1 miles you'll find yourself at the 4,817-foot Buckeye Gap and begin a 7.3-mile, 1,800-foot ascent to Clingmans Dome. Along the way you'll hit **Silers Bald** (5,607 feet) at 28 miles, where the views are quite good; Jenkins Knob at 29 miles; and **Double Spring Gap** shelter (5,570 feet) at 29.5 miles. Begin a steep ascent, pass Goshen Prong Trail to the west at 30.1 miles, summit Mount Buckley (6,582 feet) at 31.9 miles, then reach Clingmans Dome Bypass Trail at 32 miles.

If you want to top out on the 6,643-foot Clingmans Dome and hike to the top of the observation platform (recommended, especially if the weather is good), take a detour on a side trail to the east; head to the top, then back to the trail. You're now at 32.4 miles and are less than 8 miles from Newfound Gap, the end of this section of the Appalachian Trail.

Continue descending to the summit of Mount Love (6,446 feet) and Collins Gap (5,886 feet). At 35.8 miles you'll reach Sugarland Mountain Trail and **Mount Collins Shelter** (0.5 miles west). The Appalachian Trail joins North Carolina's Mountains-to-Sea Trail at the 36.2-mile mark.

Indian Gap (5,317 feet) and the intersection of Road Prong Trail await at 38.6 miles. At 39.4 miles a few openings in the trees provide views of Mount LeConte to the west. Ascend a graded trail to **Newfound Gap** (5,045 feet) and the overlook there.

Eastern Smokies
NEWFOUND GAP TO DAVENPORT GAP

Distance: 31.3 miles one-way
Duration: multiple days
Elevation gain: 4,380 feet
Difficulty: strenuous
Trailhead: Newfound Gap

Along this section you'll have 11 major climbs and descents like Mount Cammerer, Cosby Knob, Mount Guyot, Charlies Bunion, and Mount Kephart. There are five **shelters** here: Icewater Spring (mile 3), Pecks Corner (mile 10.4), TriCorner Knob (mile 15.6), Cosby Knob (mile 23.3), and Davenport Gap (mile 30.4).

Begin at **Newfound Gap,** taking a wide trail past the rock overlook and into the woods. You'll reach a viewpoint at 1.9 miles, then arrive at a junction with Boulevard Trail at 2.7 miles. The Boulevard leads to Mount LeConte, and from LeConte a day hiker can descend to Roaring Fork Motor Nature Trail via Trillium Gap Trail or descend to Newfound Gap Road via Alum Cave Bluffs Trail. Appalachian Trail hikers should proceed past the junction and reach **Icewater Spring Shelter** at the 3-mile mark.

The trail passes east around Charlies Bunion at 3.9 miles and then Dry Sluice Gap (5,375 feet) at 4.1 miles. Pass Dry Sluice Gap Trail (leading to Smokemont Campground) at 4.2 miles. Porters Gap (5,500 feet) is the next landmark at 5.8 miles, then False Gap (5,400 feet) at 6.5 miles. At the 9.1-mile mark you'll be at Bradleys View, where you'll have some of the best views of North Carolina that you'll find.

At 10.4 miles you'll reach a junction with Hughes Ridge Trail, which will take you to **Pecks Corner Shelter** to the east. There is another outstanding view at 11.3 miles, where you'll be looking down into the headwaters of Eagle Rocks Creek. Begin climbing at Copper Gap (5,478 feet), 12.1 miles in, and head on to the summit of Mount Sequoyah (6,003 feet) at 13.1 miles.

Newfound Gap to Davenport Gap

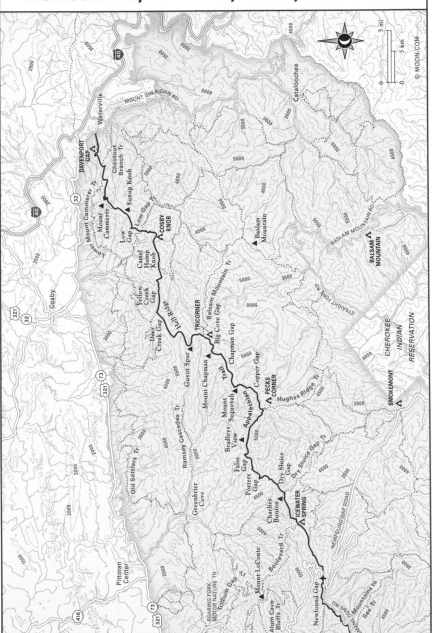

© MOON.COM

Descend to Chapman Gap (5,801 feet) at 13.8 miles, then climb again to Mount Chapman (6,218 feet) at 14.6 miles. You'll cross Big Cove Gap (5,825 feet) at 15.5 miles, and 0.1 miles farther, the trail to **TriCorner Knob Shelter.**

The junction with Balsam Mountain Trail lies at the 15.8-mile mark, and a sharp ridge at 16.2 miles. The next landmarks are Guyot Spur (6,360 feet) at 16.8 miles, Guyot Spring at 17.4 miles, and the so-called "Hell Ridge" section at 17.9 miles. The 4-mile Hell Ridge earned its name not from the tough trail but from a forest fire that raged here after pre-park logging left it particularly vulnerable; you'll notice the absence of the larger and old-growth trees seen elsewhere along the trail.

Deer Creek Gap (6,020 feet) at 18.5 miles and Yellow Creek Gap at 19.1 miles are the next two landmarks before you reach Camel Hump Knob (5,250 feet) at 20.8 miles. At 22.7 miles you'll be at the north end of Hell Ridge and pass back into a lovely deciduous forest.

Cosby Knob Shelter awaits at 23.3 miles, then Low Gap (4,242 feet) and the intersection with Low Gap Trail at 24 miles. The Appalachian Trail brushes past Sunup Knob at 25 miles, then crests the ridge and the North Carolina-Tennessee border on the slopes of Mount Cammerer at 25.9 miles. If you want to summit Cammerer and the stone fire tower there, you'll find the 0.6-mile spur trail at 26.1 miles.

There's a great view at 26.9 miles, and a spring east of the Appalachian Trail at 28.2 miles. Lower Mount Cammerer Trail comes in at 28.5 miles, then Chestnut Branch Trail at 29.4 miles. Davenport Gap Trail waits at the 30.4-mile mark; it's 200 yards or so off the west side of the trail. From here it's 0.9 miles to the **Davenport Gap Shelter.** Here you'll find State Route 1397, the Pigeon River, and I-40.

And, of course, the end of the Appalachian Trail passes out of Great Smoky Mountains National Park and turns northwest into North Carolina and toward Maine.

Tennessee Gateways

There was a time when this was the frontier,

when the Smoky Mountains stood too high and too rough to pass.

But settlers made their way across this huge green wall with what few supplies they could carry to carve out an existence in the virgin wilderness. They found coves of rich bottomland around which to settle outposts. Eventually these outposts turned into communities, which turned into towns and cities, and something like what we see today was carved out of the wild—Gatlinburg at the foot of the Smokies, Pigeon Forge on the river just a few miles distant, and Knoxville growing large on the bluffs of the deep, wide Tennessee River.

Today the setup is the same, but the inherent risks of frontier life are gone. In their place, Gatlinburg and Pigeon Forge are tourist hot

Highlights

Look for ★ to find recommended sights, activities, dining, and lodging.

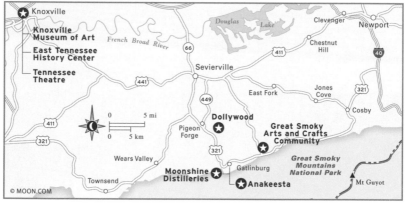

★ **Sample Moonshine Distilleries:** Moonshiners were rampant in these hills during Prohibition, but now you can sample a little legal 'shine in Gatlinburg (page 111).

★ **Shop at Great Smoky Arts and Crafts Community:** Interact with more than 120 traditional Appalachian artists, artisans, and craftspeople (page 115).

★ **Take in the View from Anakeesta:** With rides and restaurants aplenty, this mountaintop theme park captures the spirit and fun of the Smokies. (page 117).

★ **Go for a Ride at Dollywood:** At this theme park owned by the country music legend, roller coasters go hand in hand with Appalachian music, culture, and history (page 123).

★ **Uncover the Past at East Tennessee History Center:** This landmark tells the story of the Tennessee foothills through surprising exhibits (page 133).

★ **Explore the Knoxville Museum of Art:** Enjoy an impressive collection of contemporary pieces, including works by artists native to the city and the region (page 133).

★ **Step Back in Time at the Tennessee Theatre:** The official state theater is an architectural marvel offering a glimpse of Roaring Twenties opulence (page 135).

spots, or even tourist traps. (I mean that in the most flattering, fun, kitsch-filled sense of the term.) Gatlinburg is, proudly, the gateway to the Smokies, and Great Smoky Mountains National Park rubs shoulders with the town limits. Not to be outdone, Pigeon Forge is the home of Dollywood—an amusement park that's part rides, part Appalachian culture, and part homage to Dolly Parton's childhood.

The two towns are bright dots of light connected by a glittering ribbon—a sharp contrast to their next-door neighbor, the most-visited national park in the United States. Some 30 miles west of the park, Knoxville is the nearest city of any size, and it's as pretty and proper a Southern city as there ever has been. It offers a cosmopolitan respite from the wildness of the Smokies and the country kitsch of Gatlinburg and Pigeon Forge, all while maintaining its own identity as an intellectual and creative urban center that's grown up but has never forgotten its roots.

PLANNING YOUR TIME

To get a true sense of this complex place and a real taste of the cultures at work here, plan to spend at least **four days.** Spend two in Gatlinburg or Pigeon Forge. (The in-your-face faux-hillbilly attractions are so silly that you can't help but embrace them.) Pay a visit to the Great Smoky Arts and Crafts Community, where more than 120 artists, artisans, and craftspeople practice traditional Appalachian arts. Head to Dollywood for a sense of the area's history while waiting in line for a roller coaster. Taste some traditional food—from barbecue to country-kitchen standards—and clear the calendar for an evening of moonshine tasting, as most distilleries use versions of old family recipes likely made in the nearby hills.

After that, head to Knoxville for **two days** and soak in the contemporary, creative vibe of the city. You'll likely hear some traditional or bluegrass musicians, but listen closely and you'll find the ways they're making these old styles current. At the Knoxville Museum of Art and throughout downtown, the art here is certainly of the place, and seeing how it blends old with new gives you an idea of how these worlds come together. Visit the Ijams Nature Center, one of the premier urban wilderness areas in the nation, and see why several magazines have called this city one of the top outdoor towns in the South. If you're here on a weekend, Market Square is a happening spot with outdoor concerts, plenty of alfresco dining options, and a lovely farmers market.

Gatlinburg

On a typical Saturday night, when 40,000 people pack the restaurants and sidewalks of Gatlinburg, you would never know that only about 4,000 people live here. As the unofficial capital of the Smokies and gateway to the national park, Gatlinburg benefits greatly from the 10 million visitors drawn here for the views, the wildlife, the hikes, and the kitsch. And if there's anything Gatlinburg has in abundance, it's kitsch.

Gatlinburg is unabashedly a tourist town, and owning up to that fact makes it all the more charming. On Parkway, the cheekily named main drag, there are T-shirt shops, candy stores and fudgeries, taffy pullers, more than one Ripley's attraction, novelties both racy (in that family-friendly, double-entendre way) and tame, knife shops, mini golf, ice-cream parlors, restaurants, and more odd little art, craft, and gift shops than you can count. Don't let that deter you from staying (and even enjoying yourself) here. The

---

Previous: Dollywood in Pigeon Forge; the view from Anakeesta; Ole Smoky Moonshine distillery

Tennessee Gateways

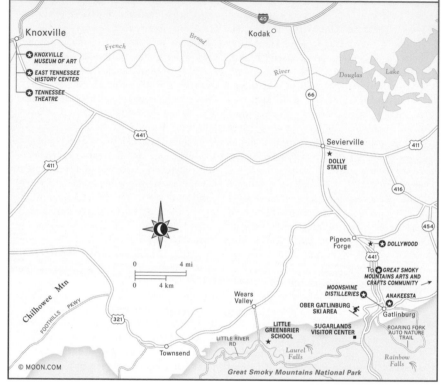

Ripley's Aquarium is quite nice, and at Great Smoky Arts and Crafts Community, you'll find modern interpretations of traditional mountain arts that were handmade nearby.

SIGHTS
Space Needle

All of downtown Gatlinburg is a sight to behold. The mountains rise all around you, that namesake Smoky mist rising from them, and the street glitters and twinkles like a sort of vacationland Milky Way. One of the best ways to take it all in is from the **Space Needle** (115 Historic Nature Trail, 865/436-4629, www.gatlinburgspaceneedle.com, 10am-9pm Sun.-Thurs., 10am-10pm Fri.-Sat., $16 adults, $13 seniors and military, $10 ages 4-11, free ages 3 and under). I know what you're thinking:

"But the Space Needle is in Seattle." Yeah, it is; this is the other one. From the observation deck 407 feet above Gatlinburg, you have truly stellar views. For the best views, get to the top shortly before sundown and watch as the mountains darken and the strip of downtown comes alive with lights. At the foot of the tower, there's a two-level, 25,000-square-foot arcade with games galore, laser tag, a gift shop, a snack bar, and restrooms.

Gatlinburg Sky Lift

Gatlinburg SkyLift Park (765 Parkway, 865/436-4307, www.gatlinburgskylift.com, 9am-9pm daily Jan.-late May, 9am-10pm Mon.-Thurs. and 8:30am-10pm Fri.-Sun. late May-early Sept., 9am-9pm Sun.-Thurs. and 9am-10pm Fri.-Sat. early-Sept.-Dec.,

Gatlinburg

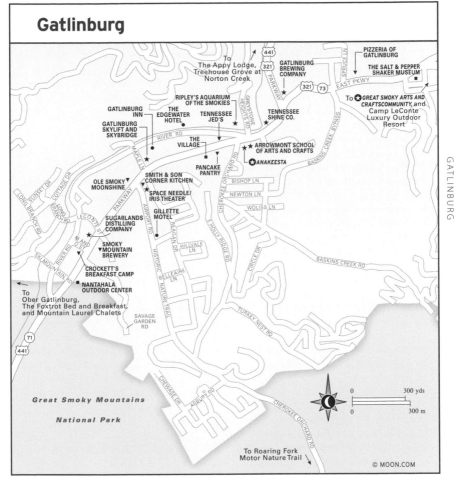

$29 adults, $24 seniors 65 and over, $19 ages 4-11, free ages 3 and under) was built in the early 1950s and was the first chairlift in the region, seeing more than 100,000 visitors by its third season in operation. The ski lift carries you 1,800 feet up the side of a mountain. You have pretty views of Gatlinburg on the way up and back down, and even better views from the top, where there are decks overlooking downtown. Also at the top, along with a gift shop and a snack bar, is the 680-foot SkyBridge. The SkyBridge spans a deep valley, and at its highest point—140 feet above the ground—features a glass bottom that affords

dizzying views. On this section of the bridge people take selfies, maintain death grips on the handrails, and shuffle across, alternately giggling, crying, turning pale, or thrilling to the experience. Nighttime tends to be the best time to ride the SkyLift. You'll find the lift in the heart of downtown; it's impossible to miss.

★ Moonshine Distilleries

Moonshine is a high-octane corn liquor made in the hills, hollows, and coves all throughout and around the national park, especially in Gatlinburg. Today moonshine is brewed legally and there are a few distilleries right in

Gatlinburg, the best of which is **Sugarlands Distilling Company** (805 Parkway, 865/325-1355, www.sugarlands.com, 10am-10:30pm daily). Sugarlands has their whole distilling process on display, and free tours are offered. If you really want to get into it, the Meet the Distiller workshop ($40) is a hands-on experience that sends you home with a full jar, and Distiller for the Day ($250) guides you through the process from start to finish. There are sampling stations ($5, ID required); the Sugarlands Cocktail Kitchen ($6), serving cocktails; a gift shop; and the opportunity to buy a quart or two. The Back Porch is the performance space, where musicians and storytellers come to sing songs and spin yarns; check to see who's there when you visit.

At the other end of downtown, **Tennessee Shine Co.** (519 Parkway, 865/325-1468, www.tnshineco.com, 10am-8pm Mon.-Wed., 10am-9pm Thurs.-Sat., noon-6pm Sun.) is one of four locations in the region. Here, and at the locations in **Pigeon Forge** (3435 Teaster Ln., Pigeon Forge, 865/366-3204, 10am-9pm Mon.-Thurs., 10am-10pm Fri.-Sat., noon-7pm Sun.), **Wears Valley** (3303 Wears Valley Rd., Sevierville, 865/286-4262, 10am-8pm Mon.-Wed., 10am-9pm Thurs.-Sat., noon-7pm Sun.), and **downtown Sevierville** (1242 Winfield Dunn Pkwy., Sevierville, 865/366-2854, 10am-8pm Mon.-Thurs., 10am-9pm Fri.-Sat., noon-7pm Sun.), you can sample moonshine and whiskey, try a cocktail, and pick up a souvenir T-shirt, shot glass, or mason jar mug. At each location, the bartenders are happy to wax poetic on moonshine and the steps it takes to transform water and corn into white lightning, but in downtown Sevierville, you can take a **moonshine history tour** ($10) that goes through the distillation process, NASCAR's ties to Prohibition's moonshine bootleggers, and the history of this legendary white liquor.

Another moonshine distillery is **Ole Smoky Moonshine** (www.olesmoky.com), which has multiple locations in the area, including **The Holler** (903 Parkway, Ste. 128, 865/436-6995, 10am-11pm daily) and

The Barrelhouse (650 Parkway, 865/325-1111, 10am-11pm daily) in Gatlinburg, and **The Barn** (131 The Island Dr., Pigeon Forge, 865/436-6995, 10am-11pm daily) in Pigeon Forge. At each you'll find plenty of 'shine to sample, as well as shirts, glasses, and mixers for sale alongside other Ole Smoky merchandise.

Ripley's Aquarium of the Smokies

Ripley's Aquarium of the Smokies (traffic light no. 5, 88 River Rd., 865/430-8808, www.ripleyaquariums.com/gatlinburg, 9am-10pm daily, $40 adults, $20 ages 6-11, $10 ages 2-5) is one of countless Ripley's attractions in Gatlinburg and Pigeon Forge. The other attractions are skippable unless you have kids in tow, but the aquarium is another story. Ripley's Aquarium is the largest in the state, with more than 1.4 million gallons of water. Exhibits include the Touch a Ray Bay, where you can touch a stingray; the Penguin Playhouse, where tunnels lead you through the exhibit, putting you eye to eye with penguins as they do their thing; and Shark Lagoon, with a 340-foot-long glide path that takes you under the lagoon, where sand tiger and nurse sharks swim with sea turtles and moray eels.

Arrowmont School of Arts and Crafts

Gatlinburg has a surprising artistic side. The artists and craftspeople here take their work very seriously. Many of them are carrying on mountain traditions, while others are finding new modes and media to express the inspiration they draw from the landscape here. Artists go to the **Arrowmont School of Arts and Crafts** (556 Parkway, 865/436-5860, www.arrowmont.org, 8:30am-5pm Mon.-Fri., 10am-4pm Sat., workshops $400-1,155) to hone their techniques. Founded in 1912 as a philanthropic project by the Pi Beta Phi

1: downtown Gatlinburg **2:** Space Needle
3: Gatlinburg Sky Lift **4:** Ole Smoky Moonshine distillery

women's fraternity, the Pi Beta Phi Settlement School sought to deliver basic education and health services to the children of the area. The schoolchildren brought the school staff homemade gifts—baskets, weavings, wood carvings—made by their parents. Recognizing the talent here, the school brought in a weaving teacher and began some vocational education. Then in 1926, the school opened the Arrowcraft Shop, a market selling crafts and wares made by the people of the region for decades until its recent closure. As this gained popularity, the idea of summer craft workshops arose. In 1945, the first of many summer workshops saw 50 students attend. Today the school holds weekend and one- and two-week workshops for adults every spring, summer, and fall. Classes include traditional and contemporary takes on weaving and fiber arts, pottery, metal and jewelry, painting, and drawing. Three galleries in the school display rotating and permanent exhibitions and are open year-round.

ENTERTAINMENT AND EVENTS
Nightlife
One spot to grab a drink other than moonshine is **Smoky Mountain Brewery** (1004 Parkway, 865/436-4200, www.smoky-mtn-brewery.com, 11:30am-midnight daily), a microbrewery with close to a dozen handcrafted beers brewed here or at one of the three nearby sister breweries. Mainstay beers include a light beer, red ale, pilsner, porter, and pale ale; they also brew seasonal and specialty beers, like the creamy Winter Warmer Ale and the Brown Trout Stout. Stop in and grab a hot pretzel and a sampler flight of beers, or stick around for a full meal ($5-30)—steaks, burgers, a few hand-tossed pizzas, and salads—and do a deep dive into that beer list.

Tennessee has an excellent craft beer scene, and as evidence I present **Gatlinburg Brewing Company** (458 Parkway, 865/412-1123, www.gatlinburgbrewingcompany. com, noon-1am daily). Now, if you're from a brewery-heavy area like I am, it's odd to find a place with only a handful of craft beer options, but this is a big deal for hop heads and suds seekers in the Smokies. The food (pizza, wings, salads, $8-15) does the trick, and the beer—Don't Feed the Bears, a brown ale; LeConte Tripel, a Belgian tripel; and IPAs like Breakfast Juice and Frog Alley Double IPA—will have you coming back soon.

Performing Arts
A number of stage shows go on nightly throughout Gatlinburg. The **Iris Theatre** (115 Historic Nature Trail, 888/482-3330, www.iristheater.com, showtimes vary, $28 adults, $20 military and seniors, $13 ages 4-11) is home to a rotating slate of performers. Expect to see family-friendly comedy and magic shows, hypnotists, and the like. Shows take place on most nights except Monday; check the schedule for times and current performers.

Festivals and Events
Throughout the year, several events draw attention to the things that make Gatlinburg the place it is. The **Spring Wildflower Pilgrimage** (www.wildflowerpilgrimage.org, $75-100 adults, $30 students, $5 ages 12 and under), usually during mid-April, is a five-day event with around 150 guided walks and presentations that celebrate the spring blooms, a photography contest, and more. From the end of September through October, celebrate **Oktoberfest at Ober Gatlinburg** (865/436-5423, www.obergatlinburg.com) with a beer hall, sing-alongs, yodeling, and authentic German food. Twice a year—two weeks in mid-July and mid-October—**Gatlinburg Craftsmen's Fair** (www.craftsmenfair. com) brings local and national artisans and craftspeople together to demonstrate their skills and to sell their wares. It's a juried show, so expect to see some fantastic work. **Gatlinburg Winter Magic** (800/588-1817) is a 120-day celebration of all things winter and holiday. From early November through February, the city is a riot of millions of LED bulbs strung up in trees and lining elaborate

Wedding Fever

To say that Gatlinburg is a popular place to get married is a gross understatement. This tiny town is second in the nation only to Las Vegas in the number of weddings held each year. On average, around 20,000 couples tie the knot here (that's 55 ceremonies a day), and the number of witnesses and guests they bring pushes the number of people in town for weddings north of 600,000. Guess that explains why Gatlinburg is called the "wedding capital of the South."

What makes Gatlinburg such a hot spot for weddings, even for celebrities (Billy Ray Cyrus, Patty Loveless, and others)? It could be that Tennessee makes it easy. No blood tests or waiting periods are required before getting married. It could be the abundance of wedding venues both natural and artificial. It could be the fact that there are plenty of romantic spots where one can retreat with their betrothed.

If being here has you in the mood for marriage, it's easy to find a place. Gatlinburg alone has more than a dozen chapels and more officiants than you can count. You can find all the information you'll ever need for planning a Smoky Mountain wedding at the website of the Smoky Mountain Wedding Association (www.smwba.com).

displays. There's a chili cook-off, carolers, a Christmas parade, and more. The Great Smoky Thanksgiving & Christmas Arts & Crafts Show adds to Winter Magic with an arts, crafts, and handmade goods show from the day after Thanksgiving through the first weekend in December.

SHOPPING

Gatlinburg's touristy side has a big personality, and plenty of shops sell T-shirts and the expected souvenirs, but for something that truly speaks to the heritage of this place, you'll need to do a little looking around.

★ Great Smoky Arts and Crafts Community

Your first stop should be the Great Smoky Arts and Crafts Community (turn right at traffic light no. 3 and go 3 miles to Glades Rd., 865/412-1012, www.gatlinburgcrafts. com, most studios and shops open 10am-5pm Mon.-Sat., call ahead for Sun. and holiday hours). Founded in 1937, it is among the largest group of independent artisans in the United States. There are more than 100 shops, studios, and galleries along this 8-mile loop consisting of Glades Road, Buckhorn Road, and U.S. 321. Look for the logo denoting membership in the community so you know that

wares you're seeing and buying are from genuine local and regional artisans. One thing that sets this community apart is the fact that you can interact with the artists in their studios and galleries. You can watch them work, ask questions, maybe even lend a hand (if asked). With 100 stops here, you can easily spend a day if you want to peek into each and every gallery, shop, and studio.

Shop artisans include candlemakers, watercolor artists, photographers, potters, and creators of traditional mountain crafts. My current favorite coffee mug came from Buie Pottery (1360 E. Parkway, Ste. 1, 865/436-3504, www.buiepottery.com), where I fell in love with the glazes and shapes in the owner's pots (and picked up my mug and a few gifts).

Artist Tim Weberding, a fourth-generation woodworker, makes religious signs and placards, wooden baskets and boxes, ornaments, and more. You can find his work at Tim Weberding Woodworking (600 Glades Rd., unit 5, 865/430-8811, www.timweberding. com). He's one of many woodcarvers here, and if you'd like to see more, try The Wood Whittlers (1402 E. Parkway, Ste. 6, 865/436-7187), the oldest continuously-operated craft shop in town.

Throughout the community there are several basket weavers, but nothing like what you'll find at **Licklog Hollow Baskets** (1360 E. Parkway, 865/436-3823). Not only does it have the strangest name, but the baskets are also superb. Whether you're buying for form or function, you'll find a basket that fits your style and probably your budget.

At **Woodland Tiles** (220 Buckhorn Rd., 865/640-9089), artisans create tiles and functional pottery pieces inspired by the leaves on the trees surrounding Gatlinburg. Custom glazes capture the jewel green of summer and the blazing colors of fall. You'll find more pottery at **Treasures in Earthen Vessels Pottery** (170 Glades Rd., no. 32, 865/430-3387, www.dhowardpottery.net), including bowls, mugs, and spoon rests. The bakeware is out of sight, but the Claydirondack—an Adirondack chair with stoneware pottery slats instead of wood—is a product like none other.

The Village

In downtown Gatlinburg, you'll find **The Village Shops** (634 Parkway, 865/436-3995, www.thevillageshops.com, 10am-10pm daily, hours may vary by shop), a collection of 27 shops centered around a courtyard in a Bavarian-style structure. Most shops cater to human clientele, but at **Bonediggity Barkery and Gifts** (865/277-9024) you'll find toys, accessories, and tasty treats for your pups. Among the shops here is **Cartoons & Toys** (865/430-8666), a kid-centric shop loaded with toys and games. **The Day Hiker** (865/430-0970, www.thedayhiker.com) provides the basic gear you need to take day and short overnight hikes in the national park. **The Silver Tree** (865/430-3573) is a silver lover's paradise with plenty of silver jewelry and accessories to peruse. Finally, you can check out a pair of shops for the hungry. **The Donut Friar** (865/436-7306, from 5am daily) is an amazing bakery making doughnuts, cinnamon bread, and other pastries; it also has the requisite coffee to go with your doughnut. And, for later in the day, **The Cheese Cupboard and Hofbrauhaus Restaurant**

(865/430-4111, $8-10) has a selection of German and Swiss cheeses and treats downstairs. Upstairs, it serves German-inspired sandwiches.

Other Shops

For a unique shop-museum (there is only one other place in the world like this, and it's in Spain), stop in at **The Salt and Pepper Shaker Museum** (461 Brookside Village Way, 865/430-5515, www.thesaltandpeppershakermuseum.com, 10am-4pm Mon.-Sat., 10am-2pm Sun., $3 adults, free ages 12 and under). The name tells you what you'll find here, but it doesn't prepare you for the more than 20,000 salt and pepper shakers from around the world and the growing collection of pepper mills. The collection began on a lark, growing from one pepper mill into this massive assembly of the most banal of kitchen accessories. It's weird, so it's worth the cost of admission, especially when you can apply your admission fee to any gift shop purchase—and who doesn't want a salt and pepper set shaped like outhouses?

Not all the shops in Gatlinburg are kitschy, mountain-themed spots. **The Gatlinburlier** (611 Parkway, D level, 865/436-4412 or 800/862-2204, https://gatlinburlier.com, 10am-8pm daily) carries specialty tobaccos, pipes, and other smoking accessories, and it has an impressive humidor. Picking from the plethora of T-shirt shops can be repetitive, but **The Soft Shirt Place** (611 Parkway, F level, 865/776-5505, www.thesoftshirtplace.com, 11am-7pm Wed.-Sun.) stands out with a better T-shirt, great design, and some actually witty illustrations and slogans. You might think that **Aunt Mahalia's Candies** (611 Parkway, F13, 865/436-7992, www.auntmahalias.com, 8am-10pm daily) is no different from the other candy stores and sweetshops in Gatlinburg, but it's been a fixture in town since 1939. With the volume of business it does, it'll likely be here until 2939, if not longer.

RECREATION

There is no end to the outdoor recreation opportunities near Gatlinburg. At **Nantahala Outdoor Center Gatlinburg** (NOC, 1138 Parkway, 865/277-8209, www.noc.com, 10am-6pm Mon.-Thurs. 10am-9pm Fri.-Sat., 10am-7pm Sun.), you'll find a huge retail store selling everything you'd ever need to gear up for an outdoor adventure. NOC is the region's leader in outdoor guide services, providing white-water rafting, float trips, and kayaking on several rivers across the region; guided hikes and fly-fishing trips; and more. Their trips vary by season, so check the website or ask someone at the store about current trips and activities.

Rafting in the Smokies (813 E. Parkway, 800/776-7238, www.raftingthesmokies.com, 8am-8pm daily Memorial Day-Labor Day, $33-44) is another white-water rafting outfitter in the area. Trips depend on the weather and water levels, so it's a good idea to call ahead or check online for current trips and reservations. Once you've gotten it nailed down, check in at the rafting outpost in Hartford (I-40, exit 447). They also have a zip line and high ropes course.

Open year-round, **CLIMB Works** (155 Branam Hollow Rd., 865/325-8116, www.climbworks.com, Mon.-Sat., reservations required, $89-99) brags that "your feet won't touch the ground for two and a half hours." And it's true: Whether you take its impressive mountaintop zip-line tour or the treetop tour, you'll be playing flying squirrel for a good part of the day, soaring from tree to tree, climbing up or down to the next platform, and taking in some impressive views.

★ Anakeesta

One of my absolute favorite places in Gatlinburg is **Anakeesta** (576 Parkway, traffic light no. 5, 865/325-2400, www.anakeesta.com, hours vary, generally 9am-9pm daily, $27 adults, $22 seniors over 59, $18 ages 4-11), a mountaintop theme park with an 880-foot treetop sky bridge, a tree house adventure village, dueling zip lines ($82 adults, $75 seniors

over 59, $69 ages 4-11, includes general admission ticket), a single-rail mountain coaster ($13-15), live music, a kids' play area, and several places to relax and take in the views.

Anakeesta is divided into four areas: Firefly Village, Black Bear Village, Vista Gardens, and Forest Adventures. There are shops, restaurants, and activities sprinkled throughout these areas, though they each have a distinct look and feel. In Firefly Village, where you'll get on and off the tram, you'll find a miniature Great Outdoor Provision Company stocked with outdoor gear. Black Bear Village has a splash pad, a photogenic fountain and bit of bear statuary, and an outdoor stage. Forest Adventures leads you to gem mining, the TreeTop SkyWalk (a series of bridges and platforms suspended in the trees), and the zip line. And in Vista Garden you have sculptures and rotating art, a photo display detailing the 2016 fires, a play area and spot where adults can hang out and admire the view, and AnaVista Tower, the highest point in Gatlinburg, where some handy signage will clue you in as to what you're seeing.

There's plenty to do here, and plenty to eat throughout the park. Pearl's Pie in the Sky scoops up ice cream for cones and shakes, and they have a heap of pies, cookies, and brownies to choose from. The Snack Shack has plain and topped funnel cake. The Watering Can carries healthy snacks, sandwiches, and drinks, and a selection of gardening goods. The Happy Camper, a cute, retrofitted camper, serves as a beverage and snack bar at the top of the hill. Serving lunch and dinner, Cliff Top has the biggest menu, with burgers, sandwiches, huge salads, and steaks (dinner only), plus a full-service bar. Grab some barbecue at Smokehouse, or try a flatbread, hot dog, or frozen yogurt at Kephart Cafe.

Locals and frequent Gatlinburg visitors should consider forgoing the standard ticket in favor of an **annual pass** ($60 adults, $55 seniors, $52 ages 4-11) that gives you a 20 percent discount on shopping, dining, and select activities as well as a free buddy pass.

Ober Gatlinburg

Ober Gatlinburg (1001 Parkway, 865/436-5423, www.obergatlinburg.com, hours vary by activity, generally 9:30am-9pm daily spring-fall, 10am-7pm daily winter, aerial tram $17 adults, $14 kids; à la carte $4-20; activity pass $39-49 adults, $35-45 ages 5-11, free ages 4 and under), the mountaintop resort that looks out over Gatlinburg, is a ski resort in winter and a mountain playground the rest of the year. There are eight ski and snowboard trails, and Ober Gatlinburg is equipped with plenty of snowmaking equipment to compensate for what Mother Nature doesn't supply. Warm-weather activities include the awesome Alpine Slide, a sort of luge that follows one of the ski slopes down the hill; a pair of raft-based waterslides; a maze; and year-round indoor ice-skating. There's also a Wildlife Encounter where you can see many of the area's native species. If you're hungry, there are several places to grab a bite, ranging from a slice of pizza to a steak.

FOOD

Dining in Gatlinburg, especially for foodies, can be tricky. In a town where, literally, millions of people pass through, you get a lot of restaurants that have stopped caring about repeat customers and seek only to provide a heaping plate of food and mediocre service at premium prices, knowing their diners will be in for one, maybe two meals during their visit. And there are plenty of major chains ready to take your dining dollars. That said, it is possible to find a good, even great, meal here.

Gatlinburg is one of those towns where a restaurant either becomes an institution and sticks around for 40 years, or scrapes by for a season. Rest assured that **Smith & Son Corner Kitchen** (traffic light no. 8, 812 Parkway, 865/430-1978 or 865/436-8878, www.smithandsoncornerkitchen.com, 11am-9pm Sun.-Thurs., 11am-10pm Fri.-Sat., $10-25) is the former. With a prime location, loads of space, and a sizable menu that remains

navigable and has brought me back for dinner a few times, they're here to stay. The salads are whoppers, and when paired with an appetizer, there's more than a meal for one. Burgers and sandwiches are fresh and filling, and the entrées—ranging from smoked chicken to meat loaf to fajitas to fried catfish—are so generous you won't mind sharing a bite or two.

A totally unexpected treat is ★ **Red Oak Bistro and Caffe** (669 Glades Rd., 865-325-1717, www.redoakbistro.net, 4pm-10pm Thurs.-Sun., $12-30), a tapas, wine, and European beer spot. The food is exceptional and unlike anything else in Gatlinburg. Thoughtfully composed cheese and charcuterie boards, fresh hummus and other spreads, bruschetta, dolmas, *kebarche* (a Bulgarian pork sausage), and beet napoleon are complemented by a wine list that may just be the best in town. There's outdoor seating, a firepit, and a fireplace, as well as couches and other places to relax; it's no wonder you need a reservation.

Delauder's BBQ (1875 E. Parkway, 865-325-8682, 4pm-8pm Thurs.-Fri., 12:30pm-8pm Sat., noon-2:30pm Sun., $5-25) will draw you in through smell alone, and once you taste the pulled pork or ribs, you won't want to leave. Other options are a Smoky Mountain Potato (a baked potato heaped with barbecue and fixings), nachos piled with barbecue goodness, and a number of sandwiches including the Holy Bologna Sandwich, a grilled bologna behemoth topped with pulled pork, onions, pickles, sweet jalapeño mustard, barbecue sauce, and cheese.

★ **Buckhorn Inn** (2140 Tudor Mountain Rd., 865/436-4668, www.buckhorninn.com, 7pm-late daily, $40) serves a five-course prix-fixe meal nightly to inn guests and visitors. The food makes creative use of regional ingredients, with meals that bring together influences from Southern, East Tennessee, and international cuisine. Dishes like roast pork with peach barbecue sauce, seared salmon, five-onion soup, almond-date cake, and fresh catch with mango butter have people making reservations as soon as they book their trip.

1: AnaVista Tower **2:** Anakeesta

As a Grateful Dead fan, I'd be remiss if I didn't pop my head into **Tennessee Jed's** (631 Parkway, 865/412-1131, www.tennesseejeds.net, 8am-3:30pm daily, $4-12), a restaurant named for one of the band's more playful songs, and I'm glad I did. The breakfast sandwich is out of sight (and travels well if you're looking for a to-go option), and the Cubano is spot on.

When you're hankering for a pizza pie or some homemade Italian dishes, get to **Pizzeria of Gatlinburg** (349 E. Parkway, 865/412-1234, www.gatlinburg.pizza, noon-1am daily, $8-28), pronto. Not only do they sell the biggest pizza in Gatlinburg—a 22-inch monster you might not be able to fit into your car—but they also have pasta, hoagies, and an assortment of appetizers ready for dunking in their house-made marinara sauce.

If there's one thing Gatlinburg has, it's pancake houses. But frankly, they all fall short of the OG pancake house, the very first one to open in Tennessee: **Pancake Pantry** (628 Parkway, 865/436-4724, www.pancakepantry.com, 7am-3pm Mon.-Fri., 7am-4pm Sat.-Sun., $6-10). They griddle up 24 varieties of pancakes and crepes, as well as waffles, omelets, and French toast. Breakfast is served all day, but if you feel like a burger or sandwich for lunch, there are a few of those too. If you're going for a hike, go easy on the pancakes—they sit a little heavy—but you can get a to-go boxed lunch made just for hikers and day-trippers into the park.

You can't miss my current favorite breakfast spot in Gatlinburg for two reasons: One, it's great, and two, there's a cast-iron skillet the size of a king bed outside. ★ **Crockett's Breakfast Camp** (1103 Parkway, 865/325-1403, www.crockettsbreakfastcamp.com, 7am-1pm daily, $2-15) sits at the eastern edge of town near the entrance to the national park and serves, predictably, breakfast. Fried cinnamon rolls (think French toast plus cinnamon roll, but the size of a baby), the Waffle of Insane Greatness, and the Thick Aretha Frankenstein's Pancakes (great pancakes, funny name), as well as biscuits and breakfast burritos, are only part of the menu. The menu itself—a keepsake that's both menu and "newspaper"—is packed with stories about the area, from legendary bear hunters to odd trivia, all of which is backed up by what they serve on the plate and the odd assortment of photographs, ephemera, and artifacts on the walls. Get here early, especially if your party is a big one.

the massive cinnamon roll at Crockett's Breakfast Camp

ACCOMMODATIONS

Something about being in Gatlinburg makes me want to stay in a cabin. Fortunately, there are plenty of options whether you're traveling solo, as a pair, or with even the largest of groups. ★ **Mountain Laurel Chalets** (440 Ski Mountain Rd., 865/436-5277, www.mtnlaurelchalets.com, 2- to 4-person cabin $249-399, 6- to10-person cabin $350-750, 11- to -24-person lodge $650-1,449) has several lodges and large houses sleeping anywhere from 10 to 24 people if you're traveling with your extended family, or smaller cabins that sleep a couple or small group on a getaway. The cabins are spread out over a huge property, so they're private in addition to being cozy. Some of the cabins, the last ones in line for a refresh, are dated, but others are quite nice inside, so check cabin descriptions online if this matters to you.

Want to stay somewhere different? Maybe relive those childhood memories of staying up all night in a tree house? Well, at ★ **Treehouse Grove at Norton Creek** (475 Norton Creek Rd., 865/409-1410, www.treehouse-grove.com, $350-600), you can. There are eight tree houses here, and by tree houses, I don't mean cabins on short pilings built near a tree. I'm talking proper tree houses that are 30 or even 45 feet off the ground. Each one has that perfect blend of cozy, comfy, cabin-y charm but without going overboard. Each of the cabins sleeps four, making them great for a small family or a couples' getaway.

Camp LeConte Luxury Outdoor Resort (1739 E. Parkway, 865/436-8831, www.campleconte.com) has a variety of accommodations that include luxury tree houses (from $211), safari tents (from $136), retro campers (from $149), RVs (from $82), and tent sites (from $37). The open-air tree houses offer views of Mount LeConte and can sleep up to four guests. The safari tents are tents on pads, similar to a glamping experience, while the cool retro campers are replica 1961 Shasta Airflytes. A pool and small general store are on-site as well.

★ **The Appy Lodge** (168 Parkway, 865/430-3659, www.theappylodge.com, $199-295) sits at the west end of Gatlinburg where it's a little quieter, making for a relaxing stay. Rooms are spacious and modern, but with enough of that rustic twist to retain that Smoky Mountain feel. It's a lovely property with a warm, friendly staff (and one of the best local travel blogs around), the kind of people who want to be sure you have a great stay in the Smokies and come back next year. Or sooner.

The Foxtrot Bed and Breakfast (1520 Garrett Ln., 865/436-3033, www.thefoxtrot.com, $190-230) is a little different from most B&Bs in that an actual chef prepares breakfast. That's just one thing that sets it apart. The Foxtrot is high on the hill, well above the noise, traffic, and bustle of downtown Gatlinburg, making it a true retreat. You can add several packages to your room, like spa packages, honeymoon and anniversary packages, cooking schools, and more.

There are a number of mom-and-pop motels and chain hotels in Gatlinburg with prices ranging from budget to mid-range. In the heart of Gatlinburg, **Gillette Motel** (235 Historic Nature Trail, 865/436-5601 or 800/437-0815, www.gillettemotel.com, rooms from $85) is a place I recall from trips to the Smokies as a kid, and I've spent more than one afternoon in their pool. The **Gatlinburg Inn** (755 Parkway, 865/436-5133, www.gatlinburginn.com, $169-359) sits one block back from the main drag and is walking distance from most everything you want to do in Gatlinburg. A solid choice is **The Edgewater Hotel** (402 River Rd., 865/436-4151 or 800/423-9582, www.edgewater-hotel.com, $141-220). You'll get a great room on the creek and be just a block away from the bustling heart of Gatlinburg, an easy walk to everything in town and an easy drive to the national park.

TRANSPORTATION AND SERVICES

Car

Most visitors arrive in Gatlinburg via Newfound Gap Road (U.S. 441) heading west from Cherokee, North Carolina, through Great Smoky Mountains National Park. From Cherokee, it's an approximately 45-minute drive through the park. Gatlinburg is easy to find: One minute you're in the park, the next minute you're in Gatlinburg.

For those driving from the north or west, I-40 is the most convenient road into town. From I-40, take exit 407 onto U.S. 66 south; this road feeds into U.S. 441 and leads past Sevierville and Pigeon Forge to Gatlinburg. This is the easiest and most heavily traveled route into town from I-40. You can avoid the peak-season crowds by taking exit 435 near Knoxville (an hour away) and following U.S. 321 south to Gatlinburg.

Coming from the east on I-40, the best bet is to take exit 443 and drive along the beautiful Foothills Parkway to U.S. 321 south, from which you cruise right into town.

PARKING

Finding parking in Gatlinburg can be quite tough. There are a number of public and private parking lots and garages where you can park your car if you're not staying at a hotel nearby. Parking rates vary depending on public or private ownership, so for affordability, it's often best to stick to the public parking garages at **Ripley's Aquarium of the Smokies** (88 River Rd., $8 per day) and the **McMahan Parking Garage** (520 Parkway, at traffic light no. 3, $8 per day).

Air

The **McGhee-Tyson Airport** (TYS, 2055 Alcoa Hwy., Alcoa, TN, 865/342-3000, www.flyknoxville.com) outside Knoxville is 42 miles from Gatlinburg. From the airport, head south to Maryville on U.S. 129. Once you're in Maryville, take U.S. 321 north to Pigeon Forge, then turn right and take U.S. 441 to Gatlinburg.

Public Transportation

Gatlinburg has a great trolley system that can get you to and from every attraction in Gatlinburg and nearby Pigeon Forge, including Dollywood. The **Gatlinburg Trolley** (88 River Rd., Ste. 101, 865/436-3897, www.gatlinburgtrolley.org, 8:30am-midnight daily, extended hours some holiday and event dates) has more than 100 stops in Gatlinburg alone. It's cheap, with most rides only $0.50, but your best bet is to pick up an All Day Trolley Pass ($2) from the **Gatlinburg Welcome Center** (1011 Banner Rd., 865/436-4178 or 800/588-1817, www.gatlinburg.com, 9am-5pm daily) or the **Aquarium Welcome Center** (88 River Rd., 9am-9pm daily).

Services

There are two visitors centers in Gatlinburg: the **Gatlinburg Welcome Center** (1011 Banner Rd., 865/436-4178 or 800/588-1817, www.gatlinburg.com, 9am-5pm daily) and the **Aquarium Welcome Center** (88 River Rd., 9am-9pm daily). On the radio, **WWST** (102.1 FM) plays the Top 40. **WSEV** (105.5 FM) is an adult contemporary station.

LeConte Medical Center (742 Middle Creek Rd., Sevierville, 865/446-7000, www.lecontemedicalcenter.com) is the nearest hospital, just over 20 minutes away. The **Gatlinburg Police** (1230 E. Parkway, 865/436-5181) are available if the need arises.

Pigeon Forge and Sevierville

The dominating presence in Pigeon Forge and Sevierville is that of Dolly Parton. Her namesake amusement park, Dollywood, is in Pigeon Forge, and she was born and raised in Sevierville, where a statue of Dolly stands in front of the courthouse. You'll see her face, hear her music, and maybe even meet one of her many cousins everywhere across these two towns.

These towns have grown a lot since Dolly was born, thanks largely to the increasing popularity of Great Smoky Mountains National Park. More growth came when the amusement park that would become Dollywood opened its doors, and again when nearby Knoxville hosted the World's Fair. But to keep more than 10 million annual visitors coming back year after year, Pigeon Forge and Sevierville had to become destinations unto themselves, and, for the most part, they've succeeded. Pigeon Forge has become one of the biggest "tourist traps" (which I say not with disdain, but astonishment—the place is a wonderland of vacation delights) on the East Coast. Want to ride go-karts and go bungee jumping at 9pm on a Wednesday? No problem. Midnight mini golf? Got it. Roller coasters, neon signs, and fudge shops? Pigeon Forge has got you covered. Don't be fooled by all the neon, hotels, and attractions, though: Pigeon Forge remains a small town, with fewer than 7,000 year-round residents.

In the midst of this swirl of touristy flotsam is a surprising center for engaging with the community's culture: Dollywood. This amusement park has been around in some form or another since the 1960s, though in the early days it was kitsch over culture. As the park matured and expanded, so did its attention to the culture of mountain living. Today the park is home to some great bluegrass and country shows and a good many shops and exhibits where Appalachian crafters showcase their skills and their wares.

SIGHTS

★ Dollywood

At **Dollywood** (2700 Dollywood Parks Blvd., Pigeon Forge, 800/365-5996, www.dollywood. com, hours vary Apr.-Dec., $69-79, parking $20 cars, $25 RVs), you might just catch a glimpse of Dolly Parton walking through the park or performing for the crowds at the park's opening. Even if you don't see Dolly, her namesake park is packed with rides, food, cultural stops, artisans, shows, and nature experiences—everything one of the world's best amusement parks should have—to keep you entertained for a couple of days.

Dollywood started in 1961 when Rebel Railroad, a small attraction with a steam train, a general store, a blacksmith shop, and a saloon, opened. By 1977, the park had grown and changed hands more than once. Renamed Silver Dollar City, the park eventually caught the attention of Dolly Parton. She became a partner and lent the park her name. Since then, it has become Tennessee's most-visited tourist attraction outside the national park and is consistently named among the top theme parks in the world.

Dollywood has a great look: one part Appalachian village, one part small Southern town. There are tree-lined streets and paths, and several streams follow their courses through the park. You don't see the rides until you're right up on them because they're tucked away in the woods. One of the best-known spots in the park is **Showstreet,** where stages and theaters are always busy with musicians, square dances, and storytellers. In addition, a bevy of master craftspeople practice their Appalachian arts for all to see: blacksmiths, basket weavers, candlemakers, and woodworkers. On Showstreet, you may see some of

Pigeon Forge

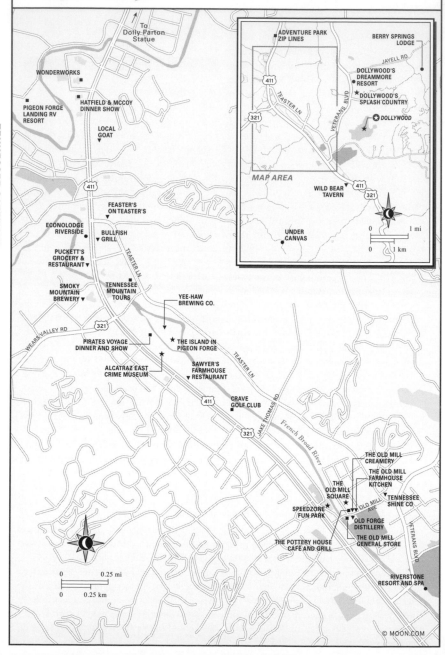

To Dolly Parton Statue

WONDERWORKS

HATFIELD & McCOY DINNER SHOW

PIGEON FORGE LANDING RV RESORT

LOCAL GOAT

411

FEASTER'S ON TEASTER'S

ECONOLODGE RIVERSIDE

BULLFISH GRILL

PUCKETT'S GROCERY & RESTAURANT

TEASTER LN

SMOKY MOUNTAIN BREWERY

TENNESSEE MOUNTAIN TOURS

YEE-HAW BREWING CO.

321

WEARS VALLEY RD

PIRATES VOYAGE DINNER AND SHOW

THE ISLAND IN PIGEON FORGE

ALCATRAZ EAST CRIME MUSEUM

SAWYER'S FARMHOUSE RESTAURANT

TEASTER LN

411

CRAVE GOLF CLUB

321

JAKE THOMAS RD

French Broad River

THE OLD MILL CREAMERY

THE OLD MILL FARMHOUSE KITCHEN

THE OLD MILL SQUARE

OLD MILL AVE

TENNESSEE SHINE CO.

SPEEDZONE FUN PARK

OLD FORGE DISTILLERY

THE OLD MILL GENERAL STORE

VETERANS BLVD

THE POTTERY HOUSE CAFÉ AND GRILL

RIVERSTONE RESORT AND SPA

0   0.25 mi

0   0.25 km

MAP AREA (inset)

ADVENTURE PARK ZIP LINES

BERRY SPRINGS LODGE

JAYELL RD

411

DOLLYWOOD'S DREAMMORE RESORT

TEASTER LN

DOLLYWOOD'S SPLASH COUNTRY

321

VETERANS BLVD

DOLLYWOOD

MAP AREA

WILD BEAR TAVERN

411

321

UNDER CANVAS

0   1 mi

0   1 km

© MOON.COM

Dolly's relatives playing and singing in shows throughout the year.

Also on Showstreet is a carriage, sled, and wagon shop called **Valley Carriage Works.** It takes orders from clients from around the world and builds beautiful, fully functional, historically accurate carriages. At the Museum of the Cherokee Indian in Cherokee, North Carolina, you can see a replica Cherokee wagon that the shop built to commemorate the 165th anniversary of the Trail of Tears.

Given that the park allows nature to be such a prominent feature in its design, it's no surprise to learn that Dollywood has partnered with the American Eagle Foundation and is authorized by the U.S. Fish and Wildlife Service and the Tennessee Wildlife Resources Agency to possess eagles and other birds for education, exhibition, rehabilitation, and breeding. The 30,000-square-foot **aviary** is home to the nation's largest group of non-releasable bald eagles (many of these birds have been injured and wouldn't survive if released into nature). Daily shows put visitors in close proximity to these incredible birds.

Spread across Dollywood's 160 acres are more than 50 rides and attractions that range from kid-friendly to thrilling. Favorites include Blazing Fury, an indoor roller coaster where you try to outrun an out-of-control fire (it was the absolute be-all and end-all of roller coasters when I was a kid); Thunderhead, a great wooden coaster; Mystery Mine, which answers the question "What if we put a death-defying roller coaster in a coal mine?"; and Daredevil Falls, a log flume ride where you can cool off and build up the nerve to take on one of the bigger rides.

In 2020, the park debuted its first **Flower & Food Festival** (mid-spring–early summer), a celebration of beautiful blooms, enormous plant sculptures, and, of course, food. The food draws on the traditions of Southern, Appalachian, and Smoky Mountain cuisine, paying homage to both folksy dishes and the flavors brought here by the region's many immigrant communities, and the sculptures and flowers—more than 500,000 blooming throughout Dollywood—are amazing.

Lighted drones and fireworks fill the air during **Sweet Summer Nights** (June-July); the **Harvest Festival** and **Great Pumpkin LumiNights** celebrations (late Sept.-Oct. 30) see more whimsical decorations and a few not-so-spooky costumes in the park; and from early November into the first week of January, **Smoky Mountain Christmas** gets the park twinkling with more than five million lights. The fireworks, Christmas- and holiday-themed shows, and special seasonal treats to eat make for an amazing visit that'll get you in the holiday spirit.

Dollywood's Splash Country

Water parks abound in Pigeon Forge and Sevierville, but the best is **Dollywood's Splash Country** (2700 Dollywood Parks Blvd., Pigeon Forge, 800/365-5996, www.dollywood.com, hours vary May-Sept., $39-49, parking $20 cars, $25 RVs). This water park has 30 waterslides, a lazy river, 3 water play areas for kids, a 7,500-square-foot leisure pool, and a 25,000-square-foot wave pool. There are also concessions, a gift shop, and stroller and locker rentals.

Dolly Parton Statue

Local artist Jim Gray sculpted a **statue** (125 Court Ave., Sevierville) that shows Dolly with a wide smile and her guitar, as if she's ready to write a song at any moment. Stop by downtown Sevierville to take a picture with the statue, located on the courthouse lawn.

Alcatraz East Crime Museum

There are more than 100 interactive exhibits at **Alcatraz East Crime Museum** (2757 Parkway, Pigeon Forge, 865/453-3278, www.alcatrazeast.com, 9am-9pm Sun.-Thurs., 9am-10pm Fri.-Sat., $27 adults, $15 ages 8-12), which offers a great audio tour and plenty to touch and see. You can "lock" yourself in a mock jail cell and attempt to crack a safe. Exhibits cover crime scene investigations and crime-fighting techniques. The most

popular displays are found in **The Notorious History of American Crime,** where you can see John Dillinger's death mask; getaway cars used by Bonnie and Clyde, Ted Bundy, and O. J. Simpson; and Al Capone's rosary. Discount tickets ($20) are available to locals, seniors over 60, and military and law enforcement personnel.

WonderWorks

WonderWorks (100 Music Rd., Pigeon Forge, 865/868-1800, www.wonderworksonline.com, 9am-10pm daily, $32 adults, $25 seniors 60 and over and ages 4-12) is another weird attraction. From the outside, the building appears to be upside down, and inside there are more than 100 interactive exhibits. Some, like the Tesla Coil and the Earthquake Café, are strange and seem dangerous, while others allow you to use your imagination to solve challenges or test your willpower.

ENTERTAINMENT
Nightlife

If you want to wet your whistle in Pigeon Forge, your options are exclusively bars in restaurants. The two best bars happen to be at Smoky Mountain Brewery and Yee-Haw Brewing Co. at The Island in Pigeon Forge. **Smoky Mountain Brewery** (2530 Parkway, Ste. 15, Pigeon Forge, 865/868-1400, www.smoky-mtn-brewery.com, 11am-midnight Sun.-Thurs., 11am-1am Fri.-Sat.) brews every drop of its draft beer in-house or at one of three sister restaurants, and it serves up some good grub. **Yee-Haw Brewing Co.** (131 The Island Dr., Pigeon Forge, 865/505-1200, www.yehawbrewing.com, 10am-11pm daily) was founded just up the road in Johnson City, and they've grown into three other locations, including this one. They brew up a Scotch ale, a pale ale, an IPA, a dunkel (a dark lager), and a kölsch (a German style of beer), plus several seasonal offerings. All of these go well with a day of exploring the park, playing 36 holes

of mini golf, or listening to some live music (which the brewery has on weekends).

Next door to Yee-Haw Brewing is one of **Ole Smoky Moonshine's** (www.olesmoky. com) three locations: **The Barn** (131 The Island Dr., Pigeon Forge, 865/436-6995, 10am-11pm daily) has plenty of 'shine to sample, as well as shirts, glasses, and mixers for sale alongside other Ole Smoky merchandise. There's more moonshine to be had at **Old Forge Distillery** (170 Old Mill Ave., Pigeon Forge, 865/908-8351, www.oldforgedistillery. com, 10am-9pm Mon.-Sat., 10am-6pm Sun.), where they cook up an original recipe from 1830 as well as flavored 'shine and some lower-proof (read: easier to sip) small-batch spirits. If that's not enough moonshine for you, then you need to mosey on over to **Tennessee Shine Co.** (3435 Teaster Ln., Pigeon Forge, 865/366-3204, www.tnshineco. com, 10am-9pm Mon.-Thurs., 10am-10pm Fri.-Sat., noon-7pm Sun.) for tastings, bottles, and the ubiquitous T-shirt, and also to learn a bit about how moonshine is made. To expand on your moonshine knowledge, the **moonshine history tour** ($10) at the downtown Sevierville location (1424 Winfield Dunn Pkwy.) digs deeper into the history, culture, legacy of 'shine.

Dinner Shows

While the **Hatfield & McCoy Dinner Show** (119 Music Rd., Pigeon Forge, 865/908-7469, www.hatfieldmccoydinnerfeud.com, 2pm, 5pm, and 8pm daily, $60 adults, $30 ages 3-9) isn't an accurate portrayal of the Hatfields (who hail from my home county in West Virginia), the McCoys (from just over the border in Kentucky), or their legendary feud (which started over forbidden teenage love, a stolen pig, or a revenge murder dating back to the Civil War, depending on who you ask), it is a good time and there's plenty of food to be had. You'll pick a side when you purchase tickets; on entering, you'll sit with the Hatfields or the McCoys, and then the show begins. Take in the songs, dances, corny but legitimately funny (and family-friendly) jokes, and a few

---

1: Dolly immortalized in bronze by sculptor Jim Gray **2:** WonderWorks in Pigeon Forge

stunts while your all-you-can-eat country buffet is served, including fried chicken, pulled pork barbecue, mashed potatoes, corn on the cob, and dessert.

Pirate's Voyage Dinner and Show (2713 Parkway, Pigeon Forge, 865/505-2469, www. piratesvoyage.com, 6pm and 8:30pm Mon.-Fri., 3pm, 6pm, and 8:30pm Sat.-Sun., $60 adults, $30 kids ages 3-9) makes pirates a bit more family-friendly than they were (I don't know any pirates personally, but I live where Blackbeard plied the seas, so I know them by reputation). If you want a show with a mix of kid-friendly and ribald jokes that (mostly) go over the heads of the youngest audience members, this is it. Cannon fire, swordplay, plank walking, pirate crew recruiting, and about a dozen other surprises await inside.

SHOPPING

Pigeon Forge got its name from a forge set up in 1820 by Isaac Love and from the incredible number of passenger pigeons the early European settlers found living along the banks of the Little Pigeon River. A decade later, Love's son established a mill, which is now a National Historic Site that you can visit: **The Old Mill Square** (175 Old Mill Ave., Pigeon Forge, 877/653-6455, www.old-mill.com, hours vary by store) is a collection of shops and restaurants in a cute restored and recreated historic area. **The Old Mill General Store** (865/453-4628, 8am-9pm Mon.-Sat., 8am-8pm Sun.) has all sorts of country provisions, including fresh-ground grains milled next door at the Old Mill. **The Old Mill Farmhouse Kitchen** (865/428-2044, 9am-9pm Mon.-Sat., 9am-8pm Sun.) also sells a variety of provisions and ingredients that you need to cook your own country meal at home. It has a nice pottery shop and gift baskets too. You can cool off with an ice-cream treat at **The Old Mill Creamery** (865/453-4301, 10am-9pm Mon.-Sat., 10am-8pm Sun., $4-6), where they keep around two dozen flavors on hand, including ones that bring in ingredients from the nearby candy kitchen and Old Forge Distillery (just be sure not to get one of these moonshine-laced goodies for the kiddos).

Pick up a pair or two of cowboy boots, a snazzy pearl-buttoned shirt, or a belt buckle at **Stages West** (2765 Parkway, Pigeon Forge, 865/453-8086, www.stageswest.com, 10am-9:30pm Mon.-Sat.). They've been a fixture in Pigeon Forge for decades, and their selection ranges from pricey Lucchese boots made with alligator leather to basic boots that'll look perfect once they get a few scuffs. Stetson and Greeley Hat Works are two top brands they carry for cowboy hats and other styles, and that's just the tip of the iceberg. If you're into Western wear for its throwback qualities, because you run deep in the world of country music, or because you actually work on a ranch, you can get your outfit together here—whether you're off to a wedding or headed out to work.

Smoky Mountain Knife Works (2320 Winfield Dunn Pkwy., Sevierville, 865/453-5871, www.smkw.com, 10am-6pm Sun.-Thurs., 10am-8pm Fri.-Sat.) has long held a reputation for quality pocketknives, hunting knives, and specialty blades. You can pick up a Swiss Army knife here, a fishing or kitchen knife, even antique and collectors' knives that can cost upward of $4,000.

The Island (131 The Island Dr., Pigeon Forge, 865/286-0119, www. islandinpigeonforge.com) has a little bit of everything, including more than 40 retail and gift shops, a number of restaurants, and countless activities, making it a one-stop shop for a lot of visitors. Not surprisingly, several shops are geared toward kids. **RideMakerz** (865/409-2722, www.ridemakerz.com, 10am-11pm daily) lets you build your own free-wheeled or remote-controlled car or truck. When I say build, I mean it: You'll select your chassis, body, wheels, and more, then put them together (with supervision, of course). Comic book fans, manga maniacs, and pop culture fanatics should visit **Kryptonite Character Store** (865/774-0065, www. kryptonitecharacterstore.com, 9am-11pm Sun.-Thurs., 9am-midnight Fri.-Sat.), where you'll find all sorts of pop culture gifts from

T-shirts and hoodies to high-end collectible figures and more. Billing itself as a "21st-century variety store," **Emery's 5 & 10** (865/365-4138, www.emery510.com, 10am-10pm daily) brings the nostalgia of the old country store to life, so expect penny candy, old-fashioned sodas and treats, and lots of yesteryear gifts. Adults will find ample shopping at The Island too, from boutiques like **Earthbound Trading Co.** (865/429-6010, www.earthboundtrading.com, 11am-7pm Mon.-Sat., noon-6pm Sun.) to **Farmhouse Decor & Gifts** (865-366-3076, 10am-10pm daily) to **Natural Comfort Footwear** (865/366-1205, 10am-8pm daily).

RECREATION

There is plenty to get into when you're in Pigeon Forge and Sevierville. Of course, you can hike in the national park, but you can also white-water raft, ride a wild alpine coaster, or even try ziplining.

If you want to get up close and personal with the Smokies and learn about the area from locals, book a tour with **Tennessee Mountain Tours** (153 E. Wears Valley Rd., Ste. 10, Pigeon Forge, 865/455-6981, www.tnmountaintours.com, $60-115, discounts offered for seniors, military, and children 5-11). It has a range of offerings, including the fall foliage Trees of Many Colors tour; Cades Cove tour; full-day Sights of the Smokies; the Vittles & Views tour; and more. Many of the tours include a meal.

One of the most interesting outdoor activities is the **Smoky Mountain Alpine Coaster** (867 Wears Valley Rd., Pigeon Forge, 865/365-5000, www.smokymountainalpinecoaster.com, 10am-11pm Sun.-Thurs., 10am-midnight Fri.-Sat., $15 adults, $15 ages 7-12, $5 ages 3-6). This odd little quasi-roller coaster puts you in a track-mounted sled with an automatic speed control and manual brakes, and then sends you down a 1-mile track, spiraling through tight turns and down a few steepish drops. It looks scary from the parking lot, but the ride is more thrilling than frightening, so give it a go.

At **Adventure Park Zip Lines** (1628 Parkway, Sevierville, 877/287-6946, www.adventureparkatfiveoaks.com, 8am-5pm daily, weather permitting, $85) the zip routes range from a measly 450 feet to a lengthy 2,000 feet. Another zip-line option is **Legacy Mountain Zip Lines** (800 Legacy Vista Dr., Sevierville, 888/869-0289, www.legacymountainziplines.com, 8am-9pm daily, $119), with 4.5 miles of zip lines and some runs as long as 2,500 feet that will take you 450 feet into the air.

With all these mountains around, it's natural to want to get out and explore, but not all of us want to hit the hiking trails. The motor-minded should take a look at what **Smoky Mountain Adventure Tours** (4874 Hooper Hwy., Cosby, 423/625-3643, www.adventuresmokies.com, $250 first 2 riders, $50 for each additional rider up to 4 total) has on tap. They rent side-by-side UTVs (Utility Terrain Vehicles) for guided trips in the Smoky Mountains, though not in the park. Don't let that deter you, as the trails will lead you into the hills and through the hollers and coves beside the park, giving you sweeping views of Mount Cammerer, Mount LeConte, and other landmarks as you explore the woods on four wheels.

SpeedZone Fun Park (3315 S. River Rd., Pigeon Forge, 888/352-7507, www.speedzonefunpark.com, 9am-11pm Mon.-Thurs., 9am-midnight Fri.-Sun., 1 track $10, 3 tracks $20) is one of many go-kart places in Pigeon Forge, but what sets this one apart is the quartet of tracks in one spot. The Slick Track is a fast, paved go-kart track where you drift around every turn. The Tennessee Twister is a curve-riddled wooden track. The Coaster Track has a steep downhill drop at the end for big speed. And the Kids Track is slower and easier; it lets little drivers get behind the wheel.

Pigeon Forge is loaded with mini golf courses (mini golf may be the only activity that rivals go-karting), and no one does it better than **Crave Golf Club** (2925 Parkway, Pigeon Forge, 865/366-3403, www.cravegolf.com,

9am-midnight daily, 1 course $14 adults, $10 children, 2 courses $18 adults, $13 children). It has an indoor course and an outdoor course on the roof, plus a pair of escape rooms, a sweet-shop, and miniature bowling (tiny pins, tiny bowling balls, short alleys—you'll feel like a giant).

The Island in Pigeon Forge (131 The Island Dr., Pigeon Forge, 865/286-0119, www.islandpigeonforge.com, 10am-11pm daily) is a tourist extravaganza. You'll find a half-dozen restaurants and as many snack shops, 35 or so stores selling everything from jerky to puzzles to gems, and rides galore. Rides and activities include the 200-foot-tall Great Smoky Mountain Wheel ($14 adults, $12 seniors 60 and over and military, $9 ages 3-11) and The Islands Ropes Course ($15), plus a mirror maze, a huge arcade, laser tag, an escape room, and more.

FOOD

At The Old Mill Square (175 Old Mill Ave., Pigeon Forge, 877/653-6455, www.old-mill.com, hours vary by store), there's a quaint collection of shops and a pair of restaurants, and the better of them is **The Pottery House Café and Grill** (3341 Old Mill St., Pigeon Forge, 865/453-6002, www.old-mill.com, 11am-9pm Mon.-Fri., 10am-9pm Sat.-Sun., $10-18). They serve everything from steaks to fried chicken livers (served with Buffalo sauce and blue-cheese dressing) and sandwiches. Rather than trout, which is offered by many area eateries, they serve catfish, which is just as good. If you like what you get for dessert, it's likely you can get a whole cake or pie to take home with you. Brunch is served on weekends.

One restaurant, **Feaster's on Teaster's** (2391 Parkway, Pigeon Forge, 865/286-5662, www.feastersonteasters.com, 4pm-9pm Mon.-Thurs., 11am-10pm Fri.-Sat., 11am-9pm Sun., lunch $10-21, dinner $11-48), brings something a little different to the plate: a touch of Native American influence. The Indian Taco, something I first had in Cherokee, features a piece of Indian fry bread topped with ground

bison and taco fixin's. Of course, there's corn-bread and Indian fry bread on the table to get you started. Other dishes include fried catfish, pulled pork, smoked prime rib, smoked chicken, and desserts like seasonal cobblers and fry bread laced with pumpkin. They also bring Native American influences into the decor, a mix of art and artifact reproductions such as wall hangings, headdresses, photos, and paintings. The dining room's sizable—as are the portions—but each table manages to feel fairly private.

A favorite for its German beer and crispy schnitzel is **Wild Bear Tavern** (4236 Parkway, Pigeon Forge, 865/868-0737, www.westgateresorts.com, noon-10pm Thurs.-Mon., $8-18). Lunch and dinner are where it's at here, when you can sit on the deck, enjoy a radler or pilsner, and chow down on a Bavarian bratwurst or traditional schnitzel (pro tip: Get it without the sauce).

★ **Puckett's Grocery & Restaurant** (2480 Parkway, Pigeon Forge, 865/285-0155, www.puckettsgro.com, 8am-9pm Sun.-Thurs., 8am-10pm Fri.-Sat., $11-32) has quite a reputation in Tennessee. No matter which location you go to, you know you're in for a simple yet hearty breakfast, solid meat-and-three meal (featuring your choice of meat and three sides), or great barbecue. You'll also be in for a musical treat if you stick around in the evenings, when things start to get a little lively.

For steaks, oysters, ribs, and seafood, plus a good wine list and prices that won't bust your vacation budget, make your way to **Bullfish Grill** (2441 Parkway, Pigeon Forge, 865/868-1000, 11am-9pm Sun.-Thurs., 11am-10pm Fri.-Sat., $14-31). This is a reservation-worthy dinner out in Pigeon Forge (reservations are especially crucial on busy Fridays in midsummer). Portions are generous, so you may be able to get by with a set of appetizers and a split entrée.

I love food with a story, and **Elvira's Café** (4143 Wears Valley Rd., Sevierville, 865/366-2263, www.elvirascafe.net, 8:30am-2:30pm Tues.-Sat., 5pm-8:30pm Fri.-Sat., $8-16) has a good one. Like a lot of seasonal workers here,

Elvira arrived from elsewhere: Russia. I guess she found the climate and the people agreeable, because after her summer stint was over, she headed home but came back as soon as she could, making this her permanent home and building a fine restaurant to boot. Hearty breakfasts; a great burger and some near-perfect chicken tenders for lunch; and blackened prime rib, chicken and waffles, and fried catfish for dinner give you plenty of menu options to explore.

For the best burger in town, go to ★ **Local Goat** (2167 Parkway, Pigeon Forge, 865/366-3035, www.localgoatpf.com, 11am-11pm daily, $8-26), where the beef is freshly ground and the buns are baked daily. This place is a rarity in the area: It's dedicated to staying as local as possible. That means 22 of its 24 draft beers are from regional brewers, and almost everything is made in-house. Expect a good burger, a great entrée salad, and fresh flavors on every plate.

For breakfast, turn to **Sawyer's Farmhouse Restaurant** (2831 Parkway, Pigeon Forge, 865/366-1090, www.sawyersbreakfast.com, 8am-2pm daily, $7-15). If you haven't figured out the "secret code" of restaurants in these parts, here's a clue: "Farmhouse" means big, filling portions, long tables, and drinks served in a mason jar of some sort. Sawyer's lives up to each and every one of these. Waffles, flapjacks, French toast; platters piled high with fried eggs, biscuits and gravy, and home fries; and even delicate crepes fill out the menu and will fill you up for a day of adventure.

ACCOMMODATIONS

There are several chain hotels in Pigeon Forge and Sevierville, and for the most part, they're all the same. **Econolodge Riverside** (2440 N. Parkway, Pigeon Forge, 865/428-1231, www.econolodge-pigeonforge.com, $65-175) sets itself apart with an indoor pool and a huge stretch of riverfront lawn where you can picnic, grill, hang out under a pavilion, and otherwise laze away the hours in comfort.

A growing number of visitors come to the Smokies with their RV in tow, and **Pigeon Forge Landing RV Resort** (455 Lonesome Valley Rd., Sevierville, 865/446-1500, www.rvoutdoors.com, tents from $56, RVs from $149) stands out as one of the best places to stay. You'll find 149 RV sites and 10 campsites spread across this 37-acre property. Level concrete pads, grills and fire rings, picnic tables, and the all-important full-service hookup—including Wi-Fi—are part of what makes this a great place to stay. The rest includes the scenery—the river runs alongside the resort—the pool, and the easy access to Pigeon Forge, Gatlinburg, and the park.

Glamping has arrived in Pigeon Forge, and one spot to give it a try is **Under Canvas** (1015 Laurel Lick Rd., Pigeon Forge, 865/622-7695, www.undercanvas.com, $250-490), where safari tents and extra-grand suite tents sit on 182 acres just a few minutes from Pigeon Forge, Gatlinburg, and the bypass to the national park. These tents are pricey, but the experience is truly glam. An on-site kitchen cooks up anything but camping grub, beds are plush and well appointed, and, even though you're camping, plenty of USB battery chargers keep your phone and camera ready to take that perfect shot.

For couples heading to the Smokies for a romantic getaway, **Berry Springs Lodge** (2149 Seaton Springs Rd., Sevierville, 865/908-7935, www.berrysprings.com, $225-320) is the move to make. Tastefully decorated in an elegant country style, the lodge has 11 rooms and two suites, including rooms with fireplaces and hot tubs, and the property—all 33 acres of it—is yours to explore. They serve breakfast every morning in the dining room and on the Mountain View Pavilion, and you can use the Pavilion and lovely back deck to enjoy lunch or dinner you've brought in or had delivered (you can order lunch up to four days in advance) or share a drink.

With facilities including a spa, indoor pool, and one- to four-bedroom condo units outfitted with fireplaces, private balconies, full kitchens, en suite laundry, and complimentary Wi-Fi, it's no wonder visitors have been talking about **RiverStone Resort and Spa** (212 Dollywood Ln., Pigeon Forge, 865/908-0660, www.riverstoneresort.com, $250-559). Other amenities like a playground, a bounce pillow, and an outdoor lazy river, plus picnic tables and grills by the Little Pigeon River, keep everyone in the family entertained.

Inspired by Dolly's own family-filled front porch, ★ **Dollywood's DreamMore Resort** (2525 DreamMore Way, Pigeon Forge, 865/365-1900 or 800/365-5996, www.dollywood.com, from $290) aspires to gives guests that same experience. In addition to its 307 rooms, indoor and outdoor pools, restaurants, and views of the Smokies, there are storytelling stations, seasonal and holiday activities, firepits, a homey outdoor movie pavilion, and plenty of things for the kids to do. It's the first hotel on Dollywood property, and staying here has its privileges, like a complimentary shuttle to the park, early Saturday entry to Dollywood, and a complimentary TimeSaver pass, wihch gives you priority spots in line on 10 different rides and attractions. Various room packages—including tickets to Dollywood and Dollywood's Splash Country—are also available.

TRANSPORTATION AND SERVICES

Car

If you've followed the Blue Ridge Parkway to this point, you'll be coming into Gatlinburg along U.S. 441 through the national park; on this route, one minute you're in the park, and the next revolution of the wheels you're in Gatlinburg.

For those arriving from the north or west, I-40 is the most convenient road into town. Leave the interstate at exit 407 and hop on U.S. 66 south, a road that feeds into U.S. 441 and leads into Gatlinburg after you pass through Sevierville and Pigeon Forge (which are, essentially, one continuous town). From Sevierville to Gatlinburg it's just 14 miles, but with traffic it can be a drive of nearly an hour; Pigeon Forge, only 8 miles from Gatlinburg, is a drive of around 20 minutes.

This is the easiest and most heavily traveled route into town from I-40. You can avoid the peak-season crowds by taking exit 435 near Knoxville (an hour away) and following U.S. 321 south into Gatlinburg.

From the east on I-40, the best bet is to take exit 443 and drive along the beautiful Foothills Parkway to U.S. 321 south, and cruise right into town.

Air

The **McGhee Tyson Airport** (TYS, 2055 Alcoa Hwy., Alcoa, TN, 865/342-3000, www.flyknoxville.com), outside Knoxville, is 42 miles from Gatlinburg. From the airport, head south to Maryville on U.S. 129. Once you're in Maryville, take U.S. 321 north to Pigeon Forge, then turn right and take U.S. 441 to Gatlinburg.

Public Transportation

Gatlinburg has a great trolley system that can get you to and from every attraction in Gatlinburg and nearby Pigeon Forge, including Dollywood. The **Gatlinburg Trolley** (865/436-3897, www.gatlinburgtrolley.org, 8:30am-midnight daily, extended hours some holiday and event dates) has more than 100 stops in Gatlinburg alone and will get you to where you need to go. Most routes cost $0.50 per ride; a few costs $1-2. There's also a $2 day pass.

Services

The **Pigeon Forge Welcome Center** (1950 Parkway, 800/251-9100, www.mypigeonforge.com, 8:30am-5pm Mon.-Sat., 1pm-5pm Sun.) is located at traffic light no. 0 on Parkway. Here, and at the **Pigeon Forge Information Center** (traffic light no. 5, 3107 Parkway, 865/453-8574, 8:30am-5pm Mon.-Fri.), you can find information on the area and volunteers ready to help you plan your time here.

The folks at the **Sevierville Chamber of Commerce Visitors Center** (110 Gary Wade Blvd., 865/453-6411 or 888/738-4378, www.visitsevierville.com, 8:30am-5:30pm Mon.-Thurs., 8:30am-5pm Fri.) are ready to help with trip planning or simply pointing you in the right direction and helping you enjoy your vacation.

If you need a hospital, **LeConte Medical Center** (742 Middle Creek Rd., Sevierville, 865/446-7000, www.lecontemedicalcenter. com) is your best bet. There are two police departments here: the **Sevier County Sheriff's Office** (106 W. Bruce St., Sevierville, 865/453-4668) and the **Pigeon Forge Police Department** (3225 Rena St., Pigeon Forge, 865/453-9063).

Knoxville

Perhaps best known among college football fans, Knoxville is the biggest city in East Tennessee and a major travel hub granting access to Great Smoky Mountains National Park and, beyond that, the Blue Ridge Parkway. Unlike Nashville and Memphis, which have national reputations as music towns, Knoxville's comes from the University of Tennessee Volunteers athletics; but the city is also home to the historic Tennessee Theatre and the Bijou Theatre, and it has a very lively music scene of its own.

In 1982, the World's Fair came along and ignited Knoxville's hometown pride, and many residents and business owners saw what Knoxville could become. By the early 2000s, downtown Knoxville resonated with business owners. Restaurants and shops opened in spruced-up buildings from yesteryear. Bars followed, and boutiques flourished. Soon, downtown had turned into what it is today—a fun cultural center for the city.

SIGHTS
★ East Tennessee History Center

In the heart of downtown is a great little museum telling the story of more than 200 years of East Tennessee's history. The **East Tennessee History Center** (601 S. Gay St., 865/215-8830, www.easttnhistory.org, 9am-4pm Mon.-Fri., 10am-4pm Sat., 1pm-5pm Sun., $5 adults, $4 seniors, free ages 16 and under, free admission on Sun.) has exhibits on the Cherokee people, local involvement in skirmishes and battles during the Civil War, notable enslaved and formerly enslaved people from the region, the origins of country music, and Knoxville throughout the years. There are also displays on logging and mining, two vocations important to the region, as well as Oak Ridge National Laboratory, where important work on World War II's Manhattan Project went on in secret.

Also note the wonderful neoclassical Italianate architecture of the building as you enter the museum. It's Knoxville's old Customs House, built in 1874. Since then, it has served several purposes—as a courthouse, post office, and Tennessee Valley Authority offices. Like many buildings around town, it's built with Tennessee marble.

★ Knoxville Museum of Art
The **Knoxville Museum of Art** (1050 World's Fair Park Dr., 865/525-6101, www.knoxart.org, 1pm-5pm Tues.-Sun., donation) is a three-story showcase of the art and artists of East Tennessee. A huge exhibition from renowned glass artist Richard Jolley, *Cycle of Life: Within the Power of Dreams and the Wonder of Infinity,* hangs on the walls and ceiling of the ground floor, and a colorful, impressive element of it—a nebula of colored glass orbs—can be seen as you walk through the museum doors. On the top level, two galleries show historical and contemporary works created by artists from or inspired by East Tennessee. The main level has another pair of galleries with rotating exhibits of national, international, and regional works as well as single-artist shows and themed collections, like the assembly of more than a dozen pieces of amazing blown and cast glass sculptures.

Downtown Knoxville

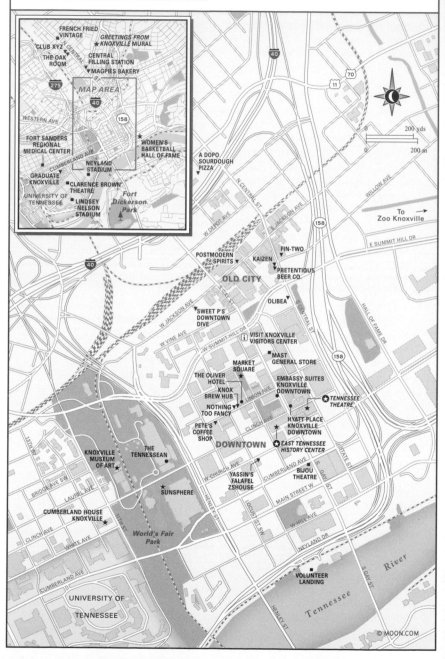

FRENCH FRIED VINTAGE
GREETINGS FROM KNOXVILLE MURAL
CLUB XYZ
CENTRAL FILLING STATION
THE OAK ROOM
MAGPIES BAKERY
MAP AREA
WESTERN AVE
FORT SANDERS REGIONAL MEDICAL CENTER
WOMEN'S BASKETBALL HALL OF FAME
NEYLAND STADIUM
GRADUATE KNOXVILLE
CLARENCE BROWN THEATRE
UNIVERSITY OF TENNESSEE
LINDSEY NELSON STADIUM
Fort Dickerson Park

To → Zoo Knoxville

0   200 yds
0   200 m

A DOPO SOURDOUGH PIZZA
N CENTRAL ST
E JACKSON AVE
E SUMMIT HILL DR
WILLOW AVE
HALL OF FAME DR
FIN-TWO
POSTMODERN SPIRITS
KAIZEN
PRETENTIOUS BEER CO.
OLD CITY
OLIBEA
W JACKSON AVE
SWEET P'S DOWNTOWN DIVE
W VINE AVE
W SUMMIT HILL DR
VISIT KNOXVILLE VISITORS CENTER
MARKET SQUARE
MAST GENERAL STORE
THE OLIVER HOTEL
EMBASSY SUITES KNOXVILLE DOWNTOWN
KNOX BREW HUB
UNION AVE
TENNESSEE THEATRE
NOTHING TOO FANCY
HYATT PLACE KNOXVILLE DOWNTOWN
PETE'S COFFEE SHOP
CLINCH AVE
DOWNTOWN
EAST TENNESSEE HISTORY CENTER
KNOXVILLE MUSEUM OF ART
THE TENNESSEAN
STATE ST
S GAY ST
YASSIN'S FALAFEL ZSHOUSE
W CHURCH AVE
CUMBERLAND AVE
BIJOU THEATRE
SUNSPHERE
MAIN STREET W
HENLEY ST
LOCUST ST SW
CUMBERLAND HOUSE KNOXVILLE
W HILL AVE
BRIDGE AVE SW
LAUREL AVE
NEYLAND DR
CLINCH AVE
WHITE AVE
World's Fair Park
River
CUMBERLAND AVE
VOLUNTEER LANDING
Tennessee
UNIVERSITY OF TENNESSEE
S GAY ST

© MOON.COM

★ Tennessee Theatre

The **Tennessee Theatre** (604 S. Gay St., 865/684-1200, www.tennesseetheatre.com, box office 10am-5pm Mon.-Fri., 10am-2pm Sat., show times and prices vary) is magnificent. In October 1928, this fabulous space opened its doors to rave reviews. The exterior features a classic marquee, and the inside puts any contemporary movie theater or music hall to shame. The Spanish-Moorish-style interior was painstakingly restored to its original grandeur. Today, when you walk into the lobby, huge chandeliers twinkle high above. The ornate ceiling and walls complement the marble floor. Twin staircases lead to the balcony upstairs, and inside the theater, there's more ornate wood and plasterwork. Onstage, there's a gorgeous Wurlitzer organ from the same era as the theater. The best part is that the theater actually has someone who knows how to play it, and play it well. Shows vary from national and international musicians to plays and stage shows to a handful of films.

Sunsphere

When the World's Fair came in 1982, the city was transformed. The most dramatic element is a recognizable symbol of the city. The **Sunsphere** (810 Clinch Ave., 865/215-8160, www.worldsfairpark.org, 9am-10pm daily, free) is a 266-foot-tall tower topped by a huge golden ball. Inside the ball are private offices, a lounge, and a great observation deck that allows a 360-degree view of Knoxville.

Knoxville Murals

Knoxville's love for the arts is on display all over downtown in the form of murals adorning buildings and alleyways. *Postcard from Knoxville* (301 S. Gay St.) by Bobbie Crews, Ken Britton, Walt Fieldsa, Curtis Glover, and Randall Starnes, on the visitors center, is the most obvious, but 43 more murals are scattered around town. Some of the best are Megan Lingerfelt's *Windows to the Smokies* (corner of Gay St. and Wall Ave.), a 50-foot-long mural of the mountains as seen through historic windows, and *Greetings from Knoxville* (1143 N. Broadway) by Greetings Tour and Dominic Corry. Also noteworthy is the collection in Strong Alley (between Union and Wall Aves.), which includes an outstanding mural of Dolly Parton originally created by Colton Valentine, with repairs by Megan Lingerfelt. There are smaller murals like Robert Felker's *Fireflies* (corner of Clinch Ave. and Locust St.) and the long, narrow view of the Tennessee River and Knoxville's bridges called *Mountains* (near the Women's Basketball Hall of Fame; artist unknown). Wander around and discover the murals on your own or use the online map or app (www.visitknoxville.com).

Zoo Knoxville

Zoo Knoxville (3500 Knoxville Zoo Dr., 865/637-5331, www.zooknoxville.org, 9am-2pm Mon.-Wed., 9am-8pm Thurs., 9am-4pm Fri.-Sun., $5 adults, $20 seniors and ages 3-12, $5 parking) has more than 900 animals from all over the world, including the expected and some surprises. There are a number of red pandas (the zoo is a breeding facility for them), a giraffe you can feed, a collection of langurs and gibbons, and Budgie Landing, an enclosed aviary in the Kids Cove Play Zone that's filled with what seem like a million budgies (parakeets) flying around.

The newest addition to Zoo Knoxville is the Clayton Family Amphibian and Reptile Conservation Campus, or ARC for short. At the ARC, visitors can see a number of critters such as Cuban crocodiles, venomous snakes, radiated tortoises, and a dozen Asian turtle species, each of them endangered. As much as the ARC's collection of animals impresses visitors, the mission—to conserve, preserve, protect, and otherwise save these animals from extinction—is even more impressive. The zoo has become a world leader in turtle and tortoise conservation, hatching a clutch of northern spider tortoises (a critically endangered species). Visitors can get a peek at some of these conservation operations, as there are a number of labs, hatching rooms, and similar facilities where workers, tanks, and terrariums are on view.

The MUSE

Adjacent to Zoo Knoxville is **The MUSE** (516 N. Beaman St., 865/594-1494, www. themuseknoxville.org, 9am-4:30pm daily, $10 ages 2-64, $5 seniors, educators, and military), Knoxville's kid-centric science museum. Some of its attractions are the only public planetarium in the city, a space exploration play area called the *U.S.S. Muse,* a tinkerer-maker space, and performance and STEM activity areas. It's a well-done museum and one of those perfect rainy day things for parents and grandparents to have in the entertainment arsenal.

Women's Basketball Hall of Fame

Given the basketball prowess of the University of Tennessee Lady Vols and famed former coach Pat Summitt, Knoxville is a fitting place for the **Women's Basketball Hall of Fame** (700 Hall of Fame Dr., 865/633-9000, www.wbhof.com, 10am-5pm Tues.-Sat. Labor Day-Apr., 10am-5pm Mon.-Sat., May-Labor Day, $8 adults, $6 seniors and ages 6-15). This facility, the only one devoted entirely to women's basketball achievements at all levels, opened in 1999 and celebrates the rich history of women's basketball. The exhibits are more than just a plaque and write-up on Hall of Fame members; there are interactive areas like the basketball court, where you can practice passing and dribbling skills or shoot a few balls at baskets both contemporary and from the earliest days of the game. Other exhibits include displays honoring current NCAA national champions and a set of mannequins dressed in uniforms from over the years. There's also a gift shop where you can pick up basketballs autographed by Hall of Fame members. The building is hard to miss—one end has the world's largest basketball, which appears to be dropping into a net.

Haunted Knoxville Ghost Tours

Haunted Knoxville Ghost Tours (36 Market Sq., 844/943-0109, www. hauntedknoxville.net, $40 adults, $35 ages 9-12, tour dates and times vary, reserve online) is more than just a person walking around telling some "scary" stories filled with local color; these guides offer one of the leading historical and investigation-based ghost tours. They've dug up some juicy, and creepy, stories that reveal a hidden side of this friendly city. And they continue to carry out investigations, bringing with them on every tour a host of tools used to gather information on the paranormal.

ENTERTAINMENT AND EVENTS
Nightlife

Knoxville's brewing scene keeps expanding, and it's getting better with each new brewery that opens. The Knoxville Area Brewers Association has the **Knoxville Ale Trail** (www.knoxvillebrewers.com), which helps you explore the city's beer scene via 25 stops (with more on the way) in and around the city. The Ale Trail works like this: Pick up a passport at one of several locations (like Knox Brew Hub), grab a pint and get a passport stamp at the breweries, and redeem your passport for cash and prizes. Okay, there's no cash, only prizes, but do you really need a reward for visiting breweries?

Downtown, **Knox Brew Hub** (421 Union Ave., 865/454-9688, www.knoxbrewhub. com, 4pm-11pm Mon., 11:30am-11pm Tues.-Thurs., 11:30am-midnight Fri.-Sat., 11:30am-10pm Sun.) serves as your Knoxville Ale Trail Passport Redemption Station and a damn good place to grab a pint and sample some of the city's best brews under one roof. They keep 23 taps flowing and have coolers full of single cans and bottles, as well as food ($2-10) of the sandwich, hot dog, and snack variety. What's good? Ask the bartender. The taps are constantly rotating new brews from breweries from here in town, across the state, and from craft breweries around the nation.

1: Sunsphere **2:** Market Square Farmer's Market **3:** Knoxville's bridge **4:** Tennessee Theatre

Abridged Beer Company (100 Lockett Rd., 865/200-8059, www.abridgedbeer.com, 4pm-10pm Tues.-Thurs., noon-10pm Fri.-Sat.) serves a little bit of everything at its flagship spot on Lockett Road: IPAs, goses, Berliner weisse beers, rice-based lagers, and more. And the kitchen puts out some snacks ($6-15), like fried green tomatoes, wings, pretzels, and sandwiches, that will help you work your way through the beer menu. Abridged Beer's brews are very good, but I'm a fan of sour beers, and their outpost, **The Oak Room** (109 W. Anderson Ave., 865/444-1949, 3pm-10pm Thurs.-Sat.), is one of my favorite places to grab a drink in Knoxville. Charcuterie boards, sandwiches, and flatbreads ($9-22) come out of a tiny kitchen, but everything seems tiny here because they have barrels of beer stacked to the ceiling. The beer is fantastic, and the sours run from the mildly tart beers that are good introductions to the genre all the way to some mouth-puckering brews. If you're a fan of sour beers or just want to see what all the fuss is about, this is your stop.

One stop on the Knoxville Ale Trail is **Crafty Bastard Brewery** (6 Emory Pl., 865/333-4760, www.craftybastardbrewery. com, 5pm-10pm Mon., 4pm-10pm Tues.-Thurs., 4pm-11pm Fri., 2pm-11pm Sat., 2pm-9pm Sun.), which has a reputation for being one of the more experimental breweries in Knoxville. Their lineup—complete with an extra-roasty Imperial Milk Stout (a cocoa- and chili-infused porter), a dill pickle sour, and even weirder things on deck—puts them on the fringe of most breweries here, but their selection of IPAs and double IPAs makes up for it. They also have food trucks every night of the week (all feature some kind of vegan or vegetarian option) and music most Friday nights. Their second location, **Crafty West** (9937 Kingston Pike, 865/770-8743), is only open on weekends.

Before you take a long, appreciative sip of your beer at **Pretentious Beer Co.** (131 S. Central Ave., 865/851-7693, www. pretentiousbeerco.com, 3pm-9pm Mon.-Thurs., 3pm-10pm Fri., noon-10pm Sat., noon-9pm Sun.), take a long, appreciative look at the glass: They make their own glassware at the hot shop next door. And what's in the glass is as excellent as the glass itself. A small brewery, Pretentious manages to cook up a wide array of beers without missing a note on any of them. Smoke on the Lager, a smoked beer, dishes up everything German beer fans might hope to find at centuries-old breweries in Bamberg. Brews in the Soda Shop series— beers devoted to the microcosm of fruited sour and sour-adjacent beers—hit with the right balance of fruit and tart, and the IPAs and DIPAs show off the hops without devolving into bitterness. Next door you can catch a glass-blowing demo and pick up a memento or two from the small shop there. Local musicians like Kelsey Walker perform on the back patio several nights a week, so your ears are in for a treat too.

Knoxville has more than breweries. Right around the corner from Pretentious is a stop on the Tennessee Whiskey Trail (www. tnwhiskeytrail.com): **PostModern Spirits** (205 W. Jackson Ave., 865/437-3190, www. postmodernspirits.com, 4pm-11pm Mon.-Fri., noon-11pm Sat., noon-10pm Sun.). In the tasting room and cocktail lounge, you can sample flights of their spirits, which include a whiskey, vodka, a trio of gins, and several liqueurs. I spent a long afternoon there and tasted just about everything on the shelf; there wasn't a bad sip in the bunch. The gins were outstanding but even better were the amari (that's plural for amaro), herbal Italian liqueurs (you may know Montenegro, Fernet-Branca, Cynar, or Averna). The depth of flavor and the variety of ingredients made for an interesting tasting, and the Amaro Alpino—a traditional, orange zest-laced amaro aged in an oak barrel—was especially memorable. Stop by for a tasting and a cocktail, then grab a bottle to take home; it's what I did.

At **The EDGE of Knoxville** (7211 Kingston Pike, 865/602-2094, 5pm-3am daily), you'll find performances of almost any kind. Live music, drag shows, karaoke? They got it. Trivia, comedy, bar games? Got

Tennessee's Unsung Music Town

Knoxville gets short shrift when folks talk about Tennessee music. Ever eclipsed by Nashville and overlooked by bluegrass and mountain string band lovers for spots like Gatlinburg and Pigeon Forge, Knoxville is often forgotten. But no more. The music scene in this hip Southern town is lively and growing livelier by the minute. Bands like metal act Whitechapel, bluesy The Black Cadillacs, pop act Jacob Whitesides, and country acts like Ashley Monroe and Kenny Chesney have been increasing the profile of Knoxville artists, playing at festivals large and small and – in the case of Chesney – earning a reputation that extends far beyond the South.

All across town you'll find buskers playing on the street and bands tucked into restaurants and bars. There are free concerts on Market Square during the summer. Jam sessions pop up, and musicians flow freely from one impromptu band to another until they find the perfect fit. Two historic venues—The **Tennessee Theatre** (the state's official theater, and a stunning place to see a band) and the **Bijou Theatre**—host concerts with clockwork regularity.

Music festivals like **Big Ears Festival** (www.bigearsfestival.com), **Smoky Mountain Music Fest** (www.smmfestival.com), and **Southern Skies Music Festival** (www.southernskiesmusicfestival.com) celebrate the sounds of the city and bring in visiting bands and music fans from all over.

Make it a point while you're in town to take in one of the daily free shows at **WDVX-FM** (www.wdvx.com), where the noontime Blue Plate Special concert series brings in local and regional acts to play for a live radio broadcast in front of a studio audience.

that too. Toss in friendly people and good drinks, and it works. Another lively LGBTQ+ gathering place is **Club XYZ** (1215 N. Central St., 865/637-4999, 7pm-3am daily, generally free but some nights and events have a small cover), where there's karaoke (Sun. and Wed.), The Queenz Bingo (Tues.), drag shows, plenty of dancing, great DJs, and a cool and welcoming vibe.

Peter Kern Library (407 Union Ave., 865/521-0050, www.theoliverhotel.com, 5pm-midnight Mon.-Thurs., 5pm-midnight Fri., 4pm-1am Sat., 4pm-midnight Sun.), the bar in The Oliver Hotel, names the drinks after literary characters. The bar is modeled after a library: To read the menu, you have to crack open an old book. It's a cozy spot with boozy and flavorful cocktails—what's not to love?

Performing Arts

The **Bijou Theatre** (803 S. Gay St., 865/522-0832, www.knoxbijou.org, ticket prices vary) is one of Knoxville's most important venues for live musical performances. Everyone from the Marx Brothers and Dolly Parton to The Ramones and Dave Matthews has played

here, and the audience at one time included President Andrew Jackson. The Bijou (well, the building anyway) dates to 1817 and has been a hotel and tavern, a place for social gatherings, and an object of some consternation for its myriad owners until it finally opened as a theater in 1908. A vaudeville stage for a long time (with a rare-for-the-time policy of admitting Black patrons to the gallery seating), the Bijou showed films on occasion, but that stopped when the Tennessee Theatre opened up the street. The builders of the Tennessee bought the Bijou, then sold it with one caveat: the Bijou couldn't be used as a theater for the next five years. After various incarnations, the Bijou reopened as a fully renovated theater in 2006.

The Concourse at The International (944 Blackstock Ave., 865/851-7878, www.concourseknox.com, showtimes and prices vary) brings in musical acts from heavy metal to rap to DJs and more. It's a cool building, once an International Harvester tractor showroom and then home to the Great Atlantic Shoe Company, that is now a concert and events venue and a good example of adaptive reuse in Knoxville. Another great place to see a show is at the **Clarence Brown Theatre** (1714 Andy Holt Ave., 865/974-5161, www.clarencebrowntheatre.com, tickets through www.knoxvilletickets.com, $18-45), home of the University of Tennessee Knoxville's theater department, which puts on several productions a year.

Festivals and Events

Knoxville holds several great events throughout the year, and two good ones are **Big Ears Festival** (www.bigearsfestival.com, Mar., general admission from $65, some individual events ticketed separately), a celebration of music and movies, and the **Tennessee Valley Fair** (3301 E. Magnolia Ave., 865/215-1471, www.tnvalleyfair.org, mid-Sept., $8 adults, $6 ages 6-11, concerts $10-100), where you'll find a traditional agricultural fair, but bigger, with funnel cakes and other fair food galore, rides, and concerts.

As with most hip cities, beer's big here, and the **Knoxville Brewfest** (www.knoxvillebrewfest.com, Aug., $20-50), a one-day, two-session tasting event at World's Fair Park, features a whopping 65-ish breweries and beer-associated exhibitors from all across the country. Come hungry in September when the **Big Kahuna Wing Festival** (www.bkwfestival.com, $20-30, VIP $200) brings dozen of wing-cooking competitors and more than 15,000 pounds of wings to Worlds Fair Park. You'll want to spring for those VIP tickets, since that's the only way to get unlimited wings and drinks.

SHOPPING

Market Square provides a central square (technically a rectangle) around which people can gather. Just one block off Gay Street, this excellent little shopping and dining district is always busy. Summer concerts, buskers, and a small fountain for the kids to play in draw folks here; sculptures liven up sections of the square and adjacent park; and the variety of people walking by and stores to peruse make it easy to kill time while waiting for your table to be ready. There are a half-dozen restaurants on the square, and close to a dozen shops, including **Earth to Old City** (22 Market Sq., 865/522-8270, www.earthtooldcity.com, 10am-9pm Sun.-Thurs., 10am-10pm Fri.-Sat.), which carries all sorts of odd and funky home decor, some of which may be more at home in a dorm room than your house; **Earthbound Trading Co.** (34 Market Sq. Suite 101, 865/219-5504, 11am-8pm Mon.-Sat., 11am-6pm Sun.), carrying clothing, home goods, and gifts; and **Fizz** (27 Market Sq., 865/851-7990, www.fizzmarketsquare.com, 11am-8pm Mon.-Fri., 10am-8pm Sat., 10am-5pm Sun.), a boutique with contemporary bohemian clothing, locally made jewelry, and some great Tennessee-themed jewelry and accessories. The **Market Square Farmer's Market** (10am-1pm Wed. May-mid-Nov., 9am-1pm Sat. mid-July-late Nov., 10am-1pm Sat. early-Dec.) shows up in late spring, bringing with it dozens of farmers and craftspeople selling their wares, edible and otherwise.

On a prominent spot on South Gay Street, the **Mast General Store** (402 S. Gay St., 865/546-1336, www.mastgeneralstore.com, 10am-6pm Mon.-Thurs., 10am-9pm Fri.-Sat., 11am-6pm Sun.) has a little bit of everything, like a good country store should. In keeping with the look and feel of the original location (in Valle Crucis, North Carolina, deep in the Blue Ridge Mountains), you can pick up everything from a sack full of penny candy to a cast-iron skillet to a housewarming gift or some new duds. There's even camping gear and rugged outdoor wear.

A barista turned me on to one of the coolest vintage shops in Knoxville, **French Fried Vintage** (1520 N. Central St., 865/599-8556, noon-6pm Mon.-Sat., noon-5pm Sun.). This is no "grabbed a box at an estate sale and slapped a price tag on everything" vintage shop; items are all handpicked and selected for their vintage chic cred. Size-inclusive clothes; knickknacks and tchotchkes; and a staff that's into the cool finds vintage offers made this a favorite. And it's in Happy Holler, a hip neighborhood with other vintage shops, breweries, restaurants, and clubs to check out.

Nothing Too Fancy (435 Union Ave., 865/951-2916, www.nothingtoofancy.com, 10am-9pm Mon.-Sat., 11am-6pm Sun.) has some very neat T-shirts and other silk-screened goods designed by local artists. Reflecting the culture, in-jokes, and vibe of Knoxville, the shirts are fun, even for those not in the know.

Nostalgia (5214 Homberg Dr., 865/584-0832, www.nostalgiaknoxville.com, noon-5pm daily) calls itself a "vintique market," as they sell both vintage items and antiques. Portmanteau aside, it's a cool shop. Inside, you'll find mid-century modern furniture, vinyl records, vintage clothing, shabby chic furniture, and more from 30-plus vendors whose booths are full of some pretty awesome treasures. And if you're into treasures, take a look at what **Architectural Antics** (820 N. Broadway, 865/411-4838, www.architecturalanticstn.com, noon-5pm Tues.-Fri. and Sun., 10am-5pm Sat.) has on hand. In addition to concert posters, retro mirrors and lamps, and other soft goods, they have a vast collection of salvaged hardware, from corbels and cornices to claw-foot tubs and doors.

RECREATION

The star of Knoxville's recreational scene is **Ijams Nature Center** (2915 Island Home Ave., 865/577-4717, www.ijams.org, grounds 8am-dusk daily, visitors center 10am-6pm daily). This 315-acre urban wilderness is laced with hiking and single-track mountain biking trails, the only outdoor rock-climbing area in Knoxville, and former quarries to explore on foot or even paddle around; it's also dog-friendly. The vast, wild space is a strange thing so close to the city, but people love it. At any time of any day, there are walkers, hikers, trail runners, bikers, families, couples, and singles on the trails here. From Ijams Nature Center, you can connect with a larger, nearly contiguous loop some 40 miles long. Grab a map when you come or download one and plan your route ahead of time, or you can just bring some water and wander.

World's Fair Park (963 World's Fair Park Dr. SW, www.worldsfairpark.org) is the best city park in Knoxville. This 10-acre park has walking paths, a small lake, open grassy spaces, soccer fields, fountains, and a gorgeous stream running right down the middle. It's the home of the Sunsphere and Tennessee Amphitheatre, and at the north end of the park, past a fantastically large fountain, is a 4,200-square-foot playground. The playground and fountain get pretty crowded with kids, but there are other places you can go if you're traveling without a few of your own.

The **University of Tennessee Knoxville** (www.utk.edu), or UT, has a loyal (some say rabid) fan base. UT fields more than a dozen varsity-level teams including football (six national championships), men's and women's basketball (eight national championships for the women's team), soccer, rowing, volleyball, and more. If you want to cheer on the UT Volunteers (the Vols, if you want to sound like a local), **tickets** (865/656-1200, www.allvols.com) are available for football season (Sept.-late Nov.), basketball season (Nov.-Mar.), tennis (Sept.-Apr.), soccer and volleyball (Aug.-mid-Nov.), and swimming and diving (Sept.-late Feb.). Men's basketball tickets cost $15-45, women's basketball $10-30. Football tickets are both difficult to come by and pricey, as most games sell out or come close; some tickets fetch upward of $1,000 a seat on resale markets. The football team plays at **Neyland Stadium** (1300 Phillip Fulmer Way), basketball at **Thompson-Boling Arena** (1600 Phillip Fulmer Way), baseball at **Lindsey Nelson Stadium** (1511 Pat Head Summitt St.), and softball at **Sherri Parker Lee Stadium** (2323 Stephenson Dr.). More information on facilities and teams is available at www.utsports.com.

Of course, UT is about more than just sports. Campus is lovely and can make for a great walk, and the **UT Gardens** (2518 Jacob Dr., sunrise-sunset daily) are filled with blooms spring, summer, and fall. The garden paths wander among trees and plantings wild and landscaped.

FOOD

Knoxville Food Tours (865/201-7270, www. knoxvillefoodtours.com, $99) shows off some of the best spots to drink and dine in downtown Knoxville. Tour dates are Thursday, Friday, and Saturday afternoons and evenings, but custom tours are available any day. On these 2.5-3-hour tours you'll walk around a mile through downtown and Old City with Paula Johnson, a local historian and author, visiting between four and six spots where they'll ensure you're well fed.

★ **Kaizen** (157 S. Central St., 865/409-4444, www.knoxkaizen.com, 11:30am-3pm and 5pm-10pm Tues.-Sat., $4-20) blends the Japanese *izakaya* style of small-plate dining with Japanese, Chinese, and Thai dishes that occasionally show a Southern streak. The eggplant steamed bun was one of the most delicious bites of food I've had in a while, followed only by the Nashville Man Bun (a fried hot chicken thigh with house pickles). The dan dan noodles are awesomely good and ideally spicy.

Oliver Royale (5 Market Sq., 865/622-6434, www.oliverroyale.com, 4pm-10pm Mon.-Thurs., 10am-10pm Fri., 9am-10pm Sat.-Sun., $12-65) extends the experience of staying at The Oliver Hotel to the dining room. Eat inside, at the bar, or on the patio, and enjoy a menu loaded with French technique and international ingredients. You can make a meal of a few appetizers (the Caribbean curry shrimp and the beef tenderloin tartare are solid options) or go for something like the short rib with smoked gouda grits and collards, the hoisin- and sorghum-lacquered pork chop, or a fantastic pasta dish. Brunch ($5-15) is available Friday-Sunday.

I've been dreaming of the breakfast I had at ★ **OliBea** (211 S. Central St., 865/200-5450, www.olibeaoldcity.com, 7am-1pm Wed.-Fri., 8am-2pm Sat.-Sun., $9-14) at least once a week since I ate there. The Tennessee Benedict—a biscuit topped with country ham (from their sister spot, a butcher shop called HenHock) and a poached egg, served with smashed potatoes—has lived rent free in my mind for a while now. Maybe it was the perfect cup of Honeybee Coffee (a local roaster) or the absolutely textbook execution of the biscuit, the ham, and those potatoes, or the positive energy of the place, but I'm ready to go back tomorrow.

There are a few food truck parks around Knoxville. If you're not familiar, a food truck park provides space for several food trucks to pull in and serve the crowds, who've come for the picnic tables and the little bottle shop you'll find in a few. **Central Filling Station** (900 N. Central St., www.knoxfoodpark. com, 5pm-9pm Wed.-Thurs., 11am-10pm Fri.-Sat., 11am-9pm Sun.) was the first full-service food truck park in the state, and it draws a crowd. Typically, 3-4 trucks show up for lunch, and 4-6 will show up for dinner, giving you a real variety of cuisines and price ranges. **Southside Garage** (1014 Sevier Ave., 865/696-9551, www.southsidegarageknox. com, 4pm-11pm Tues.-Fri., noon-11pm Sat.-Sun.) has a resident food truck, Oakwood BBQ, and they regularly have guest trucks on-site too. **The Cave Food Truck Park** (9036 Middlebrook Pike, 865/985-0326, www.heybearcafe.com, 11am-9pm Sun.-Thurs., 11am-9:30pm Fri.-Sat.) updates their food truck schedule on social media, but they always have an assortment of trucks—and bubble tea—on hand. And **35 North** (11321 Kingston Pike, 865/671-3535, www.the-35north.com, 11am-10pm Sun.-Wed., 11am-11pm Thurs., 11am-1am Fri.-Sat.) has it all: food trucks, local beer on tap, a solid cocktail and whiskey collection. At all of these spots and at others around town, you'll find trucks with barbecue, Thai food, tacos and burritos, desserts and sweets and iced treats, Greek food, burgers, fried chicken, and all the food truck things. Visit Knoxville keeps an updated list of area food trucks online at www. visitknoxville.com.

House-made pasta and seasonal Italian

food are on order at **Emilia Italian** (16 Market Sq., 865/313-2472, www.emiliaknox. com, 5pm-9:30pm Tues.-Thurs., 5pm-10pm Fri.-Sat., 5pm-9pm Sun., $12-34) on Market Square. Genovese-style fisherman's stew, pan-roasted salmon, a pork blade steak, orecchiette with Bolognese ragù, sensational gnocchi, and other pastas such as campanelle and fusilli round out the dinner offerings. Don't forget dessert, where the panna cotta and semifreddo (a type of frozen dessert) are in a perpetual competition for best way to end your meal.

When you have a hankering for falafel, hummus, or other Mediterranean flavors, look no farther than the restaurant *Reader's Digest* called "the nicest place in America," **Yassin's Falafel House** (706 Walnut St., 865/219-1462, 11am-9pm Mon.-Sat., $5-12). There are only a few things you can get, but I always consider that to be a good sign. It means they are perfecting everything on the small menu, and Yassin's has perfected, or come close to perfecting, the falafel. Whether you get falafel (just go ahead and get falafel), chicken, gyro, or vegetables in a sandwich or salad or on a plate, you'll be hooked and you'll be back. They also have a location in **West Knoxville** (159 N. Peters Rd., 865/247-7567) if you're out that way and hungry.

Knoxville is home to my current favorite pizza, the wondrous creations at ★ **A Dopo Sourdough Pizza** (516 Williams St., 865/321-1297, www.adopopizza.com, 5pm-9pm or later daily, $11-20). Red and white pizzas, all on a hand-tossed sourdough crust, fly out of the kitchen with alarming speed—seriously, my pie hit the table only a minute or two after my salad—and it's so good you'll make it disappear just as quickly. Ingredients like kale, *'nduja* (a type of cured pork sausage), Castelvetrano olives, and house-made mozzarella make the pies more interesting than anything you'll find elsewhere.

Sweet P's Downtown Dive (410 W. Jackson Ave., 865/281-1738, www.sweetpbbq. com, 11am-9pm Tues.-Sun., $5-20) serves killer barbecue. It's that simple. Owner and pitmaster Chris Ford got a taste for barbecue when he was a touring musician, and since then he's perfected his 'cue. Downtown Dive lets you get your fix of ribs, brisket, pulled pork, and sides without venturing far from the city's heart.

Pete's Coffee Shop (540 Union Ave., 865/523-2860, www.petescoffeeshop.com, 6:30am-2pm Mon.-Fri., 7am-2pm Sat., $2-8) is a diner that's dirt cheap and super tasty. The French toast is exceptional, as are the pancakes, and for lunch, Pete's Supreme (ham and melted swiss cheese on a hoagie) is excellent, as is the patty melt.

The folks at **SoKno Taco Cantina** (3701 Sevierville Pike, 865/851-8882, www.soknota. co, 11am-10pm daily, $4-10) make some bold claims about their food: "People lose their minds" for it; their selection of drinks is "more than you need." I like their attitude, and I like that they back it up. The menu is pretty basic—tacos, tamales, burritos, and quesadillas made with chicken, cod, shrimp, steak, chorizo, carnitas, or tofu—but they deliver on the plate. And those drinks? True to the boast, there's a great draft, bottle, and can selection of beer.

Central Flats and Taps (1204 N. Central St., 865/247-0392, www.flatsandtaps.com, 11am-3am Tues.-Sat., 11am-1am Sun.-Mon., $9-12), in the hip Happy Holler area of Knoxville, serves shareable pizzas as well as salads, wraps, wings, and other starters, and draft beer from their 27 taps. It's fun, tasty, and lively, and the location puts you right across the street from Club XYZ and around the corner from a few breweries and places to hang out.

There are several good places to get sushi in Knoxville, but the best might just be **Fin-Two** (112 S. Central Ave., 865/437-3105, www.fin-two.com, 11am-10pm Mon.-Fri., noon-10pm Sat., $4-14). Choices include nigiri, sashimi, and maki—in traditional and wildly inventive forms (the Appalachian Trail Roll has lettuce, carrot, shiitake mushroom, tofu, apple, avocado, and fennel)—and they have a yakitori (a type of skewered and grilled chicken) menu that serves as a great introduction to this slice of Japanese cuisine. Try the grilled corn with miso butter and *negi* (a type of onion), the *kakuni* (pork belly with shoyu and negi), and the short rib with wasabi mustard. Then order a couple of rolls just to be on the safe side.

Wild Love Bakehouse (1625 N. Central St., 865/200-8078, www.wildlovebakehouse. com, 8am-2pm Wed.-Sun., $3-12) bakes up breads and pastries every day and keeps a fresh, rotating menu. Every day the menu is a little different, so you might find a butter croissant one day and a rye reuben open-face croissant the next, or blueberries or strawberries adorning or filling a pastry. You might even find olive oil cake, tarts, and pies, or, if you're lucky, the rich Breton pastry called kouign-amann. If you're just in it for the cookies and other sweets, then stop by **Magpies Bakery** (846 N. Central St., 865/673-0471, www.magpiescakes.com, 10am-4pm Mon. and Sat., 10am-5:30pm Tues.-Fri.). The cookies and cupcakes are to die for, and I imagine that translates to their full-size cakes.

ACCOMMODATIONS

★ **The Oliver Hotel** (407 Union Ave., 865/521-0050, www.theoliverhotel.com, $165-410), an outstanding boutique hotel, has impeccable service and amazing rooms—everything is done to a luxurious, but not ostentatious, level. When you first find the hotel, you'll likely walk right past it because it blends in with the rest of the block almost seamlessly. Originally built in 1876 as a bakery, it was converted into a hotel for the 1982 World's Fair. There are 24 guest rooms with wet bars, coffee service, and fabulous bedding.

The Tennessean (531 Henley St., 865/232-1800, www.thetennesseanhotel.com, $209-599) overlooks World's Fair Park and offers rooms that are truly sumptuous. Whether you stay in an ordinary room or in the Governor's Suite ($3,000), you'll find luxe linens, tasteful decoration, and an attentive staff.

At ★ **Graduate Knoxville** (1706 Cumberland Ave., 865/437-5500 or 888/485-2881, www.graduatehotels.com, $202-280), you're just steps away from the University of Tennessee campus, and you'll find plenty of home-team pride in everything from the keycards to the decor; it's not overdone, but you'll definitely know who to root for on game day. Rooms are spacious and just upscale enough to be a great value for the price. If you need coffee or a bite to eat, the in-house coffee shop and restaurant, Saloon 16, which pays homage to UT and NFL great Peyton Manning, will do the trick.

Also near the UT campus is **Cumberland House Knoxville** (1109 White Ave., 865/971-4663, www.hilton.com, $190-450), a Hilton Tapestry Collection hotel. One block from campus, one block from World's Fair Park, a short walk from the Knoxville Museum of Art, and supremely easy to get to, it's a great hotel.

Embassy Suites Knoxville Downtown (507 S. Gay St., 865/544-8502, www.hilton. com, $220-275) is, as promised by the name, downtown, right around the corner from Market Square, a location that makes it a perfect base from which to explore the city. They've got a coffee shop and a Topgolf Swing Suite (where simulators let you practice your swing, play a round, or kick a soccer ball, regardless of the weather) for guests and visitors, and the hotel is walkable to all the restaurants and things to do downtown and in the Old City. Just down the street, **Hyatt Place Knoxville Downtown** (530 S. Gay St., 865/544-9977, www.hyatt.com, $190-290) has an excellent location near Market Square, the Tennessee Theatre, and all that the core of Knoxville has to offer. The hotel has 165 rooms and a great rooftop bar (go for the views, if nothing else), and it's pet-friendly.

TRANSPORTATION AND SERVICES
Car

Driving to Knoxville is easy. If you've followed the Blue Ridge Parkway to Great Smoky Mountains National Park, just stay on U.S. 441, which runs right into downtown. Coming from the east or west via I-40, take exit 388 for Gay Street.

From Asheville, take I-40 west for 116 miles to Knoxville, a two-hour drive. From Charlotte, where you'll find a major airport, take U.S. 74 west to I-40 west to Knoxville, a four-hour drive. Alternatively, take the same route from Charlotte but leave I-40 toward U.S. 19 and Cherokee, then take U.S. 441/ Highway 71 through the national park to Knoxville.

From the south, I-75 offers a direct route to Knoxville from Chattanooga, Tennessee (1 hour and 45 minutes), and Atlanta (3 hours). From the west, I-40 is a direct route from Nashville to Knoxville (2 hours and 45 minutes). From the north, Knoxville is accessible via I-81.

Air

McGhee Tyson Airport (TYS, 2055 Alcoa Hwy., Alcoa, 865/342-3000, www. flyknoxville.com) is 20 minutes south of Knoxville in Alcoa, Tennessee. You can get here on U.S. 129. From I-40, take exit 386-B to U.S. 129 south; it's 12 miles to the airport. Airlines serving McGhee Tyson include Allegiant, American Airlines, Delta, Frontier, and United.

If you need taxi service between the airport and Knoxville, **Discount Taxi** (865/755-5143) and **World Class Taxi** (865/406-91050) are two of the car services you can call if you're not using ride-share.

Bus

As with cities large and small, Knoxville has a **Greyhound Bus Station** (100 E. Magnolia Ave., 865/524-0369, tickets 800/231-2222, www.greyhound.com). It's not far from downtown, and taxis and ride-share services make it easy to get from the bus station to your accommodations.

Public Transportation

Once you're in town, there is plenty to walk to. **Knoxville Trolley Lines** (301 Church Ave., 865/215-7800, www.katbus.com, free), operated by Knoxville Area Transit, also run throughout downtown. Check online or call for current schedules and routes.

Services

The **Knoxville Visitors Center** (301 S. Gay St., 865/523-7263 or 800/727-8045, www. visitknoxville.com, 8:30am-5pm Mon.-Fri., 9am-5pm Sat., noon-4pm Sun.) is what visitors centers should be. It has the expected rack of maps and helpful volunteers on hand to answer questions, but what sets it apart are the gift shop filled with locally made art and foodstuffs, a kids' corner, coffee, and a radio station. This is the only visitors center I know of where you can watch a free concert every day at lunch or listen to it as a live radio broadcast.

If you need medical care, Knoxville has more than a half-dozen clinics and hospitals. The **University of Tennessee Medical Center** (1924 Alcoa Hwy., 865/305-9000, www.utmedicalcenter.org) is a 581-bed teaching hospital, and **Fort Sanders Regional Medical Center** (1901 Clinch Ave., 865/541-1111, www.fsregional.com) is conveniently located downtown.

North Carolina Gateways

A sense of otherworldliness and of magic rises up from these hills like the mist that envelops the Smoky Mountains.

Maybe it's the way the land is folded and rumpled like a quilt at the foot of the bed, or perhaps it's some element of Cherokee mythology come to life. After all, this is the ancestral home of the Cherokee and the present home of the Eastern Band of Cherokee Indians; it's possible that something in these hills and hollows remains, imprinted from their collective memories. In towns like Cherokee, the magic is thick, but it's also present in Bryson City, throughout the Nantahala National Forest, and along Maggie Valley, calling to visitors and enchanting them year after year.

The town of Cherokee sits on the Qualla Boundary at the edge of

Highlights

Look for ★ to find recommended sights, activities, dining, and lodging.

★ **Experience Cherokee Culture:** Art, history, and millennia-old culture are on display at a museum, gallery, living history village, and long-running outdoor drama in the heart of the Eastern Band of Cherokee Indians (page 153).

★ **Ride the Great Smoky Mountains Railroad:** Steam and diesel locomotives carry passengers along mountain rivers and lakes on sightseeing tours, moonshine tastings, and more (page 164).

★ **Raft the Nantahala River Gorge:** This steep gorge where Olympic athletes train is an unbeatable place for a day of white-water rafting that will leave you breathless (page 166).

★ **Fly-Fish on the Tuckasegee River:** Several outfitters can hook anglers up for a great day on the river, which conveniently flows right through Bryson City (page 166).

★ **Hike the Joyce Kilmer Memorial Forest:** This 3,800-acre forest is full of old-growth trees that show what the Smoky Mountains were like a century ago (page 171).

★ **Visit John C. Campbell Folk School:** This leader in promoting American craft heritage nurtures new generations of artists, securing the future of Appalachian traditions (page 174).

★ **Tour the Biltmore Estate:** Asheville's most popular attraction is not only an awe-inspiring palace and symbol of the Gilded Age but also home to a popular winery and a collection of great restaurants and shops, all in a beautiful riverside setting (page 176).

Great Smoky Mountains National Park. Make no mistake: This isn't a reservation; it's ancestral Cherokee land. The Cherokee are proud of the small group of ancestors who refused relocation and the travesty of the Trail of Tears, choosing instead to hide in these hills, wage a guerilla war, and ultimately win the right to set up a Cherokee government.

Other towns here abut the national park or are just a few miles away, and the Cherokee influence is felt everywhere you go. In this altogether lovely place, the mountains are tall, the roads winding, and the streams downright picturesque. It's a place people are proud to call home, whether their family has been here for 10 years or 10,000.

PLANNING YOUR TIME

To make the most of your time, spend **two days** in Cherokee (one for the casino, one for the cultural sights), set aside at least **one day** to visit the national park, and use **one day** for exploring the small towns. If camping is your thing, there are plenty of campsites in the park and some very good ones on the outskirts; if it's not, there are lovely B&Bs and funky older hotels. A more luxurious experience can be had at Harrah's Cherokee Casino.

Maggie Valley

Maggie Valley is a vacation town from the bygone era of long family road trips in wood-paneled station wagons. Coming down the mountain toward Maggie Valley, you'll pass an overlook that, on a morning when the mountains around Soco Gap are looped with fog, is surely one of the most beautiful vistas in the state.

SIGHTS AND ENTERTAINMENT

In a state with countless attractions for automotive enthusiasts, Maggie Valley's **Wheels Through Time Museum** (62 Vintage Ln., 828/926-6266, www.wheelsthroughtime. com, 10am-5pm Thurs.-Mon. Apr.-late Nov., $15 adults, $12 seniors over 65, $7 ages 6-14, free ages 5 and under) stands out as one of the most fun—and it's the only one, to my knowledge, to have Jason Momoa and Mike Wolfe visit. A dazzling collection of nearly 300 vintage motorcycles and a fair number of cars are on display, including rarities like a 1908 Indian, a 1914 Harley-Davidson, military motorcycles from both world wars, and some gorgeous postwar bikes. The collection, which dates mostly to before 1950, is maintained in working order—almost every one of the bikes is revved up from time to time.

Elevated Mountain Distilling Co. (3732 Soco Rd., 828/944-0766, www. elevatedmountain.com, 10am-7pm Mon.-Sat., tastings and tours $5) is right on the main drag in Maggie Valley, but if you decide to go for more than a quick sample or two, bring a designated driver because the moonshine—flavored or straight—is fiery. Tastings include a sample of five of the distilling company's spirits. On the fourth Saturday of each month, Elevated Mountain hosts a bluegrass jam and, in September, a small music festival.

SHOPPING

As you might expect, Maggie Valley has its fair share of touristy T-shirt shops and places where you can pick up some fudge and a refrigerator magnet. **Maggie Mountaineer Crafts** (2394 Soco Rd., 828/926-3129, www. maggiemountaineercrafts.com, 10am-5pm Sat.-Sun., Jan.-Mar.; 9am-5pm daily, Apr. and Nov.-Dec.; 8am-6pm daily, May-Oct.) and its attached sister store, **A Day in the Valley,**

Previous: Joyce Kilmer Memorial Forest; Museum of the Cherokee Indian; fall color in the Pisgah National Forest

North Carolina Gateways

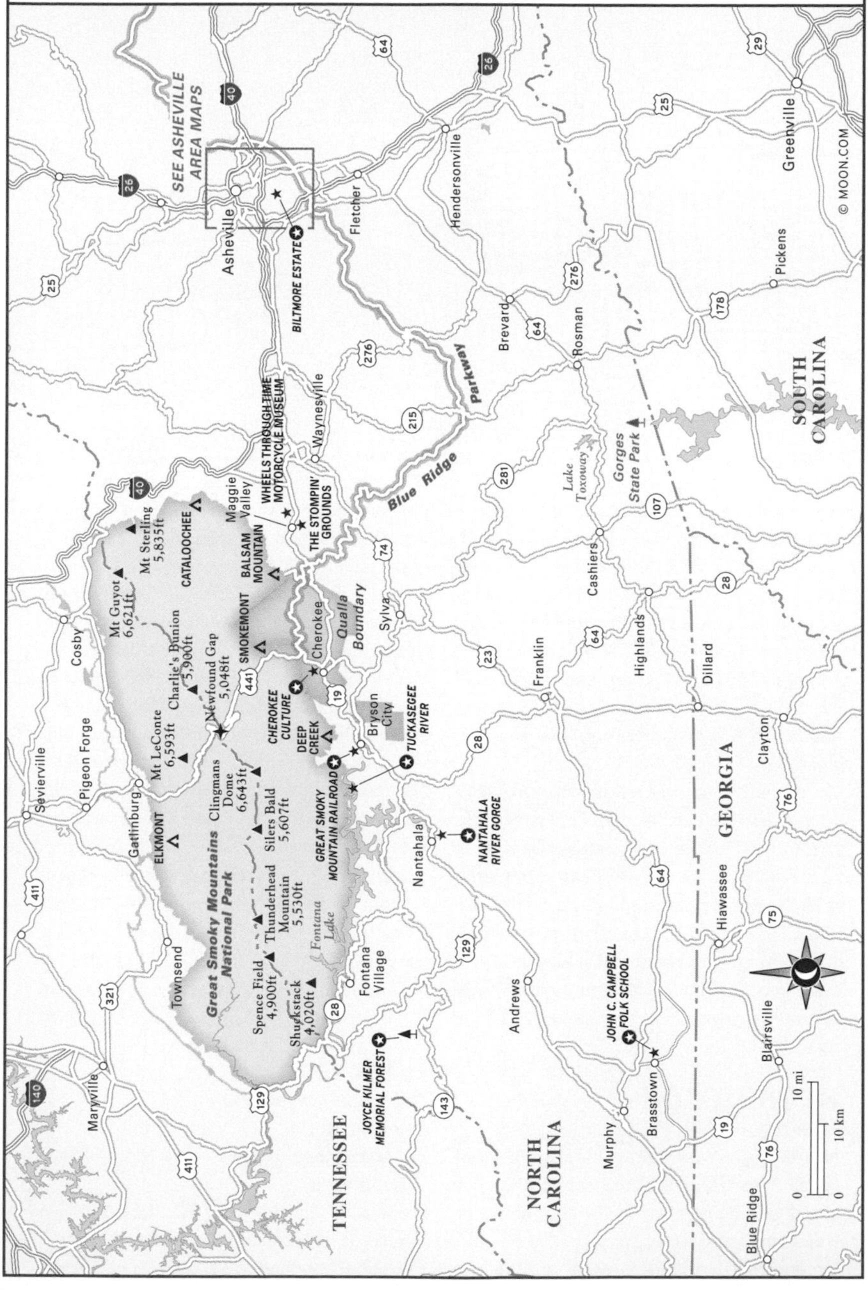

© MOON.COM

SEE ASHEVILLE AREA MAPS

Asheville

BILTMORE ESTATE

Fletcher

Hendersonville

Greenville

Pickens

SOUTH CAROLINA

Brevard

Rosman

Waynesville

Blue Ridge Parkway

WHEELS THROUGH TIME MOTORCYCLE MUSEUM

Maggie Valley

THE STOMPIN' GROUNDS

BALSAM MOUNTAIN

Lake Toxaway

Gorges State Park

Cashiers

SMOKEMONT

Mt Sterling 5,835ft

CATALOOCHEE

Mt Guyot 6,621ft

Charlie's Bunion 5,900ft

Newfound Gap 5,048ft

Qualla Boundary

Cherokee

Sylva

Franklin

Highlands

Dillard

GEORGIA

Clayton

Cosby

Mt LeConte 6,593ft

CHEROKEE CULTURE

DEEP CREEK

Bryson City

TUCKASEGEE RIVER

Clingmans Dome 6,643ft

ELKMONT

Silers Bald 5,607ft

GREAT SMOKY MOUNTAIN RAILROAD

Great Smoky Mountains National Park

Thunderhead Mountain 5,530ft

Nantahala

NANTAHALA RIVER GORGE

Pigeon Forge

Sevierville

Gatlinburg

Spence Field 4,900ft

Shuckstack 4,020ft

Fontana Lake

Fontana Village

Townsend

Hiawassee

JOHN C. CAMPBELL FOLK SCHOOL

Blairsville

Maryville

JOYCE KILMER MEMORIAL FOREST

Andrews

TENNESSEE

NORTH CAROLINA

Murphy

Brasstown

Blue Ridge

10 mi

10 km

Maggie Valley

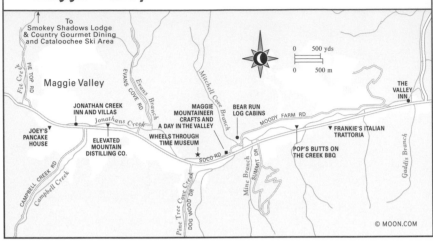

To
Smokey Shadows Lodge
& Country Gourmet Dining
and Cataloochee Ski Area

Maggie Valley

THE VALLEY INN

JONATHAN CREEK INN AND VILLAS

JOEY'S PANCAKE HOUSE

ELEVATED MOUNTAIN DISTILLING CO.

MAGGIE MOUNTAINEER CRAFTS AND A DAY IN THE VALLEY

WHEELS THROUGH TIME MUSEUM

BEAR RUN LOG CABINS

FRANKIE'S ITALIAN TRATTORIA

POP'S BUTTS ON THE CREEK BBQ

MOODY FARM RD

SOCO RD

0   500 yds
0   500 m

© MOON.COM

have all that and more. They've got plenty of fudge (and they ship; seriously, it's that good) and shirts to choose from, but they also have a pretty large selection of quilts and home decor items; knives, moccasins, and toys; and a great section of local foodstuffs like apple butter, sorghum molasses, and some seasonal treats. Throw in the deck overlooking the creek, and you have yourself a charming little souvenir store.

Antiques shopping at **Sutton and Son's Antiques** (3156 Dellwood Rd., Waynesville, 828/944-1212, www.suttonandsonsantiques.com, 10am-5pm Mon.-Sat., 1pm-5pm Sun.) is an experience best summed up by their tagline: "Treasure hunting in the Smokies." The store is large and loaded with a nicely curated selection of antiques such as mountain crafts, automotive memorabilia, kitchen goods, and records.

RECREATION
Hiking

Near Maggie Valley, the mountains become rough. Located on the valley floor, the town of Maggie Valley is surprisingly short on trails, and what trails there are can be quite strenuous. There's the 2.3-mile stroll (which you can extend to 3.8 miles) around **Lake Junaluska**, but other than that, the majority of the trails are at the crest of the mountains, along the Blue Ridge Parkway. To the east of Maggie Valley, the mountains are a little more forgiving, and there are many trails of various intensities and lengths. In the immediate area, though, you'll have to take the Heintooga Spur Road, a connector road between the Blue Ridge Parkway and Great Smoky Mountains National Park, to a mile-high campground, picnic area with unparalleled views, and the **Flat Creek Trail.** On Heintooga Spur Road, you'll pass into Great Smoky Mountains National Park and be treated to no fewer than five stunning overlooks, the best of which is the Mile High Overlook, offering a glimpse of Clingmans Dome, Mount LeConte, Mount Kephart, and Mount Guyot.

FLAT CREEK TRAIL
Distance: 5 miles round-trip
Duration: 3 hours
Elevation gain: 250 feet
Difficulty: easy
Trailhead: Heintooga Ridge picnic area off Heintooga Spur Road, accessible at milepost 458.2
Though it's named the Flat Creek Trail, you

will find a waterfall—the 200-foot Flat Creek Falls, a beautiful but difficult-to-see cascade—along the path. The main trail is easy, with little elevation gain or loss until you turn onto the short spur trail that leads to the falls. The falls trail is steep and slick, so be careful if you decide to explore in this area.

Heavy logging at the turn of the 20th century opened the forest up and allowed a thick swath of grass to grow here. Today much of the grass remains, and the forest seems to rise from it like an island in a sea of green. It's a strange sight.

Winter Sports

Maggie Valley's **Cataloochee Ski Area** (1080 Ski Lodge Rd., off U.S. 19, 800/768-0285, snow conditions 800/768-3588, www.cataloochee. com, late Nov.-mid-Mar., lift tickets $23-73, rentals $28-33) has slopes geared to every level of skier and snowboarder. Classes and private lessons are available for all ages. At Cataloochee's sister snow-sports area, **Tube World** (U.S. 19, next to Ski Area, 828/926-0285, www.cataloochee.com, late Nov.-mid-Mar., must be over 42 inches tall, $30-35), you can zip down the mountain on inner tubes and try your hand at some tricks in the terrain park. There's a Wee Bowl area for children (call ahead, $5).

FOOD

★ **Joey's Pancake House** (4309 Soco Rd., 828/926-0212, www.joeyspancake.com, 7am-noon daily, $2-9) has been flipping flapjacks for travelers and locals alike since 1966, and it's exactly what you picture: paper menu placemats, hot coffee, a little kitschy, and packed with regulars. Lines form on weekends for the pancakes, waffles, and country ham—get here early. If you're taken by the pancakes, pick up some of Joey's mix to take home with you.

My favorite restaurant in Maggie Valley is **Frankie's Italian Trattoria** (1037 Soco Rd., 828/926-6216, www.frankiestrattoria.com, 2pm-9pm Tues.-Sat., $10-24). Service is great, the wine list is more than adequate, and the

food—pizza, linguine with clams, eggplant parm—puts it over the top.

Try the local spin on barbecue at **Pop's Butts on the Creek BBQ** (1584 Soco Rd., 828/926-7885, www.popsbuttsonthecreeknc. com, 11am-8pm Tues.-Sun., $10-29). Like a lot of places in western North Carolina, they don't adhere to our state's unspoken rule that barbecue is pork only (and no ribs), and I'm glad because they have a killer rib game and their brisket and burnt ends are a welcome and beefy relief from all the pork. That said, the chopped pork is great (thanks to their butts-only approach), the spare rib dinner could feed two people, and those burnt ends are especially good on a sandwich.

ACCOMMODATIONS

Along Maggie Valley's main drag (Soco Rd./ U.S. 19), you'll see a lot of creek-side motels and mom-and-pop mountain inns. Among the pleasant independent motels are **The Valley Inn** (236 Soco Rd., 800/948-6880, www.thevalleyinn.com, from $79) and **Jonathan Creek Inn and Villas** (4324 Soco Rd., 800/577-7812, www.jonathancreekinn. com, from $74), which has creek-side rooms with screened porches.

High in the mountains—4,500 feet, to be precise—**Smokey Shadows Lodge & Country Gourmet Dining** (323 Smoky Shadows Ln., 828/926-0001, www. smokeyshadows.com) offers up **lodge rooms** (from $110) and a pair of **cabins** (from $150) in a converted grist mill that once served the Cataloochee Valley. With a long, covered porch affording some spectacular views and a yard frequented by elk, it's a special kind of place. They also have a dining room serving family-style country dishes ($35) like tomato pie, pot roast, meat loaf, and other homey fare, or you can take your meal on the porch (call and reserve a seat on the porch).

If you want to get a feel for the mountains, try one of the cabin rentals. **Bear Run Log Cabins** (1604 Moody Farm Rd., 828/926-7566, www.bearrunlogcabins.com, from $130 June-Dec., from $120 Jan.-May) has a quartet of cabins that sleep five and have Wi-Fi, a fireplace, and a small kitchen. Their decks overlook Jonathan Creek, one of the area trout streams. Cozy, comfy, and cabin-y, they're exactly what you picture when you think of a mountain cabin getaway.

Stay in a cabin at **Twinbrook Resort** (20 Twinbrook Ln., 828/962-1388, www. twinbrookresort.com, cabins $199-499, RV sites $59) or bring your RV; either way you're staying in a beautiful place. From here it's only 30 minutes to the Oconaluftee Visitor Center (a little longer if you take the scenic route on the Blue Ridge Parkway), so you're within easy striking distance of the national park and the Parkway. On-site you'll find an indoor pool and hot tub, decks with grills, a playground, and one of the namesake brooks. If your travel plans are flexible, keep an eye on the website, as the resort constantly runs specials on lodging.

There is one fantastic campground in the area: the ★ **Balsam Mountain Campground** (Heintooga Spur Rd., milepost 458.2, 828/497-9270, www.nps.gov/grsm, reservations www.recreation.gov, $18), the highest campground in Great Smoky Mountains National Park at 5,310 feet. This primitive campground has 43 sites for tents and RVs, with a dedicated tent-only section. It's a beautiful, isolated campground that's often overlooked since it's slightly off the beaten path. Because it's also a primitive campground (pit toilets, no showers), for most of the year you won't have many neighbors here. If you're driving a vehicle you feel comfortable taking on forest roads, Balsam Mountain Road, sometimes called Round Bottom Road, continues on from the campground, making a nice trip through the forest down to Cherokee. It's about two hours but worth the drive.

TRANSPORTATION

U.S. 19 is the main thoroughfare in these parts, leading from Asheville (45 minutes east) to Great Smoky Mountains National Park (35 minutes west). If you're taking your time between Asheville, Boone, or parts north, the Blue Ridge Parkway is a beautiful but slow—three hours or more, depending on where you begin—drive to this part of the state. Maggie Valley is only 25 minutes off I-40 via exits 20, 24, or 27.

Cherokee and the Qualla Boundary

The town of Cherokee is a study in juxtapositions: the cultural traditions of the Cherokee people, the region's natural beauty, a 24-hour casino, and community-wide preparation for the future. Cherokee is the seat of government of the Eastern Band of Cherokee Indians, who have lived in these mountains for centuries. Today, their traditional arts and crafts, government, and cultural heritage are very much alive, although their language seems to be disappearing. The Qualla (KWA-lah) Boundary is not a reservation but a large tract of land owned and governed by the Cherokee people. Institutions like the Museum of the Cherokee Indian and the Qualla Arts and Crafts Mutual provide a solid base for the Eastern Band's cultural life. As you drive around, take a look at the road signs: Below each English road name is that same name in Cherokee, a beautiful script created by Sequoyah, a 19th-century Cherokee silversmith. This language, once nearly extinct, is being taught to the community's youth now, and there is a Cherokee-language immersion school on the Qualla Boundary. This doesn't mean the language is not endangered: Few Cherokee people speak it fluently.

The main street in Cherokee is a classic cheesy tourist district where you'll find "Indian" souvenirs—factory-made moccasins, plastic tomahawks, peace pipes, faux bearskins, the works. In a retro way, this part

Cherokee

To
Peter's Pancake & Waffle,
Sassy Sunflowers Bakery & Cafe,
Wize Guyz Grille, Native Brews
Tap and Grill, Rivers Edge Outfitters,
and Smoky Mountain
Tube and Raft

LAMBERT BRANCH RD

TSALI BLVD

DR

WASHINGTON

JOSEPH

ACQUONI RD

BJ'S
DINER

OCONALUFTEE
INDIAN VILLAGE

FIRE MOUNTAIN
TRAILS

QUALLA ARTS AND
CRAFTS MUTUAL

MUSEUM OF THE
CHEROKEE INDIAN

Fair
Grounds

FIRE MOUNTAIN
OUTFITTERS/ MOTION
MAKERS BICYCLE SHOP

(1361)

81A HWY 1390

81A HWY 316

441

Oconaluftee River

CHEROKEE
BONFIRE

0   200 yds

0   200 m

441 19

TSALAGI RD

To Harrah's Cherokee
Casino and Resort

19

© MOON.COM

of Cherokee, with its predictable trinket shops and fudgeries, is charming.

Aside from its proximity to Great Smoky Mountains National Park and the Blue Ridge Parkway, the biggest draw in town is Harrah's Cherokee Casino, one of the largest casino hotels in the state and home to a world-class spa. The 24-hour entertainment opportunities attract visitors from far and wide, some of whom stay on the property the whole time. Others take a break from the slap of cards and the flash of slot machines

to experience the natural and cultural wonders of Cherokee.

Take all of this that you see—the casino, the tacky tourist shops, and the stereotyping signs—with a grain of salt, as they don't represent the true nature of the Cherokee people and their long history.

★ CHEROKEE CULTURAL SIGHTS

Museum of the Cherokee Indian

The **Museum of the Cherokee Indian** (589 Tsali Blvd., 828/497-3481, www.mci.org, 9am-5pm daily, $12 adults, $7 ages 6-12, free ages 5 and under) was founded in 1948 and was originally housed in a log cabin. Today, it is a well-regarded modern museum and locus of community culture. In the exhibits that trace the long history of the Cherokee people, you may notice the disconcertingly realistic mannequins. Local community members volunteered to be models for these mannequins, allowing casts to be made of their faces and bodies so that the figures would not reflect an outsider's notion of what Native Americans should look like. The Museum of the Cherokee Indian traces their history from the Paleo-Indian people of the Pleistocene, when ancestral Cherokees were hunter-gatherers, through the ancient days of Cherokee civilization, and contact with European settlers.

Many exhibits focus on the late 18th and early 19th centuries when settlers and the U.S. military began encroaching on tribal lands. This was also a time of great cultural advancement, including Sequoyah's development of the script to write the Cherokee language. The forced relocation called the Trail of Tears began near here, along the North Carolina-Georgia border, in the early 19th century. A small contingent of Cherokees remained in the Smokies at the time of the Trail of Tears, successfully eluding, and then negotiating with, the U.S. military, who were trying to force most of the Native Americans in the Southeast to move to Oklahoma. Those who stayed out in the woods, along with a few others who were able to return from Oklahoma, are the ancestors of today's Eastern Band, and their history is truly remarkable.

The best parts of the museum are the stories, legends, and myths described on placards throughout the museum. There's the story of a boy who became a bear and convinced his entire clan to become bears also. There's one about Spearfinger, a frightening creature that some say still lives in these woods. And there are tales about Selu, the corn mother, and Kanati, the lucky hunter. Cherokee member and contemporary writer Marilou Awiakta has written widely about Selu, tying the past and present together with taut lines of thought that challenge our views on culture and technology.

Qualla Arts and Crafts Mutual

Across the street from the museum is the **Qualla Arts and Crafts Mutual** (645 Tsali Blvd., 828/497-3103, https://quallaartsandcrafts.com, 8am-5pm Mon.-Sat., 8am-4:30pm Sun.), a community arts co-op where 250 local artists sell their work. The gallery's high standards and the community's thousands of years of artistry make for a collection of very special pottery, baskets, masks, and other traditional art. The Qualla co-op does a great service to this community by providing a year-round market for the work of traditional Cherokee artists. The double-woven baskets are especially beautiful, as are the carvings of the masks representing each of the seven clans of the Cherokee people (the Bird, Deer, Longhair, Blue, Wolf, Paint, and Wild Potato).

Oconaluftee Indian Village

Oconaluftee Indian Village (778 Drama Rd., 828/497-2111, https://visitcherokeenc.com, 9:30am-4:30pm Tues.-Sat. Apr.-Nov., $16 adults, $10 children, free ages 5 and under) is a recreated Cherokee village tucked into the hills above the town. Here you'll see how the Cherokee people lived in the 18th century. Tour guides in period costumes lead groups

on walking lectures, with stops at stations where you can see Cherokee cultural, artistic, and daily-life activities performed as authentically as possible. From cooking demos to flint knapping (for arrowheads and spear points) to wood carving and clay work, you'll get a look at how the Cherokee lived centuries ago. The highlight of the tour is the ritual dance demonstration, showcasing a half-dozen dances with explanations of their cultural significance.

RECREATION
Fishing

Cherokee has more than 30 miles of streams, rivers, and creeks ideal for fishing. The Eastern Band owns and operates a fish hatchery that releases around 250,000 trout into these waters every year, creating the perfect mix for fantastic fishing. Unlike in the rest of North Carolina, you don't need a North Carolina fishing license; you need a **tribal fishing permit** (www.fishcherokee.com, 1 day $10, 2 days $17, 3 days $27, 5 days $47, season permit $250), sold at a number of outlets in Cherokee. You'll find brook, brown, golden, and rainbow trout, and it's fly-rod only, so you need to have your cast down pat if you want to bring in a big one. There are both catch-and-release and catch-and-keep waters in the Qualla Boundary, but if you want to fish outside the boundary, you need a North Carolina or Tennessee fishing permit. Tennessee permits are only valid inside the Great Smoky Mountains National Park boundaries in North Carolina.

If you're unsure of your fly-fishing skills or want a guide to take you to a hot fishing hole, talk to the folks at **Rivers Edge Outfitters** (61 Big Cove Rd., 828/497-9300, www.wncfishing.com, 8am-5pm Sun.-Thurs., 7am-6pm Fri.-Sat., $25-500). Their shop's fully stocked with all the gear and tackle you need for a day on the water, and they offer lessons in casting and fly tying, and guided trips. You can go for a wading trip on local waters (2-hour, half-day, and full-day trips available); other options are half- and full-day float trips

The Story of the Cherokee

Museum of the Cherokee Indian

The Cherokee people believe that the mountains of western North Carolina have been part of their homeland dating back to at least the last ice age, some 11,000 years ago. By the time Spanish soldiers encountered the Cherokee in the 1540s, the nation controlled around 140,000 square miles across what is now the southern United States, living in log cabins in towns and villages throughout their territory. They farmed corn, squash, and beans (known as The Three Sisters); hunted elk, deer, and bears; and prospered in peacetime and warred with other nations periodically.

During the first two centuries of earnest European contact, the Cherokee were peaceful and hospitable with the colonists they encountered. Through the course of those 200 years, strings of broken treaties and concessions by the Cherokee had shrunk their once-vast empire dramatically. When President Andrew Jackson insisted that all Indigenous people in the Southeast be moved west of the Mississippi and signed the Indian Removal Act, the real trouble began.

In 1838, as Jackson's forced march and relocation of the Cherokee and other nations, known as the **Trail of Tears,** pressed on, a small group of Cherokees avoided relocation by becoming North Carolina citizens. A band of resistance fighters stayed behind near modern-day Cherokee, hiding in the hills, hollows, and caves high in the mountains. These holdouts would become the core of the **Eastern Band of Cherokee Indians.** Unable to own any land, the Cherokee turned to an adopted member to purchase and hold land in his name. He did so, and in 1870, the Cherokee formed a corporation and took control of that land, which they called the **Qualla Boundary.**

Today, the Eastern Band of Cherokee Indians has nearly 15,000 members (their counterparts in Oklahoma number 10 times as many), many of whom live within the 82-square-mile Qualla Boundary. Tribe members are fiercely proud of their heritage, traditions, stories, and language. An afternoon spent at the **Museum of the Cherokee Indian,** the **Qualla Arts and Crafts Mutual,** and the **Oconaluftee Indian Village,** followed by an evening showing of *Unto These Hills,* will give you a more complete understanding of their history.

on local waters or wading trips on private waters nearby.

Mountain Biking

Fire Mountain Trails (778 Drama Rd., https://visitcherokeenc.com, free) has 10.5 miles of trails suitable for mountain bikers, as well as hikers and trail runners. Riders of all skill levels can get in a good session here, with beginner-friendly runs that will boost your confidence and some rip-roaring single-track runs that will have expert riders catching air and finessing their way through rock gardens. The trailhead is adjacent to the Oconaluftee Indian Village.

Just across the street from where you head up to Fire Mountain Trails is **Fire Mountain Outfitters** (516 Tsali Blvd., 828/750-4196, www.firemountainoutpost.com, 10am-5pm Sun.-Mon., 10am-6pm Wed.-Sat.), an outdoor gear shop with plenty stuff to outfit you for a hiking, camping, or biking adventure. They've partnered with **Motion Makers Bicycle Shop** (www.motionmakers.com, 828/586-6925) for mountain bike sales, repairs, and rentals ($45-150 per day). If you're staying in Bryson City (it's only 15 minutes away), **Tsali Cycles** (35 Slope St., Bryson City, 828/499-9010, www.tsalicycles.com, 10am-5pm Mon.-Fri., 9am-4pm Sat., $30-50 adults, $20-25 children) can get you set up with a mountain bike rental to use here or on the Tsali Trails closer to their home base.

Golf

The **Sequoyah National Golf Club** (79 Cahons Rd., Whittier, 828/497-3000, www.sequoyahnational.com, 18 holes, par 72, greens fees from $65), five miles south of Cherokee in Whittier, is a stunning mountain golf course. Making the most of the contours and elevation, the course offers tee boxes with breathtaking views of the fairway and the Smoky Mountains. The course record is 62, an impressive feat on a normal course, but here it's something else. Holes like number 12 and number 15 test a golfer's club knowledge and course IQ. This is a tough course for first-timers because so many of the holes have blind approaches, doglegs, or both.

Water Sports

For fun on the water, try **Smoky Mountain Tube and Raft** (1847 Tsali Blvd., 828/497-4545, http://cherokeetubeandraft.com, 10am-5pm daily Memorial Day-Labor Day weekend, weather permitting, $12). It has mountains of tubes, so rent one and float down the Oconaluftee River for 2-3 hours. It also has a fleet of shuttle buses to pick you up a few miles downstream.

ENTERTAINMENT AND EVENTS

The Eastern Band of Cherokee Indians operates **Harrah's Cherokee Casino and Hotel** (777 Casino Dr., 828/497-7777, www.caesars.com/harrahs-cherokee, 24 hours daily). This full-bore Vegas-style casino has more than 3,800 digital games and slot machines along with around 150 table games, such as baccarat, blackjack, roulette, and a poker-only room. Inside the casino complex are a 3,000-seat concert venue where acts like Alicia Keys and the Black Crows have performed, a huge buffet, and a grab-and-go food court next to the casino floor. Unlike in the rest of the state, smoking is allowed on the casino floor, though certain areas have been designated as nonsmoking. Inside the hotel portion of the casino are a restaurant, a Starbucks, and the **Mandara Spa,** which offers salon and spa services like massages and facials.

Of the several outdoor dramas for which North Carolina is known, among the longest running is Cherokee's *Unto These Hills* (Mountainside Theater, 688 Drama Rd., adjacent to Oconaluftee Indian Village, 866/554-4557, https://visitcherokeenc.com, 8pm Mon.-Sat. June-Aug. 15, $28-39 adults, $18-31 ages 6-12, free ages 5 and under). Since 1950, Cherokee actors have told the story of their nation's history, from ancient times through the Trail of Tears. Every seat in the house is a good seat at the Mountainside Theater, and the play is enlightening. Be warned: There is some cannon fire and gunfire in the play.

Hear stories, learn dances, and interact with Cherokee storytellers at the **Cherokee Bonfire** (Oconaluftee Islands Park, Tsalagi Rd. and Tsali Blvd., intersection of U.S. 19 and U.S. 441, 800/438-1601, https://visitcherokeenc.com, 7pm-8pm Sun., Mon., Wed, and Sat. May-Oct., free). Bring your bathing suit and some water shoes; afterward, you may want to go for a wade or a quick dip in the Oconaluftee River, which is wide, rocky, and fun.

FOOD

Harrah's Cherokee Casino is home to one of the best restaurants in town, **Brio Tuscan Grille** (777 Casino Dr., 828/497-8233, www.brioitalian.com, 11am-10pm Sun.-Thurs., 11am-11pm Fri. and Sat., $10-36), which specializes in dishes from northern Italy. The food is great, the wine list is excellent, and the ambience makes you forget you're in a casino. There are other options in Harrah's, from the expected casino buffet to the grab-and-go-back-to-gaming food court, but **Wicked Weed Brewpub** (4pm-11pm Wed.-Fri., 11am-11pm Sat.-Sun., $8-34) has set up an outpost here where they pour their Asheville-brewed beers and serve smash burgers, hot chicken sandwiches, and even steaks and beef tartare.

With a focus on wings, pizza, and burgers, **Wize Guyz Grille** (68 Big Cove Rd., 828/497-2838, www.wizeguyzgrille.com, 11am-7pm Mon.-Thurs., 11am-8pm Fri.-Sat., $6-50) gives diners a good option away from the casino. Dozens of iterations of chicken sandwiches and burgers, a bevy of appetizers (pickle fries, anyone? Get two baskets), and 15 pizzas to choose from means you have options aplenty here.

I'd be remiss if I didn't mention the best burger in town, which comes from a roadside trailer. **BJ's Diner** (840 Tsali Blvd., 828/497-4303, www.bjs-diner.business.site, 11am-6pm Mon.-Thurs., 11am-8pm Fri.-Sat., 11am-4pm Sun., $2-9) keeps it simple: burgers with or without cheese, hot dogs, chicken tenders, and a few sandwiches. They do have a bacon cheeseburger served on a grilled cheese (which you should definitely get), but that's about as far afield as they go. If there's room at the picnic tables, grab a seat as the Oconaluftee River flows by just a few feet away. You might just see a few elk wading by.

At **Sassy Sunflowers Bakery & Café** (1655 Aquoni Rd., 828/497-2539, 9am-4pm Mon.-Fri., $3-10), you can get the usual coffee and pastry treats but also excellent soups and sandwiches. The chicken salad is especially good—and quite portable if you're hoping to picnic in the park later in the day. Just remember to bring a cooler.

Up early to hit the trail? Grab breakfast in town at **Peter's Pancakes & Waffles** (1384 Tsali Blvd., 828/497-5116, 6:30am-2pm daily, $2-11), where you can order flapjacks (the blueberry pancakes are a sure bet), eggs with bacon, or a biscuit sandwich. Offerings are cheap, filling, and tasty.

Native Brews Tap and Grill (1897 Tsali Blvd., 828/497-2739, www.native-brews.com, noon-9pm Mon.-Thurs., noon-10pm Fri.-Sat., 11am-9pm Sun., $9-20) has a quartet of their own beers—an IPA, pale ale, golden lager, and blonde—as well as spiced ales (think hard root beer, cream soda, and lemonade) and hard seltzers on offer alongside their own label of vodka, gin, and whiskey. As you taste your way through the liquid offerings, you're going to need a snack or a meal. The Colossal Pretzel is a whopper of an appetizer (not quite a wagon wheel, but still huge), the sandwiches hit the spot, and there are full-size entrées if you are feeling more than puckish.

ACCOMMODATIONS

Cherokee has many motels, including a **Holiday Inn** (376 Painttown Rd., 828/497-3113, www.ihg.com, from $113) and an **Econo Lodge** (20 River Rd./U.S. 19, 828/497-4575, www.choicehotels.com, from $75).

★ **Harrah's Cherokee Casino Resort** (777 Casino Dr., 828/497-7777, www.harrahscherokee.com, $125-510) is, without a doubt, the best place to stay in Cherokee. The hotel's 1,800 rooms are spacious, comfortable, and well kept; the casino and a number of dining options are an elevator ride away; and the spa provides an added layer of amenities you don't find at other hotels in town.

There's something about visiting a place and living where the residents live, and ★ **Panther Creek Cabins** (Wrights Creek Rd., 828/497-2461, www.panthercreekresort. com, $75-350, two-night minimum seasonally) gives you that chance. The 13 cabins range from private, two-person affairs to larger lodges that could easily sleep eight. Just outside downtown Cherokee, the quaint cabins are quiet and comfortable. Pets are welcome in most cabins, for a flat fee ($49 for the first dog, $39 for the second).

On the outskirts of Cherokee you'll find a couple of RV parks. **Happy Holiday RV Park and Campground** (1553 Wolfetown Rd., 828/497-9204, www.happyholidayrv. com) sits just to the east of town on 40 acres. They have more than 375 **tent** ($25-48) and **RV sites** ($55-75), a pool, an ice-cream parlor, and a little spot where you can grab a quick snack. Just south of town is **Fort Wilderness Campground & RV Park** (284 Fort Wilderness Rd., Whittier, 828/497-9331, www.fortwilderness.net, tent sites $35-45, RV sites $40-60), with 130 sites on 11 acres. Even though it's technically in the town of Whittier, it's only 1.5 miles to Harrah's Casino and 7 miles from the entrance to Great Smoky Mountains National Park and the Blue Ridge Parkway.

TRANSPORTATION AND SERVICES

Cherokee is located on a particularly pretty, winding section of U.S. 19 between Maggie Valley and Bryson City, 2.5 miles south of the southern terminus of the Blue Ridge Parkway. From the Blue Ridge Parkway, a six-minute drive south along U.S. 441 will take you right to the cultural center of Cherokee.

The **Cherokee Welcome Center** (498 Tsali Blvd., 800/438-1601, https://

visitcherokeenc.com, 8am-5pm daily) can help you with tickets, directions, and things to do and see. There's one radio station in Cherokee, **WNCC** (101.3 FM), a country station, although you can pick up distant stations with a wider selection.

SYLVA

The small town of Sylva, southwest of Waynesville, is crowned by the pretty Jackson County Courthouse, an Italianate building with an ornate cupola. A Confederate monument stands in the courthouse square. Visitors should stop by the **Jackson County Visitor Center** (773 W. Main St., 800/962-1911, www. mountainlovers.com) or visit online to learn more about the communities here; tourist information is available through Discover Jackson County (www.discoverjacksonnc. com).

Sights

South of Sylva, the mysterious **Judaculla Rock** (off Caney Fork Rd., www. judacullarock.com) has puzzled folks for centuries. The soapstone boulder is covered in petroglyphs estimated to be at least 500 years old. The figures and symbols and squiggles are clearly significant but as of yet are not understood. I'm fascinated by petroglyphs, and these are some of the most mysterious I've encountered. The soft rock has eroded, and the pictures are not as clear as they were in generations past, but many of them can still be discerned. To reach the rock, drive south on Highway 107 8 miles past the intersection with Sylva's Business U.S. 23. Make a left on Caney Fork Road/County Road 1737 and drive 2.5 miles to a gravel road. Turn left, and after just under 0.5 miles you'll see the rock on the right and a parking area on the left.

Shopping

Sylva's City Lights Bookstore (3 E. Jackson St., 828/586-9499, www.citylightsnc.com, 10am-6pm Mon.-Sat., 10am-3pm Sun.) is hardly a knockoff of the monumental Beat establishment in San Francisco with which it shares a name. Instead, it's a first-rate small-town bookstore with stock that has the novelty sought by vacationers and the depth to make regulars of the local patrons. In addition to the sections you'll find in any good bookstore, the selection of books of regional interest, including folklore, nature, recreation guides, history, and fiction and poetry by Appalachian and Southern authors, is excellent.

Founded by a pair of Appalachian Trail thru-hikers, **Black Balsam Outdoors** (562 W. Main St., 828/631-2864, www.blackbalsamoutdoors.com, 10am-6pm Mon.-Sat., noon-5pm Sun.) will get you geared up for a trip into the woods, whether you're looking for hard-core trail gear to use on your own thru-hike or if you're in the market for a day-hike kit that will serve you for this trip to the Smokies and many more. They know their gear, how to use it, and where to go to give it a good workout, so don't hesitate to inquire about their favorite hikes in the area and the national park.

Food

The North Carolina mountains are experiencing a booming organic foods movement, and you'll find eco-aware eateries throughout the area. **Lulu's On Main** (678 W. Main St., 828/586-8989, www.lulusonmain.com, 11:30am-3:30pm and 5pm-8pm Mon.-Thurs., 11:30am-3:30pm and 5pm-9pm Fri.-Sat., $11-30) is one of the most acclaimed restaurants in the area. The menu is American gourmet at heart, with splashes of Mediterranean and Nuevo Latino specialties. Try the cheese ravioli with tofu, the beef short ribs, or the paella. They have plenty of vegetarian options.

At ★ **Ilda** (462 W. Main St., 828/307-2036, www.ildainsylva.com, dinner 5pm-10pm Tues.-Sat and 5pm-9pm Sun., brunch noon-3pm Sat.-Sun., $8-22) you'll find rustic Italian dishes with a little bit of Appalachian twang on a menu that's perfectly representative of Chef Santiago Guzzetti and Sommelier Crystal Pace, a husband-and-wife duo who found their way back to her hometown. The food here is nothing short of spectacular. Seasonal availability drives the individual ingredients in dishes, and the mushroom risotto, mafaldini (lamb Bolognese with local greens), and rigatoni with nasturtium sausage all take advantage of what's fresh and on hand, but even in the depths of winter, the menu shines.

City Lights Café (3 E. Jackson St., 828/587-2233, www.citylightscafe.com, 8am-7pm Mon.-Sat., 9am-3pm Sun., breakfast

Jackson County Courthouse in Sylva

$2-8, lunch and dinner $5-12), downstairs from the bookshop, has some excellent crepes, a mighty good biscuit, and fun tacos, and they serve wine and beer. It's a cool, casual spot to dine and relax with your book and a bottle of wine, or to see a small local act.

If you're in the mood for coffee and something light, try **White Moon** (545 Mill St., 828/331-0111, www.whitemoonnc.com, 8am-4pm Tues.-Sat., 8am-3pm Sun., $3-11). White Moon is one street over from the main drag, so it would be easy to overlook, but that would be a mistake. Friendly folks serve coffee, café drinks, and a small but tasty breakfast and lunch menu. When you need your avocado toast fix, a savory breakfast bowl, or a sandwich, this is the spot. Their alter ego is **Dark Moon** (4pm-11pm Tues.-Sat., $6-18), the nighttime, candlelit wine and beer lounge that serves a tapas and dessert menu and makes for a classy close to the evening.

Nightlife

It's a small town, so there's not a whole lot in the way of nightlife, but **Innovation Brewing** (414 W. Main St., 828/586-9678, www.innovation-brewing.com, noon-midnight Mon.-Thurs., 11am-midnight Fri.-Sun.) has 22 beers in their regular rotation, with 10 on tap at any time. The Nitro Irish Stout, Nut Brown, and Midnight Rye-der Black IPA are mainstays, but they also make a few sours. Keep an ear out for live music in the taproom, as bands drop by often. If you're hungry, you're in luck: **Cosmic Carry-Out** (828/506-2830, www.cosmiccarryout.com, noon-9pm Mon.-Thurs., noon-10:30pm Fri.-Sat., 11am-9pm Sun., $3-9) has burgers, tacos, grilled-cheese sandwiches, and fries for your dining enjoyment.

Balsam Falls Brewing (506 W. Main St., 828/631-1987, www.balsamfallsbrewing.com, 11am-10pm Mon.-Fri., 10am-10pm Sat.-Sun.) came to Sylva by way of the Tampa, Florida, home-brew scene, where owners Corey and Laure Bryson got their start. But Balsam Falls is far from home brew. The pair went on to get their Cicerone certification (think sommelier for beer), and Corey's a certified beer judge, so the brews they put on draft are top-notch. Every beer has a fun name—Elvis Has Left the Brewpub, Fergus the Rat Chocolate Milk Stout, Petrified Dragon—and the variety runs the gamut from IPAs to barley wine to Russian imperials to lightly hopped American pale ales. They have a **restaurant** (10am-2pm daily, $12) next door, serving flatbreads, burgers, salads, and sandwiches (try the spicy fried chicken sandwich). With a range of tots, smashbrowns (think hashbrowns but little smashed potatoes), and burritos at lunch, filling up here won't be a problem.

Lazy Hiker Brewing (617 W. Main St., 828/349-2337, www.lazyhikerbrewing.com, noon-10pm Mon.-Thurs., noon-11pm Fri.-Sat., noon-9pm Sun.) is based in Franklin, North Carolina, but has a taproom in Sylva. They keep a dozen taps flowing with styles across the spectrum, each well done, and each appealing to different palates and preferences. Sour fans will find a black cherry sour as well as a gose and a Berliner weiss on tap, but dedicated IPA fans will find drafts highlighting different hops. If you like something in between, they have brown ales, blondes, and other brews to choose from.

For cocktails, head to **The Cut Cocktail Lounge** (486 W. Main St., 828/631-4795, 5pm-midnight Mon.-Sat., 6pm-midnight Sun.) in a former barber shop downtown. The drinks are excellent, the atmosphere on the right side of dive-y, and they serve food until midnight every night as a sort of potluck feast; sometimes it's chili, sometimes gourmet popcorn, sometimes barbecue.

Accommodations

The **Blue Ridge Inn** (756 W. Main St., 828/586-2123, from $110) is a great place to stay in Sylva. Located at the far end of downtown, it's an eight-minute walk to the breweries at the other end of town and a three-minute walk to dining spots like Lulu's and City Lights. The rooms are comfortable and priced right, and the staff is exceptionally polite.

DILLSBORO

Next door to Sylva is Dillsboro, a river town of rafters and crafters. **Dogwood Crafters** (90 Webster St., 828/586-2248, www. dogwoodcrafters.com, 10am-6pm Mon.-Sat., 10am-4pm Sun.), in operation since 1976, is a gallery and co-op that represents around 100 local artists and artisans. While the shop carries some of the ubiquitous country-whimsical stuff, mixed in is the work of some very traditional Blue Ridge weavers, potters, carvers, and other expert artisans, making the shop well worth a visit.

In November, Dillsboro's population grows significantly when potters and pottery lovers descend on the town for the annual **Western North Carolina Pottery Festival** (828/586-3601, wwww.wncpotteryfestival.com). This juried pottery show features more than 40 potters, a street fair, and the Clay Olympics. The Clay Olympics are timed competitions to make the tallest cylinder or widest bowl, as well as blindfolded pot making. The competition may seem odd, but the crowd and the artists get into it, making the one-day festival worth seeing.

Recreation

Dillsboro River Company (18 Macktown Rd., 828/507-2428, www.northcarolinarafting. com, 10am-2pm Tues.-Sun. June-Sept., tubing $20, guided trips $27-37), across the river from downtown Dillsboro, will set you afloat on the Tuckasegee (tuck-a-SEE-jee) River, a comparatively warm river with areas of Class II rapids; it's often referred to simply as "the Tuck." Dillsboro River Company rents rafts, "ducks," and inflatable and sit-on-top kayaks. If you'd like to hire a river rat, guides will be happy to lead you on tours twice daily, and for an extra fee you can share a boat with the guide. There are minimum weight restrictions for these watercraft, so if you are traveling with children, call ahead to ask if the guides think your young ones are ready for the Tuck.

Nightlife

Sylva's Innovation Brewing has an outpost in Dillsboro, **Innovation Station** (40 Depot St., 828/226-0262, www.innovation-brewing. com, noon-10pm Sun.-Thurs., noon-midnight Fri.-Sat.). Housed in a former train depot, it's got the right feel for this railroad town, and their generous taps—there are nearly three dozen—mean plenty of brews to choose from. Innovation also has a barrel-aging program here, and Dillsboro is home to their pilot brewhouse, so you'll likely find a few experimental brews to sample.

Food

★ **Haywood Smokehouse** (403 Haywood Rd., 828/631-9797, www. haywoodsmokehouse.com, 11am-8pm Tues.-Sat., $8-26) is a funky little barbecue shack serving some fine western North Carolina 'cue, craft beers, and house-made smoked barbecue sauces. The menu is small, but if it's pork or chicken and it can be barbecued, it's here. The Haywood Smokehouse is biker-friendly, so don't be surprised if you see a line of Harleys outside.

It's not surprising to find a restaurant bragging about their farm-to-fork philosophy these days, even in a town as small as Dillsboro, but it is surprising to find one living up to that boast and delivering great food. ★ **Foragers Canteen** (42 Depot St., 828/631-4114, www.foragerscanteen.com, 11am-9pm Mon.-Thurs., 11am-10pm Fri., 10am-10pm Sat., 10am-8pm Sun., $8-25) has fried (or grilled if that's your thing) chicken sandwiches, some inventive tacos, great salads, and bowls (steak tips over mashed potatoes or smoked gouda grits? Yes, please).

Chow down on some Greek goodness at **Kostas Express Restaurant** (489 Haywood Rd., 828/631-0777, www.kostasexpress.com, 11:30pm-8:30pm Mon.-Thurs., 11:30am-9pm Fri.-Sat., $7-28). Not everything here is expressly Greek, but it's all done with a Greek twist. Gyros, pita wraps, and baklava share menu space with burgers, pasta dishes, steak, and even barbecue, and whatever you order, you'll leave full (maybe even with leftovers) and happy to come back for another meal.

The Fly-Fishing Trail

Jackson County is the home of the first Fly-Fishing Trail in the country; it includes 15 spots on some of the best trout waters in the Smokies where you can catch rainbow, brook, and brown trout, and even the occasional golden trout. Because of its proximity to many mountain communities, the Fly-Fishing Trail has become the epicenter of fly-fishing in the region. Easy access to these waters, convenient complimentary **maps** (www.flyfishingtrail.com and http://mountainloversnc.com), and the excellent support the trail receives make it a choice spot for trout fishing, no matter which community you're visiting.

Top spots include **Panthertown Creek,** where a 2-mile walk from the end of Breedlove Road (Hwy. 1121) leads you to what some have called the "Yosemite of the East" because of its picturesque rocky bluffs. You'll catch more brook trout than you may have thought possible on this 3-mile stream, which is catch-and-release only.

For an "urban" fishing experience, try the **Tuckasegee River** as it passes through Dillsboro. You can park and fish at a number of places between Dillsboro Park and the Best Western Plus River Escape Inn, and you run a good chance of catching a large rainbow or brown trout.

The **Lower Tuckasegee River,** running from Bakers Creek Bridge to Whittier along U.S. 19/74, is around 10 miles of excellent fishing for rainbow and brown trout as well as smallmouth bass.

Fly-Fishing Trail cofounder Alex Bell, who knows the waters of western North Carolina intimately, operates **AB's Fly Fishing Guide Service** (828/226-3833, www.abfish.org, $200-450), which offers half- and full-day wading trips and float trips. AB's supplies tackle and waders if you need them, as well as extensive lessons in proper casting, water reading, and fly selection. You're responsible for securing your own North Carolina fishing license and trout stamp.

Hookers Fly Shop (828/587-4665, www.hookersflyshop.com, $200-650) guides on waters all across western North Carolina and East Tennessee, meaning they'll come out and take you fishing wherever you want to go in and around the Smokies. They offer half-day wade trips, three-quarter-day wade trips, full-day wade trips, float trips, casting classes ($30), and overnight fishing trips.

In Bryson City, the **Fly Fishing Museum of the Southern Appalachians** (210 Main St., Bryson City, 828/488-3681, www.flyfishingmuseum.org, 9am-5pm Tues.-Fri., 10am-4pm Sat., free) has displays of commonly used flies, historic rods and reels, and a Fly Fishing Hall of Fame.

If your sweet tooth is calling, give it a little satisfaction with a stop at **Dillsboro Chocolate Factory** (28 Church St., 828/631-0156, www.dillsborochocolate.com, 10am-6pm Mon.-Thurs., 10am-7pm Fri.-Sat., noon-5pm Sun.). They have truffles, chocolate, fudge, candy, and other assorted sweets, many of which they make in-house.

Accommodations

The **Best Western Plus River Escape Inn & Suites** (248 WBI Dr., 828/586-6060, www.bwriverescape.com, from $135 Mar.-Aug., from $185 Sept.-Oct., from $115 Nov.-Feb.) isn't what you think of when you think chain hotel; it's much more. The rooms are more attractive and comfortable (and more frequently updated) than you'd expect, the big patio overlooking the river includes a firepit area, and the hotel is close to Dillsboro (walkable, in fact), the road to Cherokee, and the national park.

The ever-charming ★ **Dillsboro Inn** (146 N. River Rd., 828/586-3839, www.dillsboroinn.com, $125-225) sits perched on the banks of the Tuckasegee River, giving every room in the place great views. Rooms range from spacious efficiencies to suites to something more akin to a small apartment (which means plenty of room to spread out). There are nightly fires on the deck overlooking the river, a couple of the rooms are pet-friendly, and it's walkable to Dillsboro, making a visit to Innovation Station or Foragers Canteen that much easier.

CASHIERS

Cashiers is about as quaint a mountain town as you'll find. The full-time population is small, but there are plenty of vacation and second homes here, so this little town gets busy in fall when the leaves are at their best. Fall also brings an unusual play of light and shadow on the nearby mountains. The **Shadow of the Bear,** a bear-shaped shadow that appears for only 30 minutes a day mid-October to early November when the sun hits a certain ridge just right, brings carloads of visitors to the Rhodes Big View Overlook on Highway 64 just west of Cashiers. To go "bear hunting," as the locals call it, the window is small, typically from 5:30pm to 6pm, maybe 6:15pm, but you'll want to arrive earlier to get a prime viewing spot.

In and around Cashiers you can find some truly exquisite mountain homes, cabins, and vacation rentals where you can spend upward of $1,000, even $2,000, a night. However, it's also possible to find accommodations that match this town's vibe and won't break the bank. **Hotel Cashiers** (7 Slab Town Rd., 828/743-7706, www.hotelcashiers.com, from $185), a tastefully redone motor lodge, has that classic look and feel but with modern touches like the color schemes, linens, and Instagrammable style of the rooms. From here it's only a short walk to town, the visitors center, the Cashiers Ramble Walking Trail, and both Slab Town Pizza and The Zookeeper Bistro.

There are a number of good places to dine in Cashiers, and my favorite coffee shop, **Buck's Coffee Café** (6 Hwy. 107 N., 828/743-9997, 7am-6pm daily, $2-10), serves up a great latte and has a cool little upcycled antiques shop attached. **The Zookeeper Bistro** (45 Slab Town Rd., 828/743-7711, www.thezookeeperbistro.com, 7:30am-2pm Tues.-Sat., 8am-2pm Sun., $5-16) serves breakfast, lunch, and Sunday brunch and is popular with the locals thanks to dressed-up burgers and great omelets. Billing itself as "Where Cashiers Goes for Pizza," **Slab Town Pizza** (45 Slab Town Rd., 828/743-0020, www.slabtownpizza.com, 11am-8pm Tues.-Sat., 4pm-8pm Sun., $6-18) indeed slings some quality pies, but don't skip their sandwiches and salads. Finally, **The Orchard** (905 Hwy. 107 S., 828/743-7614, www.theorchardcashiers.com, 5:30pm-late Mon.-Sat., $15-40) is one of the best restaurants around; their menu

view from a room overlooking the river in Dillsboro

of seasonally driven dishes—trout and grits, wild mushroom ravioli, bourbon-sorghum rib eye—and an outstanding wine list make this a must-dine if you're in Cashiers.

GETTING THERE AND AROUND

The towns of Sylva and Dillsboro are easily reached from Asheville by heading west on I-40, then following U.S. 23/U.S. 74 to U.S. 441 south, a drive of about an hour. Sylva and Dillsboro are five minutes apart via Haywood Road/West Main Street. Cashiers is just under 90 minutes from Asheville, and to get there, follow Highway 107 south from Sylva for 27 miles.

Bryson City and the Nantahala Forest

To look at the mountains here, you'd think that the defining feature in this part of North Carolina would be the surrounding peaks, but you're only partly right. This is a land dominated by water: Smoke-thick fog crowds valleys in the predawn hours. The peaks stand ringed in clouds. Moss, ferns, and dense forests crowd the edge of rivers and streams. When you're in the Nantahala Gorge, it feels like you've stepped into a fairy tale. According to Cherokee legends, a formidable witch called Spearfinger lived here, as did a monstrous snake and even an inchworm so large it could span the gorge. Spearfinger and her cohorts haven't been seen in years, and the Nantahala River, which runs through the narrow gorge, attracts white-water enthusiasts.

Nearby Bryson City is a river town whose proximity to white water makes it a favorite haunt for rafters, kayakers, and other thrill seekers. If you approach Bryson City from the north on U.S. 19, you're in for a strange sight: The banks of the Tuckasegee River are shored up with crushed cars.

SIGHTS
★ Great Smoky Mountains Railroad

The **Great Smoky Mountains Railroad** (GSMR, depots in Bryson City and Dillsboro, 800/872-4681, www.gsmr.com, adults from $45, children $34) is one of the best and most fun ways to see the Smokies. Using historic trains, the GSMR carries sightseers on excursions that average 4.5-hours long and take passengers through some of the region's most beautiful scenery. Trips between Dillsboro and Bryson City, with a layover at each end for shopping and dining, follow the banks of the Tuckasegee River; round-trips from Bryson City follow the Little Tennessee and Nantahala Rivers deep into the Nantahala Gorge. Many other excursions are offered, including gourmet dining; wine-, beer-, and moonshine-tasting trips; rides on a steam locomotive; autumn leaf-peeping trips; and more. There are Thomas the Tank Engine and the Little Engine That Could trips for kids, and runs to and from river-rafting outfitters.

Museums

Inside Great Smoky Mountains Railroad's gift shop is the **Smoky Mountain Trains Museum** (100 Greenlee St., 800/872-4681, www.gsmr.com, hours vary, generally 9am-4pm daily late May-Dec., 9:30am-4:30pm daily Jan.-late May, call ahead, $9 adults, $5 children, free with train ticket). The **Fly Fishing Museum of the Southern Appalachians** (210 Main St., 828/488-3681, www.flyfishingmuseum.org, 9am-5pm Tues.-Fri., 10am-4pm Sat., free) tells the story of fly-fishing on the 14,000 miles of trout waters in North Carolina and across the southern

1: Great Smoky Mountains Railroad in Bryson City 2: fly-fishing on the Tuckasegee river 3: bridge over Tuckasegee River in the Bryson City 4: Nantahala River Gorge

Appalachians. Displays of hand-tied flies, antique rods and reels, drift boats, and even live fly-tying demos round out this free museum. Across the street is the **Swain County Heritage Museum** (2 Everett St., 828/488-7857, www.swainheritagemuseum.com, 9am-5pm Mon.-Sat. and 10am-4pm Sun. Apr.-Dec; 10am-5pm Mon.-Sat. and 10am-4pm Sun. Jan.-Mar., free); downstairs is a Great Smoky Mountain Association Bookstore, and upstairs is a small but thorough museum telling the history of Bryson City and Swain County.

SPORTS AND RECREATION
★ Nantahala River Gorge
The stunningly beautiful **Nantahala River Gorge,** just outside Bryson City in the Nantahala National Forest, supports scores of river guide companies, many clustered along U.S. 19 west. Nantahala is said to mean "land of the noonday sun," and there are indeed parts of this gorge where the sheer rock walls above the river are so steep that sunlight only hits the water at the noon hour. Eight miles of the Nantahala River flow through the gorge over Class II-III rapids. The nearby Ocoee River is also a favorite of rafters, and the Cheoah River, when there are controlled water releases, has some of the South's most famous and difficult Class III-IV runs.

Outfitters and Tours
There's a lot to do in and around Bryson City beyond the borders of Great Smoky Mountains National Park. White-water rafting, kayaking, and tubing are popular ways to spend a day. Many river guide companies are located along U.S. 19. Other popular options are zip-lining, hiking, and mountain biking. Fortunately, several outfitters can help you arrange for guided tours, rentals, and just about anything else you need to make your time here memorable.

You can explore the mountains around Bryson City with the **Nantahala Outdoor Center** (13077 U.S. 19 W., 828/785-4846, www.noc.com, 8am-8pm daily, from $30),

which offers a variety of adventure options that include white-water rafting, stand-up paddleboarding on the flat-water sections of the river, hiking, mountain biking, and zip-lining. Half-day, full-day, and overnight trips are possible, and excursions like the Rapid Transit combine a relaxing morning train ride with an afternoon rafting trip.

Carolina Bound Adventures (35 Slope St., 828/788-6885, www.carolinaboundadventures.com, from $39) has guide and concierge services for a variety of outings, including hikes, mountain bike rides, overnight camping trips, waterfall tours, and brewery and winery tours. The company can assist in planning just about any aspect of your getaway, even pet-sitting if you're planning on a long day.

In addition to river guide services on the nearby Nantahala and Little Pigeon Rivers and farther afield on the Chattooga (where the 1972 movie *Deliverance* was filmed) and Ocoee Rivers, **Wildwater Rafting** (10345 U.S. 19 W., 12 miles west of Bryson City, 866/319-8870, www.wildwaterrafting.com, $50-110) leads **Wildwater Jeep Tours,** half- and full-day Jeep excursions through back roads and wilderness to waterfalls and old mountain settlements.

Endless River Adventures (14157 U.S. 19 W., Bryson City, 828/488-6199, www.endlessriveradventures.com, $45-159) guides trips on the Nantahala River, the tamest of the rivers around with Class II-III rapids; the Ocoee River, with bigger rapids and more technical challenges; and the Cheoah River, where big rapids—Class IV and above—await.

★ Fly-Fishing the Tuckasegee River
The Smoky Mountains, especially the eastern grade of the Smokies, are laced with streams perfect for fly-fishing. Anglers from all over come here to float, wade, camp, fish, hone their fly-tying craft, and learn the finer points of fly-fishing. The Tuckasegee River flows right through downtown Bryson City, and many of its feeder streams and creeks

are ideal spots to throw a line. At www. greatsmokiesfishing.com you'll find resources including license and permit information; regulations; seasonal information; maps, write-ups on lakes, streams, and rivers; and an exhaustive list of guides. To make it easy, we've put a few of the best right here.

Fly Fishing the Smokies (Bryson City, 828/488-7665, www.flyfishingthesmokies.net, $200-850) has a number of guides and options for a day or more of fly-fishing the streams on the north shore of the lake and other trout waters. Go bass fishing on Fontana for a half-day, wade the streams with them for a half-day or full-day outing, try a float trip, go fly-fishing in Great Smoky Mountains National Park, or up the ante with some backcountry camping and fly-fishing in the park.

The folks at **Nantahala on the Fly** (12121 Hwy. 19 W., Bryson City, 828/361-9386 or 828/736-0784, www.nantahalaonthefly.com, $150-400) offer half-day and full-day wading trips and float trips.

Nantahala Fly Fishing Co. (Robbinsville, 828/557-1409, www.flyfishnorthcarolina.com, $200-350) provides guided fly-rod fishing trips and private half- and full-day lessons. If you've never held one of these odd fishing rods in your hands before, there's also a fly-fishing school (2 days, $600) and private instruction. Best of all, the company has a "No Fish, No Pay" guarantee.

Fly fishers who don't need a guide can check out a number of streams that are packed with fish, but be sure to inquire about regulations for individual streams. Some are catch-and-release, while a neighboring stream might be catch-and-keep, and some have regulations about the types of hooks you can use. Once you're ready to put your line in the water, try **Hazel Creek** on the north shore of Fontana Lake, where you'll find pristine waters and a good number of fish. Other nearby creeks, like **Eagle Creek** and any of the feeder creeks that empty into the lake, are prime spots as well.

Hiking and Mountain Biking

Great Smoky Mountains National Park has more than 800 miles of wilderness trails, and with around 40 percent of the park located in Swain County, more trails than you could hike in a week are within striking distance of Bryson City. **Deep Creek Loop** is a 4.9-mile loop that passes two waterfalls on its easy, mostly flat, track. You can also take the strenuous **Deep Creek Trail** to Newfound Gap Road, a 14.2-mile one-way hike that will require a return ride. The **Noland Creek Trail** is a fairly easy 6-mile trail near the end of the Road to Nowhere (a failed road-building project from the 1930s and 1940s). At the end of the Road to Nowhere, just past the tunnel, is the **Goldmine Loop Trail,** a 3.1-mile track that's beautiful and enjoyable. The nature and lake views are especially welcome after trekking through the dark, 0.5-mile tunnel on the way in (bring a flashlight; you won't regret it).

With all these mountains, you'd think mountain biking would be a big deal around here, and you'd be right. The **Tsali Recreation Area Trail System** (Tsali Road/ NC Hwy. 28, Robbinsville, www.fs.usda.gov, $2) is only 15 miles from Bryson City and draws riders throughout the year. Named for Tsali (SAH-lee), a Cherokee martyr who led the resistance to removal at the start of the Trail of Tears, the area has four loops constituting 42 miles of trails that trace courses across the mountains. These multiuse trails are rated as moderate, and if you're up for the challenge, give these fun, flowy single-tracks a try. You'll share the road with hikers and equestrians, but there's a schedule: two trails for bikes, two for horses each day More information on area mountain biking, including an overview map showing 15 more places to ride, is available at www.greatsmokies.com.

SHOPPING

Bryson City Outdoors (169 Main St., 828/341-6444, www.brysoncityoutdoors.com, 10am-6pm Mon.-Thurs., 10am-7pm Fri.-Sat., 11am-6pm Sun.) features a well-curated selection of outdoor gear and may be the friendliest little outdoor store you've ever shopped in. Everyone here is outdoorsy—active in hiking, mountain biking, white-water rafting, kayaking, paddleboarding, fly-fishing, rock climbing, you name it—and can help you get set up for just about any activity. Next door, the store operates **BCOutdoors Taproom** (10am-9pm Mon.-Sat., 11am-7pm Sun.), offering a dozen beers on tap—mostly North Carolina brews as well as some other regional beers—plus a great selection of bottles and cans. It's a fun place to hang out, enjoy a pint, swap trail stories or fish tales, and figure out tomorrow's adventure.

There are a number of T-shirt and souvenir shops in Bryson City, but **Appalachian Mercantile** (158 Everett St., 828/488-2531, www.appalachianmercantile.net, 10am-6pm daily, call for Nov.-Mar. hours) is top on the list. Their selection doesn't overwhelm you, and there's not as much souvenir flotsam as you'll find elsewhere; instead, the foodstuffs, playing cards, games, and toys have been winnowed down to the best in each category. The owner, Lance, was a backcountry guide in the area and then a location scout for the film industry; now he's an author of local histories and a shopkeeper, and he's ready with a story if you've got a minute to listen.

FOOD

The Bistro at The Everett Boutique Hotel (16 Everett St., 828/488-1934, www.theeveretthotel.com, 4:30pm-9pm Wed.-Sun., $10-38) serves an excellent dinner that is contemporary Appalachian in nature but includes one or two vegetarian-friendly dishes, typically noodle bowls. Regardless of what you order, the flavors will be on point and you'll find a cocktail, wine, or North Carolina beer to pair with it.

You can't beat breakfast at **Everett Street Diner** (126 Everett St., 828/488-0123, www.brysoncityrestaurant.com, 7am-2pm Mon. and Wed.-Sat., 7:30am-2pm Sun., $5-14), featuring filling options that won't weigh you down on the trail, like fluffy pancakes or biscuits and gravy. For lunch, you'll find great burgers, and the light lunch—a salad and half a sandwich—is a bargain. For a real treat—Bryson City gossip and local news—sit at the counter in back.

The Appalachian Trail passes only a few feet from **River's End Restaurant** (13077 U.S. 19 W., 828/488-7172, www.noc.com, 11am-7pm Wed.-Sun., $8-23) at the Nantahala Outdoor Center. Given its proximity to the trail (really a footbridge over the river, but on the trail nonetheless) and to the center's rafting, paddling, and hiking nexus, it's a popular spot for outdoorsy sorts. The menu reflects this with dishes like the Sherpa bowls (rice, veggies, and optional meat) that are packed with protein, calories, and carbs to fuel you through a day on the trail.

For coffee and a quick breakfast, lunch, or snack, visit **Mountain Perks Espresso Bar & Café** (9 Depot St., 828/488-9561, www.mtnperks.com, 7am-3pm Sun.-Mon. and Thurs., 7am-4pm Fri.-Sat., $2-16). They make a good cappuccino, and the quiche, wraps, and bagel sandwiches hit the spot whether you eat them in-house or take them on your park adventure.

Nantahala Brewing Brewpub (116 Ramseur St., 828/585-5885, www.nantahalabrewing.com, 3pm-10pm Mon.-Fri., noon-11pm Sat. and noon-10pm Sun., Jan.-Feb.; noon-10pm Sun.-Fri. and noon-11pm Sat., Mar.-April; noon-11pm Sun.-Thurs. and noon-midnight May-Aug.; noon-10pm Sun.-Thurs. and noon-11pm Fri.-Sat., Sept.-Dec., $7-25) carries a full slate of Nantahala Brewing beer but also a menu of elevated pub grub. The salads are sizable and fresh, the pot roast and brown ale chicken are pleasant surprises, and the tacos and shareable plates exceed your bar food expectations.

Speaking of bars and bar food, **Mountain Layers Brewing Company** (90 Everett St., 828/538-0115, www.mountainlayersbrewingcompany.com, noon-9pm Mon.-Sat., noon-8pm Sun.) has an excellent rooftop deck overlooking the Tuckasegee River and a board of tasty beers to go with it. The Russian Imperial Stout, Dragon Tamer New England IPA, and Hazel Creek Blonde

Ale are top-notch. Local food trucks stop by to trade food for money with hungry imbibers.

ACCOMMODATIONS

Bryson City has a surprising number of high-quality inns and bed-and-breakfasts. Overlooking Bryson City is the ★ **McKinley Edwards Inn** (208 Arlington Ave., 828/488-9626, www.mckinleyedwardsinn.com, from $149), a lovely 12-room house and inn built in 1922. The grounds are magnificent, and breakfast, a drink, or just quiet time on the deck gazing at the mountains will convince you to come back again.

Built in 1923 and on the National Register of Historic Places, the **Fryemont Inn** (245 Fryemont St., 828/488-2159, www.fryemontinn.com, mid-Apr.-late Nov. $125-310, includes meals, late Nov.-mid-Apr. $115-215, no meals) has a cozy, rustic feel with chestnut-paneled guest rooms and an inviting lobby with an enormous stone fireplace. Suites and a log cabin that sleeps six are available.

★ **The Everett Boutique Hotel & Bistro** (16 Everett St., 828/488-1934, www.theeveretthotel.com, $199-349) has 10 suites, a rooftop hangout area, and an excellent on-site restaurant. Rooms are spacious, comfortable, and mountain chic, and the beds are so comfortable you might just want to move in. The hotel is in the former Bryson City Bank, built in 1908, and you can still see the vault door in the restaurant. It's as lovely a place to stay as you can imagine, and everything Bryson City has to offer is within a 10-minute walk.

Some river outfitters provide lodging, which can be a cheap way to pass the night if you don't mind roughing it. Many of the outfitters also offer camping on their properties. The **Rolling Thunder River Company** (10160 U.S. 19 W., 800/408-7238, www.rollingthunderriverco.com, $10-12 pp) operates a large bunkhouse with beds for its rafting customers. For large groups of 15 or more, it offers a free night in the bunkhouse Monday-Thursday. No alcohol is permitted here. **Carolina Outfitters** (715 U.S. 19, Topton, 828/488-9819, www.carolinaoutfitters.com, $80-100) offers a variety of accommodations, including two-room cabins, two-bedroom apartments, and three-bedroom cabins suitable for a large group.

Nantahala Cabins (580 Nantahala Cabins Ln., 828/488-1433, www.nantahalacabins.com, $175-325) has 10 cabins to rent, ranging from studios to 3-bedroom cabins fit for a family or group. A few minutes down

McKinley Edwards Inn

the road from Bryson City proper, closer to Almond, **Watershed Resort** (137 W. Watershed Rd., Bryson City, 877/784-0688, www.watershedresort.com, $90-700) rents cabins in just about any size, style, and configuration imaginable, within reason. There are pet-friendly cabins, cabins with a modern flair, small cabins, and cabins fit for a family reunion. Want a hot tub or a jaw-dropping view? They've got you covered. You'll find some short-term openings here and there, but if you're planning on staying for a week or more, you'll want to book well in advance. These are excellent properties and folks snap them up quick.

Camping

Among the nicest camping options available in Nantahala National Forest is **Standing Indian Campground** (90 Sloan Rd., Franklin, campground 828/524-6441, reservations 877/444-6777, www.recreation. gov, Apr.-Oct., $20-75). It has a nice diversity of campsites, from flat, grassy areas to cozy mountainside nooks. Drinking water, hot showers, flush toilets, and a phone are all available on-site, and leashed pets are permitted. The campground is close to the Appalachian Trail and sits at an elevation of 3,400 feet.

Another nice campground is the **Deep Creek Tube Center and Campground** (1040 W. Deep Creek Rd., 828/488-6055, www.deepcreekcamping.com, Apr.-late Oct., campsites $27-50, cabins $80-195), with more than 50 campsites, 18 cabins, and access to Deep Creek. The creek runs right by many campsites, and you can go tubing ($7 per day). You can also go gem "mining" here, a great mountain tradition; bags and buckets of gem-enriched dirt are sold in the camp store. The best part is that the campground is within walking distance of Great Smoky Mountains National Park.

TRANSPORTATION

Bryson City can be reached via U.S. 19 and U.S. 74, if you're coming south from Maggie Valley and Cherokee; it's only 15 minutes from Cherokee and 45 minutes from Maggie Valley. It's 20 minutes to the Great Smoky Mountains National Park's Oconaluftee Visitor Center, just north of Cherokee. Asheville is 1 hour, 20 minutes east along U.S. 74 and I-40.

Robbinsville and the Valley Towns

Between Robbinsville and the Georgia state line is another region at the heart of Cherokee life. Snowbird, not far from Robbinsville, is one of the most traditional Cherokee communities; it's common to hear the Cherokee language, and Cherokee arts, crafts, and folkways are flourishing. The burial site of Junaluska, one of the Eastern Band's most prominent leaders, is here.

As moving as it is to see the memorial to one of the Cherokee heroes, the town of Murphy is forever linked with tragedy for the Cherokee people and a dark incident in American history—the Trail of Tears. Around 16,000 Cherokee people, including warriors and clan leaders, men, women, children, older people, and the infirm, were forced to leave their homes in North Carolina, Tennessee, and Georgia. They were arrested and marched under guard to Fort Butler, here in Murphy, and from Fort Butler they were forced to walk to Oklahoma. You'll find the names of these people, many of whom died along the way, inscribed in Cherokee on a memorial at the L&N Depot in Murphy.

In addition to places of historic significance in Cherokee culture, this farthest southwestern corner of North Carolina has other compelling sights. Brasstown, a tiny village on the Georgia state line, is the home of the John C. Campbell Folk School, an artists' colony founded in 1925, where visitors can stroll among studios and along trails and stop at a gallery shop with some of the most beautiful crafts you'll find in the region. Back up toward Robbinsville, the relentlessly scenic **Cherohala Skyway** (www.cherohala. org) crosses 43 miles of the Cherokee and Nantahala National Forests. This road is a major destination for motorcyclists and sports-car drivers as well as day-trippers and vacationers.

ROBBINSVILLE

The whole southwestern corner of North Carolina is rich with Cherokee history and culture, and the Robbinsville area has some of the deepest roots of great significance to the Cherokee people. In little towns and crossroads a few miles outside Robbinsville, several hundred people known as the Snowbird community keep alive some of the oldest Cherokee ways. The Cherokee language is spoken here, and it's where some of the Eastern Band's most admired basket makers, potters, and other artists continue to make and teach their ancient arts. If you're visiting and want to enjoy an adult beverage, you'd better bring your own, as Graham County is North Carolina's one and only dry county.

Sights

Outside Robbinsville, in the ancient Stecoah Valley, is an imposing old rock schoolhouse built in 1930 and used as a school until the mid-1990s. It has been reborn as the **Stecoah Valley Center** (121 Schoolhouse Rd., Stecoah, 828/479-3364, www.stecoahvalleycenter.com), home of a weavers' guild, a native plants preservation group, a concert series, several festivals, and a great **Gallery Shop** (828/497-3098, 10am-4pm Mon.-Sat.) with local artisans' work. Concerts in the Appalachian Evening summer series, featuring area musicians, are preceded by community suppers of traditional mountain cuisine.

On Robbinsville's Main Street is the **Junaluska Memorial** (Main St., 0.5 miles north of the Graham County Courthouse), where Junaluska, a 19th-century leader of the

Eastern Band of the Cherokee, and his third wife, Nicie, are buried.

Down a winding country road 14 miles outside Robbinsville, **Yellow Branch Pottery and Cheese** (1073 Old Yellow Branch Rd., 828/479-6710, www.yellowbranch.com, noon-5pm Tues.-Sat. Apr.-Nov. or by appointment) is a beautifully rustic spot for an afternoon's excursion. Bruce DeGroot, Karen Mickler, and their herd of Jersey cows produce graceful, functional pottery and prize-winning artisanal cheeses. Visitors are welcome at their farm and shop.

Entertainment and Events

Every year on the Saturday of Memorial Day weekend in late May, the Snowbird Cherokee host the **Fading Voices Festival** (www.grahamcountytravel.com) in Robbinsville. The festival features a mound-building ceremony along with typical festival attractions—music, dancing, storytelling, crafts, and lots of food—but in the deeply traditional forms carried on by the Snowbird community.

★ Joyce Kilmer Memorial Forest

The **Joyce Kilmer Memorial Forest** (5410 Joyce Kilmer Rd., off Hwy. 143 west of Robbinsville, www.grahamcountytravel.com) is one of the largest remaining tracts of virgin forest in the eastern United States, with more than 3,800 acres of old-growth forest. Some of the tulip poplar trees are 450 years old and have grown to more than 100 feet tall and 20 feet around. The forest is named in honor of Joyce Kilmer, a soldier killed in action in France during World War I. His poem "Trees" inspired this living memorial. The only way to see the forest is on foot, and a 2-mile loop or two 1-mile loops make for an easy hike through a remarkable woodland. These easy, well-maintained paths allow visitors to experience the woods that so inspired Kilmer and his poem.

The Joyce Kilmer Memorial Forest abuts the 17,410-acre Slickrock Wilderness Area that stretches into Tennessee; **Slickrock Creek Trail**

Junaluska

One of the most important figures in the history of the Eastern Band of the Cherokee is Junaluska, who was born near Dillard, Georgia, in 1776. During the wars against the Creek Indians from 1812 to 1814, the Cherokee people fought beside U.S. forces, and it's said that the fierce young Junaluska saved the life of Andrew Jackson at the battle of Horse Shoe Bend in Alabama.

Twenty years later, Jackson, by then president, repaid Junaluska's bravery and the loyalty of the Cherokee people by signing the Indian Removal Act, which ordered that they, along with four other major Southern nations, be forced from their homelands and marched to the new Indian Territory of Oklahoma. Junaluska traveled to Washington and met with Jackson to plead for mercy for the Cherokee nation; his pleas were ignored, and in 1838, Junaluska joined 16,000 members of the Cherokee nation who were force-marched close to 1,000 miles to Oklahoma. Midway across Tennessee, he led a failed escape attempt and was captured and chained; he completed the march in leg irons and manacles. It was during this time that Junaluska supposedly said, "If I had known what Andrew Jackson would do to the Cherokees, I would have killed him myself that day at Horse Shoe Bend." In 1841 Junaluska was finally able to leave Oklahoma; he made the 17-day trip to North Carolina on horseback.

He spent his final years in Cherokee County, on land granted to him by the state of North Carolina, until his death in 1859. He and his third wife, Nicie, are buried at Robbinsville, at what is now the Junaluska Memorial and Museum. His grave was originally marked according to Cherokee tradition—with a pile of stones—but in 1910 the Daughters of the American Revolution commissioned a marker for his gravesite. During the dedication ceremony, Reverend Armstrong Cornsilk delivered a eulogy in the Cherokee language:

He was a good man. He was a good friend. He was a good friend in his home and everywhere. He would ask the hungry man to eat. He would ask the cold one to warm by his fire. He would ask the tired one to rest, and he would give a good place to sleep. Juno's home was a good home for others. He was a smart man. He made his mind think well. He was very brave. He was not afraid.

Juno at this time has been dead about 50 years. I am glad he is up above [pointing upward]. I am glad we have this beautiful monument. It shows Junaluska did good, and it shows we all appreciate him together—having a pleasant time together. I hope we shall all meet Junaluska in heaven [pointing upward] and all be happy there together.

is one of its longest trails. This 13.5-mile (one-way) trail starts out easy, but the final 5.5 miles are fairly strenuous. *Backpacker* magazine named this one of the toughest trails in the country some years ago, in part because the hike can be a 21.7-mile loop by connecting with the **Haoe Lead, Hangover Lead,** and **Ike Branch Trails.** Be forewarned that this is a big trip, but it's rewarding, with views of waterfalls (the first is only a few miles in, on the easy part) and rhododendron thickets. Its name is apt: The rocks here can be incredibly slick.

On the **Hangover Lead South Trail,** the trailhead is adjacent to the parking area at Big Fat Gap (off Slick Rock Rd., about 7 miles from U.S. 129). The trail is only 5.4 miles long (round-trip), but it's strenuous. The payoff is the view from the Haoe summit at 5,249 feet. There are backcountry campsites here, and the rule is to keep campsites 100 yards from streams and practice Leave No Trace guidelines.

A handy collection of **trail maps** for Joyce Kilmer Memorial Forest, Slickrock Creek, Snowbird Back Country, and Tsali Recreation Area is available from the Graham Chamber (https://grahamchamber.com). The maps provide a rough idea of the locations and routes of these trails, but they are not a replacement for topographic maps, which you should have with you while on any of these rugged or isolated trails. A slightly better map is available through the Partners of the Joyce Kilmer Slickrock Wilderness (www.joycekilmerslickrock.org).

Food and Accommodations

You can grab a really good steak or burger at **Moonshiner's Steakhouse** (2645 Tallulah Rd., 828/479-0708, www.moonshiners-steakhouse.business.site, 5pm-9pm Fri.-Sun., $10-26), one of the only steakhouses around. As at many of the restaurants and accommodations in these parts, you're likely to see a lot of motorcycles and sports cars in the parking lot because folks come from all over to ride several of the twisty mountain roads. Belly up to the big outdoor bar and enjoy some live music, or sit inside and talk bikes, road trips, and what your neighbors ordered with your fellow travelers.

The **Snowbird Mountain Lodge** (4633 Santeetlah Rd., 11 miles west of Robbinsville, 828/479-3433, http://snowbirdlodge.com, $310-525, meals included) was built in the early 1940s, a rustic chestnut-and-stone inn atop a 3,000-foot mountain. The view is exquisite, and the lodge is perfectly situated among the Cherohala Skyway, Lake Santeetlah, and the Joyce Kilmer Memorial Forest. Guests enjoy a full breakfast, picnic lunch, and four-course supper created from seasonal local specialties.

Another pleasant place to stay near Robbinsville is the **Tapoco Lodge Resort** (14981 Tapoco Rd., 15 miles north of Robbinsville, 828/498-2800, www.tapoco.com, rooms and suites $179-329, cabins $149-249). Built in 1930, the lodge is on the National Register of Historic Places, and it has the feel of an old-time hotel. Guest rooms in the main lodge and surrounding cabins are simple but comfortable, and the resort overlooks the Cheoah River, a legendary run for rafters several times each year when controlled releases of water form super-fast rapids. Dine here at **Tapoco Tavern** (828/498-2800, 11am-8pm Sun.-Thurs., 11am-9pm Fri.-Sat., $9-36) on pizzas, steaks, trout, fried chicken, sandwiches, and salads.

The 39-acre **Iron Horse Motorcycle Lodge** (1755 Lower Stecoah Rd., 828/479-3864, www.ironhorsenc.com) caters to motorcyclists here to ride The Tail of the Dragon, Cherohala Skyway, and Blue Ridge Parkway and to explore a number of notable routes around. A lodge ($99-165), bunkhouses ($36), fully outfitted cabins ($420-1,250) that sleep up to 20, covered wagons ($110), and tent ($20-30) and RV camping ($45-55) are available.

If you're RVing your way through the Smokies, the **Simple Life Campground** (88 Lower Mountain Creek Rd., 828/788-1099, www.thesimplelifecampground.com, Mar.-Nov., cabins $38-194, RVs $48-58, tents $22, pop-up campers $32) has cabins, RV sites, and tent sites with access to hot showers and Wi-Fi. This campground is near the Cherohala Skyway, Joyce Kilmer National Forest, and Lake Santeetlah.

HAYESVILLE, BRASSTOWN, AND MURPHY

Between Hayesville and Brasstown, you can get a really good sense of the art that has come out of this region over the years. These three small towns are along the Georgia border on U.S. 64.

Murphy River Walk

The **Murphy River Walk** is a 3-mile trail along the Hiwassee River and Valley River, winding from Konehete Park to the Old L&N Depot through the charming, tiny town of Murphy. It gives you the chance to see the town up close and personal, and it's a great way to stretch your legs after a long ride.

After a walk along the river, take a look in some of the many antiques stores in Murphy. **Marketplace Antiques** (41 Peachtree St., 828/837-1060, 10am-5pm Mon.-Thurs., 10am-6pm Fri.-Sat., noon-4pm Sun.) and **Black & White Market** (40 Valley River Ave., 828/516-1634, www.black-and-white-market.com, 10am-5pm Mon.-Sat.) will have you covered in the antiques department, and **Serenity Mountain Gift Shop** (35 Tennessee St.,

828/361-7543, 10:30am-5:30pm Tues.-Fri., 10am-5pm Sat.) has all the shirts, souvenirs, and gifts you'll want. If you're looking for beer, wine, or cigars, swing by **The Murphy Co.** (50 W. U.S. 64, 828/516-1630, 12:30pm-5:30pm Mon.-Fri., noon-4pm Sat.).

★ John C. Campbell Folk School

One of North Carolina's most remarkable cultural institutions, the **John C. Campbell Folk School** (1 Folk School Rd., Brasstown, 800/365-5724, www.folkschool.org) was created by a pair of Northern honeymooners who traveled through Appalachia over 100 years ago to educate themselves about Southern highland culture. John C. and Olive Dame Campbell, like other high-profile Northern liberals of their day, directed their humanitarian impulses toward the education and economic betterment of Southern mountain dwellers. John Campbell died a decade later, in 1919, but Olive, joining forces with her friend Marguerite Butler, set out to establish a "folk school" in the Southern mountains that she and John had visited. She was inspired by the model of the Danish *folkehøjskole*, workshops that preserved and taught traditional arts as a means of fostering economic self-determination and personal pride in rural communities. Brasstown was chosen as the site for this grand experiment, and in 1925, the John C. Campbell Folk School opened its doors.

Today, thousands of artists travel every year to this uncommonly lovely, remote valley, the site of an ancient Cherokee village. In weeklong and weekend classes, students of all ages and skill levels learn about the traditional arts of this region, such as pottery, weaving, dyeing, storytelling, and chair caning, as well as contemporary and exotic crafts such as photography, kaleidoscope making, bookmaking, and paper marbling. The website outlines the hundreds of courses offered every year, but even if you're passing through the area on a shorter visit, you can explore the school's campus. Visitors are asked to preserve the quiet atmosphere of learning and concentration when viewing the artists' studios, but you can have an up-close look at some of their marvelous wares in the school's **Craft Shop** (bottom floor of Olive Dame Campbell Dining Hall, 10am-5pm Mon.-Wed. and Fri.-Sat., 10am-6pm Thurs.), one of the nicest crafts shops in western North Carolina. You'll be wowed by what you find here. Exhibits about the school's history and examples of the work of local artists of past generations are on display at the **History Center** (8am-5pm Mon.-Sat., 1pm-5pm Sun.), next to Keith House.

Several nature trails on campus thread through this lovely valley. Be sure to visit the 0.25-mile **Rivercane Walk,** which features outdoor sculptures by some of the greatest living artists of the Eastern Band of the Cherokee. In the evenings you'll often find concerts by traditional musicians, or community square, contra, and English country dances. A visit to the John C. Campbell Folk School, whether as a student or a traveler, is an exceptional opportunity to immerse yourself in a great creative tradition.

Food and Accommodations

The western terminus of the North Carolina Barbecue Trail is in Murphy, and **Herb's Pit Bar-B-Que** (15725 W. U.S. 64, Murphy, 828/494-5367, 11am-7pm Thurs., 11am-8pm Fri.-Sat., 11am-3pm Sun., $2-30) should be your first or last stop on it. Here you can sample more than the 'cue that pitmasters in the deep mountains make—you can also order plates of tasty fried trout and chicken and thick steaks off the grill. Your barbecue tastes may be more in line with **Rib Country BBQ** (2121 W. U.S. 64, 828/837-4444, www.ribcountrybbq.com, 11am-9pm daily, $7-16), where—you guessed it!—ribs are the must-try but not the only thing on the menu. Brisket, pulled pork, fried shrimp, a rib eye, and even a fish sandwich offer distractions from the tasty, sticky ribs. The Country Feast ($41) is big enough to feed the family.

Bistro Twenty Nine (29 Tennessee St.,

Murphy, 828/361-0524, www.murphybistro29.com, 4pm-9pm Tues.-Sat., $9-32) serves some upscale but affordable meals in a surprisingly chic dining room. Warm lights, exposed brick, and local art make the perfect setting for a night out. On the menu you'll find steaks, crab cakes, burgers, shrimp scampi, and appetizers to satisfy a hungry hiker or someone ready to settle in for the night.

At **The Daily Grind & Wine** (46 Valley River Ave., Murphy, 828/835-7322, www.thedailygrindandwine.com, 8am-2pm Mon.-Tues. and Sat., 8am-8pm Wed.-Fri., breakfast $2-7, lunch $4-11), you'll find plenty of coffee and a great, cheap breakfast menu as well as a more filling lunch and snack menu loaded with sandwiches and salads, a very tasty, spicy black bean burger, and a Guinness beer brat that's top-notch. They also have a wine shop and bar serving wine and regional craft beer.

In nearby Hayesville, 15 miles east along U.S. 64, there are two spots to keep on your radar. **The Copper Door** (2 Sullivan St., Hayesville, 828/389-8460, http://thecopperdoor.com, 5pm-10pm Tues.-Sat., $16-48) is an upscale joint serving a nice selection of seafood, steaks, and other meat-centric dishes, but they can accommodate vegetarians and vegans. This elegant restaurant is run by a chef from New Orleans, and his influence is all over the menu, from crawfish to mussels to other French- and Creole-inspired creations. Over at **Nocturnal Brewing Company** (893 U.S. 64 Business, Hayesville, 828/305-7337, www.nocturnalbrewing.com, 4pm-9pm Thurs.-Fri., 2pm-9pm Sat., $5-25), they have a solid burger, a really good lentil sloppy joe, and tempeh tacos if you're hungry, and the beer—saisons, goses, pale ales, and biers de garde—is proof positive that in North Carolina, there's a great brewery anywhere you go. There's more beer to be had in nearby Andrews, where **Hoppy Trout Brewing Co.** (911 Main St., Andrews, 828/835-2111, www.hoppytroutbrewing.com, 2pm-9pm Wed.-Sat., 2pm-8pm Sun., $4-14) dishes up pizzas and snacks along with a dozen drafts. You'll get an IPA, a blonde, and an amber ale, but you'll also find things like a jalapeño and cucumber saison, barley wine, and barrel-aged stouts, so come ready to sample.

Angels Landing Inn Bed & Breakfast (94 Campbell St., Murphy, 828/360-7700, $100-120) is one of the only B&Bs in town. Fortunately, the price is right, and the breakfast is a good one. As with most B&Bs, and as with most North Carolinians, the folks here are friendly and ready with a recommendation if you're ready to explore like a local (or just get a little local gossip).

Harrah's Cherokee Casino opened a location in Murphy in 2015: **Harrah's Cherokee Valley River Casino & Hotel** (777 Casino Pkwy., Murphy, 828/422-7777, www.caesars.com, $99-499) has 300 rooms and a huge, 50,000-square-feet gaming floor with 70 table games and more than 1,000 slot machines. The dining options are mostly national chains. (Still, who comes to a casino to eat?)

TRANSPORTATION

This is the most southwestern corner of North Carolina, in some places as close to Atlanta as to Asheville. The drive from Murphy to Asheville is 2.5 hours along U.S. 74 and I-40, and to Atlanta the drive is closer to 3 hours. Robbinsville and Murphy are about 45 minutes apart along U.S. 129 and U.S. 74. It's 1 hour from Murphy to Bryson City, and the drive to the Oconaluftee Visitor Center in Cherokee from Murphy is a 1.5 hours.

Asheville

There's an energy in the mountain town of Asheville that you don't find in many other places in North Carolina. For more than a century Asheville has been a hive of progressive thinking, and it has a surprisingly cosmopolitan level of living.

With all the writers, artists, musicians, dancers, wealthy industrialists, and eclectic personalities that have inhabited this town, it's easy to understand how it earned the nickname "Paris of the South." Asheville was built on a series of hills around the confluence of the Swannanoa ("swan-uh-NO-uh") and French Broad Rivers, and commerce found its way here in the 18th and 19th centuries via water routes and a mountain stagecoach road. In the late 1800s the town experienced a boom as railroad lines began to bring vacationers by the tens of thousands. It was around that time that George Vanderbilt, scion of the massively wealthy Vanderbilt dynasty, began building his mountain home, the Biltmore, just south of downtown. From the 1880s to the 1930s the mountain town underwent a long and rapid expansion, eventually becoming a small city in its own right.

Asheville's proximity to Great Smoky Mountains National Park (it's a little more than an hour to the south and west) makes it a convenient travel hub. Use Asheville as a starting or ending point, or as a base of operations. The city also offers diverse dining and lodging options.

SIGHTS
Downtown Architecture

As beautiful as Asheville's natural environment may be, the city's striking architecture is just as attractive. The Montford neighborhood, a contemporary of the Biltmore, is a mixture of ornate Queen Anne houses and Craftsman-style bungalows. The Grove Park Inn, a huge luxury hotel, was built in 1913 and is decked out with rustic architectural details

intended to make vacationing New Yorkers and wealthy people feel like they were roughing it. Downtown Asheville has a large concentration of art deco buildings on the scale of Miami Beach. Significant structures dating to the boom before the Great Depression include the **Buncombe County Courthouse** (60 Court Plaza, built in 1927-1929), the **First Baptist Church** (Oak St. and Woodfin St., 1925), the **S&W Cafeteria** (56 Patton Ave., 1929), the **Public Service Building** (89-93 Patton Ave., 1929), and the **Grove Arcade** (1 Page Ave., 1926-1929).

The **Jackson Building** (22 S. Pack Square, built in 1923-1924) is a fine example of neo-Gothic architecture with a disturbing backstory. According to legend, on the day of the stock market crash in 1929 that started the Great Depression, one of the wealthiest men in Asheville lost it all and leaped to his death from the building. Three or four (depending on who's telling the story) more of Asheville's wealthiest followed suit. What is known to be true is that there's a bull's-eye built into the sidewalk in front of the building as a morbid monument to the story.

★ Biltmore Estate

Much of downtown Asheville dates to the 1920s, but the architectural crown jewel, the **Biltmore Estate** (1 Lodge St., 800/411-3812, www.biltmore.com, ticket office 9am-5:30pm daily, house 10am-5pm daily, gardens 9am-7:30pm daily, admission $76-96, additional fees for activities), predates that by decades. It was built in the late 1800s for owner George Vanderbilt, grandson of Gilded Age business magnate Cornelius Vanderbilt. He found himself so awestruck by the land that he amassed a 125,000-acre tract south of Asheville where he would build his "country home." He engaged celebrity architect Richard Morris Hunt to build the home in the style of a 16th-century French château. Vanderbilt also hired the

Greater Asheville

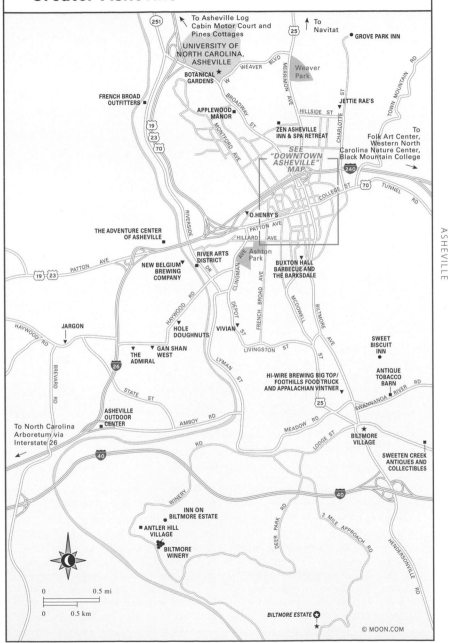

To Asheville Log Cabin Motor Court and Pines Cottages

To Navitat

GROVE PARK INN

UNIVERSITY OF NORTH CAROLINA, ASHEVILLE

Weaver Park

WEAVER

BOTANICAL GARDENS

MERRIMON AVE

BROADWAY ST

FRENCH BROAD OUTFITTERS

APPLEWOOD MANOR

HILLSIDE ST

JETTIE RAE'S

CHARLOTTE ST

TOWN MOUNTAIN RD

ZEN ASHEVILLE INN & SPA RETREAT

MONTFORD AVE

To Folk Art Center, Western North Carolina Nature Center, Black Mountain College

SEE "DOWNTOWN ASHEVILLE" MAP

TUNNEL RD

COLLEGE ST

RIVERSIDE DR

O.HENRY'S

PATTON AVE

THE ADVENTURE CENTER OF ASHEVILLE

HILLIARD AVE

Ashton Park

RIVER ARTS DISTRICT

CLINGMAN AVE

BUXTON HALL BARBECUE AND THE BARKSDALE

PATTON AVE

NEW BELGIUM BREWING COMPANY

DEPOT ST

FRENCH BROAD AVE

MCDOWELL ST

BILTMORE AVE

HAYWOOD RD

JARGON

HOLE DOUGHNUTS

VIVIAN

SWEET BISCUIT INN

HAYWOOD RD

THE ADMIRAL

GAN SHAN WEST

LIVINGSTON ST

LYMAN ST

ANTIQUE TOBACCO BARN

BREVARD RD

STATE ST

HI-WIRE BREWING BIG TOP/ FOOTHILLS FOOD TRUCK AND APPALACHIAN VINTNER

SWANNANOA RIVER RD

ASHEVILLE OUTDOOR CENTER

AMBOY RD

MEADOW RD

LODGE ST

BILTMORE VILLAGE

To North Carolina Arboretum via Interstate 26

RD

SWEETEN CREEK ANTIQUES AND COLLECTIBLES

WINERY

INN ON BILTMORE ESTATE

DEER PARK RD

3 MILE APPROACH RD

HENDERSONVILLE RD

ANTLER HILL VILLAGE

BILTMORE WINERY

0   0.5 mi

0   0.5 km

BILTMORE ESTATE

© MOON.COM

Downtown Asheville

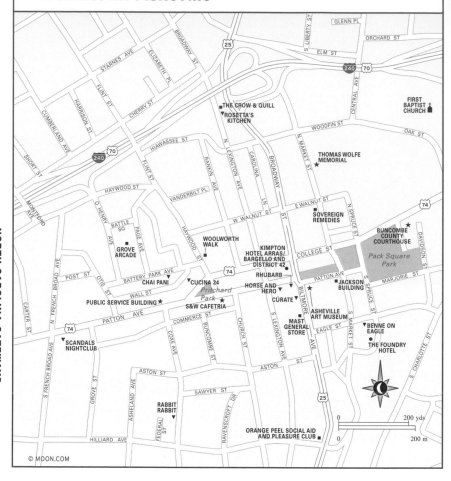

© MOON.COM

esteemed Frederick Law Olmsted, creator of New York City's Central Park, to design the landscape for the grounds, gardens, and surrounding forest.

A 3-mile-long approach road leads through manicured forests, revealing bits of the landscape and hiding the house until you are upon it, creating a sense of drama and wonder for arriving visitors. While the Biltmore Estate's original 125,000 acres are now greatly diminished—the estate comprises a little more than 8,000 acres today—it's easy to see just how big it was.

The Biltmore Estate was once the largest privately owned home in the country, and most of the house is open to visitors on self-guided tours. Other parts—like the roof and some servants' areas—are accessible on behind-the-scenes tours. As astounding as the house may be, it's nothing compared to the art collected here. There are paintings by Renoir, James Abbott McNeill Whistler, and John Singer Sargent; a collection of European antiques including Napoleon's chess set; and room upon room of masterworks in tiling, woodworking and carving, masonry, and stone carving.

Visitors can eat, shop, tour, explore, relax, and unwind without leaving the grounds, and there's easily enough here to fill a weekend. Other sights include the **Biltmore Winery** and **Cedric's** brewery in Antler Hill Village; **River Bend Farm,** which features traditional crafts; and the **Equestrian Center.**

Admission cost for the Biltmore Estate varies by season and includes the house, gardens, and winery; activities such as horseback riding, rafting, and behind-the-scenes tours cost extra. Special events, like the Christmas Candlelight Tour (Nov.-Dec.) also have additional fees. Parking is free, and a complimentary shuttle runs to the house.

Asheville Art Museum

The **Asheville Art Museum** (2 S. Pack Sq., 828/253-3227, www.ashevilleart.org, 11am-6pm Tues.-Wed. and Fri.-Sun., 11am-9pm Thurs., $15 adults, $13 seniors 65 and older, $10 students, free ages 5 and under) underwent two years of renovations to the exterior and galleries, which has allowed the museum to expand the permanent collection space by 70 percent and to double rotating exhibit spaces. The museum has been around since 1948, so this update was needed. The wing facing Pack Square is sheathed in glass and conveys from the exterior what the gallery space does inside: blend the old and the new, and invite you in for some artistic discoveries. The permanent collection includes a wide array of media and styles, ranging from photo portraits to ceramics to statuary to beautiful modern pieces. A large collection from the nearby experimental school, Black Mountain College, shows the highlights of works created by faculty and students. In addition to the galleries, there is a rooftop sculpture garden and café.

North Carolina Arboretum

The enormous **North Carolina Arboretum** (100 Frederick Law Olmsted Way, 828/665-2492, www.ncarboretum.org, 8am-9pm daily Apr.-Oct., 8am-7pm daily Nov.-Mar., Bonsai Collection 9am-5pm daily, admission free, parking $16 cars, $50 RVs) is considered by many to be one of the most beautiful in the country. The 434 natural and landscaped acres back into the Pisgah National Forest, just off the Blue Ridge Parkway. Major collections include the National Native Azalea Repository, featuring nearly every species of azalea native to the United States as well as several hybrids, and the special Bonsai Collection, comprising more than 200 bonsai plants, many of the staff horticulturists' own creation.

Bicycles and leashed dogs are permitted on many of the arboretum's trails. Walking areas range from easy to fairly rugged, but with 10 miles of trails, you will find one that suits your skill level. To learn more about the history of the arboretum and its plants, as well as the natural history of the region, join one of the guided tours (1pm Tues. and Sat.). These 2-mile walk-and-talk tours happen rain or shine, so dress for the weather. The arboretum also has a nice café, the **Bent Creek Bistro** (10am-4pm Tues.-Sun, $4-9), and gift shop, the **Connections Gallery** (10am-4pm daily).

Botanical Gardens

The **Botanical Gardens at Asheville** (151 W. T. Weaver Blvd., adjacent to the University of North Carolina Asheville campus, 828/252-5190, www.ashevillebotanicalgardens.org, dawn-dusk daily year-round, donation) is a 10-acre preserve for the region's increasingly threatened native plant species. Laid out in 1960 by landscape architect Doan Ogden, the gardens are an ecological haven. The many garden "rooms" are planted to reflect different environments of the mountains, including the Wildflower Trail, the Heath Cove, and the Fern and Moss Trail. Spring blooms peak in mid-April, but the gardens are an absolutely lovely and visually rich place to visit any time of year. Because of its serious mission of plant preservation, neither pets nor bicycles are allowed. Admission is free, but as the gardens are entirely supported by

donations, your contribution will have a real impact. On the first Saturday in May, the **Day in the Gardens** brings food and music to this normally placid park, and garden and nature enthusiasts from all around come to tour and to buy native plants for their home gardens. There is also a visitors center and gift shop (11am-3pm daily).

Western North Carolina Nature Center

Asheville, and western North Carolina generally, tend to be very ecologically conscious, as reflected in the **Western North Carolina Nature Center** (75 Gashes Creek Rd., 828/259-8080, www.wildwnc.org, 10am-4:30pm daily, $14 adults, $13 seniors 65 and over, $14 ages 13-15, $10 ages 3-12, free ages 2 and under). On the grounds of an old zoo—don't worry, it's not depressing—animals that are unable to survive in the wild due to injury or having been raised as pets live in wooded habitats on public display. This is the place to see some of the mountains' rarest species—those that even most lifelong mountain residents have never seen: cougars, wolves, coyotes, bobcats, and even the elusive hellbender. What's a hellbender, you ask? Come to the Nature Center to find out.

Folk Art Center

Anyone with an interest in Appalachian handicrafts and folk or fine art should stop by the **Folk Art Center** (Blue Ridge Parkway, milepost 382, 828/298-7928, www.southernhighlandcraftguild.org, 10am-5pm daily, free). Home to the Southern Highland Craft Guild, the Folk Art Center has around 30,000 square feet of space with three galleries, an auditorium, a research library, a tiny Blue Ridge Parkway info booth, and the Allanstand Craft Shop. Allanstand is the oldest continuously operated crafts shop in the United States. It was started in 1897 by a Presbyterian missionary and carries out

the same vision it had the year it was born: to help preserve traditional art forms and raise the visibility of the arts and crafts of the Appalachian Mountains. Although the folk arts are well represented in beautiful pottery, baskets, weaving, and quilts, you'll also find the work of contemporary studio artists in an array of media, including gorgeous hand-crafted furniture, clothing, jewelry, and toys. Bring your holiday shopping list even if it's April.

Every day, one or more members of the Southern Highland Craft Guild are on hand to demonstrate their craft at the entrance to the Folk Art Center. They may be whittling away at a chunk of wood with a pocketknife, spinning wool into yarn or weaving, or tying brooms. No matter what they're doing, they're happy to talk to you and explain their process and the history of their craft.

SPORTS AND RECREATION

Asheville is a "go out and do it" kind of town. It's not unusual to see mountain bikers, road riders, runners, hikers, and flat-water kayakers and their daredevil white-water-loving cousins all on the streets in town. A number of gear shops call Asheville home, and trails, rivers, and mountain roads are all accessed right here.

Zip-Lining

For a different perspective on the Asheville area, head north for 30 minutes along I-26 West and spend the day at **Navitat** (242 Poverty Branch Rd., Barnardsville, 828/626-3700 or 855/628-4828, www.navitat.com, 8am-6pm daily, $50-189). You can streak through the forest canopy on a pair of zip-line courses like an overgrown flying squirrel. The **Mountaintop Tour** has the tallest zip line here; it's an incredible 350 feet high—they say "don't look down," but do; it's amazing. The longest is more than 3,600 feet. Two rappels, a pair of sky bridges, and three short hikes provide interludes from all the zipping and flying, and there are plenty of opportunities for

1: Biltmore Estate **2:** signs in the River Arts District **3:** The S&W Market **4:** North Carolina Arboretum

photos and action-camera videos. A smaller course, the **Treetop Tour,** has six zip lines, rope descents, sky bridges, and timber stair climbs. Or you can combine the two courses into one giant day of adventure. Not down with strapping yourself to a steel cable and hurtling through the air? The **Guided RTV Shadow Tour** lets you take in the scenery from your seat in a Kubota RTV (that's a Residential Terrain Vehicle, think UTV but with better cupholders) and follow the zippers from the ground, safe and secure in your RTV.

If you're tempted to zip-line but want something a little less heart-pounding, consider **The Adventure Center of Asheville** (85 Expo Dr., 877/247-5539, www. ashevilletreetopsadventurepark.com, check for times, $49-89). The Adventure Center has a number of high-flying adventures to try. The **Treetops Adventure Park** has 60 challenges (read: rope swings, sky bridges, cargo nets, short zip lines, leaps from tall platforms) spread over five different adventure trails, allowing you to face the trail that presents you with the best challenges. The **Zip Line Canopy Tours** has 11 zips, three sky bridges, and so many great views you'll forget about the zip lines. **Kid Zip** is a zip-line course designed for children ages 4-10. There's also the **KOLO Mountain Bike Park** ($12-21), where you can build up your skills before you head out on some of the single-track trails south of town.

Biking

Take a tour of Asheville by bicycle. If you're thinking "It's too hilly, I'll never be able to climb that," **The Flying Bike** (meeting point 225 Coxe Ave., 828/338-8484, www. flyingbiketours.com, 9am, 10am, 1pm, 2pm, 5pm daily Feb.15-Dec.15, $62 adults, free ages 12 and under) can provide you with pedal-assisted electric bikes that make the hills easier and the flats seem like nothing at all; you'll still have to work but not as hard, as these ingenious bikes use their power to make pedaling easier. You'll start with the hill to the Grove Park Inn (which will demonstrate how

well the pedal-assist system works), the first stop on a three-hour tour around Asheville's historic and cultural sites.

There are more than 20 miles of **bicycle trails** on the Biltmore Estate, and you can bring your bike or rent one (regular or electric) in Antler Hill Village from the **Bike Barn** (828/225-1331, $20-50, estate admission not included) for two hours, a half day, or a full day and lead your own trip. You can also join Biltmore guides for a guided ride on the **Farm Trail** ($35 adults, $10 ages 9 and under) or an **Intro to Mountain Biking** ($75, ages 12 and up only). Riding on paved roads is not allowed (they're too narrow to share with cars), so stick to the marked paths, which will take you past prime photo spots and some of the most beautiful land on the estate.

In a town with as much beer as Asheville, I'd be remiss if I didn't mention the **Amazing Pubcycle** (828/214-5010, www. amazingpubcycle.com, $25, pickup at Aloft Hotel, 51 Biltmore Ave., and Renaissance Hotel, 33 Woodfin St.). Yes, it's a strange, pedal-powered pub on wheels that you see loaded down with bachelorette parties, guys getaways, and assorted rascals out to drink a heroic number of brews while working off a few of those calories as they pedal around town. On the tour you'll make two quick stops for beer; the rest is BYOB (beer and wine, no hard liquor), so pay a visit to one of the excellent bottle shops in town before you saddle up.

Water Sports

Wai Mauna Asheville SUP Tours (192 Riverside Dr., 828/808-9038, www. waimaunaashevillesuptours.com, rentals $49, tours $85-99) is a natural fit for Asheville (*wai mauna* is Hawaiian for "mountain waters"). While most stand-up paddleboarding outfitters ignore the two most beautiful parts of the day—dawn and dusk—these folks embrace them, with four tours daily at sunrise and sunset, as well as midmorning and midday.

1: floating down the French Broad River with Zen Tubing **2:** zip-lining at Navitat

As rave-worthy as sunsets are, there's something about the Dawn Patrol tour. At that time of day, the river's often shrouded in fog, the birds are waking up, and the river is as still as it will ever be; it's a perfect time to paddle. Most tours go through the River Arts District, but you can do a 7-mile trip through the Biltmore Estate, an interesting way to see the estate from a different angle.

Tubing isn't a sport, inasmuch as you simply recline in an inner tube and float from point A to point B, but it's a lot of fun and has many enthusiasts. If you want to go tubing in Asheville, do it with **Zen Tubing** (855/936-8823, www.zentubing.com, trips 9:30am-3pm, $25). The French Broad is a calm river, especially on the sections where Zen sends tubers. If you pick up a six-pack of your favorite beverage, you'll want the cooler carrier tube ($5) so you can keep drinks close at hand. Zen Tubing has two locations: downtown Asheville (608 Riverside Dr.) and south Asheville (1648 Brevard Rd.). Check the website or call ahead to see which suits your needs best.

French Broad Outfitters (704 Riverside Dr., 828/505-7371, www.frenchbroadoutfitters.com, 10am-6pm daily, rentals from $20) specializes in rentals that get you wet: namely, stand-up paddleboards, kayaks, and bellyaks—a cross between a kayak and an ergonomically designed surfboard. Bellyakers paddle like they're swimming and take the river's rapids head-on; it's a fun ride on the small but exciting rapids of the French Broad River when it's at normal levels, and a thrilling one when the river is running a little high. If you've come to Asheville equipped with your own paddleboard or kayak, French Broad Outfitters rents helmets, dry suits, personal flotation devices, kayak skirts, and more.

Asheville Outdoor Center (521 Amboy Rd., 828/232-1970, www.ashevilleoutdoorcenter.com, 9am-5pm Fri.-Sun. May and Sept., 9am-5pm Thurs.-Sun. June and Aug., 9am-5pm Wed.-Sun. July, tours $20-50) rents kayaks, rafts, and tubes to get you out on the water. They also offer shuttle services if you plan on heading out for a long paddle.

Hiking

Ready for mountain air? Join **Blue Ridge Hiking Co.** (70 College St., 828/713-5451, http://blueridgehikingco.com, $190-930) for a hike. Founder Jennifer Pharr Davis has hiked more than 11,000 miles of long-distance trails and was the first woman to become the overall record holder for fastest thru-hike of the Appalachian Trail, hiking all 2,181 miles in 46.5 days. You're not expected to have this kind of trail mobility or backpacking savvy, but Blue Ridge Hiking Co. is there to help you learn to love a hike, long or short. Join them on a private day hike or sunset hike; a group half-day hike ($80); a private full-day hike; the Brew + Brew hike, led by Jennifer's husband, Brew, and ending at some Asheville breweries; or one of their overnight hikes. The overnight hikes are often themed—women only, ages 50 or 60+, low intensity, orienteering workshops, high peaks—so pick one from the current calendar or work with the team to create a private overnight trip perfect for you and your group.

Asheville Hiking Tours (828/818-9103, www.ashevillehikingtours.com, $47-119) leads waterfall and Blue Ridge Parkway tours and wildflower and birding walks along trails in the Roan Highlands and other wild places nearby, as well as private guided hikes. Backpacking trips are also available (starting around $350) and are built around themes like fall color and destination-specific hikes. Their guides are experts in a number of fields—zoology, forest ecology, primitive skills—and are naturalists, storytellers and experienced backpackers.

Hiking on the **Biltmore Estate** can mean anything from walking the 2.5 miles of mulched paths in the manicured gardens to exploring the hills, meadows, streams, and riverbanks on more than 22 miles of trails. None are rugged, so you don't need any special equipment, just water, your camera, and maybe a walking stick. The Outdoor

Asheville and the Southern Blue Ridge

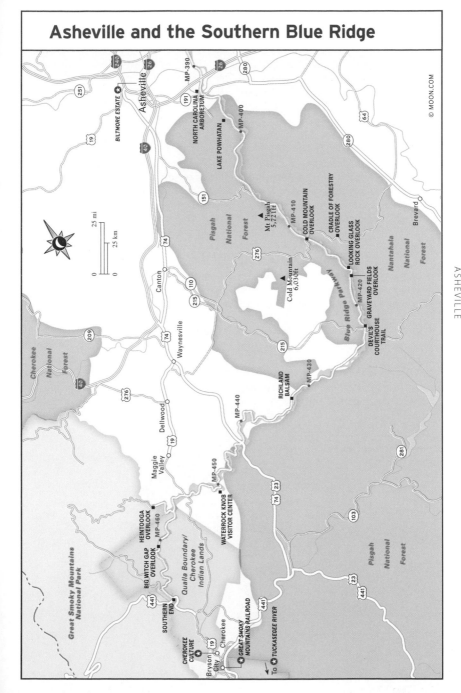

© MOON.COM

Adventure Center in Antler Hill Village has maps and can help you identify the right hike.

SHOPPING

Asheville is full of boutiques and one-off shops, and standing near the center of it all is the 1929 **Grove Arcade** (1 Page Ave., 828/252-7799, www.grovearcade.com), a storied piece of architecture that is now a chic shopping and dining destination in the heart of downtown. The expansive Tudor Revival building, ornately filigreed inside and out in ivory-glazed terra-cotta, was initially planned as the base of a 14-story building, a skyscraper by that day's standard. Inside, shops display jewelry and home decor, fossils and crystals, and clothing. **Mountain Made** (Ste. 123, 828/350-0307, www.mtnmade.com, 10am-6pm Mon.-Sat., noon-5pm Sun.) carries arts and crafts from more than 80 regional artisans, and you'll be surprised by the handiwork, fine art, and jewelry here. At **Battery Park Book Exchange & Champagne Bar** (Ste. 101, 828/252-0020, www.batteryparkbookexchange.com, 11am-9pm Sun.-Thurs., 11am-10pm Fri.-Sat.), you'll find a menu of shareable plates and snacks ($9-23); a long list of champagnes, beers, and other bubbly beverages; and a whole lot of books to browse.

There are a number of art galleries in Asheville, and two stand out as especially notable. **Woolworth Walk** (25 Haywood St., 828/254-9234, www.woolworthwalk.com, 11am-6pm Mon.-Thurs., 11am-7pm Fri., 10am-7pm Sat., 11am-5pm Sun.) has works from more than 140 artists working in a range of mediums, all in a renovated Woolworth department store; **The Soda Fountain** here (11am-5pm Mon.-Thurs., 11am-6pm Fri.-Sat., 11am-4pm Sun., $4-8) serves milkshakes and malts, sandwiches and salads à la the Woolworth lunch counter. I own and have gifted several prints from **Horse and Hero** (14 Patton Ave., 828/505-2133, www.horseandhero.com, 11am-7pm Sun.-Thurs., 11am-9pm Fri.-Sat.), a gallery that's developed a niche in Neo-Appalachian art and crafts. Woodblock prints, lithographs, digital prints, stickers, cards, shirts, and even sculptural pieces that can only be described as contemporary riffs on traditional Appalachian art make it an intriguing place to browse and buy.

One of my favorite shops is **Mast General Store** (15 Biltmore Ave., 828/232-1883, www.mastgeneralstore.com, 10am-6pm Mon.-Thurs., 10am-9pm Fri.-Sat., 11am-6pm Sun.). There are several locations around western North Carolina and a few in East Tennessee,

Asheville's Grove Arcade

but the Asheville spot is a must-visit for me. There's an area packed with bins and barrels of candy; clothes and jackets for men, women, and kids; and cast-iron cookware and Appalachian foodstuffs. The basement is full of hiking and outdoor gear and clothes.

Beer lovers should absolutely pick up some bottles and cans while they're at a brewery, but the bottle shop to check out is **Appalachian Vintner** (745 Biltmore Ave., 828/505-7500, www.appalachianvintner.com, 11am-7pm Mon.-Sat.). Their selection of beer ranges from hard-to-find European bottles (like Vichtenaar, my favorite beer ever) to the best craft beer from across the United States, and that means plenty of representation from Asheville and North Carolina. Not sure what you want? Strike up a conversation with the folks in the shop and let them lead you to a tasty discovery or two.

Art and Antiques

For lovers of vintage, retro, and aged things, the **Antique Tobacco Barn** (75 Swannanoa River Rd., 828/252-7291, www.atbarn.com, 10am-6pm daily) has more than 77,000 square feet of goodies to plunder. This perpetual winner of the *Mountain XPress* "Best Antiques Store in Western North Carolina" category has toys, art, tools, furniture, radios, sporting equipment, folk art, farm relics, oddball bric-a-brac, mid-century furniture, and all those great weird things you can only find in a collection this massive. It takes a while to explore this humongous shop, so carve out some time.

Along Swannanoa River Road, you'll find yourself in the **Biltmore Antiques District** (120 Swannanoa Rd.), a small shopping district packed with an intriguing group of antiques shops. Exploring here is always a good time because you never know what you'll find or where you'll find it. **Sweeten Creek Antiques and Collectibles** (115 Sweeten Creek Rd., 828/277-6100, 10:30am-5:30pm Mon.-Sat., noon-5:30pm Sun.) and **Screen Door** (115 Fairview Rd., 828/277-3667, www.screendoorasheville.com, 10am-5pm Mon.-Sat., noon-5pm Sun.) offer a wide selection

because their vendors and pickers number in the hundreds.

Along the Swannanoa River, many of Asheville's old warehouses and industrial buildings have been transformed into studio spaces, galleries, restaurants, and breweries in an area known as the **River Arts District** (www.riverartsdistrict.com). More than 200 artists have working studios here, and twice a year, during the first weekend of June and November, nearly every artist in the district opens their studios to the public for a two-day **Studio Stroll.** On the second Saturday of each month, many studios are open and artists are on hand, usually working (in public view) and often happy to interact with visitors.

NIGHTLIFE AND ENTERTAINMENT

A favorite spot for live music is the **Orange Peel Social Aid and Pleasure Club** (101 Biltmore Ave., 828/398-1837, www.theorangepeel.net, noon-midnight or later daily). The Orange Peel is a cool concert hall with a big dance floor, great sound, and great history. It's billed as "the nation's premier live music hall and concert venue," and it can back that up with some powerful acts taking the stage, including Bob Dylan, Smashing Pumpkins, Mickey Hart of Grateful Dead fame, Beastie Boys, and My Morning Jacket.

Asheville has another supercool music venue: **Rabbit Rabbit** (75 Coxe Ave., 828/255-4077, www.rabbitrabbitavl.com). Acts like Trey Anastasio Band, King Gizzard & The Lizard Wizard, Band of Horses, Bright Eyes, and Sylvan Esso, as well as standup comedy shows, frequent this spot, as do food trucks. On nights when there's not a big act in town, you'll find trivia, silent cinema and silent discos (where attendees wear headphones), and, of course, the house kitchen, which dishes up tacos, burritos, and the like ($3-9).

Asheville has a growing reputation as a craft-cocktail destination to match its food renown, and one big contributor to that movement is **Sovereign Remedies** (29 N. Market St.,

828/919-9518, www.sovereignremedies.com, 4pm-11pm Sun. and Wed.-Thurs., 4pm-midnight, Fri.-Sat.). The minute it opened its doors, this place became a go-to for Asheville's cocktail lovers and those hankering for delicious food (it serves dinner most nights, brunch on weekends, and light bites in between, $4-24). Between the bartenders and some local foragers, Sovereign Remedies stays stocked with wild herbs, berries, fruits, and roots, used to infuse or macerate various liquors, craft bitters, and create drinking vinegars. If it's not busy, have a seat and chat with the bartenders, and challenge them to create tasty drinks for you based around a certain spirit.

Over at **The Barksdale** (42 Banks Ave., 828/424-7449, 4pm-2am daily), Asheville's, well, Asheville side is on display. Quirky, weird, and certainly in full command of its own personality, The Barksdale is one of those places you were going to end up anyway so why not start the evening there? Cocktails here have attitude—drinks are named The Gin One or The Tequila One (ditto for whiskey and mezcal)—the music's a little loud, and the almost exclusively local crowd comes to get away from the run-of-the-mill tourists who don't want a little local flavor with their getaways. Speaking of local flavor, they serve some oddball hot dogs here. Named for former pro wrestlers and topped with things like kimchi chowchow, Takis (a spicy corn chip) dust, fried pickles, and ranch-seasoned popcorn, they have the same outsider vibe as the rest of the place.

Asheville has North Carolina's oldest gay bar, **o.henry's** (237 Haywood St., 828/254-1891, www.ohenrysofasheville.com, 4pm-2am daily). A landmark unto itself, o.henry's hosts drag shows on Saturday, throws a potluck on the first Sunday of the month, and does karaoke on Wednesdays. They also have **The Underground**, an industrial dance bar known for its "Total Gold Dance Your Ass Off" parties held the first Friday of the month. If you want more drag shows, **Scandals**

Nightclub (11 Grove St., 828/505-1612, www.scandalsnightclub.com, 10pm-2:30am Fri.-Sun.) has your back. Shows with known drag queens and up-and-comers, plus DJ-led dance parties, make this a raucous spot all weekend.

Travel writers get all sorts of tips from friends and readers, and I found **The Crow & Quill** (106 N. Lexington Ave., 828/505-2866, www.thecrowandquill.com, 5pm-midnight Tues.-Sun. by reservation) through just such a recommendation—and am I ever glad I listened. It stocks nearly 1,000 spirits, and the wizards behind the bar know how to use every one of them. The cocktails are superb, the space is lively (you might catch some live music here), and everywhere you look, there's some interesting bit of art. Note that at least one member of your party will have to become a member of The Crow & Quill and pay a small membership fee ($10)—North Carolina has some rigid laws regarding spirits, and technically only private clubs can serve them. Buy a drink for whoever ponies up.

EVENTS

Asheville's home to **Chow Chow** (www.chowchowasheville.com, tickets $15-150), a food festival celebrating the flavors of southern Appalachia. The city's biggest chefs and culinary personalities have been joined by noted guest chefs José Andréas, Vivian Howard, Ashley Christensen, and others for demos, tastings, charity dinners, and swank soirees. It's a great opportunity to taste outstanding dishes and meet some culinary legends. The festival takes place from June to September with a calendar chock-full of events small and large. Check them out, pick a time packed with things to do, get your tickets, and go.

FOOD

Asheville is a town that clearly loves its food, with 17 active farmers markets, nearly 300 independent restaurants, and more breweries

1: Orange Peel Social Aid and Pleasure Club
2: Buxton Hall Barbeque

per capita than any other city in the country. They set out to prove it at every meal.

★ Cúrate (13 Biltmore Ave., 828/239-2946, www.curatetapasbar.com, 4pm-10:30pm Sun. and Tues.-Thurs., 4pm-11pm Fri.-Sat., $5-32) is led by Chef Katie Button, a James Beard Award semifinalist who previously cooked at the legendary El Bulli restaurant in Spain. At Cúrate she serves a Spanish tapas menu, so you'll get to try a variety of flavors and textures. One of the best meals in the place is The Spanish Experience ($55, $30 for wine pairing), a multicourse feast that highlights the best of the menu. A number of vegan and gluten-free selections are also on the menu. The lively restaurant features a long bar that faces the kitchen, so you can watch Chef Button and her expert kitchen brigade work.

Chef Button and her husband and business partner, Felix Mena, also have La Bodega (32 S. Lexington Ave., 828/630-0330, www.curatetapasbar.com, 8am-8pm Wed.-Sun., $6-20), an all-day café, restaurant, and specialty foods shop just a block over. If you need to feed a crowd you need to try their paella, otherwise grab a seat and enjoy. The ensalidilla rusa "la bodega" – their spin on tuna fish – is devilishly good.

One of Asheville's most amazing restaurants—and that's quite the qualification given the food scene here—is Rhubarb (7 N. Pack Sq., 828/785-1503, http://rhubarbasheville.com, 5pm-9:30pm Sun.-Mon. and Wed.-Thurs., 5pm-10pm Fri.-Sat., also 10:30am-2pm Sat.-Sun., $9-32). Chef John Fleer is a culinary magician with a kitchen full of talented cooks. The best farmed, foraged, and pasture-raised ingredients are used to create dishes like pork belly with daylily-walnut slaw, peanut-braised collard greens, and wood-roasted whole trout.

Chef Fleer also opened Benne on Eagle (35 Eagle St., 828/552-8833, www.benneoneagle.com, 8am-10:30am daily, 5pm-9pm Tues.-Sat., $9-30) in The Foundry Hotel. Chef de Cuisine Malcolm McMillian heads up the kitchen, and he honors African American and Appalachian food traditions on the menu. Dishes like the Xawaash Spiced Wings, Berbere Spiced Chicken, and Jerk Squash draw ingredients from Africa and the Caribbean; the ramp vinaigrette, locally grown collards and peas, and Carolina Gold rice speak more directly to Appalachian and North Carolina food traditions. Situated at the heart of The Block—the center of Black Asheville around the turn of the 20th century—it's a fitting culinary tribute and hopefully the first of many restaurants to explore the nuances of African-Appalachian cooking.

What's a trip to North Carolina without barbecue? ★ Buxton Hall Barbecue (32 Banks Ave., 828/232-7216, www.buxtonhall.com, 11:30am-3pm and 5:30pm-9:30pm Sun.-Thurs., 11:30am-3pm and 5:30pm-10pm Fri.-Sat., $5-16) is old-school barbecue at its best with some new-school spins and sides courtesy of Chef Elliot Moss. Moss and company crisscrossed the Carolinas, dining in dozens of barbecue joints to create his menu. Chicken bog (chicken, rice, sausage) from the South Carolina Lowcountry is on the menu along with South Carolina barbecue hash and eastern North Carolina whole-hog barbecue. Also on the menu are smoked sausages, fried catfish, and smoked chicken. Meals are accompanied by an excellent selection of classic barbecue sides.

Italian restaurant ★ Cucina 24 (24 Wall St., 828/254-6170, www.cucina24restaurant.com, 5pm-9pm Sun.-Thurs., 5pm-10pm Fri.-Sat., $10-35), headed by Chef Brian Canipelli, is dedicated to sourcing as much as possible from local farms, ranches, and fisheries, and these ingredients are enticingly crafted into the restaurant's curated menu offerings. You can't go wrong no matter what you order, so go wild. Pizzas and veggies are roasted in a wood-fired oven, and pastas are made in-house (and come with sauces to die for). Or let the chef decide for you and get the five-course chef's dinner ($60).

If you're in the mood for a killer hot dog, a burger like no other, or a Cuban sandwich that will make you think about proposing marriage to the guy or gal operating the grill, or even a bologna sandwich (seriously), head to **Foothills Food Truck** (2 Huntsman Pl., at Hi-Wire's Big Top, 828/606-9372, www.foothillslocalmeats.com, 4pm-8pm Mon. and Wed.-Fri., noon-8pm Sat.-Sun., $8-14). I love this place and it has become one of my go-tos in Asheville. We meet friends at Hi-Wire's Big Top, grab a couple of orders of poutine and a sandwich (the cheeseburger is crave-worthy), then enjoy the beer and food and company.

★ **The Admiral** (400 Haywood Rd., 828/252-2541, www.theadmiralasheville.com, 5pm-10pm Thurs.-Mon., $16-45) has been West Asheville's prime food destination since it opened in a humble cinderblock building in 2007. The kitchen is driven by talent and culinary curiosity. On the menu you'll find an ever-evolving collection of New American dishes, like a rib eye with roasted potato and cabbage or a half-chicken with Carolina Gold rice and pole beans. The Admiral also has a great cocktail program, and this cozy spot is divey yet chic.

West Asheville's ★ **Jargon** (715 Haywood Rd., 828/785-1761, www.jargonrestaurant. com, 5pm-9pm Sun.-Thurs., 5pm-10pm Fri.-Sat., $12-45) is out to do one thing (and it does it very well): to delight diners with its techniques and ingredients. Strong relationships with farmers and food folk make the kitchen's job a little easier, and everything they serve is perfection or right next door. Grilled peaches take center stage in a summer salad, yucca gets a salt and vinegar treatment, and whether you get a vegetarian or meat-centered main, it's going to look and smell so good, you'll forget to take a picture before you dig in.

Nearby is **Hole Doughnuts** (168 Haywood Rd., 828/774-5667, www.hole-doughnuts.com, 8am-1pm Wed.-Sun., $2-3), one of my worldwide top-three doughnuts (I eat a lot of doughnuts; don't judge). Made with yeasted dough cooked to order, they're always hot, always fresh, and always interesting. My favorite from here had a sugared sumac glaze, making that yeasty little doughnut that much more tart.

In the River Arts District, **Vivian** (348 Depot St., 828/225-3497, www.vivianavl. com, 5pm-8:30pm Thurs.-Sat., 10:30am-1:30pm Sun., $9-30) delights diners with impeccable French techniques and exceptional local ingredients. Think of seared duck, pork terrine, and scallop quenelle but also venison osso buco, smoked oysters, and fried chicken. Stop by for brunch and you'll be delighted by their fried chicken biscuit, the smoked lamb Benedict, and the usual run of eggs, quiche, and smoked fish.

When you've been at the Orange Peel, the show has just let out and you need to refuel with some good food, the lights are on at **Rosetta's Kitchen** (116 N. Lexington Ave., 828/232-0738, www.rosettaskitchen.com, noon-9pm Tues.-Sun., $6-12). There's so much to recommend about this place: The food is very good, it's all vegetarian and mostly vegan, and it's made with local produce in season. They compost everything that makes its way back to the kitchen, recycle all their trash, and make sure the used vegetable oil goes to power biodiesel cars: It's Asheville's signature countercultural reinterpretation of the South, and it's one of the best vegetarian places in town. Downstairs is **The Buchi Bar,** where they serve Buchi kombucha and kombucha-based cocktails, as well as beer, wine, cocktails and all-natural sodas.

Seafood lovers take note: **Jettie Rae's** (143 Charlotte St., 828/505-4499, www.jettieraes. com , 4:30pm-9pm Wed.-Thurs., 4:30pm-10pm Fri.-Sun., $8-26) has what you want for dinner, whether it's a pile of clam strips, caviar service (a treat-yourself item at $60), or something in between. A raw bar and a menu packed with oysters, crabs, clams, fish and chips, and a lobster roll will have your stomach growling before you even get to the restaurant.

Gan Shan West (285 Haywood Rd., Ste. 20, 828/417-7402, www.ganshangroup.com, 4pm-9pm Mon.-Thurs., 4pm-10pm Fri.-Sat., $9-16) takes a broad look at Asian cuisine and serves up rice dishes, ramen, and an assortment of Asian-inspired plates from a small menu that's as intriguing as it is tasty. *Gai lan,* a broccoli-like Chinese green, gets a spicy treatment; steamed buns come served in a pair and are filled with your choice of a meat or veggie filling; and dishes like ramen and *mapo doufu* will help some diners push into new territory with this cuisine.

Take a good, long look at the gorgeous art deco S&W Building when you stop by ★ **The S&W Market** (56 Patton Ave., 828/575-1500, www.swmarketavl.com, 11:30am-9pm Sun.-Mon. and Wed.-Thurs., 11:30am-10pm Fri.-Sat.) for a bite and a drink. Originally built to house the S&W Cafeteria, it's back to its original purpose. Several vendors occupy the space. **Highland Brewing** (www.highlandbrewing.com) has an outpost here. **Bun Intended** (www.bunintendedavl. com, $5-12) added this brick-and-mortar outpost to their food truck and serves up bao buns and noodle, curry, and fried rice bowls. **Buxton Chicken Palace** (www. buxtonchickenpalace.com, $7-13), from chef and pitmaster Elliott Moss, dishes up the best damn fried chicken sandwich you'll ever eat, plus a bourbon and Cheerwine slushie. **Peace Love Tacos** (www.mountainmadreavl.com, $4-6) serves up tacos with a side of positivity. **Farm Dogs** (www.farmdogsavl.com, $5-8) is a concept from the folks at Farmburger (around the corner) and has sausages and hot dogs made from local, grass-fed beef. **The Hop Ice Cream** (www.hopicecreamnc.com, $3-6) has traditional and vegan ice-cream options available, as well as coffee and other treats. And **The Times Bar** (828/774-5028, www.thetimesbarasheville.com, 4:30am-11pm Mon.-Tues., 10am-11pm Wed. and Sun., 10am-midnight Thurs., 10am-1am Fri.-Sat.) shakes up classic and inventive cocktails for your sipping enjoyment and offers a full coffee bar (closed Mon.-Tues.) to help wake you up or clear your foggy head.

Local favorite **Chai Pani** (22 Battery Park Ave., 828/254-4003, www.chaipaniasheville. com, 11:30am-3:30pm and 5pm-9pm Wed.-Thurs., 11:30am-3:30pm and 5:30pm-9:30pm Fri.-Sun., $8-14) continues to win fans with its great food and cool atmosphere. Don't go expecting typical Indian fare; this place is inspired by Indian street food vendors and serves casual and affordable specialties from all over India, including lamb burgers, paneer and chicken and fish rolls, and more. The restaurant's name means "tea and water," a phrase that refers to a snack or a small gift, and, honestly, everything is so well put together and so tastefully made that every bite is like a gift.

ACCOMMODATIONS

The **Asheville Bed & Breakfast Association** (www.ashevillebba.com) has a constantly growing membership of inns and B&Bs in the area that band together to promote getaways, tours, and seasonal packages. Check with them for any current specials.

Asheville has a history in hospitality, and one of the longest continuously operated B&Bs in town is a real charmer. ★ **Applewood Manor** (62 Cumberland Circle, 828/254-2244, www.applewoodmanor.com, $290-310) has six gorgeous rooms (each named for a type of apple) and a great farm-to-table breakfast. The owners—a husband-and-wife team— share their interests with guests via road cycling and culinary programs. They'll set you up with a bike rental and point you toward a place to ride, or you can join them for a guided ride with a former national road race champion. If that's not your speed, you can get in the kitchen for some baking or a cooking class. If you're headed to Asheville or the Smokies with a group, look into renting the whole place ($1,700 per night) and making it your home away from home.

★ **Zen Asheville Inn & Spa Retreat** (128 Hillside St., 828/255-0051, www. ashevillespa.com, $229-479) is one of my favorite places to stay in town. Rooms are private and quiet, and all five of them come with a big, comfortable bed and a two-person hot tub. Guests can also use a sauna as well as a European steam shower. Throughout the house, comfortable seating areas make it easy to find a spot for breakfast or tea, or just to

Craft Brews in Beer City

Asheville is regarded as the epicenter of North Carolina's beer and culinary scenes, a reputation that's well deserved. Asheville itself is packed with award-winning restaurants and breweries, and every time a new one opens, it makes the news. Winner of the title "Beer City USA" and perpetually at the top of any beer geek's list of cities to visit, Asheville has an exemplary brewery scene in terms of variety, innovation, and sheer volume. When you're in town, you'll have no problem finding a brewery to visit, but this list will give you a head start on your search for the perfect brew.

- **Hi-Wire Brewing** (www.hiwirebrewing.com) has a pair of locations, on the South Slope (197 Hilliard Ave., 828/738-2452) and the **Big Top** (2 Huntsman Pl., 828/738-2451). At the Big Top you'll find their flagship brews and a great food truck, and on the South Slope you'll find experimental quaffs to try.

- **Zillicoah Beer Company** (870 Riverside Dr., Woodfin, 828/424-7929, www.zillicoahbeer. com) is new to the scene but strong with beer aged in French oak, collaboration brews with local breweries, and an exceptional kölsch.

- **Bhramari Brewing Co.** (101 S. Lexington Ave., 828/214-7981, www.bhramaribrewing.com) delivers the unexpected: black gose with orange blossom, sour pale ales, dry-hopped berliner weisse (a sour beer that tastes like fruit punch), and even a foeder-aged, honey-infused beer (a foeder is a big oak vessel).

- **Burial Beer Co.** (40 Collier Ave., 828/475-2739, www.burialbeer.com) makes intriguing brews with intriguing names. Their taproom, with its indoor and outdoor spaces, excellent food truck, and funky mural, makes it a great place to stop and enjoy one of the double IPAs.

- **Highland Brewing Company** (12 Old Charlotte Hwy., Ste. H, 828/299-3370, www.highlandbrewing.com) has the honor of being the first microbrewery in Asheville, and it's a fine one. They continue to keep their flagship brews relevant by tweaking the recipes, but they also continue to innovate, releasing an impressive set of single-hop brews.

- **New Belgium Brewing Company** (21 Craven St., 828/333-6900, www.newbelgium. com) is one of the biggest in the area, and their tour is exceptional. Most craft beer fans know Fat Tire and their other brews, but the taproom here carries specialties and barrel-aged beers not available elsewhere.

- **Archetype Brewing** (www.archetypebrewing.com) has locations downtown (174 Broadway St., 828/505-8305) and in West Asheville (265 Haywood Rd., 828/505-4177) where you'll find their interpretations of Belgian beers like a saison, witbier, strong ale, and more.

- **Green Man Brewery** (27 Buxton Ave., 828/252-5502, www.greenmanbrewery.com) has lagers, fruity IPAs, even tart berliner weisses, but their monster Rainmaker Double IPA is a hit, as are their barrel-aged and sour beers like Bootsy and Snozzberry.

- **Catawba Brewing Co.** (32 Banks Ave., 828/552-3934, www.catawbabrewing.com) has a relaxing taproom with a bevy of crushable beers on tap. Their White Zombie white ale, Drum Circle Haze double IPA, and Festbier lager are favorites.

- **Sierra Nevada Brewery** (100 Sierra Nevada Way, Mills River, 828/708-6242, www. sierranevada.com) was described to me as "the Taj Mahal of beer" and "like Willy Wonka's factory, but with beer," and it lives up to that hype. There's a good restaurant on-site, a great tour, an impressive facility, and a *long* tap list that goes beyond what you expect from Sierra Nevada.

read or talk; one lovely spot is the tatami porch overlooking a Japanese garden at the front of the house. Breakfast is a healthy, filling affair. Massage therapists and aestheticians are on call, so you can arrange for treatments of almost any kind on-site.

A truly lovely bed-and-breakfast is **Sweet Biscuit Inn** (77 Kenilworth Rd., 828/250-0170, www.sweetbiscuitinn.com, $160-275). I have to admit, I was drawn here by the name, but the place, the host, and the breakfast all conspired to make me like it even more. The seven bedrooms and carriage house are accented by tiger oak wood floors and high ceilings. Queen or king beds are comfy, and breakfast is excellent, especially the biscuits.

In recent years the face of downtown Asheville has changed with the arrival of several hotels. AC Hotel (a Marriott chain) made a splash when it arrived, as did **Kimpton Hotel Arras** (7 Patton Ave., 828/255-0303, www.hotelarras.com, $280-530). Asheville's tallest building, on Pack Square, was reduced to a skeleton and rebuilt, and the result is this stunning Kimpton that hosts works by local artists. Grab drinks and dinner at **District 42** (www.district42avl.com, $10-37) or sit for a more upscale dinner or brunch at **Bargello** (www.bargelloavl.com, $9-64), plating up Mediterranean-inspired dishes using local ingredients.

In the days of yore, before budget hotels became the norm, the motor court or cottage court was the stay-over of choice for middle-class travelers. Today these motor courts and cottage courts are relics of the past, and few remain, but the mountains of North Carolina contain a handful of fine examples. In the Asheville area, at least two are still operating, providing travelers with retro accommodations. **Asheville Log Cabin Motor Court** (330 Weaverville Hwy., 828/645-6546, www.theashevillecabins.com, $95-305, 2-night minimum stay weekends, pets allowed for a fee), 6.2 miles north of downtown Asheville, has cable TV and wireless Internet access but no phones. Some rooms are air-conditioned, but that's not usually a necessity at this elevation. Another great cabin court is the **Pines Cottages** (346 Weaverville Hwy., 828/645-9661, www.thepinescottages.com, $109-330, up to 2 pets allowed, $15 per pet), only 6.3 miles north of Asheville. How could you resist staying at a place billed as "A nice place for nice people"?

Built in a former foundry in what was once the heart of Asheville's Black neighborhood, ★ **The Foundry Hotel** (51 S. Market St., 828/552-8545, www.foundryasheville.com, $260-1,600) pays homage to the building's past, while the restaurant attached to the hotel, **Benne on Eagle** (828/552-8833, www.benneoneagle.com, $9-30), offers a hat tip to Black and Appalachian cuisine. Only a block off Biltmore Avenue, it's walkable but still gives you a separation from Asheville's bustling downtown. Exposed brick on the walls and quirky art—wallpaper and framed pieces with details, newspaper clippings, and photos from the foundry's operating years—give the hotel a bohemian touch. The bedding, lounge, gym, and other hotel amenities are decidedly upscale, though. Relax and grab a drink in the **Workshop Lounge** before you head out for the evening.

Want to stay in a tree house? How about a retro camper with a hot tub? Or a dome with skylight windows so you can watch the stars? Or a yurt? If these options sound good, you need **Asheville Glamping** (address released on booking, 828/450-9745, www.ashevilleglamping.com, $140-500). They have a trio of properties with a host of quirky but refined places and ways to stay, from safari-style tents to tree houses to yurts and more. When you book, they'll send you the address of your accommodation. It's a slight inconvenience, but it's a way to free their immensely Instagrammable campgrounds and properties from lookers and lurkers and keep them a haven to their guests.

If you've spent the day touring the Biltmore Estate, viewing the incredible splendor in which a robber baron of the Gilded Age

1: The Foundry Hotel 2: Grove Park Inn

basked, it may be jarring to return to real life (unless you're a billionaire). You can soften the transition with a stay at **The Inn on Biltmore Estate** (866/336-1245, www.biltmore.com, $340-2,000). It's everything you'd wish for from a hotel in this location. The rooms and suites are beautifully furnished and luxurious, the views are magnificent, and the lobby, dining room, and library have the deluxe coziness of a turn-of-the-20th-century lodge. In the off-season, it's possible to find rooms from about $220. **Village Hotel on Biltmore Estate** (from $220) in Antler Hill Village has 209 rooms and is a testament to the ongoing and growing popularity of the Biltmore. You can find specials for as low as $170.

Resorts

The **Grove Park Inn** (290 Macon Ave., 828/252-2711 or 800/438-5800, www.omnihotels.com, $350-1,049, spa and golf packages available) is the sort of place Asheville residents bring their out-of-town houseguests when giving them a grand tour of the city, simply to walk into the lobby to ooh and aah. The massive stone building—constructed by a crew of 400 who had only mule teams and a single steam shovel to aid them—was erected in 1912 and 1913. Eight U.S. presidents have stayed here, as has a glittering parade of early-20th-century big shots, among them Henry Ford, Thomas Edison, Eleanor Roosevelt, Harry Houdini, and F. Scott Fitzgerald.

Even if you're not staying here, it's worth a visit just to see the lobby and enormous fireplaces, and take in the atmosphere while having a cocktail or dinner at one of the many on-site establishments: **Vue 1913** (5pm-10pm Thurs.-Sun., $34-60) has French and American dishes and a few premium options like a Wagyu filet ($98) and an elk tenderloin ($75) if you're treating yourself; **Edison Craft Ales + Kitchen** (4pm-10pm Mon.-Thurs., 4pm-11pm Fri., 11am-11pm Sat., 11am-10pm Sun., $12-48) serves some high-quality bar food and craft beer; and **Blue Ridge** (7am-10:30am daily, 4:30-9pm Fri.-Sat., noon-2:30

Sun., $29-48 adults, $17-23 ages 6-12) is a farm-to-table artisanal buffet. The hotel's **Sunset Terrace** (11am-3pm and 4:30pm-10pm daily, reservations required, $13-50) has phenomenal views, allowing you to enjoy dinner and the sunset, and if you're splurging, you can go for something truly special: an A5 Miyazaki rib eye ($107), a truly exceptional cut of beef.

Being a guest at the Grove Park Inn is quite an experience. In addition to the spectacle of the lodge and its multiple restaurants, cafés, bars, and shops, for an additional charge guests have access to its world-famous **spa** (daily, day pass $244). The pass gives access to the lounges, pools, steam room, inhalation room, and outdoor whirlpool tub. The indoor pool is a fantastic place, a subterranean stone room with vaulted skylights and tropical plants. For extra fees ($180-540, most $200-300), guests can choose from a long menu of spa treatments: massages, facials, manicures, aromatherapy, and body wraps.

TRANSPORTATION
Car

From Asheville it's easy to get to Great Smoky Mountains National Park. In just over an hour you can be in Cataloochee, at the north end of the park, to camp, hike, and watch for elk in a serene mountain cove; to get there, take I-40 west to exit 20 and follow the signs. You can also take I-40 west into Tennessee: Follow the Foothills Parkway to U.S. 321 and skirt the edge of the national park to Gatlinburg, Tennessee, and the entrance to the national park (a trip of about 90 minutes). From Gatlinburg, you can make a loop back to Asheville by taking Newfound Gap Road across the national park to Cherokee, North Carolina (about 2.5 hours); then head back to Asheville via U.S. 441 to U.S. 19 to I-40, a total loop of about 3.5 hours and some 175 miles.

You can also head straight to Cherokee from Asheville and enter the national park via Newfound Gap Road there. It's an hour's drive following I-40 west to exit 27, then taking U.S. 19 south to U.S. 441, which takes you right to Cherokee. Alternately, you can take the more scenic, but much longer, route and get to Cherokee via the Blue Ridge Parkway. This route is only 83 miles, but it takes 2-2.5 hours. If you want to go this way, head south out of Asheville along U.S. 25 and pick up the Blue Ridge Parkway about 5.5 miles from town; turn south on the Parkway and drive until you reach Cherokee and the national park. And, of course, you can reverse the course if you're making that grand loop and return to Asheville via the Blue Ridge Parkway by picking it up in Cherokee and driving north.

Air

Asheville Regional Airport (AVL, 61 Terminal Dr., 828/684-2226, www.flyavl.com) is in Fletcher, a 20-minute drive on I-26 south of the city. American Airlines, Delta, United, Spirit, and Allegiant offer nonstop flights to Charlotte, Atlanta, Chicago, Washington DC, New York City's Newark and LaGuardia airports, Denver, and more. A taxi from the airport costs around $45.

Bus

There is a **Greyhound station** (2 Tunnel Rd., 828/253-8451, www.greyhound.com) in Asheville. Asheville has an extensive public bus system called **ART** (www.ashevillenc.gov, 6am-9:30pm Mon.-Fri., 7am-9:30pm Sat., 8:30am-6pm Sun., $1 adults, seniors $0.50), connecting most major points in the metropolitan area, including the airport, with downtown. See the website for routes and schedules.

BREVARD

Brevard is the pleasant seat of the improbably named Transylvania County (unlike in vampire stories, it's not creepy, but beautiful in a Gothic forest way), only 48 minutes southwest of Asheville. Brevard has a population of rather startling and odd-looking white squirrels. The local legend about their origins is that their ancestors escaped from an overturned circus truck in Florida in 1940 and made their way to Brevard as pets. More

likely, say researchers, they came from an exotic pet breeder in Florida and were acquired by a Brevard-area family. In any case, the white squirrels escaped into the wilds of Transylvania County, and you'll probably see their descendants in the area when you visit.

Recreation
DUPONT STATE RECREATIONAL FOREST

About 10 miles south of Brevard, **DuPont State Recreational Forest** (U.S. 276, 828/877-6527, www.dupontstaterecreationalforest.com) has more than 90 miles of hiking trails on 10,000 acres. Some of Transylvania County's beautiful waterfalls are located within the forest and accessible on foot via moderate or strenuous forest trails, or, for people with disabilities only, by vehicle (special permits and advance reservation required). Visitors should use caution, wear brightly colored clothing, and leave that bearskin cape at home September-December, when hikers share the woods with hunters. The Aleen Steinberg Visitor Center (89 Buck Forest Rd., Cedar Mountain, 9am-5pm daily mid-Mar.-Dec., 10am-4pm Sat.-Sun. Jan.-mid-Mar.) has restrooms and trash cans and is staffed by volunteers who are happy to help with trail recommendations. The visitors center is near the trailhead to Hooker Falls.

Many of the hiking and mountain biking trails are true rugged forest paths; others, like those that lead to a trio of waterfalls—Hooker, Triple, and High Falls—are wide, maintained avenues through the woods. The hike, or hikes, as you'll follow several trails, to Triple and High Falls can be hot, sweaty affairs in spring and summer, so bring water. But the views are more than worth it, and in fall it's a phenomenal hike. After you make this longer hike, make the shorter one to the lower Hooker Falls and go for a swim in the crisp mountain water. Already cool, the water will feel downright cold—and quite refreshing—on a hot day. If you hike the three falls, you're looking at a 2-mile loop for High Falls, a 0.4-mile trail to Triple Falls, and another

0.4-mile trail to Hooker, for a total of 2.8 miles. Downloadable maps and more information are available through **Friends of DuPont Forest** (www.dupontforest.com).

Entertainment and Events

The **Brevard Music Center** (349 Andante Ln., 828/862-2100, www.brevardmusic.org) has attracted the highest-caliber young musicians since 1944 for intensive, summer-long classical music instruction. Throughout the summer, Brevard Music Center students, as well as visiting soloists of international fame, put on world-class concerts, performing works by composers that have included Tchaikovsky as well as Gilbert and Sullivan.

Brevard Brewing Company (63 E. Main St., 282/885-2101, www.brevard-brewing.com, 2pm-10pm daily) was the first brewery in the county, and it always keeps six taps flowing with its own brews, including a Bohemian pilsner, a Munich-style dunkel, a lager, an IPA, and an American red ale. **Ecusta Brewing** (43 Pisgah Hwy., #3, Pisgah Forest, 828/966-2337, www.ecustabrewing.com, 1pm-9pm Mon.-Thurs., noon-9pm Fri.-Sat., noon-8pm Sun.) is a few miles north of town but worth the short drive. Its range of styles will please everyone from hopheads (IPAs, pale ales) to sour fans (with sours incorporating ginger and mint, blood orange, and wild yeasts).

An import from Colorado but no less welcome is **Oskar Blues Brewery** (342 Mountain Industrial Dr., 828/883-2337, www.oskarblues.com, noon-8pm Sun.-Thurs., noon-9pm Fri.-Sat.), which serves popular beers including Mama's Little Yella Pils (a Czech pilsner) and Old Chub Scotch Ale, as well as hard seltzer and the thirst-quenching Margarita Gose. If you're hungry, the **Oskar Blues Chubwagon** ($5-12) serves burgers, fries, hot dogs, and a mean chicken tender sandwich.

The Hub and Pisgah Tavern (11 Mama's Pl., Pisgah Forest, 828/884-8670, www.thehubpisgah.com, 10am-6pm Mon.-Fri., 9am-6pm Sat., 10am-5pm Sun.) is a kind of all-in-one taproom, bike shop, gear depot, and food truck stop that sits right at the edge of Pisgah National Forest. The tavern serves cold brews on tap as well as in cans and bottles. Beer choices span the country, but you'll always find a good selection of local beers. While you work on your pint, shop for a new bike or some new gear, or step outside and see which food truck is serving (if there's a line of locals waiting to order, that's a good sign).

Shopping

Brevard calls to a number of fine and folk artists, and some of the best local work is represented at **Number 7 Fine Arts and Crafts Cooperative** (2 W. Main St., 828/883-2294, www.number7arts.org, 11am-5pm Mon.-Sat., noon-4pm Sun.). This gallery has featured works by a diverse group of around 25 Transylvania County artists since 1999. Ask about the photography, textiles, oils and watercolors, sculptures, and pottery on display; the artists themselves work the register and can help you find a piece you love.

Named for Brevard's famed creatures, the **White Squirrel Shoppe** (6 W. Main St., 828/877-3530, www.whitesquirrelshoppe.com, 10:30am-5:30pm Mon.-Thurs., 10am-6pm Fri.-Sat., 11:30am-5pm Sun.) is where to go for souvenirs. The shop's got a bit of everything, so drop in and pick up a memento or two.

Outdoor gear and a solid selection of T-shirts, plus some North Carolina beer on tap—which you can sip while you shop— make **D.D. Bullwinkel's Outdoors** (60 E. Main St., 828/862-4700, www.ddbullwinkels.com, 10am-6pm Mon.-Thurs., 10am-7pm Fri.-Sat., noon-6pm Sun.) a must-stop. You'll find whatever you forgot or just realized you need on a trip along the Parkway, including backpacks, hiking poles, boots and socks, water bottles, and technical clothing. The staff are outdoors devotees, so ask any gear questions or get suggestions on where to hike, picnic, or skinny-dip.

Food

The Falls Landing Eatery (18 E. Main St.,

828/884-2835, www.thefallslanding.com, 11:30am-2:30pm and 5pm-8pm Tues.-Sat., $11-30) is a popular spot among locals. It specializes in seafood (foreshadowed by the rainbow trout on the eatery's sign), and the North Carolina trout sautéed in lemon butter is particularly good. But don't discount the burgers, steaks, or lamb chops, either, which deliver on flavor and value.

★ **Marco Trattoria** (204 W. Main St., 828/883-4841, www.marcotrattoria.com, 11am-3pm and 5pm-9pm Mon.-Sat., 11am-3pm Sun., $9-24) comes from the former owners of Hobnob, one of Brevard's top restaurants for years. Following a break to find some inspiration, Chef Marc Dambax is back with Marco Trattoria, an Italian-influenced restaurant that's quickly become known as one of the best eateries in town. Pizzas fly out of the wood-fired oven, and the menu's full of Italian classics and Chef Dambax's spin on the cuisine in dishes like North Carolina mountain trout piccata and pancetta-wrapped monkfish served over seasonal veggies.

★ **The Blind Mule at Toxaway Station** (14 S. Gaston St., 828/553-8978, www.blindmulerestaurant.com, 5pm-9pm Wed.-Sun., reservations required, $10-35) serves a menu rich in tapas and small, shareable plates. They don't forget the entrées; it's just that 3-4 are on offer at any given time. Fresh, seasonal ingredients drive the menu, which changes weekly, and whether you're ordering a salad, some poutine, a burger, an Indian-spiced lamb pot pie, or a main (their treatment of trout—often served with some great grits—is a winner), you'll leave happy you stopped by for a meal.

For an old-school shake or a quick bite, head to **Rocky's Grill & Soda Shop** (50 S. Broad St., 828/877-5375, 11am-6pm Thurs.-Mon., $5-12). This must-stop has been around since 1942, and the nostalgic counter with its line of chrome stools will transport you back to the heyday of soda fountains. Grab a malt, a milkshake, an ice-cream soda, a root beer float, or an egg cream; all are especially rewarding after a morning hike or bike ride.

When the weather's right, dining on the patio at **Jordan Street Café** (48 W. Jordan St., 828/883-2558, www.thejordanstreetcafe. com, 4pm-9pm Thurs., 4pm-10pm Fri.-Sat., 11am-2pm and 4pm-9pm Sun., $10-28) is the way to go. They serve a little bit of everything—fish-and-chips, blackened chicken sandwiches, burgers, salads, daily flatbread pizza and quesadilla specials—but the menu is simple enough to keep it focused.

There's something soothing about getting a burger at a spot like **Cardinal Drive-In** (344 S. Broad St., 828/884-7085, 10:30am-10pm Mon.-Thurs., 10:30am-11pm Sat., $3-10). Maybe it's the quaintness of the drive-in, from ordering through the little speakers to someone bringing a tray of food to your car, but it's special. As are the burgers, and the onion rings. It looks a little rough, but that's part of the charm—along with the milkshakes.

Accommodations

Slip back in time at the ★ **Sunset Motel** (523 S. Broad St., 828/884-9106, www. thesunsetmotel.com, $110-150), a kitschy throwback to the days of the classic roadside motel: It's cheap, comfortable, and has chairs right outside your door so you can visit with your neighbors. It also has the best modern convenience—free Wi-Fi. The staff is super friendly and ready to help with suggestions for places to eat and things to do. You can add on tickets to the Brevard Music Center, waterfall tours, and more when you book your room. Film buffs take note: Robert Mitchum stayed here while filming *Thunder Road.*

The Inn at Brevard (315 E. Main St., 828/884-2105, www.theinnatbrevard.com, $220-320) is spacious, beautiful, and kid-friendly. The stately 14-room B&B was built in 1885 and makes a good picture; the rooms are well appointed, and there's a full breakfast every day. Brevard's **Red House Inn** (266 W. Probart St., 828/884-9349, www. brevardbedandbreakfast.com) has six rooms ($175-235) and three rental homes ($189-350) in the area. The house has had many lives in Brevard, first as a general store in 1851 (when it was brand-new), then as the county's first courthouse, as a railroad station, a school, family home, and now a B&B. Updated to modern standards without losing its history or charm, it's a lovely and convenient spot to spend a few days.

Just a 10-minute drive south of Brevard, on 14 mountaintop acres, is **Ash Grove Mountain Cabins and Camping** (29 Ash Grove Way, 828/885-7216, www.ash-grove.com, tent and RV sites $29-49, cabins $120-160). This retreat is open year-round, unlike others in the area, so you can experience all four seasons in this lovely spot. The cabins are quaint and cozy, and the campsites well maintained. Common areas feature a bonfire pit, a few lawn games, and a tiny waterfall.

The Adventure Village & Lodgings (15 Adventure Ridge Rd., 828/862-5411, www.theadventurevillage.com) has loads of places to stay. Across the property there are 19 cabins ($89-155) and more than 50 RV sites ($44), with as many more expected to open by late 2022, and a whole heap of primitive tent-camping sites ($22). The whole property is 90 acres, all set up to help you have a good visit. Amenities include biking and hiking trails, a catfish pond, a playground, and a swimming and wading pool. Add in the super-friendly folks who run the place, and you've got an excellent spot to stay.

PISGAH RANGER DISTRICT

Just south of the Blue Ridge Parkway and north of Brevard in the town of Pisgah Forest is the **Pisgah Ranger Station** (1600 Pisgah Hwy., Pisgah Forest, 828/877-3265, www.fs.usda.gov, 9am-5pm Mon.-Sat. mid-Apr.-Oct., 9am-4:30pm Mon.-Fri. Nov.-mid-Apr.) of the Pisgah National Forest. The forest covers 500,000 acres, which is a large swath of western North Carolina, but this 157,000-acre ranger district has many of the forest's favorite attractions. A good topographic map is available from National Geographic (www.natgeomaps.com). In the ranger district are more than 275 miles of hiking trails and several campgrounds; the most easily accessible campground, and one of the most popular in the area, is **Davidson River Campground** (Davidson River Circle, campground 828/384-6666, reservations 800/444-6777, www.recreation.gov, Apr.-Dec., $28-56),

runner on a trail in Pisgah National Forest

which is 1.5 miles from the Brevard entrance. It has showers and toilets.

The **Shining Rock Wilderness** and the **Middle Prong Wilderness,** which adjoins Shining Rock to the southwest, are a rugged terrain that rises from 3,200 feet at its lowest point, along the West Pigeon River, to a towering 6,400 feet at Richmond Balsam. **Cold Mountain,** made famous by the 1997 historical novel and movie (2003) of the same name, is a real peak in the Shining Rock Wilderness, and seeing it helps make the struggles of the fictional characters more real. These mountains are steep, and the forests dense, and what trails there are have no signage. This is a popular area among experienced backwoods trekkers, but it is not recommended for casual visitors because it is exceedingly easy to get lost. At a minimum, hikers should be adept at using both a compass and a topographic map before venturing into these wilderness areas.

Not to be confused with Shining Rock, **Sliding Rock** (off U.S. 276, 7.2 miles from the Parkway, 828/885-7625) is an easily accessible waterfall and swimming spot with a parking lot ($2), bathhouse, and lifeguards (10am-6pm daily late May-early Sept.). You can actually ride down the 60-foot waterfall, a smooth rock face (not so smooth that you shouldn't wear sturdy britches), over which 11,000 gallons of water rush every minute into the chilly swimming hole below. How chilly? It's a breathtaking 55°F in the summer. Given the waterfall's proximity to the Cradle of Forestry—which is just 4 miles north—it's worth a stop with a car full of kids, especially if they are adventurous and outdoorsy.

If you have kids with you, make sure to stop at the **Cradle of Forestry** (11250 Pisgah Hwy., Pisgah Forest, 828/877-3130, www.cradleofforestry.com, 10am-4pm Wed.-Sun., mid-Apr.-early Nov., $6 adults, $3 ages 5-12, free ages 4 and under). This museum and activity complex commemorate the rise of the forestry profession in the United States, which originated here at a turn-of-the-20th-century training school in the forests once owned by George Washington Vanderbilt, master of Biltmore. Plow days and living history days give an interesting glimpse into this region's old-time methods of farming and frontier living. Self-guided trails lead through the woods to many interesting locations of this campus of America's first school of forestry. Most of what's here is geared toward little ones.

Camping

Davidson River Campground (1 Davidson River Circle, Pisgah Forest, campground 828/384-6666, reservations 800/444-6777, www.recreation.gov, Apr.-Dec., $28-56) is just outside Brevard in the Shining Rock Wilderness Area. There are around 160 sites here, some with river access. Each site comes equipped with a picnic table, fire ring, and grill. Hot showers and flush toilets are available. It's the most convenient campground for exploring the hiking and fishing in the area as well as checking out the waterfalls.

Background

The Landscape

GEOGRAPHY

The Mountain Region forms the western border of North Carolina. The ridges of the Blue Ridge and Great Smoky Mountains, both sub-ranges of the Appalachian Mountain chain, undulate like the folds of a great quilt, running northeast to southwest from Virginia along the border with Tennessee and into the southwestern corner, where the inland tip of North Carolina meets Georgia. This is a land of waterfalls, rivers, and fast-flowing creeks, and rugged, beautiful peaks of smaller mountain configurations. Hemmed in among the peaks and

hollows of the Blue Ridge and the Smokies are the Black Mountains, the Pisgah Range, and the Unka Range. The Black Mountains are only about 15 miles wide and are confined mostly to Yancey County, but they're the highest in the state, and 6 of the 10 highest peaks in the eastern United States are here, including Mount Mitchell, the highest at 6,684 feet.

This is a region rich in resources, with coal seams, limestone and marble quarries, natural gas deposits, and, surprisingly, pockets and veins of precious and semiprecious gems. The rivers here are old, with the ironically named New River, one of the oldest in the world, flowing northward from North Carolina's Blue Ridge through Virginia and into West Virginia.

CLIMATE

The mountains are much cooler than either the Piedmont or the coast, and winter lasts longer. North Carolina towns like Asheville and Boone can be blanketed in snow while the trees in Piedmont towns, less than 100 miles away, aren't even showing their fall colors. The coldest temperature ever recorded in North Carolina, −34°F, was recorded in 1985 on Mount Mitchell. Spring and fall can bring cool to temperate days and chilly nights; summer days can hit the 80s, though the evenings bring a welcome relief. The Piedmont, on the other hand, can be brutally hot during the summer and quite warm on spring and fall days, though winter is milder. The coast sees long, hot summers and cool—not cold—winters with rare snowfall.

The Smoky Mountains experience four distinct seasons, with temperatures and microclimates that can vary wildly depending on elevation and sun exposure. Temperatures can swing drastically with those elevation shifts, changing as much as 15-20°F as you go from the lowest elevations to the highest. That means on warm summer days, when cities like Asheville might see temperatures in the 80s,

Mount Mitchell, 6,000 feet above sea level, will be in the low 50s and possibly cooler, depending on the wind.

During **spring,** temperatures in this region range from the low 40s to the mid- or upper 60s, and rain or even an early spring snowfall is common. **Summer** sees higher temperatures, reaching 80 degrees with some regularity, higher on rare occasions; summer lows can dip down into the 60s and may be even lower at high elevations along the Blue Ridge Parkway. In **fall,** temperatures are similar to spring, with daytime temperatures in the 40s to 60s, and nights plunging to 30°F on occasion. **Winter** is cold, with ranges from the low 30s to the high 40s; nighttime temperatures, and temperatures in the deepest hollows, can fall into the teens and single digits. Temperatures that low are possible across the region during the coldest periods of winter, even lower at elevations where it's not uncommon to experience a few freezing days.

This is a wet place, with regular snowfall from late fall through early spring, and rains common any time of year. Winter storms can dump a few inches of wet snow on the mountains here, or they can dust it with some fine, powdery snow. Thunderstorms in spring, summer, and fall can be heavy, although the worst of the weather is only occasional; regular rain showers contribute to the 50-80 inches of precipitation falling annually.

Tornadoes, most common in the spring, can cause trouble any time of year. A rare November twister touched down in 2006, smashing the Columbus County community of Riegelwood in North Carolina, killing eight people and leaving a 7-mile swath of destruction. Even plain old **thunderstorms** can be dangerous, bringing lightning, flash flooding, difficult driving conditions, and even hail. **Snowstorms** are rare, and usually occur in the mountains. The Piedmont sees more snow than the coast, which gets flurries once or twice each winter and the occasional dusting of snow.

Geographical Vocabulary

This region has some unusual landscapes and environments, and some unusual vocabulary to describe them. As you explore, you may encounter the following terms.

HOLLER

Here's a term that's really more of a regional pronunciation than a unique word. A holler is what is on paper termed a "hollow"—a mountain cove. It's just that in the South we aren't much for rounding words that end in "ow." If you don't believe me, just beller out the winda to that feller wallering in yonder meada.

BALD

An ecological mystery, the Appalachian bald is a mountaintop area on which there are no trees, even though surrounding mountaintops of the same elevation may be forested. Typically, a bald is either grassy or a heath. Heaths are more easily explained, as they are caused by soil conditions that don't support forest. Grassy balds, though, occur on land where logically trees should be found. Some theories hold that grassy balds were caused by generations of livestock grazing, but soil studies show that they were grassy meadows before the first cattle or sheep arrived. Grazing may still be the answer, though: The balds may originally have been chomped and trampled down by prehistoric megafauna—ancient bison, mastodons, and mammoths. Today, in the absence of mammoths or free-ranging cattle, some balds are gradually becoming woodland, except where deliberately maintained.

Outside the mountains, most North Carolinians are woefully inexperienced snow drivers, and the state Department of Transportation doesn't have the equipment in coastal counties to handle much more than a little snow.

ENVIRONMENTAL ISSUES

The parklands and forests along the routes through the Smoky Mountains are preserved so future generations can enjoy nature in as pristine a state as possible. That's why there's no gas available on the Blue Ridge Parkway. It also explains the constant reminders to adhere to **Leave No Trace** (www.lnt.org) principles. Leave No Trace principles are similar to the Boy Scouts of America teachings: Plan ahead and prepare, travel and camp on durable surfaces, dispose of waste properly, leave what you find, minimize campfire impacts, respect wildlife, be considerate of other visitors. These easy rules can improve the outdoor experience for everyone.

If you pack something in, pack it out, and consider carrying a **trash bag** on trails to

pick up after less responsible hikers. If each of us would make this a habit, we could clean up a lot of litter that clutters up our view and is detrimental to the environment.

Dogs are allowed on some trails throughout this route, though they must be on leash or under physical control at all times. Please check with rangers for pet-friendly trails. If you have Fido out on the trail or let him use the grassy facilities at an overlook or wayside, be sure to pick up what he's putting down.

You'll pass several ponds and lakes as you travel this region, but unless there's a designated **swimming** area, going for a dip isn't cool. There are exceptions, but those exceptions are noted near the potential swimming hole. When in doubt, ask before you dive in.

You'll spot lots of **wildlife** on your trip. Common animals include white-tailed deer, raccoons, opossums, turtles, bobcats, and even black bears. Coyotes are becoming a more frequent sight along the way, and in certain areas of the Smoky Mountains, you can even see the occasional elk. Many times, a herd of deer will be in a pasture off the parkway. If you see deer (or any other animal), and you want to get a photograph, keep a safe distance from the animal and don't offer them any food; this makes them grow accustomed to people and can have negative impacts on their health.

Plants

In the early 1700s, John Lawson, an English explorer who would soon be one of the first victims of the Tuscarora War, wrote of a magnificent tree house somewhere in the very young colony of North Carolina.

> I have been informed of a Tulip-Tree that was ten Foot Diameter; and another, wherein a lusty Man had his Bed and Household Furniture, and liv'd in it, till his Labour got him a more fashionable Mansion. He afterwards became a noted Man, in his Country, for Wealth and Conduct.

Whether or not there was ever a tulip poplar large enough to serve as a furnished bachelor pad, the forests of North America must have seemed miraculous to the first Europeans to see them.

FORESTS

Today, after generations of logging and farming across North Carolina, few old-growth forests exist. In the Smoky Mountains, stands of old-growth timber, like the Joyce Kilmer Memorial Forest, are a sight to behold, and some of the trees almost validate Lawson's anecdote. Across the state, scores of specialized ecosystems support a marvelous diversity of plant and animal life. In the east, cypress swamps and a few patches of maritime forest still stand; across the Sandhills are longleaf pine forests; in the mountains are fragrant balsam forests and stands of hardwoods.

Both North Carolina and Tennessee are geographically and climatically varied, so there's a greater diversity in tree species. But in Great Smoky Mountains National Park, the biodiversity is incredible. More than 1,600 species of flowering plants and shrubs grow here; 450 mosses, liverworts, and hornworts; and 50 types of ferns. In short, there's a lot that grows here.

The science and profession of forestry were born here: In the 1880s and 1890s, George W. Vanderbilt, lord of the manor at Biltmore, engaged Fredrick Law Olmsted, who designed New York City's Central Park, to plan a managed forest of the finest, healthiest, and hardiest trees. Vanderbilt hired Gifford Pinchot and later Carl Schenck to be the stewards of the thousands of wooded acres he owned in the Pisgah Forest south of Asheville. The contributions these men made to the nascent field are still felt today and are commemorated at the Cradle of Forestry Museum near Brevard.

FLOWERS

In the park there are more than 1,500 species of flowering plants (the most of any North American national park), and much of the region's flora puts on great annual shows, drawing flocks of admirers—the gaudy **azaleas** of springtime, the **wildflowers** of the first warm weather in the hills, the **rhododendrons** and **mountain laurels** of the Appalachian summer. The Ericaceae family, different kinds of great woody bushes with star-shaped blossoms that include azaleas, rhododendrons, and laurels, is the headliner in the floral fashion show.

The **flame azalea** makes a late-spring appearance on the mountainsides of the Blue Ridge and Great Smokies, joined by its cousins the mountain laurel and Catawba rhododendron in May and June. The ways of the rhododendron are a little mysterious; not every plant blooms every year, and there's no sure-fire way of predicting when they'll put on big shows. The area's widely varying elevation also figures into bloom times. If you're interested in timing your trip to coincide with some of these flowering seasons, your best bet is to call ahead and speak with a ranger from Great Smoky Mountains National Park to find out how the season is coming along.

Around the end of April and into May, when spring finally arrives in the mountains but the forest floor is not yet sequestered in leafy shade, a profusion of delicate flowers emerges. **Violets** and **chickweed** emerge early on, as do the white **trillium** and the wake-robin, a trillium that looks something like a small poinsettia. Every year since 1950, around the end of April, Great Smoky Mountains National Park has hosted the **Spring Wildflower Pilgrimage** (www. springwildflowerpilgrimage.org), a weeklong festival featuring scores of nature walks that also reveal salamanders, birds, and wild hogs; there are also workshops and art exhibits. See the website for a schedule of events.

Surprisingly, one of the best places to view displays of wildflowers is along the major highways. Back in 1985, North Carolina's Department of Transportation started a highway beautification project that's still going strong and involves planting large banks of wildflowers along highways and in wide medians. The displays are not landscaped but are allowed to grow up in unkempt profusion, often planted in inspired combinations of wildly contrasting colors that make the flowerbeds a genuinely beautiful addition to the environment. The website of the state's **Department of Transportation** (www. ncdot.org) offers a guide to the locations and seasons of the wildflower beds.

FALL FOLIAGE

Arriving as early as mid-September at the highest elevations and gradually sliding down the mountains through late October, autumn colors bring a late-season wave of visitors. Dropping temperatures change trees' sugar production, resulting in a palette of colors, while simple fatigue causes the green to fade in others, exposing underlying hues. Countless climatic factors can alter the onset and progress of leaf season, so the mountains blush at slightly different times every year. The latter weeks of October tend to be the peak; during those weeks it can be difficult to find lodging in the mountains, so be sure to plan ahead. Some of the best places for leaf-peeping are along the Blue Ridge Parkway and in Great Smoky Mountains National Park.

rhododendron

Animals

The biodiversity of the animals in Great Smoky Mountains National Park is astounding: The park has 65 species of mammals, more than 200 varieties of birds, 67 native fish species, and more than 80 types of reptiles and amphibians. And researchers are finding more every year. Among the familiar wildlife most commonly seen in the state, **white-tailed deer** are out in force in the countryside and in the woods; they populate suburban areas in large numbers as well. **Raccoons** and **opossums** prowl at night, happy to scavenge from trash cans and the forest floor. **Skunks** are common, particularly in the mountains, and are often smelled rather than seen. They leave an odor something like a cross between grape soda and Sharpie markers. There are also a fair number of **black bears,** not only in the mountains but also in swamps and deep woods across the state.

In woods and yards alike, **gray squirrels** and a host of familiar **songbirds** are a daily presence. Different species of **tree frogs** produce beautiful choruses on spring and summer nights, while **fireflies** mount sparkly shows in the trees and grass in the upper Piedmont and mountains.

The Carolina woods harbor colonies of **Southern flying squirrels.** It's very unlikely that you'll see one unless it's at a nature center or wildlife rehabilitation clinic because flying squirrels are both nocturnal and shy. They're also almost unspeakably cute. Fully extended, they're about nine inches long snout to tail, weigh about four ounces, and have super-silky fur and pink noses. Like many nocturnal animals, the squirrels have comically long whiskers and huge, wide-set eyes. When they're flying—gliding, really—they spread their limbs to extend the patagium, a membrane that stretches between their front and hind legs, and glide along like little magic carpets.

Also deep in the Smokies are some herds of **wild hogs,** game boars brought to the area in the early 1900s and allowed to go feral. The official line among wildlife officials is that **mountain lions**—in this region called panthers—have been extinct in North Carolina for some time. But mountain dwellers claim there are still panthers in the Blue Ridge and Smokies, and most people here have seen or heard one—their cry sounds like a terror-filled scream. There are even tales of a panther in the inland woods of Brunswick and Columbus Counties on the southeast coast.

REINTRODUCED SPECIES

The Smokies proved a hospitable place for the reintroduction of **elk.** Now the largest animals in Great Smoky Mountains National Park, elk, which can grow up to 700 pounds, are most often observed in the Cataloochee section of the park, grazing happily and lounging in the mist in the early morning and at twilight.

AMPHIBIANS

Dozens of species of **salamanders** and their close kin, including **mudpuppies, sirens,** and *Amphiuma,* call this region home, and Great Smoky Mountains National Park harbors so many of them that it's known as the Salamander Capital of the World. Throughout the state, **frogs** and **toads** are numerous and vociferous, especially the many species of dainty **tree frogs.** Two species, the gray tree frog and the spring peeper, are found almost everywhere, and beginning in late winter they create the impression that the trees are filled with ringing cell phones.

Hellbenders are quite possibly the strangest animal. They are enormous salamanders—not the slick little pencil-thin five-inch salamanders easily spotted along creeks, but hulking brutes that grow to more than two feet long and can weigh five pounds. Rare and hermetic, they live in rocky mountain streams, venturing out from under rocks at night to gobble up crayfish and minnows. They're hard to see even if they do emerge in the daytime because they're lumpy and mud-colored, camouflaged against streambeds. Aggressive with each other, the males often sport battle scars on their stumpy legs. They've been known to bite humans, but as rare as it is to spot a hellbender, it's an exponentially rarer occurrence to be bitten by one.

REPTILES

Turtles and **snakes** are the most common reptiles. **Box turtles,** found everywhere, and **bog turtles,** found in the Smokies, are the only land terrapins. A great many freshwater turtles inhabit the swamps and ponds, and on a sunny day every log or branch sticking out of fresh water will become a sunbathing terrace for as many turtles as it can hold. Common water turtles include **cooters, sliders,** and **painted turtles. Snapping turtles** can be found in fresh water, so mind your toes. They grow up to a couple of feet long and can weigh more than 50 pounds. Not only will they bite—hard!—if provoked, they will actually initiate hostilities, lunging for you if they so much as disapprove of the fashion of your shoes. Even the tiny hatchlings are vicious, so give them a wide berth.

The vast majority of snakes are shy, gentle, and totally harmless to anything larger than a rat. There are a few species of venomous snakes that are very dangerous. These include three kinds of **rattlesnake:** the huge diamondback, whose diet of rabbits testifies to its size and strength; the pygmy; and the timber or canebrake rattler. Other venomous species are the beautiful mottled **copperhead** and the **cottonmouth or water moccasin,** famous for flinging its mouth open in hostility and flashing its brilliant white palate, although you'll rarely see a cottonmouth or moccasin in the Smokies.

Most snakes are entirely benign to humans, including old familiars such as **black racers** and **king snakes** as well as **milk, corn,** and **rat snakes.** One particularly endearing character is the **hognose snake,** which can be found throughout North Carolina but is most common in the east. Colloquially known as a spreading adder, the hognose snake compensates for its total harmlessness with amazing displays of histrionics. If you startle one, it will first flatten and greatly widen its head and neck and hiss most passionately. If it sees that you're not frightened by plan A, it will panic and go straight to plan B: playing dead. The hognose snake won't simply lie inert until you go away, though. It goes to the dramatic lengths of flipping onto its back, exposing its pitiably vulnerable belly, opening its mouth, throwing its head back limply, and sticking out its tongue as if it had just been poisoned. It is such a devoted method actor that should you call its bluff and poke it back onto its belly, it will fling itself energetically back into the mortuary pose and resume being deceased.

Local Culture

TOURISM

In the mountains, the main industries have been mining and logging, agriculture, and tourism. As the way we care for our environment has evolved, mining and logging have largely fallen by the wayside and been replaced by small pockets of manufacturing from national and international companies or larger local companies. During this transition, the importance of tourism has increased. The region has always drawn visitors to its mountains, waters, and cities, and as the economy evolves, the tourism sector has become vital to the area's well-being. In the mountains, **Great Smoky Mountain National Park** is a recognizable, even marquee, name for visitors, and **Asheville,** with its superb dining and much-lauded craft beer scene, is atop many visitors' lists. Heritage tourism is helping small towns as visitors follow quilt and craft trails across rural counties. This is helping grow interest in lesser-known cities and small towns throughout the mountains.

INDIGENOUS CULTURES

In the Great Smoky Mountains, the town of Cherokee on the Qualla Boundary, which is Cherokee-administered land, is the governmental seat of the Eastern Band of Cherokee Indians. The Eastern Band are largely descended from those Cherokee people who escaped arrest during the deportation of the Southeast's Native Americans on the Trail of Tears in the 19th century, or who made the forced march to Oklahoma but survived and walked home to the mountains.

The early 19th century in North Carolina was a good deal more peaceful than the previous hundred years had been. Yet despite the relative peace, there was also conflict. Andrew Jackson's administration presided over the passage of the Indian Removal Act in 1830, which assigned reservations in the Indian Territory of present-day Oklahoma to the "Five Civilized Tribes" of the southeastern United States—the Cherokee, Choctaw, Creek, Chickasaw, and Seminole. Thousands of Cherokee people were forced out of western North Carolina, northern Georgia, eastern Tennessee, and Alabama and marched west on the Trail of Tears. About 4,000 died along the way. Another 1,000 or so Cherokee people, through hiding, fighting, and negotiation, managed to win the right to stay in North Carolina—an act of resistance that was the birth of the modern Eastern Band of Cherokee Indians, still centered on the town of Cherokee on the Qualla Boundary in North Carolina's Great Smoky Mountains.

The Cherokee people depict emblematic episodes in their history in the outdoor drama *Unto These Hills,* in production since 1950. It's especially important to note that among the characteristics of outdoor drama in North Carolina is the fact that the cast, crew, and often the producers and playwrights are members of the communities whose stories the plays tell.

Throughout the town of Cherokee, North Carolina, you'll see many street and commercial signs written in English and a set of pretty, twisty symbols that look like a cross between Khmer or Sanskrit and Cyrillic. This is Cherokee, written in the alphabet famously devised by Sequoyah in the early 19th century. Cherokee also survives as a spoken language, though typically among the elders in traditional communities. To combat the slow death of the language, Eastern Band of Cherokee Indians leadership has started a program to teach tribal youth to speak and write the language, though the pool of fluent speakers is very small.

ARTS AND CRAFTS

Several communities are known worldwide for their local traditions, and countless individual artists, studios, and galleries can be found across the region.

Cherokee craft is an important aesthetic school comprising a wide range of techniques and media such as wood and stone carving, fiber arts, traditional weaponry, and avant-garde sculpture and painting. **Qualla Arts and Crafts Mutual,** located in the town of Cherokee, has a wonderful sales gallery that will dazzle lovers of fine craft.

Asheville is an epicenter of the arts, the heart of a vast community of artists that stretches throughout western North Carolina and includes such major folk schools as **John C. Campbell** in Brasstown, near the Georgia state line, and **Penland,** close to Tennessee in the northeastern mountains. In Asheville you can see and purchase an infinite variety of crafts, such as handmade baskets, quilts, furniture, clothing, jewelry, and iron architectural elements. The **Southern Highland Craft Guild** (www.southernhighlandguild. org), an old and accomplished organization, deserves a lot of the credit for the thriving craft movement. Its website has a great deal of information about contemporary master crafters and their work.

Understanding Local Lingo

Regional speech features delightful and sometimes perplexing regional vocabulary and grammar. Following are some of the common phrases most likely to stump travelers.

- **Bless your/his/her heart:** A complex declaration with infinitely varied intentions, interpreted depending on context or tone. In its most basic use, "Bless your heart" is a sincere thank-you for a favor or a kindness paid. It's also an exclamation of affection, usually applied to children and older adults, as in, "You're *not* 92 years old! You are? Well, bless your heart." Frequently, though, hearts are blessed to frame criticism in a charitable light, as in, "Bless his heart; that man from New York don't know not to shout."

- **buggy:** a shopping cart, as at a grocery store.

- **carry:** convey, escort, give a ride to. "I carried my mother up to the mountains for her birthday."

- **Coke:** any soft drink; may be called "pop" in the mountains.

- **come back:** often uttered by shopkeepers as a customer leaves, not to ask them to return immediately, but simply an invitation to patronize the establishment again someday.

- **dinner:** the midday meal.

- **evening:** not just the twilight hours, but all the hours between about 3pm and nightfall.

- **fair to middling:** so-so, in response to "How you?"; a holdover term from North Carolina's moonshining days, the term originally applied to grading 'shine by examining bubbles in a shaken mason jar.

- **fixing to:** about to or preparing to do something. "She's fixing to have a baby any day now."

As people become more accustomed to a world where almost every object we see and use was mass-produced far away, we develop an ever-deeper appreciation for the depth of skill and aesthetic complexity that went into the production of everyday objects in past generations. The artists of this region have always been great crafters of utilitarian and occupational necessities. As you travel, keep an eye out for objects that you might not immediately recognize as art—barns, fishing nets, woven chair bottoms—but which were made with the skill and artistry of generations-old traditions.

MUSIC

Asheville's a music-loving town if ever there was one. And the music scene revolves around the lauded, almost legendary **Orange Peel Social Aid and Pleasure Club.** Everyone who's anyone in rock and improvisational music has played or will play here. The cool downtown venue offers shows just about every night of the week, including local and regional acts in addition to major players and the "next big thing" bands. **Rabbit Rabbit** has become one of the coolest spots in town to catch a show. One of the biggest annual shows in Asheville is the **Warren Haynes Christmas Jam,** an all-star concert fund-raiser featuring a lineup of some of the top rock musicians playing with their bands, with one another, and in any mix imaginable.

If there is an epicenter of traditional Appalachian music, it may just be Gatlinburg and Pigeon Forge. Traditional music has been played here since the first European settlers arrived. As tourism increased and the towns grew into that "aw-shucks, we're hillbillies" character, traditional music also played a role. Today you can hear everything from very strict traditional music to bluegrass covers of

- **holler:** hollow, a mountain cove.

- **mash:** press, as a button. "I keep mashing the button, but the elevator won't come."

- **mess:** discombobulated, in a rut, not living right. "I was a mess until I joined the church."

- **piece:** a vague measure of distance, as in, "down the road a piece" (a little way down the road) or "a fair piece" (a long way).

- **poke:** a bag, such as a paper shopping bag. Used especially in the mountains.

- **reckon:** believe, think. Often used in interrogative statements that end in a falling tone, as in, "Reckon what we're having for dinner." (That is, "What do you suppose is for lunch?")

- **right:** quite, very. Variations include "right quick" (soon, hurriedly), "right much" (often), and "a right many" or "a right smart of" (a great quantity).

- **sorry:** worthless, lame, shoddy. "I wanted to play basketball in college, but I was too sorry of an athlete."

- **supper:** the evening meal (as opposed to "dinner," the midday meal).

- **ugly:** mean or unfriendly, spiteful. Sometimes referred to as "acting ugly." "Hateful" is a common synonym.

- **wait on:** to wait for.

- **y'all:** pronoun used to address any group of two or more people.

- **yonder:** over there.

modern pop songs being played and sung on the streets and in any number of small theaters and shows. There's no marquee venue; the closest thing is Dollywood, which draws a big crowd and will do a lot to get a musician or band's name out there.

Knoxville has a busy college music scene; major musical acts roll through town, but smaller, no-less-talented bands come through as well. Traditional music is heard throughout the city; musicians from novices to virtuosos saw on fiddles, pluck banjo strings, and slap out bass rhythms on the street, in bars, and in concert halls like the **Tennessee Theatre** and **Bijou Theatre.**

FOOD

Up in the Great Smoky Mountains, the early spring is the season for **ramps,** sometimes called skunk cabbage—very pungent wild onions that grow along creek beds in the deep mountains. They're another of those foods passionately defended by those who grew up eating them but greeted with trepidation by outsiders. The reason they're feared by the uninitiated is their atomically powerful taste, which will emanate from every part of your body for days if the ramps are too strong or not prepared correctly. Ramps taste like a cross between regular onions, garlic, leeks, shallots, and kryptonite. When they're young, they're perfectly pungent—not too overwhelming, but still powerful enough to let you know they're in the dish. Folks skillet-cook them, fry them up in grease, boil them with fatback, or just chomp on them raw. For a special treat and a gentle introduction to ramps, stop in at the Stecoah Valley Center near Robbinsville, North Carolina, and pick up a bag of the Smoky Mountain Native Plants Association's special cornmeal mix with dried ramps, and then make yourself a skillet of deliciously tangy cornbread. You can also try them at the local ramps festivals held in Robbinsville and Cherokee in spring. A growing number of restaurants from Asheville to Wilmington are buying ramps and **morel mushrooms** from mountain foragers and preparing them every way from skillet fried to pickled, so ramp lovers can get a taste of this springtime mountain delicacy even on the coast.

Vegetarians and devotees of organic food, fear not; most places are unusually progressive when it comes to healthy and homegrown grub. Nevertheless, if you want to avoid meat, you have to be cautious when ordering at a restaurant: Make sure the beans are made with vegetable oil rather than lard, ask if the salad dressing contains anchovies, and beware of hidden fish and oyster sauce. Traditional Southern cooking makes liberal use of fatback (cured pork fat) and other animal products; greens are often boiled with a strip of fatback or a hambone, which can also find their way into most soups and stews. Even piecrusts are still made with lard in many old-time kitchens.

You'll find organic grocery stores in the major cities. Ingles, Earth Fare, and Whole Foods are common chains, but there are also plenty of small independent markets. Farmers markets and roadside stands are so plentiful that they almost have to fight for space.

Essentials

Transportation

GETTING THERE
Car

The north-south interstates I-81 and I-75 meet in Knoxville, Tennessee, just 30 miles northwest of the western entrance to Great Smoky Mountains National Park. Coming from the south, I-75 is a natural route from Chattanooga, Tennessee, and Atlanta; I-81 cuts a south-southwest diagonal through Virginia along the Shenandoah Valley, passing by or through Winchester, Lexington, Roanoke, Blacksburg,

and Radford, Virginia, before hitting Bristol and Johnson City, Tennessee, and finally Knoxville.

Running east-west, I-40 carries westbound visitors directly by Asheville, across the Tennessee border just north of the national park, and to Knoxville; eastbound drivers will find Little Rock, Arkansas, and Memphis and Nashville, Tennessee, on the route.

To enter Smoky from Gatlinburg, follow I-40 to exit 407 for Sevierville, which connects to Highway 66 south. Upon reaching the Sevierville junction, stay straight to continue on U.S. 441 south, which becomes Newfound Gap Road on its way into the park.

From Cherokee, North Carolina, I-74 connects with U.S. 441 north into the park, where it becomes Newfound Gap Road.

CAR RENTAL

Rental cars are available at every airport, and if you take a train to your departure point, you'll find rental agencies in or near the station. Since many bus and train stations share a facility or are near one another, the same is true if you arrive by bus. The major rental players—Hertz, National, and Enterprise, among others—will be readily available with their standard fleet of cars, but if you are looking for a specific vehicle, like a 4WD or a convertible, check availability with the agencies and reserve your vehicle. Most of these vehicles will be available for one-way rental, allowing you to rent a car at one end and drive it to another, returning it there before boarding a plane or hopping a bus or train back home. Before you embark on a long one-way trip with a rental vehicle, be sure you can return it at the other end. Check with your car rental agency about additional fees for one-way rentals, because some charge hefty fees for this type of rental.

Air

Most visitors to Great Smoky Mountains National Park arrive by car, but for those flying in, several airports offer reasonably convenient access to the surrounding regions.

Asheville Regional Airport (AVL, 61 Terminal Dr., 828/684-2226, www.flyavl. com) is located south of the city in Fletcher, North Carolina. The next closest airport in North Carolina is **Charlotte Douglas International Airport** (CLT, 5501 Josh Birmingham Pkwy., Charlotte, 704/359-4013, www.cltairport.com), two hours away. Charlotte Douglas is the eighth-largest hub in the United States, with nonstop flights to and from more than 125 destinations worldwide.

The **Greenville-Spartanburg International Airport** (GSP, 2000 GSP Dr., Greer, SC, 864/877-7426, www.gspairport. com) is 80 minutes south of Asheville in South Carolina. Airlines serving Greenville-Spartanburg include Allegiant, American Airlines, Delta, Southwest, and United. It's a drive of a little over an hour from Greenville-Spartanburg to Asheville.

McGhee Tyson Airport (TYS, 2055 Alcoa Hwy., Alcoa, TN, 865/342-3000, www. flyknoxville.com) in Alcoa, Tennessee, is about two hours from Cherokee, North Carolina, and about 20 minutes south of Knoxville. Airlines serving McGhee Tyson include Allegiant, American, Delta, Frontier, and United. Gatlinburg and the western entrance to Great Smoky Mountains National Park are just over one hour away; Knoxville is closer, a drive of 20 minutes without traffic.

Bus

You can take a **Greyhound bus** (800/231-2222, www.greyhound.com) to Knoxville and Asheville, but other than those two cities, service is limited. Once you arrive, you'll need a rental car because meaningful public transportation in this region is virtually nonexistent. The **Knoxville Greyhound station** (100 E. Magnolia Ave., 865/524-0369) is not far from downtown, and taxis and ride-share services make it easy to get from the bus station to your accommodations. To get to the national park or North Carolina's Smoky Mountains, you'll need a rental car. The **Asheville Greyhound station** (2 Tunnel Rd., 865/436-1200) is far from the real heart of downtown, and again, you'll need transportation once you arrive.

GETTING AROUND
Driving
SEASONAL CONSIDERATIONS

From where the Blue Ridge Parkway crosses the North Carolina line through to Gatlinburg, Tennessee, the weather can slow and stop traffic or even shut down sections of the route. Generally, though, the weather is quite pleasant, and **winter** is the only time when there are widespread closures of the Blue Ridge Parkway. This route is high and exposed, making it vulnerable to ice and snow. With the expense of the equipment necessary for proper snow and ice removal, wintertime closures are inevitable. Newfound Gap Road through Great Smoky Mountains National Park is a public highway and is maintained throughout the year. It may still close if heavy snowfall is expected or is more than road crews can cope with, but closure is rare. More often you'll be delayed as crews clear the road. Road conditions are available by contacting the **National Park Service** (865/436-1200).

Spring generally brings a good amount of rain. During the earliest months, and even toward the first part of April in the highest elevations, you can experience road closures if a spring snowstorm visits the high passes. The rest of the season, it may rain, but it doesn't impede traffic.

In the **summer,** there is a chance of thunderstorms and, on rare occasions, hail. Most likely you'll encounter a rain shower or fog. The fog can be quite dense, so slowing down or even pulling off at a socked-in overlook is advisable.

In the **autumn,** there are occasional rainstorms, and in the latest part of the season rare high-altitude snowstorms dust the tops of the mountains white. Autumn sees the highest number of visitors to Great Smoky Mountains National Park, and leaf-peepers often slow down well below the speed limit, causing some congestion on the roadways. Autumn color seekers also fill overlooks and line the sides of the road to snap pictures and take in the views, slowing traffic in these busy areas.

SPEED LIMIT

On Newfound Gap Road in Great Smoky Mountains National Park, the speed limit is 45 miles per hour, though it does slow in areas. Please observe the posted speed limit. Maintaining the speed limit allows you time to stop or avoid wildlife, debris, or other hazards on the road surface as well as pedestrians or other vehicles. Since long sections of the road are unprotected—read: no guardrails to break up the view—obeying the speed limit has the added benefit of keeping you and your passengers safe from leaving the roadway on an unexpected downhill trip. And if you think you can speed on the parkway or in the national park because rangers can't pull you over, think again: They can, and they will, delivering hefty fines to reckless drivers.

One reason for the low speed limits along this scenic drive is to keep wildlife free from harm. You'll see a number of woodland creatures on your drive, and as your route cuts through the forests where they live, you'll see many animals on or near the roadway. Be extra vigilant at dawn and dusk, when wildlife is most active. If you must stop in the road to allow an animal to cross, use your hazard flashers to alert other drivers, and try not to stop in blind curves or just over the crest of a hill where you'll be difficult to see.

PARKING

In Great Smoky Mountains National Park, parking is usually limited to designated parking areas at overlooks and trailheads; parking is permitted along the road shoulder, provided all four wheels are off the road surface and your vehicle doesn't impede traffic. On interstates and other highways, stop only when necessary, and when you do, be sure to pull fully off the road so you're not a danger to passing motorists and so you don't put yourself in harm's way.

FUEL

You won't find any fuel inside Great Smoky Mountains National Park, but you will find it in Cherokee and the other towns on the North Carolina side. Gas stations are plentiful on the Tennessee side once you leave the national park.

Recreation

BACKPACKING

To go backcountry camping anywhere in the park, you'll need a permit and a reservation from the **Backcountry Information Office** (865/436-1297, https://smokiespermits.nps. gov, 8am-5pm daily, permits $4 pp per night, $20 maximum). The office can answer any questions about backcountry campsites, trail access, and trail shelters.

The **Appalachian Trail** (AT) runs nearly 2,200 miles from Georgia to Maine. The AT has 71.6 miles of trail in Great Smoky Mountains National Park, and stepping foot on it is a highlight for thru-hikers, segment hikers, and day hikers.

No fees or permits are required to hike the Appalachian Trail; however, there are requirements when you hike the AT in Great Smoky Mountains National Park. Thru-hikers are defined as those who begin and end their hike at least 50 miles from the border of the park and only travel on the AT while in the park. Thru-hikers are eligible for a **thru-hiker permit** (https://smokiespermits.nps.gov, $20). Segment hikers must get a permit from the Backcountry Information Office. Day hikers do not require a permit.

For information about the Appalachian Trail, contact the **Appalachian Trail Conservancy** (www.appalachiantrail. org) or visit the **National Park Service's Appalachian Trail website** (www.nps.gov/appa) for trip-planning information, maps, trail reports, and more.

For AT thru-hikers, there's only one place to stay in Great Smoky Mountains National Park:

Appalachian Trail shelters. Four spots are reserved for thru-hikers at all trail shelters, but they're first-come, first-served. If you're thru-hiking and a shelter is full, you can pitch your tent next to the shelters. Segment hikers and backpackers can reserve spots in AT shelters or at any of the numerous backcountry campsites along and near the Appalachian Trail.

FISHING

There are 2,900 miles of streams within Great Smoky Mountains National Park, and some 600 miles of waterways are ready for anglers to come wet a line and see what they catch. While many think of these mountain streams as perfect for trout fishing with fly rods (these anglers are not mistaken; the Smokies are perfect for fly-fishing), just as many forget that smallmouth bass and rock bass are fairly abundant in these waters.

Smallmouth bass like a rocky-bottomed stream with lots of nooks and crannies where they can hide, so roots, boulders and rock formations, and debris fields are ideal. They also like deep pools where slow-moving currents make it easier to feed. In this region of the Smokies, look for smallmouth along the West Prong of the Little Pigeon River near Gatlinburg and the park's western entrance. You'll also find them in the Little Pigeon River near Greenbrier. Other places you'll find smallmouth and rock bass in the park include the Little River on the way to Cades Cove, Abrams Creek, and Fontana Lake, specifically the feeder creeks like Noland, Hazel, and Eagle Creek.

Fishing in the park is year-round, 30 minutes before sunrise to 30 minutes after sunset, and you can fish any stream in the park provided you have a license. Since Great Smoky Mountains National Park is in both North Carolina and Tennessee, a valid license from either state is accepted within the park, and there's no trout stamp requirement. A special permit is required to fish in Cherokee and Gatlinburg. **License requirements** for North Carolina can be found at www. ncwildlife.org; requirements for Tennessee can be found at www.tn.gov/twra. Though both states offer online license sales, a license can be obtained in person at most sporting goods stores near the park.

As for daily possession limits, you're able to possess five fish—brook, rainbow, or brown trout; smallmouth bass; or a combination—in total. Rock bass are the only exception; you're allowed to possess 20 of these in addition to the five-fish limit. There's no minimum size on rock bass, but smallmouth and trout are required to be at least 7 inches.

With regard to tackle, you're allowed one handheld rod and can only use single-hook artificial flies or lures. That means no fish bait, no liquid scents, and a healthy list of prohibited baits (including minnows, worms, corn, cheese, bread, and even natural baits you find alongside the stream). A full list of fishing provisions for Great Smoky Mountains National Park can be found online (www. nps.gov/grsm).

WATER SPORTS

Swimming and inner tubing are not recommended in the park due to a number of serious injuries and hazards—drowning is a leading cause of death in Smoky. Deep Creek (in the southern section of the park, near Bryson City, North Carolina) permits tubing on its waters.

White-water rafting outfitters are located in Gatlinburg, Tennessee, and in Bryson City, North Carolina. In North Carolina, Smoky Mountain Tube and Raft in Cherokee rents tubes on the Oconaluftee River, and Dillsboro River Company will float you on the Tuckasegee River.

Your best option for white-water rafting, however, is the beautiful Nantahala River Gorge just outside Bryson City in the Nantahala National Forest. Nantahala Outdoor Center is one of several outfitters and guide services that will get you out onto the river in this stunning gorge.

Travel Tips

INTERNATIONAL TRAVELERS

Visitors from other countries must present a valid **passport** and **visa** issued by a U.S. consular official to enter the United States. Visas are not necessary for citizens of countries eligible for the Visa Waiver Program. For more information on traveling to the United States from a foreign country, visit www.usa.gov.

International visitors who wish to drive should obtain an **International Driving Permit,** which is available from the nation that issued your driver's license. Driver's licensing rules vary from state to state. It's a good idea to familiarize yourself with the driving rules in the states that you'll be visiting (you can do this at www.usa.gov). Throughout the United States, drivers drive on the right side of the road, and distance and speed are measured in miles. Speedometers display both miles and kilometers; road signs display only miles.

If you're traveling to the United States from another country, you'll need to exchange your currency at the airport, a bank, or a currency exchange in your destination city, or, even easier, exchange your cash for dollars before you leave home. Attractions, restaurants, and

Leave No Trace

PLAN AHEAD AND PREPARE

· Know the regulations and special concerns for the area you'll visit.

· Prepare for extreme weather, hazards, and emergencies.

· Schedule your trip to avoid times of high use.

· Visit in small groups. Split larger parties into groups of 4-6.

· Repackage food to minimize waste.

· Use a map and compass to eliminate the use of marking paint, rock cairns, or flagging.

TRAVEL AND CAMP ON DURABLE SURFACES

· Durable surfaces include established trails and campsites, rock, gravel, dry grasses, or snow.

· Protect riparian areas by camping at least 200 feet from lakes and streams.

· Good campsites are found, not made. Altering a site is not necessary.

In popular areas:

· Concentrate use on existing trails and campsites.

· Walk single file in the middle of the trail, even when wet or muddy.

· Keep campsites small. Focus activity in areas where vegetation is absent.

DISPOSE OF WASTE PROPERLY

· Pack it in, pack it out. Inspect your campsite and rest areas for trash or spilled foods. Pack out all trash, leftover food, and litter.

· Deposit solid human waste in cat holes dug 6-8 inches deep and at least 200 feet from water, camp, and trails. Cover and disguise the cat hole when finished.

· Pack out toilet paper and hygiene products.

· To wash yourself or your dishes, carry water 200 feet away from streams or lakes and use small amounts of biodegradable soap. Scatter strained dishwater.

LEAVE WHAT YOU FIND

· Preserve the past: Examine, but do not touch, cultural or historic structures and artifacts.

lodgings on the route accept U.S. dollars only. Credit cards are widely accepted, but for moments when you need cash, there are plenty of ATMs in cities and towns in this region (though they will likely charge a fee for each transaction). Though ATMs are sorely limited in Great Smoky Mountains National Park, you will find them at some visitors centers.

TOURIST INFORMATION
What to Bring

Depending on the season, you'll need slightly different clothing, and your supplies will depend on the activities you plan to include as part of your trip. No matter what, you'll want sunscreen and bug spray if you're traveling in the spring, summer, or fall, and sunscreen if you're visiting in winter (especially for skiers).

- Leave rocks, plants, and other natural objects as you find them.

- Avoid introducing or transporting nonnative species.

- Do not build structures or furniture or dig trenches.

MINIMIZE CAMPFIRE IMPACTS

- Campfires can cause lasting impacts to the backcountry. Use a lightweight stove for cooking and enjoy a candle lantern for light.

- Where fires are permitted, use established fire rings, fire pans, or mound fires.

- Keep fires small. Only use sticks from the ground that can be broken by hand.

- Burn all wood and coals to ash, put out campfires completely, then scatter cool ashes.

RESPECT WILDLIFE

- Observe wildlife from a distance. Do not follow or approach them.

- Never feed animals. Feeding wildlife damages their health, alters natural behaviors, and exposes them to predators and other dangers.

- Protect wildlife and your food by storing rations and trash securely.

- Control pets at all times or leave them at home.

- Avoid wildlife during sensitive times: mating, nesting, raising young, or winter.

BE CONSIDERATE OF OTHER VISITORS

- Respect other visitors and protect the quality of their experience.

- Be courteous. Yield to other users on the trail.

- Step to the downhill side of the trail when encountering pack stock.

- Take breaks and camp away from trails and other visitors.

- Let nature's sounds prevail. Avoid loud voices and noises.

This copyrighted information has been reprinted with permission from the Leave No Trace Center for Outdoor Ethics. For more information or materials, visit https://lnt.org or call 800/332-4100.

Bring your binoculars and a camera with a zoom lens so you can enjoy the wildlife up close without disturbing it, keeping all parties safe.

If you plan to hike, dress in layers so you can easily regulate your temperature, and have a sturdy pair of hiking boots on hand; trekking poles or a hiking staff aren't a bad idea either. Throw in some rain gear and a day pack with your first-aid kit, extra water, and some snacks, and you're good to go.

Many visitors enjoy water activities here, whether it's white-water rafting, wading in the streams, or going for a float on the river, and so you'll want a swimsuit. Since the white-water rivers can be cold even in summer, bring something warm, preferably a lightweight wool shirt; wool dries quickly and keeps you quite warm.

Other than these basics, you should pack any specialty gear that caters to your wants, needs, and plans—golf clubs, disc golf gear, skis, maps, rock-climbing gear, whatever it may be.

Maps

One of the best resources for exploring a new region is a good map. DeLorme's atlas and gazetteers are indispensable. The detail provided is enough to plan short day hikes or longer expeditions, and they point out everything from trailheads and boat launches to campgrounds, hunting and fishing spots, and back roads of all types. Look for the *North Carolina Atlas & Gazetteer* (Yarmouth, ME: DeLorme, 2019) and the *Tennessee Atlas & Gazetteer* (Yarmouth, ME: DeLorme, 2017). If you're doing any backcountry camping, these guides will give you a good overview, but you may want to get quadrant maps for greater detail. Excellent guides are available from any good outdoor retailer, and since Great Smoky Mountains National Park is the most-visited national park, quality maps are always on hand.

Accommodations and Camping

In Great Smoky Mountains National Park, no unauthorized backcountry camping is allowed. Reserve a spot at a backcountry shelter or campground, or get a spot at a front-country campground. Adhere to Leave No Trace principles, and absolutely follow regulations and restrictions for campfires. Due to the hazard of fire, campfires are generally only permitted in front-country campsites. If you are front-country camping, be aware that you can't bring in your own firewood; you'll need to purchase or gather it on-site. This rule is to prevent the spread of insect infestations, parasites, and diseases that may harm local plants.

For much of the year, you should be able to travel without reservations, though even in the off-season you may not be able to get into your first choice of campgrounds, lodges, hotels, or B&Bs. During peak seasons, namely October and late summer, you'll need reservations because visitors flood the area to see the autumn color show or squeeze in one more summer getaway. For some of the most popular campgrounds and lodging in the area, you should book months in advance.

PEOPLE OF COLOR

Over the years, the landscape of Great Smoky Mountains National Park has not changed, but the visitors have. They have grown increasingly more diverse, and what was once a rare sight—hikers and park visitors who aren't white—has become much more common. Since 2015, GSMNP has had its first Black superintendent, Cassius Cash, who worked in the U.S. Forest Service and joined the National Park Service in 2010. It's a positive sign that the message "national parks have something for everyone" is spreading and gaining traction.

In the areas surrounding the park, urban centers like Asheville and Knoxville, which tend to be more liberal and open, rub up against deeply rural areas, which tend to be more conservative and closed. Knoxville's population sits just under 190,000, with 76 percent being white, 17 percent Black, 5 percent Latinx, and the balance Asian, Native American, and mixed-race residents. Statistics from a City of Knoxville crime survey conducted in 2020 revealed that most violent crime in Knoxville occurs in the east part of town, away from places the typical visitor is likely to explore. No incidents of hate crimes or race-based crimes were evident in the survey, and newspaper and database searches for hate- and race-based crimes showed little of note, revealing no patterns, only isolated incidents.

The City of Knoxville maintains a list of organizations that serve racial, religious, and ethnic minority groups, including:

- **East Tennessee Civil Rights Working Group** (865/602-7250)

- **Arab American Club of Knoxville** (https://arabamericanclubofknoxville.org)
- **Muslim Community of Knoxville** (www.muslimknoxville.org)
- **Centro Hispano** (www.centrohispanotn.org)
- **HoLa—Hora Latina** (www.holahoralatina.org)
- **Knoxville Branch of the Tennessee Chapter of the NAACP** (www.knoxvillenaacp.org)
- **Hindu Community Center** (https://hinducommunitycenter.wildapricot.org)
- **Knoxville Chinese Culture** (www.knoxvillechineseculture.org); **East Tennessee Chinese Association** (https://sites.google.com/site/etcaknox/home)
- **Knoxville Area Korean Association** (see their Facebook page)
- **Tennessee Istanbul Cultural Center** (www.knoxvilleturkish.org)

You can find more details on the city's website, www.knoxvilletn.gov, under the Residents > Health and Human Services > Immigration & Citizenship Information > Organizations tab. (It's not easy to find; that's bureaucracy and antiquated information architecture for you.)

Smaller, more rural, and without a major university in the city limits, Asheville has demographics that look a little different from Knoxville's but are largely reflective of the region. In the metro area (the city and surrounding suburbs), 84 percent of residents are white, 7.3 percent are Latinx, 4.7 percent are Black, and 1.6 percent are Native American or multiracial. The percentage of Native Americans increases in Swain County, where Cherokee sits inside the Qualla Boundary and is surrounded by Eastern Band of Cherokee satellite communities. In Asheville, the Racial Justice Coalition (www.rjcavl.org) maintains a list of organizations working on race- and equality-based issues. These include the Asheville-Buncombe NAACP, which maintains an active social media presence; SONG,

an acronym for Southerners On New Ground (www.southernersonnewground.org); and the ACLU of Western North Carolina (www.acluofnorthcarolina.org).

Sevier County, Tennessee, which includes communities like Gatlinburg, Pigeon Forge, and Sevierville, has just over 98,000 residents, with 90 percent of the population identifying as white. Here, and in the rural counties surrounding the park, you'll likely encounter individuals who proudly fly the traitorous Confederate flag. Unfortunately, many of the related political sentiments are reflected in the cheap T-shirt and hat selection at souvenir shops. Fortunately, the instances of violence or harassment for race-based reasons are low. Expressions of political disdain and mild harassment for more liberal political views—eyes rolled at your T-shirt slogan, the occasional barely-in-earshot comment, horns honking at your bumper sticker—are more common.

Other resources for Black travelers include Diversify Outdoors (https://www.diversifyoutdoors.com/), Black Folks Camp Too (www.blackfolkscamptoo.com), We Go, Too (http://wegotooworld.com), Travel Noire (https://travelnoire.com), and EatOkra (www.eatokra.com).

GAY AND LESBIAN TRAVELERS

LGBTQ+ travelers may be pleasantly surprised at how tolerant the region is, despite being rural and, in some areas, part of the Bible Belt. In Asheville and Knoxville, you'll find open and active LGBTQ+ culture, and in most spots along the way the culture is open and accepting. This isn't to say everyone you meet is open to every lifestyle choice made, but it is to say that those less-accepting individuals are fewer and farther between with each passing year.

Coronavirus in Great Smoky Mountains National Park

At the time of writing in December 2021, Great Smoky Mountains National Park and the surrounding towns and cities in North Carolina and Tennessee had been significantly impacted by the effects of the coronavirus, but the situation was constantly evolving. Neither state had vaccine requirements and the percentage of fully-vaccinated adults was low.

Now more than ever, Moon encourages its readers to be courteous and ethical in their travel. We ask travelers to be respectful to residents, and mindful of the evolving situation in their chosen destination when planning their trip.

BEFORE YOU GO

- Check local websites (listed below) for local restrictions and the overall health status of the destination and your point of origin. If you're traveling to or from an area that is currently a COVID-19 hotspot, you may want to reconsider your trip.

- If possible, take a coronavirus test with enough time to receive your results before your departure. Some destinations may require a negative test result before arrival, along with other tests and potentially a self-quarantine period, once you've arrived. Check local requirements and factor these into your plans.

- If you plan to fly, check with your airline and the destination's health authority for updated travel requirements. Some airlines may be taking more steps than others to help you travel safely, such as limited occupancy; check their websites for more information before buying your ticket, and consider a very early or very late flight, to limit exposure. Flights may be more infrequent, with increased cancellations.

- Pack hand sanitizer, a thermometer, and plenty of face masks, at least one fresh (or freshly washed) mask for each day, or more if you plan to engage in activities that will get the mask wet or sweaty like hiking. Consider packing snacks, bottled water, a cooler, or anything else you might need to limit the number of stops along your route, and to be prepared for possible closures and reduced services over the course of your travels.

- Expect general disruptions. Events may be postponed or cancelled, and some tours and venues may require reservations, enforce limits on the number of guests, be operating during different hours than the ones listed, or be closed entirely.

- Assess the risk of entering crowded spaces, joining tours, and taking public transit.

RESOURCES

Centers for Disease Control and Prevention
www.cdc.gov

Great Smoky Mountains National Park
www.nps.gov/grsm

North Carolina
https://www.nc.gov/covid-19

Tennessee
https://covid19.tn.gov

ACCESS FOR TRAVELERS WITH DISABILITIES

The overwhelming majority of trails in Great Smoky Mountains National Park are not accessible for travelers with disabilities, particularly those that impede mobility. The one exception is the Sugarlands Valley Nature Trail (on Newfound Gap Rd.). The wide, paved trail makes a 0.5-mile loop alongside the West Prong of the Little Pigeon River near the Sugarlands Visitors Center. Designed with those who have mobility disabilities in mind, this path provides a taste of nature on a safe, easy-to-navigate path. A huge number of attractions, accommodations, and restaurants are accessible, however. All visitors center restrooms are wheelchair-accessible.

TRAVELING WITH CHILDREN

There's no shortage of kid-friendly activities in Great Smoky Mountains National Park. Along the route, there are kid-friendly hikes, Junior Ranger programs, animals galore, and visitors centers and gift shops where you can pick up a little something to keep the youngest traveler occupied while in transit. In the cities, you'll find children's museums, parks, zoos, and playgrounds.

SENIOR TRAVELERS

Aside from stubble-faced and bearded bikers, one of the most common sights in the park is the gray-haired couple tooling about in their Subaru, RV, or truck towing an RV. Many attractions, accommodations, and dining options offer senior discounts, so flash that AARP card and save a few bucks. Overall, the driving routes described in this guide are safe and leisurely ones.

HEALTH AND SAFETY

For the most part, your trip should be unremarkable as far as health and safety are concerned, provided you're attentive to your situation and surroundings, but there are a few things you should know. Those going on long hikes would also be wise to familiarize themselves with the **10 essentials** (https://www.nps.gov/articles/10essentials.htm).

Emergencies

For emergencies anywhere in the United States, dial **911** on your phone for immediate assistance. In North Carolina, dialing *77 connects you to the state police and *67 puts you in contact with the highway patrol. In Tennessee, dial *847 for police assistance. If you have to call, try to note your mile marker or a nearby exit or landmark as a reference point for any assistance that's headed your way.

Wilderness Safety

Hikers should beware of **ticks,** some of which can transmit Lyme disease. An insect repellant and some thorough body checks (use a partner for more fun) should keep you tick-free after a jaunt through the woods. If you do get a bite or if you notice a red circular rash that's similar to a bull's-eye, consult a physician; Lyme disease can be life-threatening in the worst cases.

You'll encounter woodland animals, including bees, wasps, yellow jackets, and hornets, so if you're allergic, be sure to have an **EpiPen** on hand. A number of **snakes,** including rattlesnakes and copperheads, live in these woods. Be alert and keep an ear open for that warning rattle, and if you unexpectedly smell cucumbers in the woods, you may be near a copperhead. In either case, back away slowly and detour around. **Spiders** can be a concern in places, namely woodpiles and some backcountry shelters. Most are harmless, though the brown recluse is seen from time to time, and the more commonly seen black widow spider is easily identifiable by the red hourglass on the female's abdomen.

Two of the most popular animals to look for in the park are **elk** and **black bears.** I've seen both many times, and frequent visitors can attest that they're quite the sight, but only when you're doing your wildlife viewing from a safe distance. That means staying 50 yards

(150 feet) from these animals. Why 50 yards? Because that's close enough for a good look but far enough away to keep the animals calm and keep you safe. If you see a bear or elk, keep an eye on it and monitor its movement; don't approach it; and try to maintain a safe distance between you and any wildlife. Most of the time, bears and elk will take a look at you and get back to whatever they were doing. If your presence causes the animal to alter its behavior (it stops feeding for more than a moment, moves toward or away from you, locks eyes and stares you down), you're too close. If you see any aggressive behavior (bears will run toward you, make loud sounds, or swat the ground), don't run. Instead, slowly back away and keep your eyes on the wildlife. Never, ever for any reason disturb or come between a bear or elk and their young; separating the mother and cub or calf, or coming between them, is often taken as an aggressive move on your part and may cause mom to get angry and do what angry moms do: protect her babies.

Because some visitors don't follow the rules and decide to feed bears and elk or elect to move closer for a better photo, some of these animals act differently around humans. If bears or elk follow you without making aggressive overtures, you need to take action. For bears, first try changing your direction of travel (head back down the trail or back to the car); stand your ground and talk loudly or shout; or make yourself large by standing on something, raising your hands over your head, or even by raising your backpack overhead. As last resorts you can throw nonfood objects (rocks, sticks) at the bear or even defend yourself with a stick or hiking pole. If an elk approaches, retreat to your car or a safe spot, or put something like a tree between you and it. Bears that become accustomed to humans and associate us with food, as well as bears or elk that have an aggressive encounter with humans, are often euthanized, and we don't want that.

Along the trails and roadsides you'll likely encounter **poison ivy, poison oak,** and **poison sumac,** all of which deliver an itchy blister when you come in contact with the oils they secrete. These oils are active for several months, so if you walk through a field of poison ivy, be sure to wash your pants, socks, and boots well lest you inadvertently get poison ivy a month later. You may also come upon **stinging nettles,** which leave itchy welts akin to mosquito bites; these are harmless and generally go away quickly.

Resources

Suggested Reading

HIKING AND FISHING

Adams, Kevin. *Hiking Great Smoky Mountains National Park*. Guilford, CT: Globe Pequot Press, 2013. An excellent hiking-only guide to trails and on-foot sights in Great Smoky Mountains National Park, from Falcon Guides.

Brewer, Carson. *Day Hikes of the Smokies*. Gatlinburg, TN: Great Smoky Mountains Natural History Association, 2002. This pocket-size guide covers 34 day hikes in the park, with maps, elevation profiles, and photos.

Johnson, Randy. *Hiking the Blue Ridge Parkway: The Ultimate Travel Guide to America's Most Popular Scenic Roadway*. Guilford, CT: Globe Pequot Press, 2010. A thorough trail guide to the Blue Ridge Parkway, from Falcon Guides.

Rutter, Ian. *Great Smoky Mountains National Park Angler's Companion*. Portland, OR: Frank Amato Publications, 2002. Everything you need to know about fishing Smoky Mountain creeks and streams, as well as fishing methods and seasons, written by a fly angler with deep knowledge of the waters in and around the park.

Wise, Ken. *Hiking Trails of the Great Smoky Mountains*. Gatlinburg, TN: Great Smoky Mountains Natural History Association, 2001. This hiking guide includes an overview of more than 125 trails in the park,

with trailhead directions, maps, and points of interest along the way.

HISTORY AND CULTURE

Brill, David. *Into the Mist: Tales of Death, Disaster, Mishap and Misdeeds, Misfortune and Mayhem in Great Smoky Mountains National Park*. Gatlinburg, TN: Great Smoky Mountains Association, 2018. A look at some of the park's more macabre moments and how the rangers and local authorities responded.

Fisher, Noel C. *The Civil War in the Smokies*. Gatlinburg, TN: Great Smoky Mountains Natural Association, 2005. How the Civil War impacted the region that is now the park, written by the winner of the Peter Seaborg Award for the best nonfiction Civil War book.

Hall, Karen J. *Building the Blue Ridge Parkway*. Charleston, SC: Arcadia Publishing, 2007. Narrative and archival photos combine to tell the story of the early days of the Blue Ridge Parkway, including construction, folkways, and cultural tidbits.

Holland, Lance. *Fontana: A Pocket History of Appalachia*. Robbinsville, NC: Appalachian History Series, 2001. This book explores the history, people, and stories of the Fontana region of North Carolina's Smoky Mountains, including the changes brought by the building of Fontana Dam and Lake.

TRAVEL

Duncan, Barbara, and Brett Riggs. *Cherokee Heritage Trails.* Chapel Hill, NC: University of North Carolina Press, 2003; online companion at www.cherokeeheritage.org. A fascinating guide to both the historical and present-day home of the Eastern Band of the Cherokee in North Carolina, Tennessee, and Georgia, from ancient mounds and petroglyphs to modern-day arts co-ops and sporting events.

Fussell, Fred, and Steve Kruger. *Blue Ridge Music Trails of North Carolina: A Guide to Music Sites, Artists, and Traditions of the Mountains and Foothills.* Chapel Hill, NC: University of North Carolina Press, 2013. A guide to destinations—festivals, restaurants, opries, church singings—in North Carolina, where authentic bluegrass, old-time, and sacred music rings through the hills and hollers. An accompanying CD gives you a chance to hear some tunes rather than just read about them.

Maynard, Charles. *Going to Great Smoky Mountains National Park.* Helena, MT: Farcountry Explorer Books, 2008. A kid-friendly guide to the plants and animals in the park.

North Carolina Atlas and Gazetteer. Yarmouth, ME: DeLorme, 2019. Since I was in Boy Scouts, I have always been partial to DeLorme's state atlases. This series represents in great detail the topography and other natural features of an area, providing users with far more helpful and comprehensive information than the standard highway map.

Simmons, Nye. *Best of the Blue Ridge Parkway: The Ultimate Guide to the Parkway's Best Attractions.* Johnson City, TN: Mountain Trail Press, 2008. Beautiful photography of some of the most iconic and picturesque spots along the Parkway is accompanied by write-ups of some of the highlights.

Tennessee Atlas and Gazetteer. Yarmouth, ME: DeLorme, 2017. An exceptional resource with details like fire towers, Forest Service roads, boat launches, campsites, and more.

Internet Resources

GENERAL TOURIST INFORMATION
North Carolina
North Carolina Division of Tourism
www.visitnc.com
This comprehensive guide contains trip itineraries in each region, including a dedicated section on the Blue Ridge Parkway. The site is rich with photos and videos, and it contains a wide-ranging index of accommodations, attractions, and more.

Explore Asheville Convention & Visitors Bureau
www.exploreasheville.com
The official website for Asheville, with lists of restaurants, breweries, accommodations, and an online visitors guide.

Brevard—Transylvania County Tourism Development Authority
www.explorebrevard.com
The online guide to Brevard and Transylvania

County, including an index of waterfalls, restaurants, and accommodations.

Bryson City—Swain County Chamber of Commerce
www.greatsmokies.com
The online visitors portal for Bryson City, including an index of restaurants and attractions, accommodations, trip ideas, and an online visitors guide.

NC Tripping
www.nctripping.com
A North Carolina-centric travel blog with trip ideas, hikes, scenic drives, recommendations on restaurants and accommodations, and more.

Visit NC Farms App
www.visitncfarmstoday.com
An app developed by the North Carolina Department of Agriculture and Consumer Services to connect farms, farmers markets, local foods, and agritourism (including farms to visit and to stay at) with visitors and locals.

Tennessee
Tennessee Department of Tourist Development
www.tnvacation.com
The official site of Tennessee's state tourism office is user-friendly, allowing you to narrow your focus on one region with just a couple of clicks. Resources for the Smokies and East Tennessee include interactive maps that provide a great overview of the region's offerings, from natural sights to built attractions.

Gatlinburg Convention and Visitors Bureau
www.gatlinburg.com
The official website for Gatlinburg, with a list of restaurants and attractions, a hotel booking portal, and an online visitors guide.

Knoxville Tourism & Sports Corporation
www.visitknoxville.com
The official website for Knoxville, with lists of restaurants, hotels, and an online visitors guide.

Pigeon Forge Department of Tourism
www.mypigeonforge.com
The official website for Pigeon Forge, including a list of restaurants and attractions, a hotel booking portal, an online visitors guide, and links to their social media.

NATIONAL PARK INFORMATION
Great Smoky Mountains National Park
Great Smoky Mountains National Park
www.nps.gov/grsm
The park's official website: an extensive history of the park, with details on flora, fauna, and natural features as well as downloadable maps and contact information for rangers and park offices.

Friends of the Smokies
www.friendsofthesmokies.org
Friends of the Smokies works to raise funds for park initiatives, trail maintenance and improvement, and a variety of other needs. They accept donations of time and money, so if you had a good time in the Smokies, consider lending them a hand or a few bucks.

Great Smoky Mountains Association
www.smokiesinformation.org
A nonprofit partner of Great Smoky Mountains National Park, the group operates retail stores in and benefiting the park; provides guidebooks, maps, logo-emblazoned clothing and gear, and other gifts; and helps with expenses associated in promoting the park.

OUTDOORS
Appalachian Trail
Appalachian Trail Conservancy
www.appalachiantrail.org
The Appalachian Trail Conservancy provides support to the Appalachian Trail, which parallels and even crosses the Blue Ridge Parkway

in many places. The trail also passes through part of Great Smoky Mountains National Park.

Hiking

www.gatlinburg.com

This website has a brief list of hikes and waterfalls in the region of the park near Gatlinburg.

www.nchikes.com

All things hiking-related in North Carolina, including trails, books, and trip recommendations.

Sierra Club

https://nc.sierraclub.org

www.sierraclub.org/tennessee

Find information about upcoming hikes and excursions as well as an overview of each state's natural areas and environmental issues.

State Parks

www.ncparks.gov

https://tnstateparks.com

A number of state parks provide alternative camping options near Great Smoky Mountains National Park. Many travelers use the parks' campgrounds and facilities as resources and waypoints along their journey.

Wildlife

North Carolina Wildlife Resources Commission

www.ncwildlife.org

Information on fishing and boating in North Carolina, including easy-to-understand hunting and fishing regulations and online license procurement.

Tennessee Wildlife Resources Agency

www.tn.gov/twra

Need-to-know information regarding hunting and fishing regulations and licenses.

Index

List of Maps

Photo Credits

All photos © Jason Frye except title page photo: © Jon | Dreamstime.com; page 3 © (bottom) NPS; page 6 © (top right) NPS Sam Hobbs; (bottom) © Sean Pavone | Dreamstime.com; page 7 © (top) NPS Gary Carter; (bottom right) Douglas Weilfaert | Dreamstime; page 9 © (bottom right) Jon Bilous | Dreamstime.com; page 10 © alexandr grichenko /123rf.com; page 12 © (top) Carol Hudson | Dreamstime.com; © (bottom) Narint Asawaphisith | Dreamstime.com; page 13 © (top) Dfikar | Dreamstime.com; © (bottom) NPS Gary C. Webster, Sr.; page 14 © Guoqiang Xue | Dreamstime.com; page 15 © (top) Steven Bridges; page 18 © James Vallee | Dreamstime.com; page 21 © NPS; page 23 © Jon Bilous | Dreamstime.com; page 24 © Dfikar | Dreamstime.com; page 29 (bottom right) © Sayran | Dreamstime.com; page 32 © (top right) NPS; page 38 © bottom) NPS; page 46 © (top) Jon Bilous | Dreamstime.com; (bottom) NPS; page 53 © (top) Anthony Heflin | Dreamstime; page 73 © Ehrlif | Dreamstime.com; page 75 © (right middle) NPS; page 107 © Cynthia Mccrary | Dreamstime.com; page 108 © (top right) Sean Pavone | Dreamstime.com; page 113 © (left middle) Ritu Jethani | Dreamstime.com; (right middle) Sgoodwin4813 | Dreamstime.com; (bottom) Sean Pavone | Dreamstime.com; page 126 © (bottom) Anthony Totah /123rf.com; page 137 © (top) Gilles Malo | Dreamstime.com; (bottom) Jakub Zajic | Dreamstime.com; page 146 © Jilllang | Dreamstime.com; page 147 © (top left) Pkodada | Dreamstime.com; page 165 © (left middle) Shester171 | Dreamstime.com; (right middle) Jill Lang /123rf.com; (bottom) Dpiano | Dreamstime.com; page 180 © (top) Florentino David | Dreamstime.com; (bottom) Jill Lang | Dreamstime.com; page 213 © daveallenphoto/123rf.com

Craft a personalized journey through the top national parks in the U.S. and Canada with Moon Travel Guides.

MO◉N

USA NATIONAL PARKS

THE COMPLETE GUIDE TO ALL
63 PARKS

BECKY LOMAX

MO◉N

ACADIA
NATIONAL PARK

SEASIDE TOWNS · FALL FOLIAGE
CYCLING & PADDLING

HILARY NANGLE

MO◉N

ARCHES & CANYONLANDS
NATIONAL PARKS

HIKING · BIKING
SCENIC DRIVES

JUDY JEWELL & W. C. MCRAE

MO◉N

BANFF
NATIONAL PARK

HIKE · CAMP
SEE WILDLIFE

ANDREW HEMPSTEAD

MO◉N

DEATH VALLEY
NATIONAL PARK

HIKING · SCENIC DRIVES
DESERT SPRINGS & HIDDEN OASES

JENNA BLOUGH

MO◉N

GLACIER
NATIONAL PARK

HIKING · CAMPING
LAKES & PEAKS

BECKY LOMAX

MO◉N

GRAND CANYON

HIKE · CAMP
RAFT THE
COLORADO RIVER

TIM HULL

MO◉N

GREAT SMOKY MOUNTAINS
NATIONAL PARK

HIKING · CAMPING
SCENIC DRIVES

JASON FRYE

MO◉N

JOSHUA TREE
& PALM SPRINGS

HIKING · SCENIC DRIVES
DESERT GETAWAYS

JENNA BLOUGH

MO◉N

ROCKY MOUNTAIN
NATIONAL PARK

HIKE · CAMP
SEE WILDLIFE

ERIN ENGLISH

MO◉N

SEQUOIA & KINGS CANYON

HIKING · CAMPING
WATERFALLS & BIG TREES

LEIGH BERNACCHI

MO◉N

YELLOWSTONE
& GRAND TETON

HIKE, CAMP,
SEE WILDLIFE

BECKY LOMAX

MO◉N

YOSEMITE
SEQUOIA & KINGS CANYON

HIKING · CAMPING
REDWOODS & WATERFALLS

ANN MARIE BROWN

MO◉N

ZION & BRYCE

WITH ARCHES, CANYONLANDS, CAPITOL REEF
GRAND STAIRCASE-ESCALANTE & MOAB

HIKING · BIKING
SCENIC DRIVES

JUDY JEWELL & W. C. MCRAE

MOON

THE BEST TRAIL TOWNS, DAY HIKES, AND ROAD TRIPS IN BETWEEN

APPALACHIAN TRAIL

TIMOTHY MALCOLM

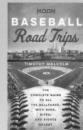

MOON

BASEBALL
Road Trips

TIMOTHY MALCOLM

THE COMPLETE GUIDE TO ALL THE BALLPARKS, WITH BEER, BITES, AND SIGHTS NEARBY

MOON

BLUE RIDGE PARKWAY
Road Trip

WITH SHENANDOAH & GREAT SMOKY MOUNTAINS NATIONAL PARKS

JASON FRYE

MOON

CALIFORNIA

SAN FRANCISCO, YOSEMITE, LAS VEGAS, GRAND CANYON, HOT ANGELES, & THE PACIFIC COAST HIGHWAY

STUART THORNTON

MOON

NASHVILLE TO NEW ORLEANS
Road Trip

NATCHEZ TRACE PARKWAY, MEMPHIS, TUPELO, MISSISSIPPI BLUES TRAIL

MARGARET LITTMAN

MOON

NEW ENGLAND
Road Trip

SEASIDE SPOTS, MAJESTIC MOUNTAINS & FALL FOLIAGE, COZY GETAWAYS

MILES HOWARD

MOON

NORTHERN CALIFORNIA
Road Trip

CRUISE ALONG THE COAST, REDWOODS, AND MOUNTAINS WITH THE BEST STOPS ALONG THE WAY

STUART THORNTON & KAYLE ANDERSON

MOON

OREGON TRAIL
Road Trip

HISTORIC SITES, SMALL TOWNS, AND GIANT LANDSCAPES ALONG THE LEGENDARY WESTWARD ROUTE

KATRINA EMERY

MOON

PACIFIC COAST HIGHWAY
Road Trip

CALIFORNIA, OREGON & WASHINGTON

IAN ANDERSON

MOON

PACIFIC CREST TRAIL

THE BEST TRAIL TOWNS, DAY HIKES, AND ROAD TRIPS IN BETWEEN

CAROLINE HINCKLIFF

MOON

PACIFIC NORTHWEST
Road Trip

OUTDOOR ADVENTURES AND CREATIVE CITIES FROM THE COAST TO THE MOUNTAINS

ALLISON WILLIAMS

MOON

ROUTE 66
Road Trip

JESSICA DUNHAM

MOON

SOUTH FLORIDA & THE KEYS
Road Trip

WITH MIAMI, WALT DISNEY WORLD, TAMPA & THE EVERGLADES

JASON FERGUSON

MOON

SOUTHERN CALIFORNIA
Road Trip

DRIVE ALONG THE BEACHES, MOUNTAINS, AND DESERTS WITH THE BEST STOPS ALONG THE WAY

IAN ANDERSON

MOON

SOUTHWEST
Road Trip

LAS VEGAS, ZION & BRYCE, MONUMENT VALLEY, SANTA FE & TAOS, AND THE GRAND CANYON

TIM HULL

MOON

U.S. & CANADIAN ROCKY MOUNTAINS
Road Trip

DRIVE THE CONTINENTAL DIVIDE AND EXPLORE 9 NATIONAL PARKS

BECKY LOMAX

MOON

U.S. CIVIL RIGHTS TRAIL

A TRAVELER'S GUIDE TO THE PEOPLE, PLACES, AND EVENTS THAT MADE THE MOVEMENT

MOON

YELLOWSTONE TO GLACIER NATIONAL PARK
Road Trip

JACKSON HOLE, CODY, THE GRAND TETONS & THE ROCKY MOUNTAIN FRONT

CARTER G. WALKER

MOON

Road Trip
USA
25TH ANNIVERSARY EDITION

CROSS-COUNTRY ADVENTURES ON AMERICA'S TWO-LANE HIGHWAYS

the OPEN ROAD

50 BEST ROAD TRIPS in the USA

From Weekend Getaways to Cross-Country Adventures

JESSICA DUNHAM

Great Road Trips From Moon

MOON.COM | @MOONGUIDES

MAP SYMBOLS

═══ Expressway	○ City/Town	ⓘ Information Center	♠ Park
═══ Primary Road	◉ State Capital	℗ Parking Area	⚲ Golf Course
═══ Secondary Road	⊛ National Capital	♣ Church	✦ Unique Feature
═══ Unpaved Road	✪ Highlight	❦ Winery/Vineyard	☇ Waterfall
---------- Trail	★ Point of Interest	TH Trailhead	Λ Camping
············· Ferry	• Accommodation	⊜ Train Station	▲ Mountain
━━━━ Railroad	▼ Restaurant/Bar	✈ Airport	⚡ Ski Area
═══ Pedestrian Walkway	■ Other Location	✈ Airfield	Glacier
▥▥▥ Stairs			

CONVERSION TABLES

°C = (°F - 32) / 1.8
°F = (°C x 1.8) + 32
1 inch = 2.54 centimeters (cm)
1 foot = 0.304 meters (m)
1 yard = 0.914 meters
1 mile = 1.6093 kilometers (km)
1 km = 0.6214 miles
1 fathom = 1.8288 m
1 chain = 20.1168 m
1 furlong = 201.168 m
1 acre = 0.4047 hectares
1 sq km = 100 hectares
1 sq mile = 2.59 square km
1 ounce = 28.35 grams
1 pound = 0.4536 kilograms
1 short ton = 0.90718 metric ton
1 short ton = 2,000 pounds
1 long ton = 1.016 metric tons
1 long ton = 2,240 pounds
1 metric ton = 1,000 kilograms
1 quart = 0.94635 liters
1 US gallon = 3.7854 liters
1 Imperial gallon = 4.5459 liters
1 nautical mile = 1.852 km

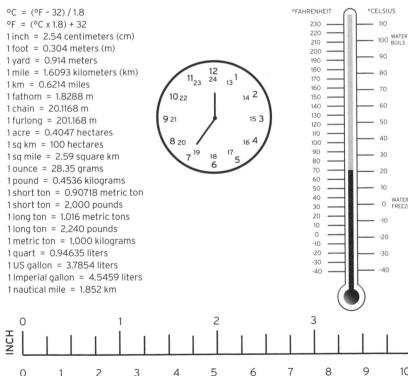

MOON GREAT SMOKY MOUNTAINS NATIONAL PARK

Avalon Travel
Hachette Book Group
1700 Fourth Street
Berkeley, CA 94710, USA
www.moon.com

Editor: Rachael Sablik
Acquiring Editor: Nikki Ioakimedes
Series Manager: Kathryn Ettinger
Copy Editor: Linda Cabasin
Graphics and Production Coordinator:
  Suzanne Albertson
Cover Design: Kimberly Glyder Design
Map Editor: Karin Dahl
Cartographers: Lohnes and Wright, and Karin Dahl
Indexer: Rachel Kuhn

ISBN-13: 9781640496439

Printing History
1st Edition — 2017
3rd Edition — September 2022
5 4 3 2 1

Front cover photo: Sunset from Clingmans Dome
  and obervation tower © Jon | Dreamstime.com
Back cover photo: Clingmans Dome © William
  Moneymaker | Dreamstime.com

Printed in Malaysia for Imago

Avalon Travel is a division of Hachette Book Group,
Inc. Moon and the Moon logo are trademarks of
Hachette Book Group, Inc. All other marks and logos
depicted are the property of the original owners.